ROBBING US BLIND

THE RETURN OF THE BUSH GANG
&
THE MUGGING OF AMERICA

Steve Brouwer

Illustrations by Matt Wuerker

Common Courage Press   Monroe, Maine

Copyright © 2004 by Steve Brouwer.
Cover work by Erica Bjerning
Cover art by Matt Wuerker
Cartoons by Matt Wuerker
Flag illustration by Jan Brouwer

Library of Congress Cataloging-in-Publication Data is available from the publisher on request.

ISBN 1-56751-238-0 paper
ISBN 1-56751-239-9 cloth

Common Courage Press
Box 702
Monroe, ME 04951

(207) 525-0900; fax: (207) 525-3068
orders-info@commoncouragepress.com

See our website for e-versions of this book.
www.commoncouragepress.com

First Printing

Printed in Canada

This book is dedicated to my mother, Tory Evans Brouwer, who moved here to be near her grandchildren and was living with us when she passed away two years ago, in the spring of 2001. Throughout her life she inspired many people with her sense of fairness and her sense of humor, while displaying an amazing ability to balance deep friendships with a strong dedication to social justice. She always spoke her mind clearly, and when necessary, forcefully, but without scolding those who were neither as consistent nor as open-minded as she was. She always maintained her ideals and followed through on her commitments, both personal and political. Through her I learned to trust in the power of love and the potential for humans to really care for one another. Since she believed in the regenerative strength of the earth and all its life, she would be pleased to know that a year after her death, her first great-grandchild, Jackson Brouwer, was born. May her spirit live on with him and all of us.

Acknowledgments

Thanks to a great many people who keep asking good questions and keep me looking for some answers. Thanks to the many writers and scholars who labor away, digging up the stories and the reliable information that the major corporations would rather have us forget. I appreciate the exemplary editorial attention to my manuscript by Greg Bates at Common Courage Press. Not that I listened to all of his sage advice, but I probably should have. I am very glad that Matt Wuerker has chosen to help us with his incisive illustrations and cartoons, which help set a sharp and funny tone for a book that would otherwise be too serious and scary. (And thanks to Mark Twain for providing us with the verbal equivalent of Matt's drawings).

Jan and Ari, my two sons who are at home, have been very tolerant throughout (especially when I had to commandeer the family computer), and they also know when to tease me and lighten my mood. My older children, Anna and Chris, have kept encouraging me from afar. Above all, I once again thank Susan for sustaining me and the family as I wrote another book.

Contents

One

The Robber Barons Return As the Bush Gang

Get money. Get it quickly. Get it in abundance. Get it in prodigious abundance. Get it dishonestly if you can, honestly if you must.

—Mark Twain

NUMBER OF AMERICANS WITH NO HEALTH INSURANCE	YEAR	NUMBER OF BILLIONAIRES IN THE USA
25 million	1982	13
43.6 million	2002	229

When the world's richest nation decides not to provide medical care to a substantial part of its population, and instead multiplies the number of billionaires almost twenty times over, this is no accident. Somebody is robbing us blind.

The Bush Gang Returns

A band of rich thugs has mugged the United States of America. For the second time in twenty years, the Bush Gang—otherwise known as The Family or The Dynasty—is pilfering our pockets and emptying the public treasury. Under the direction of George W, Dick Cheney, and Donald Rumsfeld, the members of this criminal clique are plundering our country again, just as they did in the 1980s and early 1990s. What is more, as the nation slips inex-

orably toward economic chaos, the Bush Gang is drowning out criticism with the noise of war drums and blinding the American people with a frenzy of waving flags. Rather than fix things at home, they want to enlist our help in plundering the world.

America's destiny is now linked to the reckless and selfish pursuits of a corporate elite who are disregarding the well-being of the United States. Like the "Robber Barons" in the late nineteenth century, the Bush Gang is devoted to the business of fleecing the American people and buying out the last vestiges of honest government. Through their policies, their political alliances, and their personal behavior, the members of Bush Gang I encouraged various kinds of criminal behavior in the 1980s—massive financial fraud in the Savings and Loan industry, "junk bond" scandals on Wall Street, and widespread government malfeasance. When they left office in the early

1990s, they saddled us with a long recession and a tremendous national debt. When Bush Gang II returned to the scene in 2001 and 2002, we immediately became aware of their participation—at Harken and Halliburton, Enron and Arthur Andersen—in a massive corporate crime wave that included many of the nation's biggest accounting firms, insurance companies, manufacturers, and financial institutions.

On top of this corporate criminality, the members of the Bush Gang were the central agents in thievery of even greater magnitude, the "mega-crime" of our era. They began to engineer the systematic robbery of the income and wealth of American working people during the 1980s, then pressured a weak Democratic administration to acquiesce to most of their demands in the 1990s, and finally resumed their project with renewed vigor with George W. Bush's election in 2000. This mega-crime has resulted in the wholesale redistribution of money to a very small minority of wealthy Americans, thus leading to inexcusable levels of economic and social inequality in the United States. Consequently, our political system now resembles, as it did a century ago, a plutocracy—a government of the rich, by the rich, and for the rich.

The Bush Gang has a two-fold character. First of all, it is an actual band of opportunistic, anti-democratic operators assembled by the two Bush presidents. For 16 out of the past 24 years (and soon it may be 20 out of 28), someone named George Bush has been sitting at the controls of the U.S. government. While Ronald Reagan served as a popular figurehead during two presidential terms, much of the day-to-day operation of his government was left to others. This was evident two months after the start of the Reagan/Bush era, in March of 1981, when James Brady, White House press secretary for Ronald Reagan, told United Press International that "Bush is functioning much like a co-president."[1] Later that same month Bush assumed the leadership of the White House Special Situation Group; *The Washington Post* reported that "it has been decided that Vice President George Bush will be placed in charge of a new structure for national security crisis management, according to senior presidential assistants. This assignment will amount to an unprecedented role for a vice president in modern times."[2] Throughout the next eight years, as Reagan's health and attention span deteriorated, George Bush Senior, his friends and associates asserted more and more control over the country.

Secondly, and more importantly, the Bush Gang represents a much larger group, the ultra-conservative, corporate upper class that has taken over our country just as they did a century ago. The last time a tiny, self-centered minority held so much power, dominating the United States through their control of "Money Power" and the Republican Party, they were called the "Robber Barons." Though it might seem unfair to pick on a particular family by re-casting the Robber Barons as the Bush Gang, these guys deserve the attention. The roots of Bush family power extend back to the beginning of the 20th century—George W and Jeb really are the great-grandchildren of the Robber Barons. The Bush family has a long record—their involvement in upper-class investment schemes, their promotion of dangerous intrigues in foreign affairs, their long-time participation in Republican politics, and their membership in a variety of elite institutions—that makes them ideal examples of how the corporate upper class maintains and wields its power in the United States.

Can We Really Call Them Robbers?

Most Americans, being hard-working people of modest means and moderate temperament, are fairly tolerant of wealthy Americans, and are not likely to call them "robbers" just because they are fortunate enough to get rich or be born rich. On the other hand, there is a long and noble tradition in our country, built on our distinct notions of equality, liberty, and justice, that requires us to notice when some people are using the system to benefit themselves at the expense of everyone else. The Bush Gang is a throwback to "The Gilded Age," that time over a hundred years ago when wealth was worshiped in all its forms and the nation was ruled by a band of notorious financiers and capitalists, which is why people called them Robber Barons. Today, a glance at any daily newspaper confirms that massive fraud has been taking place in our economy. While the story of the ethical lapses of powerful CEOs is important, the bigger and largely untold story is about the milieu in which they operate, where powerful corporations, a good share of the political elite, and plenty of America's richest families are clearly making out like bandits.

Should we restrain our anger and refrain from calling them "robbers?"

Of course not. The economic and social evidence is overwhelming: the Bush Gang and the new generation of thieves have orchestrated a massive redistribution of America's wealth. They have taken from the poor, from the working class, and from a wide swath of the middle class, and given to the rich—that is, to themselves. The share of national income that goes to the bottom nine-tenths of the American people, the large majority who reside at the base of the economic pyramid, shrank from 67% of the total in the late 1970s to about 52% twenty years later. Analysis of statistics kept by the Internal Revenue Service shows that almost all of this missing income was redistributed to the very richest Americans, the top one percent of our population—in fact, their take of the loot, already a robust 9.3% of all American income in 1979, had more than doubled, to 20.8%, by 2000.[3]

When you are being dispossessed, when your assets and income are shrinking due to the activities of others, then you are being robbed. When the perpetrators organize themselves purposefully to dispossess you, when they plunder your savings, then it is fair to call them a "gang." One dictionary definition fits them perfectly: "Gang—a group of people working together for criminal, disreputable ends."

Our whole notion of freedom in the United States is based upon a the willingness of citizens to speak up and throw self-satisfied elites out of power. Those who fought against the "Money Power" in the past, such as the Kansas farmers who helped invent the term "Robber Barons" in the 1880s, never apologized for calling them a criminal class. Mary Ellen Lease, an outspoken Populist leader of the time, told her Midwestern audiences that they could not afford to be shy. "Raise less corn and more hell!" she said.

She also told them where to go to recover their lost farms and stolen wages: "Wall Street owns the country. It is no longer a government of the people, by the people, or for the people, but a government of Wall Street, by Wall Street and for Wall Street."[4]

Over the past few decades in the United States, there has been little popular criticism of the "elite," the small class of people who dominate corporate ownership and management. Obviously many critical voices are blocked by the corporations themselves, since they have successfully monopolized the major media. But there is another factor. There are no prominent politicians castigating members of the monied elite and calling them "malefactors of great wealth." And though some of us have heard vague references to "The Gilded Age," we seldom hear it applied to the society we live in today. Was the slogan invented by cranky losers who missed out on the American success story?

Not so. The United States' most famous and humorous writer of the nineteenth century, Mark Twain, wrote his wickedly satirical novel, *The Gilded Age*, in 1873, thus giving a name to the first great wave of American corporate and financial thievery. The theme reappeared constantly in his writing for over forty years. When one of the most famous criminals of the era, the railroad scam artist and financier known as Jay Gould, died in 1892, Twain offered a mock eulogy:

> The people had desired money before his day, but he taught them to fall down and worship it.... The gospel left behind by Jay Gould is doing giant work in our days. Its message is 'Get money. Get it quickly. Get it in abundance. Get it in prodigious abundance. Get it dishonestly if you can, honestly if you must.'

In those days, the powerful indictments of a variety of outraged Americans—populist Democrats, trade union organizers, progressive Republicans, home-grown and immigrant socialists—changed our political culture. With their strong sense of morality and their powerful voices, they condemned "Money Power" for creating a culture of greed and dishonesty. The struggle against the corrupt supremacy of the rich went on for so long, roughly from 1865 to 1935, that three or four generations of Americans had to rebound from discouraging defeats before they finally triumphed. Along the way, they recruited the help of people from all social classes. One of them, President Theodore Roosevelt, the descendent of a wealthy New York family and a Republican, had the courage to defy a substantial sector of his own party and say: "We hold it to be a prime duty of the people to free our government from the control of money." In the same fashion, Woodrow Wilson, a fairly conservative Democrat, echoed the rhetoric of the populist chorus: "The masters of the government of the United States," he said, "are the combined capitalists and manufacturers of the United States."

Even with such contributions at the presidential level, the popular campaign to promote more honest politics and progressive taxation faltered in the early decades of the 20th century. After World War I, the rich counterattacked by mounting an extraordinary celebration of the glory of their own money. Their exuberant excesses—cutting taxes, speculating in finance, and buying every possible extravagance (three attributes which reappeared in the 1980s and 1990s)—eventually brought the Roaring Twenties down to earth with an abrupt crash.

The Great Depression led to the disgrace and the downfall of the aristocracy of money. Franklin Roosevelt, backed by a massive popular coalition of working people, realized that it was in the interests of his party to keep the rich at bay and he was determined to keep it that way after his re-election in 1936: "I should like to have it said of my first Administration that in it the forces of selfishness and lust for power met their match. I should like to have it said of my second Administration that in it, these forces met their master."

That never quite happened. But for decades the equality and dignity fostered by the New Deal kept the nation focused on the health and happiness of middle-class and working-class Americans. The ultra-rich paid their high taxes, and lo and behold, they survived quite well, just slightly less wealthy than before. No aristocrats were marched off to the guillotine, nor did the nation's industries and businesses starve for capital. In fact, the United States lived through a golden era, from the 1940s to the 1970s, in which most of its citizens enjoyed unprecedented levels of economic growth and prosperity.

In recent decades, citizens of the United States of America developed amnesia about the financial piracy of the past. Many of us slipped into a delusional state, worshiping the gods of finance and luxury, tantalizingly displayed in ubiquitous advertising but not really within our reach, while forgetting that our real priorities still concerned work, family, and community. Some, it seemed, were bowing down before the false idols of Dow Jones and Wall Street and chanting the incantations they found in *Money, Invest,* and *Fortune*. Meanwhile most families were struggling to stay afloat, with mothers and fathers working many more hours per week simply to avoid slipping behind and going further into debt.

The "Bush Gang" Represents Unrestrained Upper Class Power

For years a number of authors, myself included, have written about the growing inequality in America. In the 1980s, I criticized the ultra-conservative path pursued by the Reagan/Bush administrations. And in the 1990s I took the Clinton administration to task for doing too little to reverse this reactionary

course, for all too often they simply acquiesced to the demands of powerful corporate interests.[5] Many thoughtful writers were raising similar warnings—from moderate, liberal, and left perspectives—but, all in all, they barely touched the consciousness of most Americans. During the euphoria generated by the enormous Internet and stock market "bubble" of the late 1990s, it was difficult to get anyone to pay attention to the pressing problems of real life on earth, such as repairing the social fabric of our country and fairly sharing the fruits of our labor.

From the vantage point of a new century, we can see that our worst suspicions have been confirmed. Economic analysis shows that the increasing inequality in the United States was not an unfortunate or transitory phenomenon, but the result of systematic plundering by the rich. Historical perspective places the Bush family and its political associates at the heart of this privileged elite. For this reason, the "Bush Gang" becomes a convenient and accurate metaphor for describing how the corporate upper class and the ultra-right wing of the Republican Party have manipulated the economy and the government for their own selfish ends.

From the moment the first George Bush took over leadership of the Task Force on Regulatory Relief in 1981, the Bush Gang mounted a very effective program of dismantling the rules and regulations that had controlled the predatory instincts of big business ever since the Great Depression. This led to the emergence of a new, low-wage corporate model that utilized every possible method of exploiting working people. In later chapters, we will explore how diverse corporate actors—Wal-Mart, the meat-packing industry, and for-profit health care providers—used a combination of business deregulation and the outright coercion of labor to make their employees work harder, faster, longer, and for less pay. Squeezing working people—this is the legacy of the Bush dynasty. They did not do this primarily to be cruel; they did it to make more money.

And since we are talking about an upper class gang whose prime objective in life is money, we will devote considerable time focusing on how the rich have been getting it and keeping it—their methods of hauling in income; their preoccupation with accumulating wealth and capital; their obsession with avoiding taxes in order to augment their income and wealth all the more; and their insatiable appetite for other people's savings and Social Security.

We will also look at some important ideological elements that have helped the Bush brand of capitalism win out over American democracy. Their belief in the value of capital takes priority over all other human values; their support for the anti-democratic legal apparatus of corporations protects their class advantages; their isolation in elite organizations warps their ideas and social relations (the Bushes' Skull and Bones club is a prime example); and their monopolization of news and information in the corporate media spreads their views widely among the general population.

Finally, we will consider political questions that are of immense importance to the future of American democracy. What kind of lust for power and profit is driving the Bush Gang's compulsion to take over the world? Do the American people realize that they are rapidly losing both their money and their ability to influence their government?

George W and the Renewed Urge to Plunder and Pillage

Ever since the 1980s, grave damage has been done to the institutions that promote democracy and equality. The ultra-conservative program of serving the wealthy and punishing lower income Americans became so well-entrenched, even among many Democrats, that it ultimately gave free rein to corporate thievery. During the Clinton years, the Democratic Party occasionally tried to limit the most egregious methods which the corporate class used to bilk the majority of working Americans, but in most respects they fell under the influence of the Bush Gang, too. Frightened off by the vicious attacks mounted by the Republican Congress and the pit bulls of talk radio, Democrats attended to the agenda of their own wealthy campaign donors. For this reason, there was no effective Democratic opposition to the initiatives of the Bush Administration in 2001, even though the Democrats won more popular votes in the 2000 election.

This abdication of responsibility by the Democrats allowed the reassembled Bush Gang to pursue the same objectives that guided the United States when Ronald Reagan and the first Bush Gang took office twenty years earlier. They wanted to 1) give huge tax breaks to the wealthy and the corporations; 2) begin a military build-up that reaps very high profits for defense industries; 3) ignore the increasing indebtedness of the private sector and the federal government; 4) disregard the general welfare of most citizens and their natural environment; 5) deregulate almost all corporate activity and financial markets; 6) limit constitutional freedoms and the rights of working people.

When the younger Bush was inaugurated,

the U.S. government had a federal surplus of $129 billion. But less than two years later, by the autumn of 2002, the deficit hit $157 billion and kept growing, with shortfalls of over $450 billion predicted for 2003 and 2004. As the stock market continued on its crash course and the unemployment rate began shooting up, many people noticed that their shrunken pensions and mutual fund holdings would no longer support their retirement plans; others found that their modest stock holdings and 401(k) plans were worth nothing at all. Although the Clinton administration ought to share some responsibility for pushing the stock market to unrealistic heights, it is Bush's Republican Party that refuses to reverse the course of favoring the wealthiest Americans at any cost. The major feature of Bush's 2001 tax bill was a ten-year reduction of taxes for the upper class. Even though tax revenues plummeted in 2002, the Bush Gang continued to propose fiscal measures in 2003—the abolition of the inheritance tax, more cuts in corporate and upper bracket income taxes, another cut in the capital gains tax, the elimination of the tax on corporate dividends—that were just as irresponsible as those that were adopted in the Reagan/Bush years. Huge and lasting federal deficits are now being incurred again.[6]

The ambitions of the plutocrats are not confined to the borders of the United States. The events of September 11 have provided Bush Gang II with an opportunity to pump up their sense of "manifest destiny" and think about boldly imposing the will of the USA on the rest of the world. The control of fossil fuels and natural resources of any kind is high on the Bush agenda—this is, after all, a gang of oil men and one woman who used to have a Chevron oil tanker named after her. The Bush Gang displays

an unprecedented eagerness to dominate arms development of every kind—conventional, space-based, nuclear, and chemical/biological. The political techniques that are required for this new era of global conquest are being modeled on the successful reassertion of our dominion over Central America in the 1980s. In fact, the same criminal element—Abrams, Poindexter, Reich, and Negroponte—that helped carry out those illegal and immoral operations, including our state-sponsored terrorism against Nicaragua, have been rehired for the global job.

Bush Gang II is following in the footsteps of Bush Gang I by concentrating on foreign adventures in order to distract us from their miserable economic performance at home. But this time around there is a heightened sense of global mission, for the administration announced that it is ready to engage an ever-expanding list of "evil enemies" that supposedly threaten the interests of the United States. The wars for Afghanistan and Iraq bolstered George II's standing in the public opinion polls and helped the Republicans recapture control of the Congress. In a flurry of activity after November 2002, Bush appealed to working Americans to keep making wartime sacrifices and proclaimed that it is necessary to curtail federal wage increases, privatize federal jobs, allow pension agreements to be discarded, and otherwise renew attacks on the livelihood and economic security of the great majority of America. This is a cover, a ruse, for the Bush Gang's real objectives: to reward the corporations and the rich with further tax cuts and instigate a long-lasting, imperial policy that will be supported on the backs of working-class and middle-class people. This arrangement not only threatens to permanently lower the standard of living of the average American, it also creates the possibility of over-reaching so far in foreign affairs that we will be faced with even greater hostility around the world.

The corporate upper class and the Bush Gang simply do not care if the future is very harsh for most of us. They seem convinced that they can continue to reduce the quality of life of many Americans without political repercussions. They may be right, since no one is asking for the rich to make any sacrifices at all, even though the American tradition during wartime used to be that the wealthiest citizens had to accept substantial increases in their taxes.

They are indeed "robbing us blind." It is time to discard the red, white, and blue glasses, and visit the crime scene. In the chapters that follow, we will catalog the offenses of people Theodore Roosevelt called "the malefactors of great wealth, the wealthy criminal class." Above all, as we comprehend that the economic and social damage was not accidental, but the result of purposeful Gang activity, we must resolve to put some limits on the behavior of this tiny minority of Americans.

Two

Small-Time Crime

Bush and Cheney, The Chief Executive Officers of America, Set A Fine Example

> Why do we need government?
> *To protect us from the crooks and scoundrels.*
> —Mark Twain

> Executive compensation has become highway robbery—we all know that.
>
> —Geoffrey Colvin,
> *Fortune* June 2001

Maybe some governments can offer what Twain wanted: protection from the crooks and scoundrels. But what if "the crooks and scoundrels" are the government? Obviously, the state of the nation is already threatened when incompetent lawmakers allow private interests to bulldoze them into an unwise course of action. Worse still is the state of affairs when legislators are bought off by big business so that selfish projects turn into public policy and no one can tell the difference between bribery and lobbying. This is what we might call the market theory of politics, also based on an observation by Mark Twain about American government:

> I think I can say with pride that we have legislatures that bring higher prices than any in the world.

Which brings us to the worst of all states —the final step to political decadence is when we can no longer tell the difference between the corporate crooks, the rich crooks who pay for government, and the crooks who run our government.

In the past couple of years, there has been a flood of corporate villains vying for the title of most notorious. At last count, as of Spring 2003, Bernie Ebbers of WorldCom was the leading contender for the title of sending the most hundreds of billions of dollars down the tubes. Kenneth Lay and his higher minions at Enron thought they had laid claim to that title the previous year. But Enron still seemed to be leading in another category—most corrupting influence within a Republican administration.

In this author's neighborhood, the state of Pennsylvania, the rich have a long history of taking working people to the cleaners and then taking vengeance against them—hanging the

Molly Maguires in coal country, machine gunning the Homestead strikers outside of Pittsburgh, and generally crushing all steelworkers and railroad unions for many decades in the late 19th and early 20th centuries. Lately the head of the Tyco Corporation, Dennis Kozlowski, has become a popular candidate for most dastardly chief executive, at least in the south-central part of the state where I live (in Philadelphia, the Rigas family that looted the Adelphia corporation are prime contenders).

Koslowski once was featured on the cover of *Business Week* and highly praised thoughout the nation's business press as a leader of great vision. He claimed that his background in accounting allowed him to spot worthy companies and make them more valuable by slimming down their workforces. Koslowksi took Tyco, a diversified company, on a wild buying spree that extended all over the world in 1999. In the process he snatched up AMP, a quiet, but good-sized manufacturer of electrical connectors headquartered in the Harrisburg area. The parent corporation then immediately sold off several factories and laid off 8,000 AMP workers, 2,100 in central Pennsylvania.

Three years later, in 2002, one of the more honest and determined politicians in America, Attorney General Elliot Spitzer of New York state, took notice of what Kozlowski was really doing. After nabbing him for avoiding sales tax on expensive artwork, Spitzer got down to business. A grand jury handed down criminal indictments against Koslowski and his second in command, Mark Swartz, on the excellent, but seldom-used criminal charge of "enterprise corruption;" that is, making use of a corporation to commit a crime. The men were alleged to have stolen $600 million since 1995 through stock fraud, unauthorized bonuses, and false expense

accounts. Besides $170 million in outright theft, they were accused of making $430 million by using accounting gimmickry to inflate the price of the shares of the company, which they promptly sold. After that, the stock sank 70 percent.

What is most horrendous about this performance was that it was not unusual, but representative of the state of the U.S. business world. In late 2001 and all through the following year, the American people watched dumbfounded as a great number of very large corporations, most of them highly celebrated in the business press for several years previously, began to collapse. From Enron to WorldCom to Arthur Andersen, they all suffered from fraud at the top. And in the rubble of their demise, an underlying, rotten structure of deceit and dishonest business practice was revealed, most of it directly linked to the ethics of the men who ran these companies and to the lax business regulations that encouraged them to try to get away with their crimes.

The CEOs, the corporate chief executive officers, suddenly fell from grace. Many of those who had once adorned the covers of *Business Week, Fortune,* and the major newsweeklies, receiving the adulation usually accorded to movie stars and great athletes, were now despised. They had colluded in crime with each other, with their accountants, with directors on the corporate boards, and with whomever else could help them produce illusory "paper profits." They cooked the corporate books while simultaneously bilking their workers, their shareholders, and the public. In the process they also awarded themselves astronomical compensation in the form of salaries, bonuses, stock options, fake loans, or unlimited expense accounts and retirement packages designed to meet the most extravagant whims that anyone could imagine. Robert Brenner, director of the Center for Social Theory and Comparative History at UCLA, added up the staggering dimensions of this crime spree in early 2003:

> Between 1995 and 1999, the value of stock options granted to US executives more than quadrupled, from $26.5 billion to $110 billion, or one-fifth of non-financial corporate profits, net of interest. In 1992, corporate CEOs held 2 percent of the equity of US corporations; today, they own 12 percent. This ranks among the most spectacular acts of expropriation in the history of capitalism.[1]

Perhaps the corporate executives thought of themselves as a new kind of royalty, granted immunity from the restrictions placed on lesser mortals and ready to assume the mantle of divine right. Clearly the business culture and the political culture that supported the business world had led them to believe that there were no bounds to money-making behavior.

Business crime? No such thing.

The CEOs' sense of entitlement, the feeling that the world owed them everything, may seem insane, but it was, in a way, understandable. For, in a few heady years from 1995 through 1999, and into early 2000, the values of corporate stock on Wall Street kept soaring so extravagantly that once-prudent economists were getting giddy with the idea that the market could keep flying higher and higher, out of this world. In the mid-1990s, Republican Speaker of the House Newt Gingrich declared that "the so-called business cycle," the ups and downs of the market, had no right to exist any more. When the Dow Jones Industrial Average reached 10,000, two fellows at the American Enterprise Institute, James K. Glassman and Kevin A.

Hassett, wrote a popular book with the extravagant title *Dow 36,000*, a prospect that they and their readers seemed to take quite seriously.[2] In this rarified atmosphere, there seemed to be no need to regulate business at all, and every reason to grant big businessmen their every wish. This immense license for crime led the CEOs to take everything they could, and ultimately their compensation had very little regard to do with their job performance, with the exception of one curious relationship. All too often bad performance was rewarded with very high pay.

An interesting analysis by United for a Fair Economy (UFE), which specializes in interpreting economic trends for a popular audience, looked at the compensation of corporate CEOs whose companies were being investigated for improprieties by the Securities and Exchange Commission, the US Justice Department, and other authorities. In the 23 major companies examined, including AOL Time Warner, Bristol-Myers Squibb, Kmart, Lucent Technologies. and Xerox, the CEOs were paid a combined total of over $1.4 billion from 1999 through 2001, or an average of $62.2 million each for the three year period. In contrast, the average CEO at the top 500 US corporations had cumulative earnings averaging $36.5 million for the same period of three years. Crime, it seems, was paying well, double the going rate for more honest executives. For the shareholders of these 23 companies, there was a different story—they lost $530 billion in stock value, or more than 73 per cent. Many workers at these companies, 162,000 of them, fared the worst—they lost their jobs.[3]

In September of 2002, *Fortune* surveyed 1,035 large companies whose market value had dropped at least 75 percent and found that insiders had cashed out to the tune of $66 billion since January 1999. The feature writer, Mark Gimein, wanted to impress upon the reader the idea that this kind of looting had spread throughout the corporate world, and wrote that "greed suffused the business world far beyond Enron and Tyco, Adelphia and WorldCom." The end of the stock market bubble brought out the worst in people, according to Gimein: "The not-so-secret dirty secret of the crash is that even as investors were losing 70 percent, 90 percent, even in some cases all of their holdings, top officials of many of the companies that have crashed the hardest were getting immensely, extraordinarily, obscenely wealthy."[4]

"Obscenely wealthy!?" What kind of language is this, used in public by one of the premier American business magazines, which has made its living for nearly a century by adoring, not condemning, the fortunes of the corporate rich?

What had finally grabbed the attention of the business press? The utter depravity of some chief executives? Or the ordinariness of the crimes, the fact that they were occurring everywhere?

I suspect it was really the stock market, not the CEOs, that got the attention of the editors at *Fortune* and the rest of the newly converted moralists. The greatest crash in history, in terms of total dollars lost, was taking place. Six... seven... eight... nine trillion dollars were dissolving into thin air. By early October of 2002, the Standard & Poor's 500, a wide-ranging index that is a more reliable gauge of the overall stock market than the Dow Jones, would fall to half the value it had reached in March of 2000, indicating a total loss of almost $9 trillion. In any event, the business press had finally noticed the all too rational theft that lay behind the "irrational exuberance."

Although some CEOs were penalized for the poor performance of their companies in 2001-2002, the median pay for top executives did not collapse like the stock market. It continued to go up in 2002 by a modest 6%. There was, however, one group that kept making out like bandits, according to United for a Fair Economy (UFE). They reported that the median compensation of CEOs at the 37 largest military contractors went up 79% for the same year. This reflected the priorities of the Bush administration, which had increased defense spending by 14% and continued to favor one of its favorite constituencies, the military-industrial complex. While the average total compensation of an army private was $19,585 in 2002, the average CEO in the weapons racket was pulling down 577 times as much, or $11,297,585 per year. A related finding demonstrated the efficacy of the revolving door system of government that has benefited Dick Cheney at both ends of the military-industrial game—UFE calculated that the size of the defense contracts won by the big companies was overwhelmingly connected to the size of their political campaign contributions.[5]

Chief Executives Look Out For One of Their Own

Naturally, in this kind of criminal environment, there are many guilty parties, as well as a number of other social actors or institutions that helped induce them into crime. But for our purposes, which is to come to some understanding of the Bush Gang, we need to examine why George W. Bush rose so quickly to the top of the political world. The rich and powerful knew that his father had led the charge for business deregulation, higher defense spending, and lower capital gains taxes throughout the three terms of the Reagan/Bush administrations. The son was a man prepared to deregulate anything that was not already deregulated, to lower every tax on private capital and wealth that had not already been eliminated. His idea of American leadership was to be CEO of the whole country. After all, he was the first candidate with an MBA from Harvard who had ever applied for the job.

Businessmen and corporations swarmed around Bush at the end of the 1990s, lavishing cash donations upon him in the greatest profusion because they knew that this was a man who would never refuse to grant them a favor. The pile of loot grew so high that Bush actually refused to accept matching campaign funds from the federal government. Why? Because federal law would have required Bush to limit the amount of private money he could raise during the very busy presidential primary season of 2000. According to Federal Election Commission data, Bush received more than twice as much as Gore in individual campaign contributions for the 2000 election. He took in $101 million to Gore's $45 million.[6] In order to gain this $56 million advantage, the Bush campaign sacrificed about $15 million in federal funds.

In retrospect, given the level of crime in the corporate suites in 2002, we can assume that the donors knew they were running a man for office who had a high tolerance for financial chicanery. Bush, and his vice presidential choice, Cheney, were familiar with the give and take of the corporate world, and had done some personal taking of their own. They advertised their own corporate accomplishments and suggested that they were the men who could understand the values and priorities of big business. How true.

The Morally Challenged Duo, Sleazy and Oily

Bush and Cheney were granted an immense favor in 1999 and 2000—very few in the news media were interested in looking into the darker regions of the candidates' pasts and examining their shady backgrounds. If the media had been doing their job, they would have realized that these men were trailblazers in corporate irresponsibility.

A decade earlier, George W. Bush had successfully unloaded stock in an oil company, Harken Energy, because he had inside information that the value of the company was about to plummet, the details of which we will examine below. Cheney's experience was somewhat similar, except that his company, Halliburton, also part of the oil industry, was a global giant. Perhaps this was why the terms of his departure were a good deal richer than Bush's.

George W. Bush spent a good part of his adult life drinking too much while getting in and out of the half-baked oil businesses that abound in his part of Texas (Bush has been quite forthright about his past drinking problem with his biographers; he was less forthright about getting arrested in Maine for drunk driving). One of his last business ventures, financed like all the others by Bush family relatives, rich friends, and political connections, was Spectrum 7, a tiny oil company which continually lost money. As CEO, he was able to negotiate a sale of the company to a somewhat larger firm, Harken Energy, in 1986; in turn he was rewarded with shares in Harken, a salary of $120,000 a year, a seat on the board of directors, and a place on the auditing committee. The President of Spectrum 7, Paul Rea, knew that Harken had an important use for the young Bush. "George's name," he said, "would be a big help to them."[7]

Shortly thereafter, in 1989 when the elder George Bush was President, Harken began losing money. The board of directors decided that they had better hide their losses by selling a subsidiary, Aloha Petroleum, for a tidy sum. In a stroke of genius that would have done the officers of Enron proud ten years later, the directors decided to sell Aloha to a group of Harken insiders; they raised most of the cash for purchase by borrowing money from Harken. On the books it then appeared that Harken had made a tidy profit, while in effect it had merely sold the Aloha subsidiary to itself. In 1991, the Securities and Exchange Committee (SEC) would rule that this was really not a profitable sale of assets at all, but a bookkeeping trick. Harken was forced to restate its earnings and declare a loss of $12.6 million for 1989.[8]

Before Harken's troubles became known, however, and before the price of George W. Bush's stock could fall, he rushed to sell it for $848,000 in June of 1990. Less than a month later, bad economic news about the company became public and the value of Harken Energy stock fell fast. Bush failed to inform the SEC, as required by law, that he had made what is known as an insider trade. It was quite likely that Bush, since he was a member of the auditing committee, was aware that public revelation of the accounting trick would cause the stock price to drop, so he wanted to get out with his money while the getting was good. Harken's law firm had been kind enough to offer a legal opinion at the time of the sale; it was not favorable, but Bush chose to ignore it.

Men at Enron, WorldCom, and Arthur Andersen should have been taking notes. (Maybe they were, since Andersen was Harken's accounting company.)

"Unless the favorable facts clearly are more important than the unfavorable, the insider should be advised not to sell"—so read the memo issued by the law firm of Haynes and Boone to its client, Harken Energy Corporation, one week before George W. Bush sold his stock. A prudent person, already knowing that the *facts* about Harken were clearly *unfavorable*, would have decided, as the lawyers implied, *not to sell*.

The role of the board of directors, of which Bush was a member, is to safeguard the investments of its owners, the shareholders. Apparently, Bush didn't see it that way: the stock that he sold for $848,560 at $4 per share would fall to $1.25 per share in December of 1990. The price bounced up and down for a while, but eventually Harken settled into the Texas dust. The firm still existed in 2002, sort of. The bankrupt company's stock was said to be worth the equivalent of 2 cents per share and Bush's investment, had he held on to it, would have been worth $4,243.

In 1991, more than a year after the Harken sale was completed, the Securities and Exchange Commission got around to investigating the Harken case, found that Bush had violated the laws about filing on time, but "concluded there was insufficient evidence to recommend an enforcement action against Bush for insider trading." SEC staff, some with close ties to the Bush family, closed the case on August 21, 1991, the day before the SEC obtained a copy of the memo from Haynes and Boone that warned about the dangers of insider trading.[9]

Could the case have been stacked to protect the President's son?

SEC chairman Richard Breeden, appointed by President George Bush, was a former Baker & Botts attorney and longtime Bush administration aide. The SEC's general counsel was James R. Doty, who had represented George W. Bush in his purchase of the Texas Rangers and also was a partner with Baker & Botts. Bush's defense attorney in the SEC investigation was Robert W. Jordan, another lawyer with the Baker & Botts law firm and a former partner with Doty. (About a decade later, Jordan would be confirmed as President George W. Bush's choice as U.S. ambassador to Saudi Arabia.) Then there was James Baker III, Secretary of State under the first President Bush and his closest advisor, and the leading "Baker" in Baker & Botts, the biggest and oldest corporate law firm in Texas. Baker & Botts has been around for a long time; those interested in keeping track of the interlocking interests of elite families and institutions (see Chapter 14) should note that corporate law firms, like corporations, can live forever. Baker & Botts fought on the side of the railroad monopolists and Robber Barons such as E.H. Harriman when they were running roughshod over Texas at the end of the 19th century; individuals from the law firm have been directly tied to the interests of the Eastern Establishment (such as the Bush and Harriman families) and giant corporations (including oil companies and Enron) ever since.

"I'm all name and no money"— George W. Bush, 1986[10]

There are many things to be learned from the story of Harken and Bush, but the main lesson goes beyond the question of George W. Bush's guilt. Whether his behavior was legal or not, the Harken history reveals how cronies act in their own collective self-interest, especially in the absence of close regulation; it shows how politically powerful families connected to the main lines of "The Money Power" can help a

wayward son get along in the world. All the way to the White House.

After the Harken Energy experience, George W. Bush finally did have a little money and was ready to parlay the family name into bigger and better deals. When he invested $600,000 in the Texas Rangers, he liked to think of himself as a "managing partner," while in reality he was more of a figurehead. Texas billionaire Richard Rainwater was recruited by baseball commissioner Peter Uberroth so that ownership of the Texas team would have a sizeable Texan component. Other out-of-state partners included William DeWitt, an old family friend who had invested in Bush's failed oil ventures and a member of the very rich Cincinnati family that once owned baseball's Reds, and investor Richard Betts, a wealthy college buddy from Yale. Because those who put up the big money prefer to hire management people who have actually had previous success, Rainwater brought in one of his own associates, Rusty Rose, to keep track of day-to-day business affairs. But they did need a man who liked to appear in front of crowds, who liked to show up at the ballpark every day and act as the company cheerleader. Bush's one successful job up to that point in his career had been as a cheerleader; when he attended Phillips Academy at Andover, a boys' prep school in New England, he was chosen head cheerleader for the football team. The Texas Rangers' partnership, recognizing the skills that went along with his name, paid Bush a tidy annual salary for this high-visibility job, which in turn gave him the public exposure he needed to run for Governor of Texas five years later in 1994.

His business partners also made him pretty rich. When the Texas Rangers franchise was sold in 1998, his partners did well on their overall investment, for they had tripled their money in nine years. But Bush did even better, for his partners were especially generous and authorized a $15.4 million payout to him, twenty-five times as much as his original investment.

The partnership made their speedy score by using an old sports trick. It was a sleazy but legal maneuver that sports team owners have been pulling on the public all over the United States. In Arlington, Texas, it worked this way: after acquiring the team for $86 million, the Rangers convinced the citizens to raise their own local taxes in order to pay for the construction of a snazzy new baseball stadium costing $191 million. The stadium agreement stated that the Rangers would pay rent until 2002 (about $60 million in total payments), then the town would give them the ballpark. Not quite free, but close. When the partnership sold the team franchise in 1998 to Texas billionaire Tom Hicks, the new owner paid a greatly inflated price, $250 million, because he would inherit the stadium three years later.

Dick was Trickier

Dick Cheney was not born in a Texas oil town. Nor did he waste his youth drinking and hawking useless oil drilling deals in the Southwestern sun. Yet he was much more successful in oil than his running mate. He had delayed his search for the "black gold" until after he left George Bush Senior's White House, where he had served as Secretary of Defense in the early 1990s. He landed at the oil giant Halliburton, which employs over one hundred thousand people in oil production services around the world, and he served as their chairman and chief executive from 1995 to 2000 before resigning to run for vice president.

Appointing Cheney to the top position proved lucrative for Halliburton. Because of his Washington connections, he landed many more government contracts for Halliburton than the company had previously enjoyed and he arranged foreign business dealings where his predecessors had found little success. For example, through its two Dresser drilling subsidiaries, Halliburton did more business than any other American company in 1998-1999 with Saddam Hussein's Iraq.[11] (In an earlier reincarnation, Dresser Industries was a company associated with Prescott Bush, George W. Bush's grandfather, and his financial benefactors, the Harriman family. Through one of the family friends, Dresser Industries gave George Bush Senior a job in the late 1940s when he was a young graduate of Yale looking for a way to make a fortune in the Texas oilfields.)

The Halliburton and Saddam story was one of the most overlooked issues of the 2000 presidential campaign. On one occasion Cheney was asked about Iraq by Sam Donaldson of the ABC News "This Week" program. "I'm told, and correct me if I'm wrong," said Donaldson, "that Halliburton, through subsidiaries, was actually doing business in Iraq."

Cheney replied, "No, no, I had a firm policy that I wouldn't do anything in Iraq—even arrangements that supposedly were legal."

For some reason ABC News and the rest of the major media never followed up on the future vice president's bald-faced lie, even though the business activities were easily traceable in the corporate records of Halliburton. In the previous year Halliburton had done $23.8 million in business with Iraq through its subsidiaries at Dresser Industries.

But it was another example of corporate intrigue that brought Cheney's name into court in 2002. A conservative watchdog group,

Judicial Watch, filed a lawsuit against Dick Cheney and Halliburton for fraud, alleging that they had overstated earnings by $445 million from 1999 to 2001. At the same time, the SEC launched a probe to see if profits had been exaggerated, for they might have been used to fatten the generous package of severance pay that Cheney received when he chose to run for vice president in 2000. Cheney certainly left the world of private enterprise at the right moment. The stock price had risen to $52 per share in 2000 and he was able to cash in his newly acquired stock options to the tune of $36 million. There was ample chance of something being amiss, since Cheney had employed the corrupt accountants at Arthur Andersen to prepare his books. He was so pleased with their work that he volunteered to appear in a video promoting Andersen. Cheney described Andersen's accounting as: "over and above the just sort of normal by-the-books audit arrangement."

We cannot fault him for accuracy. By the summer of 2002, Arthur Andersen had collapsed and disappeared. Halliburton stock was selling for $12 per share, less than one quarter of the price that Cheney had received when he sold his shares two years earlier. Halliburton stockholders were left holding the bag.

According to *New York Times* reporter Mary Williams Walsh, Cheney's retirement deal was timed perfectly. The board of directors "had voted to award him early retirement even though he was too young to qualify under his contract. That flexibility enabled him to leave with a retirement package, including stock and options worth millions more than if he had simply resigned." Other people were not treated so well. In 2002, Halliburton arbitrarily cut pensions in half for a group of employees who had

been persuaded to retire before they were sixty-five. Halliburton was able to save about $25 million by short-changing this lower class of employees.[12]

Leading By Example—A Fitting Connection to Enron

The corporate life of Cheney and Bush reads like a primer course for their friends at Enron, the giant Houston energy firm that from its inception was closely tied to the Bush family and the Bush presidencies. One of the priorities of George Bush I's administration was to pass the Energy Act of 1992 that allowed for the deregulation of energy markets. This law opened the door for Enron, with its wild patchwork of energy trading and transmission contracts all over the United States and the world, to become a major economic and political force. Enron became George Bush II's biggest backer and corporate contributor, breeding such familiarity that the younger Bush liked to call Enron's CEO "Kenny Boy." With no political embarrassment for either the candidate or the company, Enron frequently loaned its corporate jet to Bush for his long trips on the campaign trail.

This is typical turn-of-the-21st-century sleaze. Although the executive officers at Enron engaged in fraud and mismanagement on a larger scale than did the presidential duo, the thievery at Enron also revolved around tricks practiced by Bush and Cheney. First, there was quick insider trading that leaves others to take the losses. Second, paralleling Halliburton's treatment of its employees, Enron engaged in misleading and dishonest handling of retirement investments. Since Enron has become one of the outstanding examples of scurrilous corporate behavior, its connections to the Bush administration have become quite scandalous. No wonder that Vice President Cheney refused to release the minutes of his meetings with the Presidential Energy Task Force even when the government itself, through the General Accounting Office of the Congress, sued him for that information. The energy task force included many employees from Enron, as well as many government representatives who previously worked at Enron. The House of Representatives nearly succeeded in getting the documents when lower court judges ordered Cheney to turn them over; but in the end a higher, Bush-friendly court prevailed and said the administration could be as secretive as it liked.

One of President Bush's prominent appointees was Thomas White, Secretary of the Army. His efforts shed new light on the revolving door process which enables those in private industry to go to work in the public sector and assist the companies and industries that previously employed them. A former Enron executive, White sold $12 million of Enron shares between June and November of 2001, just before the company collapsed. He had been vice-chairman of Enron Energy Services, which was implicated in manipulating electricity costs in the California power crises. Substantial legal evidence has been accumulated showing that Enron and allied companies, such as El Paso Natural Gas, consciously bilked the citizens of California out of billions in overcharges. Investigative reporter Greg Palast, in his book *The Best Democracy Money Can Buy*, calculated the long-term financial damage: "The Bushes' hard work has paid off—and now, California will pay back at the rate of $2 billion a year for thirty years."[13]

The recruitment of White into Army service had more to do with his energy expertise than his military expertise. One of his first activities as Secretary of the Army was to explore new ways in which to consolidate government contracts for electricity use—Army bases are, after all, big consumers of energy—so they might be served by private companies. This followed logically from White's preoccupations at the time he left his former employer: at the time he took his job as Secretary of the Army, Enron had seven energy bids pending at the Pentagon.

Larry Lindsay, chief White House Economic Advisor, and Robert B. Zoellich, Bush's chief U.S trade representative, had also served as paid advisors to Enron before Bush took office. When Lindsay was devising Bush's economic policies during the 2000 election campaign, he was still on Enron's payroll as a company consultant.

Enron, it seems, even had religious significance for Bush during his campaign. At the urging of Bush's political guru, Karl Rove, Enron hired Rex Reed, the former leader of the Christian Coalition, as a corporate consultant. It was not clear whether the Bush campaign was merely trying to do a favor for Reed, who had been a very successful political lobbyist on a range of conservative religious issues, or whether they were consciously trying to keep him under wraps, paying him handsomely so he would not rush off to work for one of Bush's erstwhile Christian rivals for the Republican nomination.[14]

Theft and Plutocracy

Were all the crooks Republicans and Republican sympathizers? Of course not. Lobbyists and corporations were dangling the bait for all comers throughout the 1990s. Many Democrats were scared silly that they would fall far behind the levels of political funding achieved by their rivals. They had good reason; they had lost badly in the money-raising races during the Reagan/Bush I years. So off they went, scurrying after big business, currying favor in the most obsequious ways. Clinton, with his "New Democratic" image that kept working people and unions at arms length, was quite adept at using the power of the White House to attract corporate donations, particularly from the burgeoning financial sector that loved his Secretary of the Treasury, Wall Street dynamo Robert Rubin.

Probably no one on the Democratic side outdid Joe Lieberman, the 2000 candidate for vice president and long-time devotee of the pro-business contingent known as the Democratic Leadership Council. He was a major supporter, often working hand-in-hand with Republicans, of changes in accounting rules and tax preferences that led directly to abuses of stock options and corporate bookkeeping. When the Senate pushed through rules stipulating that stock options given to employees (and in particular, to CEOs) did not have to be reported as expenses, this allowed corporate boards to keep grossly overcompensating their chief executives while inflating the levels of corporate profits at the same time. Many CEOs then went so far as to drive up the price of their newly acquired stock with bookkeeping tricks and sold off their inflated holdings through insider trading schemes before the stock values fell. After these scandals became public in 2002, Lieberman pretended to be appalled at the lack of corporate oversight by public watchdog agencies. But Arthur Levitt, the former head of the Securities and Exchange Commission, had been deeply frustrated when Lieberman and others undermined his attempts to catch fraudulent behav-

ior. He called the Democrat to account when he said:

> Where was Lieberman? He was busy tying up the SEC in knots over auditors' independence, over the budget, and over options accounting.[15]

Clinton and his henchmen did not cause the corporate crime wave, but were reacting to the burgeoning "Money Power" that had enveloped American politics. They felt they had no choice but to bargain with the big-time corporate brokers who had been feeding at the Republican trough throughout the 1980s. The "New Democrats" seldom showed the slightest interest in reviving the substantial ideas of the Old Democrats, such as instituting universal health care or restoring the rights of laboring people, themes that date back to the robust promises of the New Deal. In general, the Democrats were easily frightened back into line by a rabidly right-wing Congress and were held prisoner to the economic course that was dictated by big business.

Bush and Cheney and the rest of their crew demonstrated, through their personal ties and their behavior, a higher level of commitment to the corporate program. Their enthusiasm for robbing the American people surpassed the weaker level of criminal collusion exhibited by the Clinton Democrats. In 2000, Bush Gang II was ready to extend this program with a vengeance. Because their aims are irrevocably linked to the prosperity of the upper class, their strategy is simple and brutal: to steadily raid the income and assets of the classes below them. This kind of criminal strategy, the same one that characterized the actions of Bush Gang I from 1981 to 1992, takes us far beyond the individual examples of corporate thievery and mischief touched on in this chapter. Even though these thefts were awfully large, they were "small-time crime" compared to the realm of what can be aptly called *Mega-Crime*. The corporate class as a whole, led by the Bush Gang, has decided it is outside the law, that it is so powerful that it is free to plunder and pillage at will.

Historian Sidney Schama thinks the current state of American social and political leadership has sunk to new levels of moral degradation, even lower than when big money was last ensconced in power a century ago:

So we should not wonder at the aversion to debate, for the United States Inc. is currently being run by an oligarchy, conducting its affairs with a plutocratic effrontery which in comparison makes the age of the robber barons in the late 19th century seem a model of capitalist rectitude.[16]

DEJA VOO DOO

M. WUERKER

Three

Mega-Crime

Three Decades of Class Piracy

Nearly 100 years ago, robber barons hijacked our country and our wealth by taking advantage of the legal and regulatory voids created by our change from an agricultural society to an industrial society. Now we're faced with 21st century corporate pirates who took advantage of our transition from an industrial to an information economy to kidnap working families and take us back to the past.

—John Sweeney, president of the AFL-CIO,
at a rally on Wall Street, July 30, 2002

THE INVOLUNTARY REDISTRIBUTION OF AMERICAN INCOME

Shares of All Income Going to Different Segments of the U.S. Population

Year	The Richest 1%	Next 9%	The Rest of Us, 90%
1979	10%	25%	65%
2000	22%	26%	52%

(Based on IRS statistics and analysis by Emmanuel Saez and Thomas Piketty)[1]

What a great country the United States of America can be. Take the time when William Jefferson Clinton, George Walker Bush, and this author grew up, the 1950s and 60s, the era of the baby-boomers. Things seemed to be getting better for almost everyone.

The economy steamed along for three decades, from 1947 to 1979, although it began to slow down in the 1970s as energy prices and inflation began to rise.[2] The gross domestic product of the U.S. grew at a lively rate, about 3.4% per year, the most prosperous time in American history. What was also unique was that most Americans shared in this material progress—low-income, middle-income, and high-income households made very substantial gains, and at nearly the same rates. By the 1960s, many working class Americans were able to enjoy a "middle class" life—they had the opportunity to own a home, drive their own cars (maybe even two of them), take regular vacations, and send their children to college.

The incomes of all Americans more than doubled over three decades, except for the top 5%, whose percentage gain was just slightly less than everyone else's (adjustment for inflation is figured into the following chart). For the working class and the middle class, this was the Golden Age. The richest citizens, however, were beginning to squirm, because they did not share the same vision of economic bliss.

GROWTH OF INCOMES FOR AMERICANS, 1947-1979						
income category	bottom 20%	second 20%	middle 20%	fourth 20%	Next 15%	Top 5%
Percentage growth	116%	100%	111%	114%	103%	86%

(Sources: United for a Fair Economy, Economic Policy Institute)

The Skies Darken —Grim Times Ahead

From 1973 to 1979, there were a number of reasons that the American landscape did not look so bright: the grim experience of Vietnam came to an inglorious end; a disgraced President, Richard Nixon, resigned; and the economy slowed down a bit, buffeted by "oil shocks" and ill-conceived attempts to "whip inflation now." Two presidents, the conservative Republican Ford and the moderately conservative Democrat Carter, stewed anxiously about how to put the country back on track. A few Americans, notably the chief executives of America's biggest corporations and many of the richest owners of corporate and banking stocks, were particularly disgruntled. Morgan Guaranty reported to its investors in 1978 that "the need is to cut the growth of wages by increasing unemployment." Corporate profits after taxes were lower than they would have liked, about 5% per year instead of the 8% they had enjoyed in the 1960s. Since this kind of return on investment did not seem to be increasing their wealth holdings sufficiently, they rallied to conservative suggestions that the control of the investing class was slipping and that dangerous ideas were infecting average citizens.

Americans in the 1970s were starting to make demands that seemed unreasonable to the most powerful leaders of our economic institutions. Citizens groups agitated and petitioned for many things, and among their demands were

the following: clean up the environment and stop burning so much oil; use workers' pension funds, which were burgeoning, to govern corporations in a more democratic manner; free up the labor process and wake unions up from their lethargic state; promote more opportunities and better wages for minorities and women; restrict the kinds of imperialistic policies that had led to the Vietnam War; and keep progressing on civil rights.

The prospect of a more democratic America was threatening to the rich in the early to mid-1970s. The bastion of big business, The Business Roundtable, which represented 200 of the largest American corporations, was formed under the guidance of John Connally, President Nixon's Secretary of Treasury. Connally's influence in Washington turned out to be a harbinger of the rightward shift that would dominate the United States over the next three decades. Leonard and Peter Passell, writing in *The New York Review of Books* in 1971, accurately described the kind of conservative Texas thinking that would sweep over the capital with the arrival of the Bush Gang a full decade later: "One aspect of the new economic program of Nixon and John Connally should not have been unexpected: its benefits for the rich and disdain for the poor. Connally, in particular, has brought to the Administration a blunt favoritism for big business that calls to mind the way things are done in Houston."[3]

Nixon and Connally helped the Business Roundtable get started on plans to reassert corporate power and use the vast resources of big business to mold public opinion. The Roundtable asserted that "chief executives of major corporations should take an increased role in the continuing debates about public policy." Elite organizations dominated by Wall Street bankers, executives, and lawyers, such as the Council on Foreign Relations and the Trilateral Commission, began discussing the problem of "too much democracy" in both industrialized and developing countries.[4] They were finding it difficult to control the new varieties of political movements that were springing up everywhere. And new think tanks, such as the Heritage Foundation, or obscure ones given new life, such as the American Enterprise Institute, were suddenly funded in lavish style by a bevy of ultra-conservative, ultra-rich families such as Coors, Mellon, Bradley, and Olin. They were ready to launch their highly ideological, right-wing agenda into the middle of American politics.

As the moderately conservative elite and the very conservative foundations mounted their offensive, they were joined, for various reasons, by a number of middle-class allies: fundamentalist evangelists who proclaimed the moral decline of the United States; "nativist whites" who worried that they would lose ground if economic and political opportunities were extended to Hispanics and Blacks and Asians; and a variety of home-owners and small business owners who were being pinched financially and wanted to have their taxes reduced, and so naively threw in their lot with big business.

Morning in America? Or the Dark of Night When Robbers Roam the Land?

The Arrival of Bush Gang I

In the '80s, these economic and political forces combined to establish a new ultra-conservative, Republican era of government that has dominated the United States ever since. This power shift to the extreme right, with its unabashed devotion to the needs of rich Americans and the biggest corporations, has been attributed to various factors over the years—for instance, to the "Reagan Revolution" in the early '80s, the "New Christian Right" in the late '80s, or Newt Gingrich's "Conservative Revolution" in Congress in the mid '90s. Looking backwards from the 21st century, however, it is apparent that this has been the era of the "Bush Gang." The Bush family and their political allies have been the dominant influence in and around the White House and they are perfect representatives of the ascendant upper class. This plutocratic elite has dictated most policies of the United States government over the past quarter century, even when Democrats nominally held power. In this wider sense, the members and allies of the "Bush Gang" are analogous to the "Robber Barons" of the late 19th century: they are openly engaged in the outright looting of the American economy and no one seems able to stop them.

In 1980, the gathering ultra-right forces chose to back Ronald Reagan, the actor who had trained for years as a conservative business spokesman for the General Electric Company and then had won the hearts of conservative Republicans when he was Governor of

California. He managed a narrow victory in a three-way presidential race against Democrat Jimmy Carter and moderate Republican John Anderson. When Reagan took possession of the White House, a right-wing regime swung into action. Vice-President George Bush and his long-time friend and political ally, James Baker, immediately took charge of some of the most important functions of the presidency. Bush assumed leadership of the president's Special Situation Group that oversaw national security issues. At the very same time, Bush also decided to take over an equally important domestic job: paying back corporate America for their support. He headed up the Task Force on Regulatory Relief, which aggressively intervened to deregulate American business and relieve big corporations of the cost and bother of abiding by environmental restrictions and labor rules. Meanwhile Jim Baker took over as Chief of Staff at the White House, where he successfully controlled access to the president. He would later become Reagan's Secretary of the Treasury.

Ronald Reagan had a romanticized vision of America that harked back to the 1920s, the time of his boyhood, when Calvin Coolidge was President and his Secretary of the Treasury, Andrew Mellon, was enthusiastically cutting the taxes of the very rich. For Reagan, the "Twenties" had been a wonderful time of free markets and freedom from government interference, and this vision of the past fit in perfectly with his fondest wish: "What I want to see above all," he said, "is that this remains a country where someone can always get rich."[5] He chose not to remember that there was a major downside to the 1920s: a small segment of the population, enriched at the expense of the struggling majority, celebrated their overabun-

dance of wealth with utter recklessness and went on a rampage of financial speculation that led to economic disaster.

Once in office, the Reagan and Bush regime immediately embarked on a campaign to lower taxes on the rich, cut regulation of business, restrict the activities of organized labor, and cut back on federal assistance for education, health, and other social needs. Their rationale was that the activities of government were obstructing the lives of all Americans and that the whole population would prosper when these obstructions were removed or when government services were privatized. The conservatives promised that the rising tide of a growing economy would lift all boats.

This was not to happen. Twenty years later, only the yachts of the well-to-do rode high in the water.

Although average incomes grew by 32% over the next two decades, this growth was not nearly as robust as in the period from 1947 to 1979. Unfortunately, the labor of most hardworking American families was hardly rewarded at all, or not nearly in proportion to their efforts. Only the top 20% of the population made significant gains over the period from 1980 to 1999. Even among these fortunate people, most (the 15% below the top 5%) had average increases in income (29%) that did not keep up with the average growth in household incomes. However, that one small group, the top 5%, saw their incomes increase at twice the rate of the overall economy.

Mega-Crime

In the previous chapter, it was noted that the current leaders of the Bush Gang, George W and Dick Cheney, had a proclivity for "small-

GROWTH OF INCOMES FOR AMERICANS, 1979-1999

Income category	bottom 20%	second 20%	middle 20%	fourth 20%	Next 15%	Top 5%
Percentage growth	-5%	3%	8%	15%	29%	64%

Sources: United for a Fair Economy, Economic Policy Institute; preliminary figures from the U.S. census indicate that things only became worse after 1999; all income categories except the top 5% had declining incomes by the end of 2002.

time crime," including insider trading, corporate fraud, and generally sleazy accounting. Many of their political donors, such as the executives at Enron, piled up fortunes through the plunder of selected companies. The corporate swindles were but a dim reflection of the realm of "mega-crime", where one of the biggest heists in history was taking place. The most egregious "mega-crime" of all was the intentional reversal of many of the measures that had turned the United States into a much more equal society from the 1930s to the 1970s.[6]

This mega-raid, the plundering of working Americans by the upper class, was all the more galling because it was, for the most part, carried out within legal boundaries. Although the pirates continually violated the spirit of democracy and fairness, they usually operated under the cover of law. For example, the National Labor Relations Board (NLRB) was established in the 1930s to protect the right of Americans to bargain for a fair wage. The Reagan-Bush team did not abolish labor laws or the NLRB; it simply stacked the Board with appointees who were sure to take the side of big business in any disputes with labor unions. This tactic, combined with a reluctance to enforce regulatory laws on pollution and safety, allowed corporations to increase their profits without raising wages at the same time. Then, to make those profits even more valuable, income taxes on corporations and rich individuals were sharply

cut. At the same time, many Americans experienced a decline in their wages and their standard of living, while almost all Americans were working more hours than they had in the 1970s and paying higher social security taxes.

Their first time through, riding into Washington on the coattails of Ronald Reagan, the Bush Gang and their associates pulled off a two-pronged assault on the stability of the economy. They approved large spending increases that benefited military contractors (their former business associates) by an inordinate amount. They let their campaign contributors and political pals play fast and loose with the nation's banking system. And through it all they got much richer.

Despite the shaky state of both the economy and the average family's finances at the end of the 1980s, the first Bush Gang kept basing its decisions on a very narrow foundation defined by parameters of accumulated wealth. When George I became President in 1989, he brought in three especially trusted associates with him: Secretary of Treasury Nicholas Brady, Secretary of State James Baker, and Secretary of Commerce Robert Mosbacher. These old friends not only shared Bush's upper class training and background, but they also had a collective net worth of about $250 million between them.

By 1991, the average American family with the median income of $37,340 was working much more than it had twelve years earlier (two-earner families increased their working hours by about 10%), but hardly making more than they had in 1979 (less than a 3% increase; according to figures provided by the U.S. Census Bureau, the gain was less than a thousand dollars). This typical family was paying 27.6% of their income in combined federal, state, and local taxes.

The richest Americans fared much better, increasing their before-tax incomes by over 60% over the same period, while their overall tax rates continually declined until they approximated those paid by average citizens. One prominent example was the household of President George H.W. Bush, whose income varied from $0.5 million to $1.3 million per year from 1989 to 1991. Their total tax rate—state, local, and federal—ranged from 18% to 27%. The rate would have been higher except that George I listed his residence as a hotel in Texas, not the White House or the family home in Maine. Texas has no income tax, whereas the District of Columbia and the State of Maine levy a healthy income tax on the rich.[7]

By 1992 most Americans were left with a very bad taste in their mouths. Not only had they been deprived of growth in their incomes but they were also saddled with a worrisome federal deficit and a steep recession. Twelve years of Reagan and Bush budget deficits, largely caused by a failure to collect sufficient taxes from the rich and by the expense of a ballooning defense budget, had more than quadrupled the federal debt. It climbed from less than $1 trillion when they took office to more than $4 trillion when they left. The American economy was a wreck—the commercial banking and financial system had barely survived numerous scandals, while the savings and loan system had

been so thoroughly looted that taxpayers were left to pick up the bill that would climb to $500 billion (when annual interest payments were applied).

It was time to kick the Bush Gang out of town.

President Bill, Numerous Appetites, But No Stomach For a Fight

The American people were so disgruntled with the record of the Bush Gang in 1992 that they gave twenty percent of their vote to a grumpy but entertaining billionaire, Ross Perot, who had an undying hatred for the first George Bush and a passion for charts that explained some things about the economic decline of the country. Bill Clinton was no dummy. He talked the talk, too. In the 1992 campaign, he got considerable mileage by seeming to offer a populist challenge to the regime of the rich. In a speech announcing his candidacy for president in October of 1991, he put the matter bluntly: "The 1980s ushered in a Gilded Age of greed and selfishness, of irresponsibility and excess and of neglect."

Following Clinton's victory, the Democratic Party rallied briefly in defense of working Americans and increased taxes on the rich by a modest amount, from 31% to 39.6%, the highest marginal rates. This was nowhere near the levels of taxation—70% to 91%—that had been set for very wealthy individuals from the 1940s through the 1970s. Still the tax increases of the 1990s, combined with cuts in social spending, were sufficient to enable the Clinton Administration to balance the federal budget by the end of the decade.

During the Clinton years a combination of factors—higher rates of taxation on the rich, the Earned Income Tax Credit granted to many low-paid workers, an increase in the minimum wage, and a period of lower unemployment—seemed to slow the growth of income inequality. But on many other issues, Clinton caved into the pressure of the mounting challenges from the conservatives. His willingness to lower the capital gains tax from 28% to 20% signaled an enthusiasm for aiding the big financial and investment institutions and the people who profited from them. His unwillingness to keep pursuing health care reform betrayed most Americans, and especially lower-income working people.

Rich individuals, corporations, and conservative foundations took offense at the modest tax increases. Their old wealth, plus the fresh wealth they had accumulated in the 1980s, was immediately employed against the Democrats. They promoted scurrilous personal attacks on Clinton, long before his troubles with the Monica Lewinski affair, and waged battles against specific Democratic programs. Wealthy conservatives funded Newt Gingrich's successful bid to win control of the Congress in 1994 and this put the Clinton administration on the defensive. Since these contributors still had plenty of cash to spare, the Democrats, being a party with very little backbone, gladly held out their own hands. The money did not just trickle down—it showered upon them.

Clinton and Gore abandoned the natural constituency of the party that had been built up by the followers of Franklin Roosevelt during the Depression and the Second World War. That is to say, the Democrats were so busy trying to compete with the Republicans in wooing the wealthy and the upper-middle class that

UNDER BUSH GANG I, THE FEDERAL DEFICIT EXPLODED FROM 1980-1991

1980 -2.7%   1983 -6.0% 1986 -5.0%   1991 -6.3%

(The negative percentages indicate how much of the United States Gross Domestic Product, GDP, was devoted to paying off Federal deficits.)

WHY DID THIS EXPLOSION OCCUR?

Income tax revenues went down
11.3% of GDP in 1980
9.3% of GDP in 1991

Defense spending went up
4.9% of GDP in 1980
6.2% of GDP in 1991

UNDER CLINTON, THE FEDERAL DEFICIT GRADUALLY DISAPPEARED

1992:	6.0% Deficit
2000:	+2.7% Surplus

WHY DID THE PROBLEM GO AWAY?

Income tax revenues went up
9.3% of GDP in 1991
12.2% of GDP in 2000
Military spending went down
6.2% of GDP in 1991
2.9% of GDP in 2000

(Source: Robert McIntyre, Citizens for Tax Justice.[8])

they did little of substance to serve working Americans. In fact, they often sided with the allies of the Bush Gang in promoting reactionary policies, such as the so-called "welfare reform," that punished the poor. No one was helping the wage and salary earners, the farmers and small business people, and the retired people who had depended on strong government advocates to ward off "the malefactors of great wealth" ever since the Great Depression (very few political leaders in the 1990s would have dared to think, let alone utter the words, "malefactors of great wealth").

In the late 1990s, the United States was intoxicated by a huge "bubble," a massive misallocation of speculative wealth, most of it thrown into the stock market. Democrats helped the Republicans pump the "bubble" up to magnificent and unrealistic proportions by joining the campaign to deregulate banks and investment houses, loosen the accounting procedures of corporations, and lower the taxes on capital gains. From within the Democratic Party, many voices joined the conservative chorus of praise for those corporate masterminds, the CEOs, who supposedly deserved every penny of their outrageous incomes.

In short, the Clinton administration, despite it record of deficit reduction, was a government of weak-willed and mixed intentions, one that could not reverse or contain the assault on the well-being of average Americans. The richest one percent of the population relentlessly grabbed more and more of the nation's personal income.

Class Warfare or Class Piracy?

A few perspicacious and popular commentators, such as the syndicated columnist Molly Ivins, have identified this mass reallocation of income as "Class Warfare." In her column of August 15, 2002 in *The Chicago Tribune*, she wrote:

> When the Newt Gingrich Republicans mandated that the IRS spend more of its resources auditing working-class people who get the Earned Income Credit than it does auditing millionaires who use countless tax evasion schemes, *that's class warfare*…when the 400 richest Americans between 1982 and 1999 increased their average net worth from $230 to $2.6 billion, over 500 percent in constant dollars, *that's class warfare*.

It was unusual to see words such as Ivins' in a major newspaper, because political discussion in the United States is usually restricted to the moderate to conservative range that precludes discussion of class conflict. If "class warfare" is mentioned, it is because a conservative wants to suggest that certain matters should be kept off-limits in American political discussion. For instance, in the months before the 2000 elections, when Al Gore got brave enough to suggest that Bush's tax plan favored the rich once again, Bush rebuked him for "being a candidate who wants to wage class warfare in order to get ahead."

In late 2002, however, things were changing. There was an unusual upsurge in straightforward economic analysis as other liberals in the media were willing to follow Ivins' lead. On October 20th, *The New York Times Sunday Magazine* placed a very uncharacteristic title on its cover: "The Class Wars, Part I: The End of Middle-Class America (and the Triumph of the Plutocrats)." In the corresponding article, the newspaper's own columnist and resident economist, Paul Krugman, wrote that he was delving into a matter that had been largely verboten over the two previous decades—"even bringing up the subject," he wrote, "exposes you to charges of 'class warfare,' the 'politics of envy,' and so on."

Krugman noted that "the permissive capitalism of the boom destroyed American equality" and that the United States had suffered through "the Undoing of the New Deal." The incredible shifts of income and wealth, all to the advantage of the very rich, could not be attributed to "globalization," "skill-based technological change," or the "superstar" status of CEOs. These explanations, argued Krugman, had been trotted out regularly by mainstream pundits during the 1980s and 90s, but simply did not account for the magnitude of the transformation of American society. He wrote that the rich, including the leaders of the great corporations, had established a "new gilded age" for themselves, one in which it was socially acceptable to rake in the fruits of economic activity at the expense of everyone else. How did they do it? For one, he wrote, "money buys political influence; used cleverly, it also buys intellectual influence."

Doesn't the process of the rich reasserting their dominance over American society constitute "class warfare?" If the people who control capital completely undermine the social position of those who contribute almost all the labor, haven't they been waging a class war?

I admit that I, too, used the term "class war" in 2001. When describing the transformation of our political economy over the previous two decades, I suggested that we call it: "The Great Class War of 1980–2000: the Upper Class Wins Big, The Working Class Forgets to Show Up." The explanatory numbers demonstrate just

how astoundingly one-sided this class war had been.

In retrospect, I think there is a problem with characterizing this assault as a "Class War." There is no denying that something transpired for twenty years that resulted in a massive victory—the margin was one thousand to one—and that it was planned and executed by a small cadre of forces at the top of the social pyramid. But should this be characterized as "Class Warfare" when one side did not even get to fight? The losing side, the 90% of Americans at the bottom of the income pyramid, never made it to the battlefield. In reality, the statistics that illustrate how "Capital Clobbered Labor" do not depict a struggle or a war; rather they portray a one-sided and unprovoked *class assault* perpetrated by *upper-class brigands* against a law-abiding and unwary populace.

"Class War" is the wrong choice of words for what transpired, because the eventual winners never declared war and their sustained raid

CAPITAL CLOBBERS LABOR, 1000 TO 1

The Winners:
The CEOs of the Fortune 500
and upper class investors
CEO pay went up 1030%
from 1982 to 1999
and stock prices went up 1017%
from 1982 to 1999

The Losers:
The American working class
Average hourly pay rose only 1%
from 1982 to 1999
even though productivity per hour went up more
than 35%

(Source: United For A Fair Economy)[9]

on the nation's assets provoked very little response until it was too late. In contrast, "Class Piracy" fits the leaders of the raid much better. For a century the Bush family and their associates have been flying the pirate flag, Skull and Bones, the banner of their exclusive club at Yale. It indicates the cavalier attitude of the privileged elite and their wanton disregard for their fellow citizens. The banner of the rich proclaims, *We're entitled, let's take whatever we want.*

The Return of the Bush Gang

After the presidential election of 2000, the Bush crew came sailing back into town. Their return was aided by the fact that Gore and Clinton themselves had adopted the posture of groveling at the feet of the rich in the previous eight years, excelling at such activities as renting out the Lincoln room at the White House for $100,000 per night and arranging international junkets for corporate bigwigs who wanted to move their factories and jobs to low-cost labor areas overseas. The failure of the Clinton/Gore team to identify the Bush Gang as the leading agents of a new generation of Robber Barons eventually led to their downfall.

The reassembled Gang added staunch reinforcements from ultra-conservative circles, and they made a no-holds-barred grab for the Presidency. Their leader, George W, followed in the Bush tradition by choosing decision-makers and advisors who had also accumulated great wealth. According to *The Washington Post*, the president, the vice president, and their cabinet were the richest men ever to take over the executive branch of government. In particular, five of them—Vice President Dick Cheney, Secretary of Defense Donald Rumsfeld, Secretary of the Treasury Paul O'Neill,

Secretary of Commerce Donald Evans, and Secretary of State Colin Powell—were together worth about $600 million dollars, according to their own self-disclosure statements.[10] George W's own wealth was a little more modest, in the $20 to $30 million range, but that estimate did not take into consideration large sums he might inherit from his parents some day.

Most of these men, and the larger raiding party they brought into government with them, had already served loyally under the Reagan/Bush I administrations and they knew the routine very well. In the first half of the year 2001 they immediately reverted to the modus operandi that had been set forth back in 1981:

- Give extraordinary tax relief to very rich citizens and corporations.
- Build up the military with rapid increases in defense spending and weapons procurement.
- Assert a very aggressive posture in international relations.
- Offer every possible kind of deregulation of business activity.
- Overlook the criminal activity of the businessmen who support their agenda.
- Disregard the very real possibility of large federal deficits.

Tax cuts for the rich have been the centerpiece of Republican policy for two decades, so the Bush II administration acted quickly. The tax legislation of June 2001 promised tax savings for all, which was only true to the extent that many average taxpayers enjoyed a small rebate on their 2001 tax payments (due to an amendment that originated in the Progressive Caucus in the House of Representatives, not in the Bush administration). The real money, however, was written into the full ten-year program—52% of the tax benefits went to the richest 1% of Americans, the same people who had run off with the loot over the previous two decades.[11]

Bush pushed for new weapons systems, including the revival of "space-based" military options, and made plans to instigate a major build-up of American forces long before the September 11 attacks on the United States occurred. Cheney and Rumsfeld, with their long-standing ties to defense industries and the Department of Defense, were adamant about building American power up to levels that were unprecedented, even in the Reagan/Bush years of 1981-1992.

Their purpose was to establish a new level of international aggressiveness, a plan laid out in advance in their "Project for the New American Century" in 1997 (see Chapter 17). This plan envisioned a new posture for the United States in world affairs, whereby it would dispense with the pretense of multi-lateral consultation with allies. Instead, as the world's single remaining superpower, it would insist upon special displays of deference from all other nations. The Bush administration immediately renounced a series of foreign agreements, including the Kyoto Agreement on Global Warming and the International Criminal Court, that would have held it to true international standards. It also signaled the United Nations that it did not necessarily intend to comply with future U.N. decisions.

On the home front, the Bush administration sent a clear message to corporations that enforcement of environmental standards would be loosened and that health and safety standards for workers would be weakened. For example, the Labor Department immediately abandoned guidelines drawn up under the Clinton administration to protect workers from repetitive stress syndrome, the most common debilitating injury in the workplace. The officials who were selected to oversee regulations in agriculture, finance, industry, and forestry were generally veteran lobbyists from those same industries; they favored non-enforcement of existing laws and regulations in order to lessen the expenses of their big business allies.

Even as the big corporate scandals were starting to emerge, the Bush administration kept working closely with a bevy of Enron boys, then refused to release notes of the proceedings after Enron began to collapse. Similarly, George W. Bush tried to avoid strict government oversight of corporate accounting once the magnitude of the fraud at the nation's companies became apparent. Instead he decided to push Harvey Pitt, a long-time advocate of leniency toward corporate boards, into the chairmanship of the Securities and Exchange Commission.

As the depth of the economic downturn became apparent, the Bush administration did not pursue a broad-based plan of economic stimulus. Although they might have used deficit spending in a positive way to revive the incomes of average Americans or invest in public infrastructure, the Bush Gang chose instead to follow the exact same course that had led to very wasteful deficits throughout the 1980s and early 1990s. They kept expanding the tax cuts for the rich at the same time they were increasing expenditures on defense and new weaponry. Thus, within their first year of retaking office, Bush Gang II relinquished the entire government surplus that had been so carefully cultivated in the previous few years and set a pattern for incurring large deficits for the coming decade.

In short, the Bush Gang immediately delivered the goods in 2001 that wealthy Republican supporters had paid for in advance. But their job was not complete. Since the attacks of September 11 and the ensuing "War on Terrorism" allowed them to distract public attention from the disastrous performance of the economy, they were able to take control of Congress by the end of 2002. This opened up the opportunity that the pirates had dreamed about for decades, a wholesale assault on all forms of progressive taxation.

While they were considering many enticing possibilities for reducing the obligations of the richest capitalists—an end to dividend taxes, more cuts in capital gains taxes, accelerated depreciation on business holdings, etcetera —they were especially excited about one caper that not even George W's father had dared to contemplate. Bush Gang II wanted to eliminate the federal estate tax, the levy on inherited wealth that that falls almost exclusively on the very rich. Currently, inheritance taxes only affect the top 2% of the population, and for most of those people who leave estates under $5 million, the consequences are generally mild. Estate taxes are designed to take the biggest chunk from a much tinier segment of the populace, the super rich—people like George H.W. Bush and George W. Bush. In 1999, for instance, half of all federal inheritance taxes were paid by only 3,300 estates that had an average value of $17 million apiece.

After piling up the plunder for almost two and a half decades, the rising plutocracy knows that it can insure its dominance long into the future if it can safeguard its immense fortunes. Putting an end to inheritance taxes could represent the coup de grace for the Bush Gang, a perfect finale to the long spree of class piracy. On the other hand, their success might herald a new level of confidence among the new Robber Barons, meaning that a whole new round of thefts could be yet to come.

Four

Stealing Our Livelihood

Labor is prior to, and independent of, capital. Capital is only the fruit of labor, and could never have existed if labor had not first existed. Labor is the superior of capital, and deserves much the higher consideration.

—Abraham Lincoln, in his first annual message to Congress, 1861

If we look back to the beginning of the 20th century, around the time the Internal Revenue Service began keeping reliable income statistics, it is clear that a huge share of American income was controlled by the very rich, the top 1% of the population, and the upper middle class, the 9% below them. The trend reached its height during the runaway stock market boom of 1925-1929 when the top one-tenth raked in 47%-50% of all income. This happened in part because Andrew Mellon, the Republican Secretary of the Treasury throughout the 1920s, had succeeded in slashing the taxes of the upper class in 1926. This unleashed rampant financial speculation on the part of the rich. In 1928, just before the stock market crash of 1929, the top one tenth of Americans grabbed exactly half of the income, with the top one per cent gobbling up almost a quarter, or 24%, all by themselves. This left just 50% of all income for the large majority of Americans, the bottom nine tenths who did not benefit from the financial boom.

Although the Great Depression and the stricter regimen of the New Deal dampened the spirits of the rich throughout the 1930s, no one threw those "robber barons" in jail. But they did have to relinquish some of their power. Taxes were raised dramatically on the wealthiest citizens and the government provided work for masses of unemployed people through a variety of public programs. Most important, the U.S. labor movement for the first time in history was allowed to operate and organize freely after the Wagner Act was passed in 1935; it set up the National Labor Relations Board to protect workers' democratic rights and allowed the newly formed CIO to organize millions of factory workers and miners in industrial unions. Still, it took almost a decade for these measures, followed by the massive increases in industrial production required for World War II, to really shift the economic playing field so it benefited the great majority of Americans. By the 1940s, economic outcomes were much more favorable for working people, whether they were wage earners, small proprietors, or salaried employees. Even then, the richest one percent of Americans still consumed a very large portion, around one-tenth, of the economic pie.

The world had definitely improved for the people who made their living by their labor rather than through their ownership and control of capital. Although the government and the business structure remained profoundly pro-capitalist in the United States and Western Europe, there was a new kind of oppositional power exerted by unions and populist political organizations, ranging from liberal New Deal Democrats in the U.S. to coalitions of social democrats, centrists, and other leftists in Europe. This kind of working people's power restricted the options of the mighty owners of capital and promoted real gains for average citizens throughout the advanced capitalist countries. For a remarkably long time, for over four decades from 1942 to 1985, the income share of the top 10% of American households was corralled within the range of 32-34%, while working people brought home a much bigger chunk of the bacon, 66-68%, than they had ever enjoyed before. Their high point, 68% of all personal income, was reached in the early 1950s. It was no accident that this occurred precisely when the percentage of union members among all employed people reached the level of 35-38%, which was an all-time high in the U.S. At the same time in some European countries, the rate of unionization rose as high as 60% to 90%, and included most white collar as well as blue collar workers.[2]

Well-organized labor unions meant that ordinary people could bargain for fair wages and an increasing share of the economic pie. Even though union membership declined somewhat in the 1960s and 1970s in the United States, working people—that is, the wage and salary earners and small proprietors who make up the ranks of the bottom 90% of income earners—maintained their more favorable share of personal income, about two thirds of the total.

Why, in a democracy, would this overwhelming majority of people ever want to go back to the bad old days? They never knowingly voted for the fate that would befall them under Reagan and Bush, and most people did not seem to realize that a negative income shift was being foisted upon them toward the end of the 20th century. It all culminated at the end of the past decade, the 1990s, when an astounding stock bubble was created by the excess amounts of capital being dumped into the New York Stock Exchange, NASDAQ, and a wide variety of financial instruments. Just as in the 1920s, workers and their bargaining organizations had already been beaten down through a combination of harsh corporate practices, deregulation of business, and unsympathetic treatment by government agencies. In addition, the levels of taxation on the very wealthy had fallen so sharply that the worst sorts of speculation and corporate gambling were encouraged. The Bush Gang and their fellow travelers (including many conservative Democrats) had managed to accomplish the same things that Calvin Coolidge and Andrew Mellon had engineered back in the Twenties.

By 1996-2000, the very wealthy and the upper middle class, the top 10% of the American population, were again collecting well over 40% of all personal income, finally reaching a level of 44% to 48% in 1999-2000. This meant that the ninety-percent majority had lost a 10% to 15% share of all national personal income. Seen in

HOW INCOME WAS SHARED THROUGHOUT THE 20TH CENTURY IN THE UNITED STATES

(the changing income shares of three different groups; percentages show the range for each time period)

	1900-1942	1942-1984	1985-2002*
The Rich (top 1%)	16-24%	9-13%	13-22%
The Upper Middle Class (next 9%)	24-28%	21-25%	24-27%
The Rest of Us (the 90% Majority)	50-59%	66-68%	52-60%

(based on research of Emmanuel Saez and Thomas Piketty.[1])
*preliminary IRS figures for 2000-2001 and Bush administration policies suggest that these trends will continue at least through 2004.

terms of their own proportion of income, the reduction from the 66-68% range to the 52-56% range meant that working people's incomes were more than 20% less than they would have been if the mid-century, New Deal norms had been maintained. The impact of these lost wages might have been greatest on the bottom 20% of the population, who were very poorly paid to begin with. Their share of all income declined from 4.2% in 1973 to 3.5% in 2001. However, the size of the decline in earnings share that was sacrificed was even more substantial among middle income Americans. Census figures (which tend to understate, not exaggerate the losses of average households) show that households in the second quintile (the 21st to 40th percentiles) saw their income share decline from 10.5% to 8.7% over the same time period. The middle quintile, 40-60%, experienced a big loss in their share, which fell from 17.1% in 1973 to 14.6% in 2001. Even the fourth quintile, who are better off than 60% of American households, lost a meaningful chunk due to wages that did not keep up with economic growth—their income share declined from 24.6% in 1973 to 23% in 2001.[3]

Who was stealing our livelihood?

Capital Says It Is Superior to Labor

The smallest share of the money taken from working people and redistributed upward, about 2.5% of all income, went to the 9% of the population that I have labeled above as upper middle class. Since these people primarily earn their living from work, usually from labor performed in the offices of the corporate and business sector, they do not necessarily like the implication that they are different from "working people." On the other hand, they know that their jobs have a privileged status, and they tend to be proud of the special services they perform. Many manage the legal and administrative matters of the corporations and, on occasion, have to follow orders from above that impose harsh measures upon lower-paid salaried and wage earners. For their loyalty they are given rewards, albeit modest ones, whenever capital makes tremendous gains at the expense of labor. This is particularly true of the people in the 96-99th percentiles of income—the upper-middle class and the almost rich—who filed tax returns with adjusted gross incomes of $125,000-$325,000 in 2002. They saw their share of national personal income rise from 12.5% to 14.5% over two decades. The five percent below them in the 91st-95th percentiles, those who declared $90,000-$125,000 in earnings per year, just barely merit the description of being privileged over others, since their share of all income in the1980s and 1990s increased by a mere one half of 1%, from 11.5% to 12%. In many parts of the country where the cost of living is high, such as metropolitan New York, Boston, San Francisco, or Washington D.C., these people would not think of themselves as "upper middle class" at all, but more representative of the struggling middle income sector of the population. Of course, the contrary is also true: in the rural environs of many U.S. states, people with incomes over $100,000 would be perceived as "downright rich."

And how much did capital gain? In terms of clear-cut corporate profitability after paying the salaries of the upper middle class, capital claimed an extra 4% of all national income as the profit rate rose from 6.4% in 1979 to 10.4% in the late 1990s.[4] This is a very sizable chunk for the owning class, an increase in profitability of over 60%; it shows up on the national account books as a huge gain for capital income.

But there is another large transfer of income that is misleadingly labeled as wages and salary on the corporate balance sheets. This is the extraordinary increase in the incomes of the top 1% of earners, most of them chief executive officers or other top managers and functionaries of the corporate world, that is, all those whose incomes averaged over $1 million per year in the year 2000. Their share of all personal income shot up from 8.03% in 1979 to 14.58% in 1999. This 6.55% amounts to about half of what was redistributed upwards from the working classes (a total of 10-15% of all nation-

al personal income) and constitutes a monstrous income share gain for this segment of the elite, (81.6% to be exact).[5] Please note that this particular calculation of income does not include capital gains, which were also very significant for high-end earners.

In fact, most of these incredible gains were concentrated among an even smaller group, the top one-tenth of 1%, whose income share skyrocketed from 2.16% to 6.04% of all income earned by all people in the United States. This money was, for the most part, a self-reward, the bonus money taken by CEOs and their close buddies with the full sanction of their boards of directors. They took the loot in the form of straight salary, stock options, and a host of special perks. (This number, too, as calculated by Emmanuel Saez and Thomas Piketty, does not include other very large sums collected as capital gains.) These earnings are, in effect, the hidden share of the capital extracted from the labor of working people; the money did not show up as profit on the corporate account books, but instead was written off as an expense. As long as the CEOs could drive stock prices upward, few in the business world were criticizing them for their outrageous levels of remuneration. They were being cheered wildly by most big and small stockholders and the business press, and were almost never excoriated as immoral, criminal scum (at least, not until the market collapsed).

As noted in the previous chapter, the total compensation of the Fortune 500 CEOs rose by over 1000% over a period of two decades, staying in perfect tandem with stock prices. The reason these gains were so big was that the productivity of labor grew handsomely (44.5%), while the remuneration of the median laboring person hardly increased at all (1%). In other words, wages stayed flat while the value produced by each worker in a given hour of labor shot up. This was due to technological advances, to increases in the skill levels and education of employees, and, quite often, to the intensity of work demanded by managers.

Finally, on top of all this, there was another sizable amount of income directly attributable to capital. It came from the sale of individually held property that is realized as capital gains. Capital gains income is more erratic than other kinds of income because the sales of property (especially stocks) increase in boom times or when special tax favors are granted to the richest citizens. The Congressional Budget Office found that capital gains taxes generated 12% of all income taxes reported in 2000, and had sustained a high level of 10%-12% for the boom years 1997-2000.[6] Capital gains were generally much lower two decades ago, generating 4%-5% of all income tax from 1976-1982, and then 5%-7% from the 1980s through the mid-1990s. (Because of the up and down, cyclical nature of capital gains, some economists like Emmanuel Saez and Thomas Piketty have chosen to set them off to the side when they are analyzing income trends for the very rich.)

Capital gains can be large—for instance, they constituted over 10% of all personal income in the year 2000—and they invariably favor the rich. IRS charts show that almost 75% of capital gains went to the richest 2% of Americans in 1999 and 2000; 60% went to the top 1%; and the lion's share, a full half of all capital gains income, was gathered by those with incomes of $1 million and up, the quarter of a million households who comprise one-sixth of 1% of the population. This is the Bush League, the tiny proportion of families that have fortunes of $10 million and up (see Chapter 5). The majority of these big-time winners were not the CEOs of the Fortune 500 companies (although some of these characters did rip off big chunks of money when they cashed in their stock options), rather they were the employers of those CEOs, the rich investors and family trusts that indirectly control the business world because of their dominant ownership position in America's corporations. Fully 58% of all capital gains came from the sale of directly held stock in 2000; a much lesser amount went to stocks owned in mutual funds or pension plans (the primary form of stock ownership for upper-middle class Americans)[7] and to other forms of property such as real estate.

The stock market, though supposedly "democratized," is still primarily serving the immediate needs of the very rich. Mainstream press accounts have thoroughly exaggerated the amount of stock ownership among average Americans. It is true that more than 52% of Americans owned stock in some form in 2001, either through direct ownership or indirect means, such as mutual funds, retirement accounts, 401(k)s, and defined contribution pensions. On the other hand, their amounts of ownership were pitifully small. In 1998, the average stock holdings of people on the bottom rungs of economic ladder, the lowest 40%, were just $1,700 (only about 6% of this near-majority of Americans owned any stocks or mutual funds at all). The average stock holdings of someone in the middle 20% only amounted to $9,200; but the amount of stock held by the richest 1% was extraordinarily high, an average of $2,525,200, according to economist Edward N. Wolff. These very rich citizens held 48% of all publicly traded corporate stock, so were necessarily the big beneficiaries of capital gains made on sales of stock in the financial markets.[8]

Preliminary findings for the years 2001-2002, issued by the Federal Reserve in January 2003, indicate that the holdings of the rich probably improved by about 18% from 1998 to 2002 in spite of the stock market crash. Meanwhile the meager average holdings of citizens in the middle 20% had declined a bit, to about $8,000.[9]

The principal money making activity of those with incomes of above one million dollars was indeed capital gains, which produced nearly half, or 42% of their income in 2000 (the last year, as of this writing, for which the IRS did high-income analysis). The salaries of these very rich people were not negligible, but accounted for less than a third, or 32%, of their income. Another 12% flowed from other sorts of investments such as rental income property, dividends, bank trusts and annuities, and other kinds of business ownership. The final 14% of the million dollar incomes came from a variety of partnerships and small corporations, many of which have been created to shelter or hide the income of rich Americans, legally or illegally, from the Internal Revenue Service.[10] This means that the amount reported as income in this category was certainly much less than these partnerships really produced (see Chapter 6, concerning taxes, for some indication of the enormous amount that is stolen from the federal treasury each year in the epidemic of tax cheating that has been fostered among the rich).

The Labor of Ordinary Americans Gets No Consideration At All

The percentages above are meaningful, but may look unduly abstract. There is another, more concrete way of portraying the consequences of this shift in income for American families.

The numbers below indicate the actual incomes of typical American households over a twenty-three year period, 1979-2002. The after-tax incomes of low-income American households hardly changed at all. Middle-income earnings only rose 12% even though the average income of all citizens increased by 32% (the average rose from approximately $44,000 to $58,000 when adjusted for inflation in constant 2002 dollars).

Meanwhile, the after-tax incomes of the very rich exploded, with the top 1% experiencing a 157% gain from 1979 to 1997 (and by 2002, even with stock market losses, they were still expanding, being approximately 195% higher than 1979 according to preliminary income figures). The gains enjoyed by this tiny elite accounted for almost two-thirds of the increase in all incomes. The very rich were hogging two-thirds of the expanded economic pie, thus enjoying one of the biggest "free lunches" of all time.

Some would say this was unfortunate, even scandalous. Others would say it is criminal.

CHANGE IN AFTER-TAX INCOMES FOR DIFFERENT HOUSEHOLDS

(Incomes in 2002 dollars, adjusted for inflation)

Income Group	1979	1989	1997	2002*
Lowest 20%	$12,200	$12,100	$12,200	$12,500
Middle 20%	$37,800	$39,400	$41,600	$42,500
Top 1%	$295,000	$555,000	$760,000	$875,000

*(2002 figures, based on preliminary IRS, Census, and SCF data, are very approximate)[11]

WHAT REALLY GOES ON WITHIN THE TOP 20%?

(Income group)	Income Growth, '79-'97	Average After-Tax Income, 1997
81st to 95th percentiles	28%	$78,200
96th to 99th percentiles	46%	$143,800
The 100th percentile	157%	$677,900

(For clarification: the 100th percentile indicates the top 1%; the 95th to 99th percentiles indicate the 4% just below the top 1%; and the 81st to the 95th percentiles indicate the 15% just below the top 5% of all households. These figures are derived directly from the CBO study done in 2001. I am not including estimates for 2002 in this table because information on income growth between 1997 and 2002 is too sketchy to differentiate clear percentages for the top 1% and the next 4%. The trend shown here continued, however, and the top 5% made significant gains compared to the 15% below them, who by 2001-2002 were starting to experience income losses, mostly due to increases in unemployment just like the bottom 80% of the population.)

Statistics and "Damn Statistics"

Over the past two decades many reports on income, from the Census and elsewhere, have been presented in ways that obscure the incredible wealth that was collected at the very top. Often a very large group of Americans, the 20% of citizens earning the highest incomes, are lumped all together. If these households, more than 25 million strong, are treated as if they are one homogeneous mass, then it appears as if they were grabbing all the income gains from our economy at the expense of everyone else in the United States. This may be statistically true, but only if we ignore the gigantic income transfers that only benefited the uppermost 1%. If we separate out the upper-upper crust and expose its monopoly on the big money, we can get a much more accurate view of the entire situation.

The figures in the table above tell us that the income growth rate for three-quarters of the top 20% of the population, the 81st to the 95th percentiles, was only 28%. By coincidence, this happens to be precisely the increase in average income for all American families from 1979 to 1997; that is, this relatively well-off group did not gain at an excessive rate; they simply enjoyed the income gains that should have been available to all Americans over two decades. How can that be?

The skewing of income statistics was so extreme because those in the top 1% were treating themselves to an enormous windfall of 157%; their gains, in turn, make the earnings of the whole top 20% look out of line. By separating the very rich from those immediately below them, the next 19%, we find that it is more difficult to condemn the 19% for stealing from the rest of us. To tell the truth, $78,200 per year in 1997, the average income of 15% of that top quintile, does not look like a lot to get upset about. For that matter, even $143,800, the average chunk taken home by the 4% immediately above this 15% and immediately below the very rich, is not a terribly distressing number.

So, what does the rest of the population need from nineteen out of twenty people in the top 20%? Not their money. We need their help in catching and reining in the 1% at the very top. These thieves have raked in so much that most Americans have gained little or nothing ever since the first Bush Gang appeared on the scene at the beginning of the 1980s.

Capital Eyes Labor and the "Union Premium"

Business leaders of the 1970s (as was pointed out in the previous chapter) were upset by their mediocre returns on investment and wanted to increase corporate profitability. Elite organizations such as The Business Roundtable, the Council on Foreign Relations, and the Trilateral Commission favored conservative approaches from Democrats and Republicans alike. For instance, many of them backed Jimmy Carter for president in 1976. Paul Volcker, who served as chairman of the Federal Reserve under Carter and Reagan and was a Trilateral Commission member, determined that "the standard [of living] of the average American has to decline"[12] and proceeded to raise interest rates to very high levels, thereby inducing massive unemployment, a deep recession, and the transfer of money from working people who borrowed money to the money-bags who loaned it out. This strategy raised the profitability of most major banks and financial corporations, while other major American businesses looked for further assistance.

The quickest way to higher profits was the low-wage path. The most conservative corporate leaders looked to the Republicans, Ronald Reagan, and the Bush Gang to lead them down this low road. Upon taking office in 1981, the Reagan/Bush administration immediately designated working people—in particular, unionized citizens—as the enemy. As a demonstration of their resolve, they first attacked PATCO, the air controllers' union and forced all employees to resign; then they packed the National Labor Relations Board with anti-labor members.[13] Unions, in their view, were a major cause of their mediocre profits. These businessmen and friends of big business tended to ignore the overriding international reality, that profits had fallen because capitalist industry worldwide had built up a tremendous overcapacity of production, thus competition between countries and corporations was driving down profit rates. This has been the classic example of capitalist crisis ever since Karl Marx identified it 150 years ago. Obviously, our captains of industry seldom read Marx or the able critics of capitalism who have followed in his wake up until the present day.[14]

The perfect short-term solution for sluggish business, according to corporate America, was to ignore international reality and attack the gains made by labor unions over the previous forty years. Members of labor unions not only were enjoying much higher wages than non-union workers, but they also had the advantage of much better total compensation because of their health insurance and pension benefits. This advantage, which stems directly from the power of collective bargaining, is known as the "union premium."

The anti-labor onslaught never stopped. Business and government have teamed up to push unions out of some old industries and keep them from organizing workers in newer industries, while generally harassing them unmercifully with union-busting law firms and consultants.[15] Over two decades, the percentage of union workers in private industry has declined to less than one in ten, and the percentage of unionized workers in manufacturing fell by more than half, from 38.8% in 1973 to 17.6% in

1995.[16] Still, the union premium remains significant today—in 2002 union members received 28.4% higher wages and 39.1% more in employee benefits when compared to non-union workers. This held true, though at lower rates—an 11.5% advantage in wages, and about 30% for health and pension coverage—when researchers meticulously allowed for all variables such as region of the country, type of industry, education level, and years of employment.[17]

The anti-union strategy got results. Immediately after the Bush Gang arrived, the median wage began declining by about 1% per year. By 1984 to 1986, the overall rate of profit pushed up from 6% to 7%, thanks in part to the layoffs and givebacks demanded by employers, especially from blue collar employees. Throughout the three presidential terms that Bush I was on the scene, the average wage of all the production and non-supervisory workers, those who make up more than 80% of the total workforce in the United States, dropped from $13.92 in 1980 to $13.19 in 1992 (figures in inflation-adjusted dollars), an overall decline of 7%. The productivity of labor increased about 25% over that same period.

This combination, lowering wages while taking advantage of productivity gains (even though they were rather weak gains by historical standards), caused the profit rate to keep climbing back, until it reached 8-9% in the late 1980s. Then deep recession, bad fiscal policy, and the other negative effects of the Reagan/Bush policies caused the economy and the profit rates to decline from 1989 to 1993. When the economy recovered in the mid-1990s, the corporate profit rate did rebound sharply, and reached an apex of around 10% in 1997, the highest since the mid-1960s. None of

this gain was passed on to working people by U.S. corporations.

Throughout the 1980s, the overall wage situation was aggravated by the low value of the minimum wage, which fell sharply and never recovered completely in the 1990s. If we adjust it for inflation and state the value in 2003 dollars, the minimum wage was worth $6.81 in 1979; fell to $4.80 in 1989; was boosted to $5.61 in 1991 and $5.89 in 1997, and was stuck back at $5.15 in 2003. Since this amounted to a 29.5% drop in the 1980s, and 24.4% drop overall, the pay of low-income workers was kept artificially low, with no allowance for low wage workers to be paid in accordance with the growth in the economy. (If the minimum wage had been indexed to the productivity of labor and the rate of increase in Gross Domestic Product in the United States, then the minimum in 2002 would not have been $5.15, but around $10.00 an hour. Obviously capitalist corporations in America did not want this kind of change, for it would have encouraged all wage workers to ask for increases, too.)

By the early 1990s, the corporate anti-union campaign was supplemented by the overwhelming popularity of "downsizing" among corporate executives, who started laying off their employees like crazy, often dumping as many white collar employees as blue collar. The lay-offs and increased pressure on remaining workers were two of the factors that helped push profit rates up by the mid-1990s. The median wage for American men was $11.62 in 1995, exactly $2.04 below the male median wage in 1979, when its value was $13.66 (figures adjusted for inflation in 1995 dollars).[18]

Then, during the late 1990s, a combination of factors boosted wages. There was the efficient computerization of many industries and the higher productivity of labor created by new investment. The speculative growth in the stock bubble fueled temporary growth in the internet and telecom companies, and this led to lower unemployment rates that caused employers to bid wages upward. All these things combined to raise wages about 10% over five years—a gain of about 2% per year after inflation but not enough for wages in 2000 to surpass the values they had reached (when figures are adjusted for inflation) thirty years earlier, way back in 1973. That is, the improvements from 1996 to 2000 were too little, too late. Working people's minor gains were due mostly to a temporary boom in the technology sector, not to sound choices made by the U.S. government. Since the policies of the Clinton administration were either pro-corporate or ineffectual in regard to most labor issues, they hardly altered the overall direction that had been set by big business and the Bush Gang. With three years of economic decline, from 2000 to 2003, the United States was in the same condition that Larry Mishel, Jared Bernstein, and John Schmitt had described in *The State of Working America, 1996-1997*:

> The panorama of indicators of economic performance and economic well-being that we present in this book suggests *that we have already taken the low-wage path*. No one in the government or business has explicitly announced a program of lowering American wages and working conditions in order to become "competitive;" nevertheless, the cumulative impact of both government policy and business strategies has achieved a lowering of wages and the standard of living of most Americans.

In summary, the people who benefited the most throughout this whole era were the top managers and the large stockholders.[19] Their increased shares of income were capital earnings driven by the stock market frenzy, not by their contributions of labor. All in all, the stagnant wages of the whole era constituted an outright theft from labor, because the U.S. economy had not been sitting still. It had been growing, not as spectacularly as in the previous thirty years, but at a steady rate nevertheless. According to the Economic Policy Institute analysis, the economy was producing 60% more goods and services per person by the year 2000 than it had in the late 1970s.[20] Economist Mark Weisbrot of the Center for Economic and Policy Research gave a comparable figure for a slightly longer period. He made this dismal appraisal of working people's progress in an essay written just before Labor Day, 2002:

> The real median hourly wage in 1973 was $12.45—measured in 2000 dollars. In 2000, it was about $12.90. Considering that the U.S. economy grew by 72 percent on a per-capita basis during that period, somebody got shafted. Anyone who is old enough to have lived through the 1950s, '60s and '70s knows that it was not uncommon for a typical wage earner to buy a house, support a family, and even put the kids through college with just one income. That doesn't happen anymore.[21]

How could most Americans, men or women, expect to support a family on one income, when many could not support a family on two incomes? The median wage for women was 78% of the median male wage in 2001. And the median wage for men was 3 cents lower than it had been twenty-eight years earlier.[22]

Working More... and More ... and More

With wages either falling or stagnant for most people over the 1980s and 90s, the only way a family could keep slightly ahead was to work more hours. Economic Policy Institute findings for one sub-group of Americans—married-couple families with children—demonstrate that there was a sizable increase in working hours for 80% of American families. Those couples who made up the top 20% of earners were already working over 4,000 hours per year (the equivalent of two full-time jobs) back in 1979, and they kept working at the same pace for the next two decades. But everyone else had to scurry to catch up by working hundreds of hours more each year, with almost all the extra hours being supplied by the wives in the families.

Obviously, there was no reward for diligence and effort. Among the top fifth of the families, the really big gains for a relative few pushed up the average; very high earnings due to a high return on capital, not hours worked, inflated the incomes of the top 1% (see earlier table). Those in the bottom 40% were trying to bail out a sinking boat, for even though they worked harder, their incomes sank in relation to everyone else. Families in the third fifth, or middle quintile, increased their incomes, but almost all of the gain was due to an enormous amount of effort, 20% more hours worked. The fourth fifth, with higher than average wages, were not punished as much; their increase in income, 33.6%, minus their increase in hours, 10.5%, yielded an overall gain of 23.1% per hours worked. But this is still less than it should have been if the average increase in household income, about 30%, had been spread out evenly among all families (as had been the case in an earlier era, from 1947 to 1979).

CEOs Against Workers

In 1980, the CEOs of the Fortune 500 companies earned 42 times as much as the average American worker; by 1999, they earned 531 times as much. How was this possible?

It happened because the CEOs, with the help of senior managers working under them and the backing of elite conservative political supporters, were able to break or bypass the bargaining power of workers' unions and then harness all the desperate labor power of the unorganized. The CEOs did their job, according to the dominant ideology among the owners of capital,[24] which was to maximize profits and stock value while minimizing labor costs.

When layoffs and pay cuts did not suffice, whole divisions of corporations were closed down. When plants could not produce their share of profits, production was moved abroad to low-wage nations, contracted out to low-wage sub-contracting companies, or relocated to non-union areas of the United States. Jobs either left the United States or migrated within the United States, and in the process a great many good working class jobs were turned into

WORK EFFORT OF MARRIED COUPLES, AGED 24-55, WITH CHILDREN[23]

Income Category	Bottom Fifth	Second Fifth	Third Fifth	Fourth Fifth	Top Fifth
Hours worked, 1979	2,354	3,013	3,272	3,757	4,256
Hours worked, 2000	2,727	3,557	3,932	4,149	4,231
Change in hours	+15.9%	+18.1%	+20.2%	+10.5%	- 0.6%
Change in income	+10.8	+17.5%	+25.8%	+33.6%	+ 55.6%

crummy jobs and the overall level of wages and benefits declined. As profits climbed, the absolute number of jobs retained at many of the biggest corporations hardly grew at all. This was particularly true among the world's largest 200 corporations, most of which are American.

Between 1983 and 1999, the number of people employed by top 200 firms grew 14.4%, an increase that is dwarfed by the firms' 362.4% profit growth over this period.[25] Some workers and their unions were successfully frightened into submission, for there were enough plant closings and other examples of corporate flight to make strikes a threatening proposition—the threat was not to the corporation but to the future of working people who wanted to stay settled in their hometowns.

To round out this picture of stagnant and falling wages, there was a new influence among the new big shots of the Fortune 500 corporations. Joining the movers and shakers were low-wage enterprises of a new breed. The largest employers in the country were no longer companies such as General Motors, which paid a wage that could support a family, but corporations such as Wal-Mart and Manpower, which hired disposable employees and paid wages that were so low that they were often insufficient to support a single person, let alone help support a whole family.

Why Pay for Labor?

Paying for labor, in short, was not popular among America's corporate leaders and owners. Or to put it another way, they realized that *not paying for labor* was the most direct path to profits. This tactic has been a favorite of the owners of property ever since the great empires of antiquity imposed slave labor upon their subjects and the people they conquered. Feudal arrangements were hardly better, for the noble owners of productive property, the land, were always tempted to see just how little food and other necessities were required to sustain their working peasants. And in the primitive stages of capitalism, when globalization of trade by the Europeans opened up vast new opportunities to exploit labor, slavery was reintroduced as a method of extracting the highest return on investment. In the extreme, some plantation owners, for instance the English on their sugar islands in the Caribbean, found it "economical" to simply work their slaves to death, then acquire new ones.[26]

Slave owners occasionally made a calculation that was remarkably similar to the one that was so popular with American CEOs operating in the supposedly "advanced" mode of late 20th century capitalism. Plantation overseers, especially those who were hired to produce very fast profits by absentee owners, decided it was more "efficient" to work people so hard that they were simply discarded, dead or alive. No one cared about the long-term health of the working people, the condition of the land, or the economic enterprise because those in charge—both plantation managers and owners—wanted to get their money quickly and get out.

This is not to say that contemporary American capitalists have determined that working people will be whipped and beaten until they keel over and die at their typewriters or cash registers. But clearly they did notice that American workers, being among the best-paid people in the world, could labor more hours and survive on less money than we did before. In the eyes of the corporate class of the late 20th century, the wages, salaries, and incomes of the large majority of Americans were downwardly flexible, and could bend and yield so that capital could be well served. Paying capital, at the highest rate possible, was in great favor because first, it is the primary job of capitalists to cultivate their capital. Secondly, as they experimented with limiting wage growth, restricting labor organizations, and subjecting workers to more stress, pollution, and injuries in the work place, there was not enough outrage expressed on the part of the general public and the forces of organized labor had become too weak to muster resistance all on their own. With relatively small expenditures of money, most conservative members of the owning class supported this reactionary change in our political economy. They found it easy to bankroll anti-labor campaigns within corporations and pro-wealth campaigns on the political circuit.

Unfortunately, there was no Mr. Lincoln on hand, who would have shamed the elite by speaking up for the value of labor. Instead we had a totally different breed of Republican in charge, led by the Misters Bush, and they cheered for capital at every opportunity.

Five

Hiding the Loot

Hoarding the Wealth, or Burning it Up?

Behind every great fortune is a crime.

—19th century French novelist Honoré Balzac

I think we've hit the jackpot with this one.

—Ronald Reagan, 1981, on signing the law
deregulating the savings and loan industry

While Martin Luther King had a dream that won him a Nobel Peace Prize and transformed the country, Ronald Reagan had one that inspired the wealthy and those who aspired to be wealthy. Reagan said, "What I want to see above all is that this remains a country where someone can always get rich."

The Reagan dream, however, was distorted by the actions of his administration and the presidents who followed him, and transformed into a national nightmare: *we have become a country where people who are already very rich get much richer, while average citizens have great difficulty accumulating even modest amounts of wealth.* There were 13 billionaires in 1982 in the United States; 52 in 1988 (the end of Reagan's second term); 170 by 1996; and by 2000, the number had jumped to 298, although a few of them, 69 to be exact, would fall into centi-millionaire status by 2002 due to the stock market collapse that marked the beginning of the 21st century.

Still, the multiplication of billionaires by a factor of almost twenty, from 13 to 229, was

CHANGES IN THE OWNERSHIP OF WEALTH AT THE TOP AND BOTTOM, 1982-2002

The average wealth of the 400 richest Americans went up 409%

1982:	$428 million	2002:	$2.18 billion

The average wealth of poorest 80% of American families went up 18%

1982:	$54,100	2002:	$63,800

(The Forbes 400, listed every year in *Forbes*; figures adjusted for inflation in 2002 dollars)[1]

quite an accomplishment, for such a rapid accumulation of wealth in so few hands only takes place in eras of rampant upper class thievery— for instance, the Gilded Era that began after the Civil War. Not only did the billionaires seem to be reproducing themselves like bunnies in the 1980s and 1990s, but the richest of them expanded their fortunes exponentially. If we translate money values into inflation adjusted to 2002 dollars, we find that in 1982 the Forbes 400, the four hundred richest individuals in the United States, were worth $171 billion between them, or an average wealth of $428 million each. By 1998 the four hundred richest Americans had increased their worth many times over to $812 billion, or an average of $2.03 billion each (in 1998 dollars). Very briefly the stock market bubble carried their collective worth over the trillion dollar mark for the two years 1999-2000. Then, even after the stock market collapse that ushered in the 21st century, the Forbes 400 were maintaining a level of wealth that was ahead of their 1998 levels; in 2002 they weighed in with average fortunes of $2.18 billion each, meaning they had achieved a modest gain of 7.4% over 1998. But we do not need to feel too sorry for them, for after adjusting for inflation their fortunes were 409% greater than they had been twenty years earlier.

Over the same period, most American families had not done nearly so well. If the large majority of American, the poorest 80%, had increased their wealth at the same rate, 409%, as the Forbes 400, then the large majority of American families would have been sitting pretty. Their average wealth (adjusted for inflation in 2002 dollars) would have increased from $54,100 in 1982 to $261,800 twenty years later. Unfortunately, nothing like this happened. The deck was stacked against average families

because twenty years of business and government policies were punishing ordinary wage and salary earners. Even though they were working many more hours per year in 2002 than they had in 1982, these families' average net worth only went up $9,700 over two decades, from $54,100 to $63,800, a very meager increase of 18% for the entire period.

Who is Rich? Who is Not?

The unsatisfactory gains of the majority, and the failure of the capitalist system to promote wealth growth among all Americans, reflects the pattern of very unequal income growth that was discussed in the previous chapter. Distortions in wealth, however, are even more extreme than inequalities in income, and this makes it difficult to comprehend exactly who the "the rich" really are. There are, of course, many more super-rich Americans than just the top 400 that *Forbes* celebrates every year; perhaps 5,000 families have fortunes over $100 million according to Kevin Phillips. His latest book, *Wealth and Democracy*, provides a treasure trove of information on the wealthy in America, both historically and in the present. He notes that the number of families with $10 million or more, the group that George W. Bush now belongs to, jumped from 66,000 in 1982 to 274,000 at the end of the 1990s.[2] This group, the aforementioned Bush League, amount to just one-quarter of one percent of our population. In addition, there is another very well-off group of people, numbering about 750,000 households, who have a net worth ranging from roughly $3 million to $10 million. When their numbers are added to the ranks of the super-rich above them, we then have the richest 1% of the population, families with average fortunes of about $12 million as of 2002.

Obviously, it is a bit arbitrary to decide that the "truly rich" are the top 1%, the top half of 1%, or the top tenth of 1%. To a great many Americans, any family with savings of $200,000 and up looks pretty rich. To the family with $200,000 salted away in home equity and retirement accounts, their holdings seem very modest compared to those with $3 million or more. Because income and wealth statistics are collected for the top 1%, and because this elite group owns about half of all financial assets and half of all publicly traded stock in the United States, this book has settled upon them as "the rich." They wield the bulk of economic power.

Below them, another 9% of the populace is not doing badly, since they hold 38% of all stock in their hands and about as much of all financial assets.[3] In the eyes of everyone but the top 1%, this 9% seems quite rich because the assets of the families in this group average about $1.1 million (ranging, in very rough terms, when all their assets, houses and possessions are included, from less than $600,000 to more than $2,000,000). Their average wealth is more than ten times as much as the average wealth holding among the bottom 90%. I would suggest that we not get too exercised about the wealth of what I am choosing to call the "upper-middle class," and my reasoning is very much the same as I expressed in the previous chapter on wages. For

the most part these are people who did relatively well on the basis of their labor, not their capital, and they are citizens of a very rich country. We should not necessarily begrudge them their savings, even if the sum approaches a million dollars or so, when they may have worked for fifty years to accumulate that tidy nest egg. Why?

Because the United States is so rich! In 2001 the *average wealth* of all American households was $394,000 (although it would fall to $341,000 when the stock market kept sinking in 2002). When the average is this high, it does not seem particularly greedy for some citizens to accumulate twice that amount. As is the case with incomes, the 9% of the people residing below the richest 1% on the wealth charts do not constitute the major problem. The real problem is the growing share of wealth that falls into the laps of the very rich.

The average wealth of the top 1% was over $10 million per family in 1998, climbed to over $14 million in 2001, and settled back to around $12 million in 2002. They control enormous economic resources that the next 9% can only dream about. Obviously, with this kind of superiority in wealth, roughly twelve to one, over the average wealth held by the nearly rich or the upper-middle class (or whatever else one chooses to call the well-off folks below the top 1%), the truly rich are in the driver's seat.

1920S, HERE WE COME: WEALTH SHIFTING BACK TO THE WEALTHY

(The percentage of all wealth held by the richest 1%)

1929	1949	1969	1979	1983	1989	1998
44.2%	27.1%	31.1%	20.5%	33.8%	37.4%	38.1%

(Edward N. Wolff, *Top Heavy*, NY: The New Press, 1995; *The State of Working America*, 2002-2003)

The rest of us, the poorest 90% of the population, only own about 14% of corporate stock and 20% of all financial assets, even when indirect ownership through pension funds and retirement accounts is considered.[4] Many of us choose not to gamble directly in the stock market, but instead have very modest shares of ownership through participation in mutual funds, 401(k)plans, and other kinds of pensions. This indirect ownership raised the share owned by the bottom 90% to 13.9% of the stock market in 1998, somewhat more than the paltry 9.6% they held in 1983.

This small trend of accelerating stock ownership may already be over, since the most recent Survey of Consumer Finances shows that the median value of shares held by middle-income families fell from $9,200 in 1998 to $8,000 in 2001; almost certainly it is less in 2003. Thus the notion that there was a great democratization of the stock market appears even more nonsensical than it did in the mid-to-late 1990s.[5] Just because the proportion of people who had some connection to corporate stock assets—through direct ownership, pensions, retirement plans—rose to 52% (about the same proportion as the number of adults who vote in presidential elections), that does not make ownership of corporations democratic. There is no "one person, one vote" rule in the world of corporations, because people do not rule. Capital rules: "one share equals one vote." Consequently, the number of votes you have depends on how much money you've been able to invest in America's corporations—an inherently anti-democratic mechanism. On average, there are approximately 300 shares voting for each rich person, while a single share votes for each of us among the overwhelming majority of Americans, the bottom 90% on the wealth charts.

Boom and Bust Didn't Hurt the Rich Very Much

The overall value of publicly traded stock went from approximately $3 trillion in 1988 to $5 trillion in 1992, to over $10 trillion in 1997, and finally peaked at $17.8 trillion in March of 2000. Since many of the richest 1% of the population were so heavily invested in the stock market when it began its ascent, they did very well indeed, even if they did not pull their money out of the market in time to avoid the bursting bubble. Some people, no doubt, especially among the CEOs and corporate insiders, managed to take their money and run before the stock market came crashing back to earth in October of 2002. For instance, insiders within the telecommunications industry cashed in $18 billion of stock between 1997-2000, most of it in 2000 when stock prices peaked. The entire telecom sector then collapsed over the next two years. A great many of the richest Americans, the Forbes 400 among them, probably took some losses. But because most of them had been invested so long, their overall gains—spanning ten, fourteen, or twenty years—were still very handsome indeed.

The crash of the stock market alerts the rest of us to the fragility of our savings, which are not exactly solid. They can be eroded by inflation even if they are safely locked in the bank, but when we invest them in volatile markets, derivatives, commodity futures, and currency exchanges, we are in fact gambling. This has always been a favorite activity of the very wealthy, for it is hard to resist the temptation of magnificent returns on a segment of one's wealth, especially when absolutely no labor is required. In this regard, the rich had two distinctive advantages over many of the middle class and upper middle-class citizens who invested in the stock market in the 1990s.

For one thing, a great many rich people have been heavily invested for a long time because so much of their wealth is inherited or accumulated through long association with those at the top of the corporate ladder. As already mentioned, the richest 1% owned almost 50% of corporate stock long before the boom and they still owned more or less the same amount afterwards. They reaped a good share of the nearly three-fold return on investments in the stock market between 1988 and 2002. Among long-term investors (this would include some modest equity owners as well as the rich), those who sold their shares or exchanged shaky stocks for solid ones in 2000 would have enjoyed the maximum gains, about five times their original investment. The worst-hit were certainly the new investors who entered the market between 1995 and 2000, gambled a substantial amount of their savings on the riskiest stocks, such as new dot.coms, but did not sell off fast enough.

This brings us to the second big advantage of the very rich. They could be big-time players in the stock market without being hurt very much by the risks. Most all of them had substantial sources of savings and income outside of stocks to back them up. For instance, Edward N. Wolff calculated in 1998 that the richest 1% of Americans had huge stock holdings averaging slightly more than $2.5 million, but these were backed up by more than three times as much wealth, worth nearly $8 million, that was invested in other kinds of assets. This kind of money allows them to wait out swings in the markets. Preliminary data on wealth ownership for 2001 suggest that this is just what happened from 1998 to 2002. The assets of the richest 1% went up from $10.2 million in 1998 to $13-14 million in 2001, only to settle back to about $12 million in 2002 after the biggest stock market losses were sustained.[6]

Data from *Forbes*, the magazine that likes to call itself the "capitalist tool," reveal that most old family money did very well during the run-up in the stock market. These families outlasted many of the upstart billionaires in the high tech industries. For instance, the Rockefeller family trust saw its portfolios rise from $3.3 billion to $8.5 billion and the Mellon family fortune ballooned from $1.6 billion to $10 billion between 1982 and 2000. While these extremely rich families might well have sustained losses in the first years of the 21st century, their dominant ownership position in the country remained intact. Over the previous two decades, both Federal Reserve and scholarly studies have demonstrated a steady increase in the percentage of wealth belonging to those at the very top. They improved on the position they held in the prosperous 1960s when they held 31.1% of all net worth, moving up to 37.5% in 1989, and then hitting 38.1% in 1998. This wealth shift can be seen for households of different income classes thanks to the careful calculations of Professor Edward N. Wolff of New York University and others; the figures below illustrate the changes in wealth for different segments of the population.

CHANGE IN WEALTH BY CLASS 1983-1998			
	1983	**1989**	**1998**
Top 1%	$7,175,10	$9,101,700	$10,203,700
Middle 20%	$55,500	$58,800	$61,000
2nd lowest 20%	$12,500	$10,200	$11,100
Bottom 20%	-$3,200	-$18,200	-$8,900

(Adjusted for inflation in 1998 dollars.)[7]

The folks at the bottom, being hooked by the slew of credit offers thrown at them by the banks, and trying to fight the effects of their falling wages, ended up further in debt. The next group up, the not entirely poor people in the 20th to 40th percentiles, have surprisingly low assets that have actually shrunk. And the middle stratum of working Americans, in the 41st to 60th percentile range, have a modest chunk of money that is usually tied up in the equity of their houses. There was hardly any growth in wealth for them. Their holdings had only increased from $55,500 to $61,000 over fifteen years. The whole sum of their savings could easily be swallowed up by a severe family illness or a lengthy layoff from work.

One good way to get an appreciation of the modest nature of wealth accumulated by most Americans is to look at the situation of those who are somewhat above the median, those in the 50th to 75th percentiles according to the Survey of Consumer Finances conducted by the Federal Reserve Board in 2001. The median wealth of this group was $156,000 in 2001, most of which was housing equity of $120,000 (for the 91% of this group who were homeowners). Their financial holdings were small: only 20% owned stocks directly; 17% owned mutual funds; and 63% had retirement accounts. For those who had retirement accounts, the median amount was $30,000 in 2001, down from $35,000 in 1998. In stocks, for those who had them, the median holdings were just $8,300, down from $8,700.

But then, in 2002, their median net worth took a hit, losing an average of $11,000 due to the drop in the financial markets. Overall their net worth was still ahead, about 10% more in 2002 than in 1998, but all of that gain was due to the increase in the market value of their homes.[8]

Wealth in a Democracy

Natural wealth is comprised of the earth's resources which are at our disposal for as long as we care for and restore the land, air, and water, and the species that they sustain. Human wealth generally consists of things that we have grown, created or built, things that can be accumulated and saved. We can pass down a home and other assets to our children in ways other animals cannot, and can manipulate nature in ways that increase our wealth. These savings have enabled human societies to develop their own resources over time, to invest in new technologies and the development of cities, agriculture, and industry. This surplus also allows us the leisure time necessary to develop new knowledge and amuse ourselves.

Once accumulated, what shall we do with our wealth? And in a democracy, who should control it?

One answer is to consider the savings, or capital, as something produced by all human labor in its various forms. In the United States this is more or less in line with the ideas of founding fathers like Jefferson, progressive Republicans like Lincoln, and New Deal Democrats like Franklin Roosevelt. Another faction maintains that democracy is more limited, and that wealth and capital ought to be in the safe keeping of an intelligent elite. These rich citizens supposedly know better than the great majority of the people when it comes to managing society's money. This view is more in keeping with the American tradition of conservative Federalists like Alexander Hamilton and conservative Republicans like Andrew Mellon. The more egalitarian group tends to think that people in democracies can make informed decisions about the use of wealth. The more elitist group favors elevating a few people to positions where they control the wealth produced by society. What they share in common is the idea that wealth, which has been created by all the working people in American society, should be used and invested wisely.

In the case of the United States and most other advanced capitalist countries, the bulk of accumulated private wealth resides in a few hands, and a tiny minority of people has an overriding obligation to do useful things with these funds. The capitalist owners of business must make timely investments in new factories, machinery, and innovative research in order to raise productivity, maintain profitability, compete in the international arena, and augment the wages of their workers. (The last item was essential to the economic development of all advanced industrial nations throughout the 20th century. Owners had to share some of their gains in increased productivity with working people in the form of higher wages. This enabled average citizens to purchase the increasing amounts and variety of commodities and services produced by private business.)

As for the society as a whole, it has a duty, too. It must use its democratic institutions to impose sufficient taxes on the rich, so that the people can accumulate the wealth sufficient to build up public assets that benefit everyone. When the public sector gains the capacity to create more efficient transportation, better schools, and good health care, this has obvious benefits, not only for all citizens but also for private businesses. Employers gain from increased productivity when they have healthier and better educated employees who can conveniently get to and from work.

When we look back over the past twenty years, there were some exciting moments—innovation in computer and internet capabilities, for instance. But when we consider where the bulk of our resources went, the era does not seem particularly productive compared to the rest of the 20th century. For instance, we spent trillions of dollars on glorified pick-up trucks, the SUVs, that are a step backward in automotive technology and waste an inordinate amount of fuel. Another chunk of our national savings has been funneled into houses, a more stable form of middle-class wealth than the stock market, but there is now some justified fear that this market also may be on the verge of popping a smaller speculative bubble.[9] A related use of our savings, the cost of filling in farmland with subdivisions and shopping malls, does constitute wealth invested in the built environment, but it may be a cost that our environment cannot sustain.

All the above investments are closely related to personal consumption, which has been encouraged across all social classes by our commercial culture. Naturally the rich were eager to consume, too. The high degree of luxury fever had them panting for more, consuming four, five, or ten times the amount spent by other families on daily expenses, plus throwing one McMansion on a nearby hillside and another on a mountain in Colorado. Even so, the rich households should have had lots of excess income left over for investment and savings, for real wealth creation. What have they done with it?

Many of the wealthy went on a binge of speculation and looting.

The 1980s—More Loot, More Crime at the Top

The crimes of reckless money only compounded the sins that criminologist Raymond J.

Michalowski described in his 1985 book, *Order, Law, and Crime*, a compendium of the ways that corporations choose to disregard laws to the detriment of the whole society. He surveyed a broad range of white collar crimes, environmental crimes, and crimes that were injurious to workers and consumers, then concluded that "crimes of capital constitute the greatest source of untimely death, injury, illness, and economic loss faced by American citizens."[10]

The corporate grasp on American culture, which has elevated amoral or immoral business people into heroic figures, has been encouraged by the Bush Gang since the 1980s. The big CEOs and investors could do no wrong because there was no wrong. Eager students applauded Ivan Boesky, the master of junk bond mergers, during his 1985 commencement speech at the University of California-Berkeley's School of Business Administration, and laughed when he said, "Greed is all right, by the way. I want you to know that. I think greed is healthy. You can be greedy and still feel good about yourself."[11] The students would later learn another lesson from Boesky: crime pays. Boesky went to jail in 1980s, paid a huge settlement, yet still was a near-billionaire when he was released from his relatively comfortable stay in a low security prison.

Those Berkeley students raced out with their MBAs in the late 1980s, eager to plunder the country. But they scarcely had the opportunity because others had beaten them to it. The disastrous financial scandals of the decade, fueled by the wave of deregulation brought on by Reagan and the Bush Gang, had cleaned out much of the investment capital and a good chunk of ordinary citizens' savings, helping to induce the worst economic downturn since the Great Depression of the 1930s. Economist Ravi

Batra called this period, from 1989 to 1995, the "quiet Depression" and John Kenneth Galbraith labeled it the "Recession cum Depression."

The looting of the savings and loan industry caused the failure of an entire wing of the banking industry. The S&Ls were originally created for the legally designated purpose of serving community homeowners. They promptly shifted gears as soon as they were deregulated in 1981, and began investing heavily in risky real estate development schemes instead. Their subsequent collapse left American taxpayers with a staggering bill to pay off, $500 billion when interest was included. The commercial real estate collapse in America's big cities and suburbs was set up by similar circumstances—a combination of deregulation, a stampede of legally questionable limited partnerships, changes in accelerated depreciation rules, and the manipulation of other tax laws. The losses of the large commercial banks were estimated to be even greater than the S&Ls, at $1 trillion and up. In this case, because the whole economy was at risk, corporate giants like Citibank were rescued through huge injections of capital from the Federal Reserve banks and very rich foreign investors.

In the 1980s, there was a warning sign about the nature of the Bush clan that should have been heeded. The family was showing a pronounced tendency to involve themselves in the wave of piracy that was endangering the financial health of the whole nation. While our current president was one case in point, and his Uncle Jonathan was banned from selling brokerage securities, the example of Neil Bush, brother of George W, was the most blatant. Neil probably had as many failed business ventures as George W, but some were more spectacular, especially the Silverado Savings and Loan in

THE GREAT SAVINGS AND LOAN ROBBERY—SILVERADO EPISODE, 1987

Loss of Taxpayers' Money at Silverado S&L ($1 billion)	$1,000,000,000
Damages collected from Neil Bush and other directors	$49,500,000
Losses from all armed bank robberies in the U.S., 1987	$37,000,000

Colorado, which lost more than $1 billion when it collapsed in the late 1980s.[12]

From the figures above the reader can appreciate the fact that the fines assessed against Neil and his ganglet were far less than the real criminal damage to the economy and the taxpayers' pocketbooks. Moreover, Neil and his buddies did not really pay the damages, for the entire $49.5 million was paid off by liability insurance on their S&L and a special "legal defense fund" the Silverado directors had wisely created even before the institution collapsed and they were investigated. The cost of this one white-collar crime was far greater than all the armed bank robberies committed in the United State in 1987.

Neil Bush had found a way to pass on millions in unsecured loans to his friends, but did not seem to profit much himself from this criminal escapade. Undeterred, he promptly went out and signed up for a loan from the Small Business Administration, and received $2.35 million to finance his next endeavor, Apex Energy. That business flopped and he never repaid the loan.[13]

Neil Bush's transgressions were but light snowflakes atop the tip of a giant corporate iceberg of crime, most of which stayed hidden from sight. The large majority of savings and loan irregularities were not properly investigated or prosecuted, even though the Federal Home Loan Bank Board found evidence of fraud and other criminal activity by managers and direc-

tors at 75% of the failing S&Ls. When the Office of Thrift Supervision was investigating Neil Bush's tricks in 1990 and decided not to prosecute, this undoubtedly had something to do with his father, George H.W., being president of the United States. The Bush family could have rightly claimed that their son was not getting preferential treatment because almost all the criminals working the same territory, the savings and loan racket, were going unpunished.

The first Bush administration let them all walk free! This gets to the essence of the Bush Gang's criminal influence over the past twenty years. More important than their own personal transgressions has been their propensity to let anything go. They deregulated and then looked the other way because these were their friends at work. The decade of the 1980s had produced theft, fraud, and undisciplined gambling with America's vast wealth. Business values had deteriorated to the point, said *Business Week* in a famous cover story, that America had become a "Casino Society."[14] It was endangered by the irresponsible game of economic roulette played by those at the top of the social pyramid.

The 1990s:
More Scams, Bigger Casino

From the mid-1980s through the early 1990s, corporate ethics continued to deteriorate, as witnessed by the case of the Prudential

Insurance Company. It permitted its agents to persuade millions of customers that they should cash in or borrow against existing insurance policies and buy new ones. What made this a wonderful scam, known as "churning," was that neither the Prudential management nor their agents informed their clients that they were getting less coverage at a higher cost. In 1996 the Justice Department determined that Prudential owed 10.7 million people a total of $410 million in damages (a sum which was not satisfactory to state prosecutors, so they filed for additional settlements.) The same pattern emerged among other giants of the insurance industry such as John Hancock, Metropolitan Life, and New York Life. According to *The New York Times,* "These cases have embarrassed the industry, and, many executives say, contributed to a decline in sales."[15]

While these big-time operators enjoyed perpetrating millions of such small-time frauds, there was other entertainment to be found at the brokerage gaming tables where people wagered huge amounts of money. In one case, Merrill Lynch enticed the treasurer of Orange County, California into putting $21 billion of publicly generated wealth (including retirement money for county employees) into tricky new investment vehicles known as financial derivatives, then sat back and watched as the county went bankrupt. Merrill Lynch earned huge fees by selling two-thirds of those securities and by underwriting $875 million worth of bonds that Orange County issued, but it also broke the law. At one trial Merrill Lynch, Wall Street's largest investment bank, was charged with fraud for its duplicity[16] and had to pay $437 million to Orange County and private parties. In another appearance in court, also related to the Orange County scam, Merrill Lynch was lucky enough to secure the services of Harvey Pitt. This is the guy who was later picked to head the regulatory Securities and Exchange Commission under the second president Bush.

Harvey Pitt had spent 10 years training as a Securities and Exchange Committee (SEC) lawyer before switching to the much more lucrative practice of using this expertise to defend corporate clients against lawsuits, criminal charges, and the SEC itself. His firm had gained fame in the 1980s for getting Ivan Boesky off with a mere $100 million fine, thus preserving the bulk of his fortune. Pitt succeeded in getting the case against Merrill Lynch reduced to a charge of "unintentional fraud" (though no one has ever explained how fraud can be anything but purposeful). The company's executives then pled guilty and were given a light slap on their collective wrist, a $2 million civil sanction.

Later in the decade, corporate profits began to soar, as did corporate immorality. Once the stock mania had been stoked in 1990s, there was no holding back the CEO maniacs. Greed and irrational bookkeeping were glorified. *Fortune* called Enron the most innovative company in America, not once, but six years in a row. Bill Clinton, to his credit, vetoed a bill in 1995 that would have made it harder to sue executives for the misdeeds of corporations, but the Republican Congress and some eager-beaver Democratic Senators overrode his veto. The accounting industry also successfully lobbied Congress to change corporate accounting into something else altogether, and they called it "business consulting." The table was set.

Alan Greenspan later claimed that he knew that corporate leaders were hungry: "It's not that executives got more greedy," he said. "They were already greedy. But they were more able to skirt the law, to avoid deregulation." True, but not only was the law unregulated, but so was the flow of money. Greenspan, with his hand on the money spigot (and with the encouragement of almost everyone else in positions of power in the banks and the government) brushed aside the fact that corporate profits started falling steadily after 1997 and kept pouring more and more easy money into the economy. As Robert Brenner has demonstrated in his book, *The Boom and the Bubble,* the Federal Reserve Board kept pumping up the money supply even though it was clear that corporations were not performing.

The easy cash, often available to corporations which wanted to buy back their stock and then redistribute it to executives, led to irresponsible behavior and led to corporate malfeasance at Enron, WorldCom, Tyco, and a host of other companies. This completely dwarfed the levels of business crime that Prudential, Merrill Lynch, and others had committed during the early to mid-1990s. (Merrill Lynch did keep coming back to the trough in the late '90s and was implicated in a variety of fraudulent stock offerings, as were many of the nation's giant banks such as Citicorp and JP Morgan Chase). Mr. Pitt, meanwhile, kept gaining fame as the smartest of the smart. He defended the practices of corporate bookkeepers who were setting the betting odds higher and higher, as well as the accounting firms who were called in to justify their excesses. Ultimately, just as the house of cards of devious capital was collapsing, the Bush Gang needed a man to head up the Securities and Exchange Commission. Who did they choose? Harvey Pitt.

Pitt started his job by lifting a term from the lips of George Bush Sr. He suggested that the government take a "kinder, gentler" approach to uncovering crime in the corporate world. However, when more and more multi-billion dollar scandals erupted from corporate balance sheets and an irate Congress passed the Sarbanes-Oxley Bill to fight crime in the suites, Pitt had to change his tune. The Bush administration and Pitt contended they would start cracking down by setting up a "Public Company Accounting Board" within the SEC.

To give the appearance of really fighting crime, Pitt appointed William Webster—who had been a federal judge, the boss at the FBI, and chief at the CIA—to head this new board. Pitt overlooked the fact that Webster had never taken a bite out of corporate crime; the fact was that the man was a corporate lap dog. Webster had served on the boards of various shaky corporations, including a stint as chairman of the audit committee at United Technologies, which had fired an outside auditor for criticizing its "financial controls." The company was near bankruptcy and under fire from shareholders for fraudulent behavior at the very moment Webster joined the SEC Accounting Board. All this embarrassed the Bush Gang, so both Pitt and Webster resigned in November 2002.

Voters were too distracted by the War on Terrorism to be bothered by the special coddling and outright friendship extended by the Bush administration toward the corporate criminal class. The Democrats refrained from raising the issue of the scandalous misuse of America's wealth in the 2002 campaign, and the Republican Party cleaned up by taking over all of Congress. And since there is actually a kind of honor among thieves, the Bush Gang was ready to repay the new generation of Robber Barons.

Tax cuts always make a suitable gift.

Six

Taxes

Would Robbers Cheat?

The primary objective should be to put a constantly increasing burden on the inheritance of those swollen fortunes, which it is certainly of no benefit to this country to perpetuate.

—Theodore Roosevelt in his annual message to Congress, 1906

The subjects of every state ought to contribute toward the support of the government, as nearly as possible, in proportion to their respective abilities; that is, in proportion to the revenue which they respectively enjoy under the protection of the state...

—so wrote Adam Smith, in *The Wealth of Nations*, 1776, then he added, just so no one would mistake his intentions:

... as Henry Home (Lord Kames) has written, a goal of taxation should be to 'remedy inequality of riches as much as possible, by relieving the poor and burdening the rich.'

How would Teddy Roosevelt, who is said to be one of George W. Bush's heroes, react to the Bush Gang's attempt to do away with inheritance taxes? How would Adam Smith, icon of capitalism, react to the priorities of the Bush Gang and their allies? They would be appalled at the unrelenting desire for lower taxation on the part of the rich, who seek to relieve the tax burden from themselves and their corporations and shift it onto the backs of working people.

Corporations, which are predominantly owned by the rich, saw their share of federal taxes systematically lowered even though their profits were generally rising from 1970s until 2000. At the same time, income earned by labor, which after the 1970s did not increase very much at all, was providing more and more of federal revenue through Social Security and

other withholding taxes.

Bush Gang I was instrumental in this process, and when Bush Gang II returned to office in 2001, they immediately pushed more corporate tax reductions for big business through Congress.[1]

Huge cuts in the corporate income tax rates were matched by equally generous reductions in individual income taxes for the very wealthy. When the Bush Gang moved into Washington in the 1980s they initiated another massive tax giveaway for themselves and their friends. Maximum tax rates on the richest individuals were lowered from 70% to 50% to 28%, so they were able to keep a bigger share of their rapidly growing pre-tax income.

Effective taxation on high incomes has always been lower than the official top rates because of the special tax categories and tax shelters granted to the rich. Therefore even when the Democrats increased the top marginal income tax to 39.6% in 1993, it produced a much more modest increase, from 22% to 27%, in the amount of taxes actually collected from the wealthiest Americans in 1996. When Bush Gang II returned to Washington in 2001 they immediately took up the task of individual tax reduction again, once again favoring themselves and other wealthy Americans by lowering their effective tax rate to 25% for 2001, with further reductions to 23% slated a few years down the line. They were simply resuming the program that was instituted during the reign of the Reagan/Bush administrations: in those 12 years the Bush Gang had engineered a staggering reversal of the American tradition of progressive taxation.

EFFECTIVE FEDERAL INCOME TAX RATE ON THE RICHEST 1%

1979: 34%   1986: 22%   1996: 27%   2001: 25%

(source: IRS)[2]

Worker's payroll taxes, the main source of federal revenues from low and middle income Americans, have increased dramatically, bringing in over 34.9% federal revenues in 2001 as opposed to just 6.9% in the 1950s. These rev-enues compensated for the drastic drop in corporate income taxes from 26.5% in the 1960s to 7.6% of federal revenue in 2001. In fact, it was the middle and working classes that were suffering higher taxation with very little representation, brought to them courtesy of Alan Greenspan, who was chairman of the Republican Council of Economic Advisors in 1983. That group successfully pushed for raising the rate of FICA withholding taxes (Social Security and Medicare) by about 20% between 1980 and 1990.[3] In 1987 Greenspan was chosen to be chairman of the Federal Reserve Board, a post he was still holding sixteen years later under Bush II.

Over the long run, federal taxes on working families had doubled, going from 9% of their income in the 1950s to 18%, or even 20% in the mid 1990s. Because of the large social security increases, a small reduction in federal income taxes on working families in the 1980s did not offset this overall trend. There was a really big change, however, when it came to the income taxes of the rich.

With guidance from the Bush Gang, Ronald Reagan returned to that glorious decade of Coolidge and his youth, when the rich ran rampant and their income tax rate was below

THE BURDEN SHIFTED FROM CORPORATIONS TO WORKING PEOPLE

(Percentage of all federal revenues collected from each source)

Year	Corporate Income Taxes	Workers' Payroll Taxes
1950	26.5%	6.9%
1970	17.0%	18.2%
2000	10.2%	31.1%
2001	7.6%	34.9%

(Sources: Congressional Budget Office, IRS. Most other federal revenue comes from individual income taxes.)

30%. In 1986 the top marginal rate dropped to 28%. The results, compiled by the IRS a few years later, were striking:

TAX SAVINGS IN 1989 RESULTING FROM "TAX REFORM" OF 1986		
Household income	% cut	Tax savings
$30,000-40,000	11%	$467
$75,000-100,000	18%	$3,034
$1,000,000 and up	31%	$281,033

(IRS data from 1989 tax returns)

Though these tax cuts for the rich were very generous, the federal tax system remains mildly progressive overall, in the sense that most rich people still pay a higher percentage of their income than do the poor. But at the state and local level, the rich won the taxation battle long ago. Many regressive state taxes, like the sales tax, end up penalizing the poor much more than the rich. The middle class, too, is taxed at a much higher rate than the richest 1% of taxpayers (see next table). State legislatures, even when they are not populated with anti-tax reactionaries, are very wary of insulting multinational corporations or very rich individuals by raising their taxes, since then they might move to another state or another country. Although most states have some form of income tax, many do not apply it too rigorously. As might be expected, the Bush boys gravitated to two of the six states that have no income tax at all, Texas and Florida. Jeb Bush's Florida ranks number two in terms of having the most unfair combination of state and local taxes in the nation. Texas, though not far behind, has slipped to number five (it was number three before Dubya moved to Washington).

Progressive Taxation versus the Robber Barons: A Brief History of the Income Tax

The U.S. Congress first passed a very minimal income tax in 1894, imposing a tax rate of 2% on the richest five or six per cent of the population. The Supreme Court immediately struck the law down in 1894, calling it "an assault on capital." Since the Court continued to act as a bastion of upper class sentiment in the early 1900s, a progressive coalition of Republicans and Democrats used other means to go after the income that the 19th century Robber Barons and their children were hoarding. They instituted the Federal Income Tax by passing a constitutional amendment in 1913. The tax started out as a levy on a small minority of well-off cit-

THE MOST REGRESSIVE TAXES—THE BUSH STATES LEAD THE WAY			
Combined state and local tax rates paid by different households			
income levels	Average for all states	Florida	Texas
poorest 20%	11.4%	14.4%	11.4%
middle 20%	9.6%	9.8%	8.4%
richest 1%	5.2%	3.0%	3.5%

(figures from Institute on Taxation and Economic Policy for 2002)[4]

izens, with multimillionaires paying at the highest rate of 6%. With the beginning of World War I, however, there was the necessity of paying to arm the country, so those earning over $1 million per year were required to pay much higher taxes. Their tax rate rose to 67% in 1917.

The top rate stayed high after the war. This infuriated Andrew Mellon, the oil and banking heir from Pittsburgh, and one of the richest men in the country. Over the twelve years between 1920 and 1932, he relentlessly pursued his mission in life, to lower the income tax. And he was in a position to do so. He served as the Secretary of the Treasury for three Republican presidents: Harding, Coolidge, and Hoover. In 1921, the top rate on income was reduced from 73% to 56%; with the tax "reform" law of 1924, the rate sank to 46%; and finally with the Revenue Act of 1926, Mellon hit the jackpot: the tax on the richest citizens was reduced to 25% and the estate tax was cut in half, from 40% to 20%. The corporate profits tax was reduced by a stunning three quarters.

Mellon's efforts immediately gave solace to the wealthy, for the fortunes of the Robber Barons came roaring back. In 1920, there had been only 33 Americans who earned $1 million per year. In 1928 there were 511 of them. And just below them, in the $100,000 to $1 million category, the ranks of the rich swelled from 3,616 to 15,466. But this did not mean that wealth was being generated for all Americans. Most working people were left far behind as their wages stagnated or fell.

With money flowing so freely upward, the fresh crew of millionaires and their minions flew into a wild orgy of financial speculation, taking the stock market higher and higher until it crashed in 1929. The rich, including Mellon, had to do penance for their sins, for they were blamed by many for bringing on the Great Depression. The highest marginal income tax rates went up to 79% in 1936, hit 88% during World War II, and topped out at 91% in the 1950s.

TAX RATES AND ECONOMIC PERFORMANCE DURING THE PAST HALF CENTURY

Tax rates on highest incomes		Economic performance of the United States
1951:	91%	For most of this period, 1951-1973, this was
1964:	77%	the most prosperous time in U.S. history;
1965-1980:	70%	there was a fall-off in growth 1974-1980.
1981-1986:	50%	Bush Gang arrives:
1987:	38.7%	Lowest taxes since the 1920s,
1988-1990:	28%	worst economic growth since the Depression.
1991-1992:	31%	
1992-2000:	39.6	Slow recovery, then higher growth 1996-2000.
2001-2003:	35%-38%	Bush Gang returns:
2004-2010:	35% (or less?)	a very poor start.

Even though Andrew Mellon was a conservative and an unapologetic defender of upper-class interests, it would be a mistake to suggest that he stooped as low as the ultra-conservatives who came creeping in with the Bush Gang fifty years later. While he wanted to reduce the taxes of the wealthy, Mellon nevertheless said that there was an intrinsic "fairness of taxing more lightly income from wages and salaries." As he put it:

> Surely we can afford to make a distinction between people whose only capital is their mental and physical energy and the people whose income is derived from investment.
>
> —Andrew Mellon, in his book, *Taxation: the People's Business*.

The Bush Gang thinks much differently. Not only did they promote the steep cuts in income taxes in the 1980s and again at the beginning of the 21st century, but they, unlike Andrew Mellon, are very comfortable with the idea of transferring the tax burden from income based on capital investment to income derived from human effort in the workplace. Their lack of moral consideration for laboring people is easily condemned, but what about their reading of recent economic history? There is very little evidence that lowering taxes on capital and the rich is helpful to the economy as a whole. In fact, the relation of taxes to strong economic growth in the last half century seems to be the opposite.

While there is no way of proving that high taxes lead to prosperity, lowering taxes on the rich certainly did not help the U.S. economy over the past 50 years.

Capital Guys Do Not Prefer Capital Gains Taxes

In 1996, the Republican Congress and Clinton joined forces to enact one of the fondest dreams of George Bush I, lowering the capital gains tax. Bush Senior had pushed for a reduction from 28% to 15% during his presidency, 1989-1992, but no one listened because the country was sitting in a deep, deep deficit. Later, with the economy in recovery and the deficit declining rapidly, the capital gains rate was lowered to 20% in 1996. In 2003 Bush Gang II declared it should be lowered again. They were also anxious to eliminate all other taxes on capital income, whether in form of dividends from corporate stock, capital gains, or taxes on the nation's largest estates.

One of the great successes of contemporary conservatives has been to eliminate the distinction that even Andrew Mellon acknowledged was an element of fairness, the one between the "earned" income produced by one's labor and the "unearned" income produced by one's capital. By eliminating this conceptual barrier to all-out greed, the Bush forces have mounted a full scale attack on wages and salaries even though they are the product of a person's active work (even the bloated pay of the big CEOs is generally connected to showing up at work every day). The income of investors, however, is passive, the byproduct of wealth already amassed.

This passion for taxing work more heavily than non-work has allowed the very richest Americans to enjoy lower tax rates than ordinary, run-of-the-mill rich folks. In 1999, the million dollar earners, with average incomes of about $3.2 million, paid a 27.9% effective rate in federal income taxes. The sub-millionaires, rich people with incomes of between $500,000 and $1,000,000, paid a slightly higher effective rate on taxes, 28.4%, because their average income of $677,000 had a smaller component of capital gains (only 21%, compared to the millionaires' 42%) and a higher component of wages. As for the 400 richest taxpayers, they realized 7% of all the capital gains in the nation, or well over $30 billion. Because of the lower rate for capital gains income, the fat 400 had a very modest rate of effective taxation at the federal level: 22%. Professor Joel Slemrod of the University of Michigan found that the highest 400 incomes also paid the 22% rate in 1998. This was a very sharp reduction from the 30% rate they paid in 1995; Slemrod calculated that the change in the capital gains rate saved the top 400 about $3 billion in 1998.[5]

Many highly ranked Republicans as well as Federal Reserve Chairman Alan Greenspan, have long been enthusiastic about eliminating the capital gains tax altogether. "I've always been supportive of either lowering the capital-gains tax or preferably eliminating it completely," Mr. Greenspan once told the Senate Banking Committee.[6] Does anyone still recall that Greenspan, besides being very conservative, was once a Wall Street investment banker? Bankers prefer working for the richest 1% of the population because they own the most capital, and naturally the bankers make more money when capital is not taxed.

Did the 1996 reduction in the capital gains tax rate encourage wild behavior in the stock market? Since the gains on stock sales were going to be taxed at a low rate, 20%, while some of the other choices open to the rich were taxed at 39.6%, why not invest more in the stock market? Generally, tax advantages do cause people, especially those with lots of money, to real-locate their financial resources. Huge sums of money were thrown at stocks by the rich, bolstered by legions of small investors who longed for big gains themselves. The roulette wheel was spinning faster and faster. IRS tables show that the share of capital gains collected by the richest 1% was three quarters of all capital gains collected by all taxpayers in both 1999 and 2000; in those two years the share of all capital gains produced by stock sales mushroomed, swelling to 58% from a rate of 40% in the mid-1990s.

How to Get More: Returns from the Dead

There are four pillars of progressive taxation that really aggravate the Bush Gang because they are direct or indirect taxes on capital: the capital gains tax, the corporate income tax, the progressive tax on all individual income (because the highest incomes also tend to have the highest shares of capital income), and the estate tax that is levied at the death of very rich citizens. All of these were imposed in the first half of the 20th century so that there would be little chance for the wealthy owners of America's corporations and financial institutions to divert money from one kind of investment to another, thereby wiggling out from under the long arm of the tax man. If the Bush administration can destroy these restraints on capital, all remaining semblance of democracy in America will collapse, leading to outright victory and permanent domination by a committee of plutocrats.

Since headway had already been made against the capital gains tax before Bush Gang II took office, they immediately moved on to measures that reduced both the corporate and the personal income tax rates in 2001. The cuts made were so big that in the first decade of the 21st century they are likely to produce deficits like the ones that reaped fiscal disaster in the 1980s. By the fall of 2002, the Congressional Budget Office was projecting a $3.8 trillion deficit for the period from 2002 through the year 2011; $2.4 trillion of that deficit was going to be due to reduced taxes, and a smaller portion, about $1.4 trillion, caused by increased military spending and "homeland security."[7]

George W, like his father, will be a direct beneficiary of his own policies. After all of the 2001 tax cuts are put in place, the wealthiest 1% of the people will receive 52% of the benefits. By 2010, the tax reductions will be worth $234 billion per year, with $121 billion going to the very rich. Average families will get tiny reductions, but the substantial benefits will go to families like the Bushes (George W and Laura) whose annual income ranged between $800,000 and $2 million from 1998 to 2001; measured on that basis their future tax cuts will run about $100,000 per year.

This leaves one more target for George W. Bush. Like many of his wealthy supporters, he longs to get rid of the upper class's worst enemy, the estate tax or inheritance tax that is levied upon wealthy Americans at death. The Bush tax cuts of 2001 included a measure to phase out the federal estate tax over ten years. But the measure did not eliminate the tax forever. A bill to abolish the estate tax came within four votes of passing the Senate in 2002 and will almost certainly be coming back for further consideration. Some rich Americans are concerned about making sure their children live in luxury, while others, like George W, have parents who are considerably richer than they are, probably in the over-$100 million crowd. That money represents intergenerational power, something the

Bush family takes very seriously. They feel, like many other wealthy people, that they are being discriminated against. This is true.

Inheritance taxes are particularly useful to a democratic society because they can help break up the very largest estates, those worth tens of millions and more. This can prevent, or at least limit, the passive ownership of the productive forces of society from being handed down within the same family for generations. The federal estate tax was signed into law in 1916, just after the income tax was installed as part of the Constitution in 1913. Without these two measures, it would have been impossible to break up the old plutocracy of political power that had been created during the Gilded Age.

One of the favorite arguments of contemporary conservative opponents of estate taxes is that estates represent income that has already been taxed. The opposite is true—most big multi-million dollar estates tend to be formed from investments that were purchased years ago and have become many times more valuable. For instance, consider a large swath of farmland or a pile of company stock that was purchased (or received as a gift) thirty years ago when it was worth $1 million; thirty years later, with little or no effort expended by the owner, the property is worth more than $50 million and is left as an inheritance. The heirs are receiving $49 million that was not earned by anyone's labor; they are benefiting from huge unrealized capital gains, purely passive income from property that has never been taxed because it was never sold and cashed in by the deceased.

Today some conservatives, such as Grover Norquist's Americans for Tax Reform, refer to the estate tax as the "Death Tax" because they feel it unfairly taxes people who want to leave a legacy to their children. Since it is only levied on 2% of all estates, they are obviously concerned about a special class of children. They claim that it prevents parents, particularly those who own farms and businesses, from leaving their property to hard-working children and grandchildren. Organizations like the American Farm Bureau insist that this tax poses a grave threat to the family farm (which is actually being destroyed by corporate factory farms, not by taxes), yet are unable to offer one case of a family that lost their farm because of estate taxes. Neil Harl, an agricultural economist at Iowa State University who gives frequent tax advice to Midwest farmers, has never heard of any farms lost because of inheritance taxes nor could he find any record of such loss. He offered this explanation, "It's a myth." [8]

Real data shows that the big story with estates has little to do with small business holders. The Department of the Treasury has found that only 3% out of the 47,482 taxable estates in 1999 had family-owned businesses or farms that were equal to half of the gross estate.[9] Since there are a number of ways to reduce or eliminate estate taxes on most proprietors' farms or businesses, they are not especially endangered by estate taxes. The real threat of the "death tax" is to the estates of the plutocrats. According to a study by the Center on Budget and Policy Priorities, those inheritances reside in a very few hands—there were just 467 estates that were above $20 million in 1999, and they paid 25% of all federal estate taxes, or about $7 billion.[10]

This suggests a more realistic scenario concerning the tough choices imposed on a family by the inheritance tax. Let us say that a Wall Street mogul has decided to leave his children a fortune of half a billion dollars, including the small change he invested in a 50,000 acre ranch out West. He kicks the bucket. Since inheritance taxes on the very richest Americans average 25% (good tax lawyers can usually figure out how to lower the rate from the maximum 45% to 55%), the sons and daughters will have to give up something. Will they feel forced into selling the "family farm" in Montana? Or will they choose to give up the yacht and the mansion on the Riviera instead?

Interestingly enough, some of the richest Americans, including those who have had to exert their energies or their brains to make their fortunes, think large inheritances should be curtailed. Warren Buffett, the nation's second richest man in 2002, argues that democracy cannot tolerate a system based on inheritance: "Without the estate tax, you in effect will have an aristocracy of wealth, which means you pass down the ability to command the resources of the nation based on heredity rather than merit." Andrew Carnegie had even stronger feelings a century ago, for he felt that rich people had a moral duty, to their own children and to the general public, to give their money away. At the end of his book, *The Gospel of Wealth*, he wrote: "The man who dies rich dies disgraced." William H. Gates, Sr., father of Microsoft founder Bill, has written a book with Chuck Collins (of United for a Fair Economy) called *Wealth and Commonwealth: Why America Should Tax Accumulated Fortunes*.[11] Their book carefully corrects people's misconceptions about estate taxes; it also argues that American society provides so many benefits to those who get very rich that they should be happy to repay that debt in the form of inheritance taxes.

The Roosevelt cousins, Theodore and Franklin, had similar feelings about wealth even though they were surrounded by the trappings of privilege when they were growing up. Perhaps they had witnessed too much idleness and waste on the part of the rich parents and spoiled young people around them. They developed such a profound antipathy for inherited power that they were compelled to fight against their own class interests.

"The transmission from generation to generation of great fortunes by will, inheritance, or gift is not consistent with the ideals and sentiments of the American people," said Franklin Roosevelt in 1935.

"The primary objective should be to put a constantly increasing burden on the inheritance of those swollen fortunes, which it is certainly of no benefit to this country to perpetuate," said Theodore Roosevelt in his presidential message to Congress in 1906.

That year Roosevelt failed to get a progressive tax on inheritances passed, and thus began his disillusionment with the powerful business interests that controlled his Republican Party. They were disillusioned with him, too, and more than a little frightened, since in the spring of 1906 he called for a tax on the great fortunes and those who held them. He did not care whether he rounded them up dead or alive (he proposed revenues collected after death by an estate tax or before death by a wealth tax), and his language indicated he was aiming directly at those forefathers of the Bush Gang, the Robber Barons. He referred to his targets explicitly as "malefactors of great wealth, the wealthy criminal class."[12]

Would Robbers Cheat?

"In some years, reported property income is less than half of what the national income and product accounts indicate it should be," according to New York University economist Edward N. Wolff, one of the foremost experts on the growing inequality of income and wealth.[13] Property income is income produced by capital in any form—money, stock, land, derivatives, limited partnerships—that is unconnected to the owner's labor. The problem with tracking such income-producing assets is that the rich find it easy to cheat, or better yet, to pay someone else to cheat for them.

David Cay Johnston, who has followed the tax dodge business for some time in the pages of *The New York Times*, reported a dire warning from IRS Commissioner Charles O. Rossetti in the summer of 2002. "Up to 82 percent of those who cheat on taxes are getting away with it because the IRS lacks the auditors to pursue them,"[14] said the commissioner. Way back in 1991, because of pressure from the first Bush Gang, the IRS had already abandoned its strategy of chasing down rich tax evaders. On tax day of that year, April 15th, *The Wall Street Journal* reported that the IRS was concentrating its audits on middle-class tax payers because the returns of the rich and the corporations were too complicated and too easily contested in court.

The trick for the rich—or in reality, for their accountants and lawyers—was to invent tax scams that were so intricate or murky that it would be too expensive for the IRS to track them down. This trend was accelerated later in the 1990s by the Bush Gang's Republican allies who were dominating Congress. Newt Gingrich's "Conservative Revolution" targeted the Internal Revenue Service as an enemy of the people, calling it a tyrannical force which intruded needlessly into the lives of ordinary Americans. While there were undoubtedly some cases of over-zealous agents harassing beleaguered middle-class Americans, there was another, more important reason for the elevated rhetoric. The Republicans were trying to discredit the IRS and let wealthier taxpayers roam free. The IRS had its funding and its investigative staff reduced to the point it could no longer carry out as many audits, particularly the more expensive audits of the rich that end up revealing large chunks of unreported or misreported income.

By 2000, the tax auditing process was seriously curtailed by these cutbacks, for 1% or less of people with incomes over $100,000 were being audited as opposed to 5% in 1990 and 12% in 1988. What was even more ridiculous was that the IRS was giving up on pursuing middle-class evaders, too, and concentrating most of their energy on low-income Americans who had filed "overclaims" on their Earned Income Tax Credit (EITC) that characteristically pay poor working families $500 to $3,000 per year.[15] By 2002, the Bush administration was encouraging the financially strapped and under-staffed IRS to conduct a higher percentage of audits on the poor than on the rich.

One cannot deny that low-income people, if given the opportunity, will cheat on taxes, too. The problem is that EITC "overclaims" represent a tiny portion of the tax cheating that takes place in the United States; in 1998 they amounted at most to $11 billion out of the $195 billion that the IRS estimated it did not collect. Just one of the scams for the protected rich folks—hiding their dough in foreign bank accounts—was said to cost $20 to $40 billion per year.[16]

Another favorite scam involves "swap funds" or "exchange funds," which are financial entities that were created to serve only the richest investors; by law one must own $5 million in stocks and bonds and agree to pool at least $1 million of one's loot with other very wealthy investors. Within the tight little "fund swapping" clubs, people can trade stocks for free without ever having to declare a sale. Later, when they withdraw stocks from the pool, they tend to conveniently overlook any gains they may have made. Big investment firms are fond of this racket; just two of the specialists, Eaton Vance and Goldman Sachs, manage over $18 billion in pledged assets that are devoted to "swap funds."

The Bush II administration had no objection to this particular exercise in immorality. They were not going to close the legal loophole according to Mark Weinberger, the chief of tax policy in the administration, because "we are against taxes on capital gains in general." After performing his brief stint of public service for the wealthy, Weinberger returned to his old firm, the accounting giant Ernst & Young, to assume a more lucrative job as vice-chairman.[17]

In August 2002, shortly before IRS commissioner Rosetti quit his job in frustration over the lack of support coming from the White House and Congress, he managed to shut down one great fraud of the rich that involved currency trading. Accounting firms had been advising clients to invest in foreign currency transactions in such a way that they could fabricate very large and fictitious "paper" losses. In one typical marketing proposal for very wealthy people, Ernst & Young suggested that a $5 million dollar fee was appropriate if they developed a strategy that would save the clients $20 million a year in tax obligations. Another promised people with salaries of $20 million or more that they could live tax free. In June, just before the IRS declared them illegal, one of the accounting company's spokespersons claimed that these currency schemes must be legal because the government had not closed them down yet. This kind of sleaziness indicates that the richest Americans will seldom be charged with tax fraud because there is an army of accountants and lawyers defending them and inventing new evasions. If one kind of scam is outlawed, then they conjure up new ones.

Try the Bermuda Angle: Money Disappears

"Everybody's annoyed at big American corporations that renounce their citizenship and move to Bermuda to avoid taxes," wrote Robert S. McIntyre in his column, "The Taxonomist." Despite negative media publicity, it seems that the Republicans were very reluctant to give up on the Bermuda angle, which was a popular scheme of incorporating on sunny, offshore tax havens and avoiding the patriotic duty of supporting the homeland with corporate income taxes. Right-wing ideologues at the Cato Institute, the Heritage Foundation, and Americans for Tax Reform (and about thirty other conservative groups) sent a letter in August of 2002 to Representative Bill Thomas (R-California), the Chairman of the House Ways and Means Committee. They praised him for his past record of promoting offshore corporate relocation, which they see as an exercise in economic freedom, and warned that it would be a mistake to even briefly curtail the practice. Laws creating "barriers against companies that wish to re-charter," they wrote, would be "misguided" and could only "undermine economic growth."[18]

Meanwhile, other prominent Republicans were lining up to do favors for companies which should have been hiding in disgrace. The former chairman of the Ways and Means Committee,

Bill Archer of Texas, found employment opportunities at PriceWaterhouseCoopers, another one of the accounting giants. His job was to lobby on behalf of two Houston companies that renounced their U.S. citizenship in favor of staying tax-free abroad. When he wasn't out peddling Viagra, Bob Dole was defending Tyco Corporation's efforts to make money disappear in Bermuda. Tyco had moved its corporate headquarters to the sunny isle back in 1997, but one should not think that the tax evasion practice was just another crime invented by the company's ex-CEO, Dennis Kozlowski. In March of 2003, the annual stockholders convention voted overwhelmingly to stay in Bermuda because it was their American right to avoid taxes. Some large shareholders resisted, notably giant union pension funds associated with the American Federation of State, County and Municipal Employees and "Calpers," the California Public Employees' Retirement System. They pushed a resolution to make Tyco return to the United States and comply with its moral obligations. But wealthy private investors carried the day for tax avoidance, garnering 76% of the votes. One investor, who controlled more than six million Tyco shares, scolded CalPERS and said their concern was "ill-informed."[19]

According to Martin A. Sullivan, a former Treasury Department analyst, by 1999 the amount of corporate profits shifted to offshore havens to avoid taxes was $92 billion, or 11.5% of all corporate profits ($804 billion), that were declared that year. Of course, none of the U.S. corporations actually makes or sells anything in Bermuda or the Cayman Islands. Some companies do claim that they are storing their "intellectual property" in the tiny offices they rent there. They then attribute a large part of their revenue to the "value" of this intangible item, thus enabling them to declare that a substantial share of their overall profits are created outside of the U.S. and are not taxable.[20]

These tax haven tricks are not illegal and are available to most well-known multinational corporations. For example, a corporation such as Nike can choose to keep its "swoosh" in a tax haven. Since that symbol allows the company to sell shoes for a lot more than its generic competitors, Nike can claim that the swoosh is collecting billions in income as a piece of intellectual property. And if the swoosh moves to Bermuda it can avoid the tax man. (Is the "swoosh" really stretched out and relaxing on those pink sand beaches? Better ask Nike.)

The fact that such a travesty is considered a legitimate activity instead of blatant criminal behavior is a tribute to the Bush Gang's persistence in deregulating business for more than two decades. Easy money appeals to all sides: wealthy individuals and corporate players, their well-paid servants in law and accounting firms, nearly all Republicans and a disturbing number of Democrats. Not only is "The Money Power" strong enough to erode moral principles, but it is persistent enough to wash away the shame of the guilty, who increasingly see themselves as innocent players in the only game in town. Daniel Gross, a financial columnist for *Slate*, has concluded that our government will not crack down on "Corporate Tax Dodgers" because cheating has become the norm, not the exception. "Congress," he wrote, "may have enough resources to investigate one Enron that is slyly ducking its income taxes, but it certainly doesn't have enough to investigate a whole Fortune 500 that is doing the same."[21]

The Bush Prince Tries to Defy History—Whatever Happened to War Taxes?

Something is rotten in the 21st century. A brief look at the historical record of the United States reveals what always happened in time of major war: taxes went up. Especially for the rich. During the Civil War, the Union had to invent an income tax so that the wealthier Americans could pay for the Army of the Potomac, the vast piles of munitions, the horses and wagons and uniforms, and a hundred other costs of war. The tax stayed in place for seven years after the war, until 1872, in order to help pay off the national debt. By 1917, the United States committed itself to the Great War and the rate of income tax on the richest Americans shot up from 6% to 67%.

There were some underlying reasons for this "sacrifice" that were implicitly understood by most Americans, rich and poor alike: 1) if the United States and its Allies were going to win this struggle, then those who had the means to pay for it would have to step forward like honorable men; 2) the United States, in its support of other countries, particularly Great Britain, was protecting the foreign investments and the future international investment opportunities of a minority of its citizens, the wealthy ones; 3) a democratic country, mostly made up of small farmers and shopkeepers and wage laborers, might be able to tolerate capitalism, but only if the wealthiest capitalists paid handsomely for the privilege of accumulating their fortunes (which, by the way, were often augmented through their production and control of war-time supplies and armaments).

In the 1940s we had to pay for a Second

World War that was even bloodier and more expensive than the first one. For the first time in history, working class people were also required to pay federal income taxes as well as withholding taxes. The tax rates in the United States did not go down. In fact, the top rate on millionaires went up to 91% and stayed there, a fact that drove a few ultra-conservative families such as the Mellons and the Buckleys into a state of permanent right-wing apoplexy. Then there was a war in Korea to pay for in the early 1950s, followed by various big Pentagon projects, and another serious war in Vietnam. A healthy income tax was required to pay for all these adventures and the top rate was kept high at 70%.

Now the Bush administration has become involved in a long and frustrating war in which the enemy, "terrorism," is very illusive. The level of armament purchases and the amount being spent on domestic security are very high, just as they would be in a large conventional war. If we are embarking on a never-ending and very expensive war against terrorism, why is no one suggesting the obvious? Why is no one talking about doubling the taxes of the rich?

This is the ultimate and most offensive tax dodge by the new Robber Barons, a slap in the face to American tradition and to common citizens who expect that they will be the ones who will fight the fires, fight the criminals, and fight the wars, if necessary. They are always ready to sacrifice. Where is the sacrifice of the rich chickenhawks? If the members of the Bush Gang are not ready to put their bodies on the line, why aren't they lining up to pay higher taxes instead?

That would be the day. When Congressman Hudson of Kansas spoke on behalf of the Income Tax Act of 1884, he bluntly explained why he thought the rich would have to be coerced (by law) into paying for the common good:

> This method [the income tax] lays the burdens on those possessing the ability to pay, and compels those who reap the harvests...to give more of that harvest for the common good. I know that many wealthy men are generous and charitable...On the other hand, the majority of the very wealthy are haughty, overbearing, autocratic, mean, and it is that class in particular that the income tax is designed to reach.

Seven

Breaking and Entering

How to Lose Your Retirement and Social Security

> The low level which commercial morality has reached in America is deplorable. We have humble, God fearing Christian men among us who will stoop to do things for one million dollars that they ought not to be willing to do for less than two million.
>
> —Mark Twain

Privatize? A Reality Quiz

Step One:
Check out the 1,073 corporations that had the greatest losses in the recent stock market crash.

Step Two:
Notice that the officers of these companies conspired to cash in stock worth $66 billion just before the market tanked.

Step Three:
Consider the pension funds that invested in these same stocks. In just one three month period, the second quarter of 2002—$469 billion gone.

Ask Yourself:
Do I trust the CEOs of corporate America to make wise and honest decisions? Do I trust the fund managers—the very ones who picked Enron and Global Crossing—to safeguard my pension money?

One can consider the picture in the longer term and it looks even worse. The value of the stocks known as Standard & Poor's 500, an index much more representative of the overall stock market than the Dow Jones average of 30 stocks, hit its high number, 1553, in March of 2000. By early October of 2002, the stock market had lost exactly 50% of its value, for the S&P 500 index had fallen to a low of 776.76. This meant the market value of all stocks reached $17.8 trillion in 2000, then lost $8.9 trillion over the next two and a half years. Just before the stock market began its rapid descent from its high point in 2000, the Federal Reserve Board calculated that the total of privately held wealth of the United States amounted to $43 trillion. Therefore the $8.9 trillion in stock market losses represented more than a 20% reduction in the nation's accumulated wealth.

For many people, particularly long-term investors, much of the wealth that disappeared amounted to "paper losses." The prices of their stocks had increased very rapidly for five or ten years, then dropped suddenly (thus on paper they were worth less than they had been two years earlier), but overall they were still ahead of the game. Others, who were more recent entrants to the market in the late 1990s, either suffered real losses or were lucky to break even on their corporate equities. But among both groups, those with real losses and those with "paper losses," there were a great many people who had made their retirement plans based on the rosy predictions of escalating stock values. Some had borrowed against the value of their stocks, or had borrowed money from elsewhere (with home equity loans or credit cards) to purchase more shares.

This was the largest financial loss of all time. The markets recovered slightly in late fall of 2002, but not enough to diminish the effect very much, and the long-term outlook for stocks did not look so bright going into the year 2003 (price-to-earnings ratios and other historical measures of corporate profits suggested that, if anything, share prices might have to drop some more). At this point we do not know how many of the insiders and billionaire investors sold out when the prices were high, and how many neophyte small-time investors were left holding the bag. Did the sophisticated managers of the giant pension funds act quickly enough, or were they also bamboozled by the high-flying CEOs and their accountants? It will probably be a couple of years before investigators can sort through the wreckage and see who lost what. But one thing is certain, the scene could have been worse. What if billions of dollars from millions of individual Social Security accounts had been invested in the market early in 1998 or late 1999?

To Market, to Market, to Buy a Fat Pig

In the summer of 2002, when investment banks and brokerage houses were scavenging for business, Charles Schwab & Co. decided to run TV ads demeaning the performance of their rivals, such as Merrill Lynch, which had to pay $100 million in penalties for deviously recommending ugly stocks to its customers. In the ad, the office manager at a fictional investment house tells his underlings that they have to make a stock look good even though its performance stinks. Then, in the line that made the ad famous, he orders them to "Put Some Lipstick on that Pig."

There was a much bigger hog for sale at the end of the 1990s and even into the early part of 2002. The make-up crew was immense—the investment banks, the business press, the Clinton administration, and almost every financial advisor and economist in the country who received any attention. They kept dressing up and pumping up the whole stock market into a gigantic blimp of a pig that floated over the heads of most Americans. They said, "Wouldn't you like to be up there, wouldn't you like a piece of that pig?" Then the army of lobbyists and politicians tried to drag the majority of American people to market to buy that fat pig with their most enormous asset, their Social Security.

There had been a great clamor about the crisis in Social Security earlier in the 1990s. For instance, Peter G. Peterson, former Secretary of Commerce during the Nixon administration and a prominent investment banker, wrote books in the 1990s such as *Facing Up* and *Will We Grow Up Before We Grow Old?* He claimed that the whole basis of our government retirement system was in danger of imminent failure. Allied with him was the Concord Coalition, an influential group of moderately conservative Democrats and Republicans who were convinced that major Social Security reform was the number one priority in the United States.

When the stock market took off in the late '90s, the Congressional Republicans and some allies of the Clinton administration, such as Joe Lieberman, thought they had found the perfect solution. Having been persuaded about the unreliability of the federal system, it seemed obvious to them that the stock market was the perfect device for rescuing our government retirement system. They saw Social Security as heavy-handed and inefficient, so earthbound and slow that it was vastly inferior to that swollen pig, the stock market, that was floating around in the sky. The only solution was for citizens to take money out of Social Security quickly, before it was too late, before that big, beautiful pig floated off into the stratosphere without them.

As soon as the Bush Gang took office in 2001, they jumped on the bandwagon, too. They urged major changes in how Social Security funds were handled, in particular recommending that some of the money collected from each paycheck be shifted into "private accounts" that could be invested in the stock market. The idea had an immediate appeal: why should poor working stiffs, for whom Social Security is the major part of their savings, be closed off from those phenomenal gains that other people were getting in the stock market? There was considerable support throughout the news media for this idea, and articles stoked the anxieties of the public. "Public opinion polls consistently show that a large share of the working age population does not believe that Social Security will be able to pay them benefits when they retire," wrote Dean Baker of the Center for Economic and Policy Research.[1]

The pig, of course, was no more than an enormous bubble. And when the stock market went on its crash diet, slimming down by half, the Bush Gang and its allies on Wall Street stopped trying to sell this not-so-sweet-looking hog to the general public. There were mid-term elections coming up, and the talk of making Social Security more "market friendly" had begun to frighten many Americans. After the November 2002 election, most Americans were wary of federal retirement accounts. A *Los Angeles Times* poll asked respondents to say yes or no to the following proposal: "Allow workers to divert a portion of their Social Security taxes into individual retirement accounts that they could invest in stocks and bonds." 55% voted no, 38% approved.[2]

Still there was talk, among the Bush Gang and elsewhere, about dire threats to Social Security and the need to take drastic action soon. Phrases like "personal choice" and "individual protection" were bandied about, suggesting that the idea of privatization of the system into individual accounts would be coming back again.

What was going on?

The widely respected economic think-tank, the Economic Policy Institute, pointed out some answers in their article, "Social Security is Not Broken: Why Does Wall Street Want to Fix It?"[3] Their projections showed that the Social Security system will be in sound shape until 2030 and judged that if some tinkering becomes necessary, the solutions will be simple. On the other hand, they pointed to the motivation driving the "privatizers"—profit. In the most common schemes put forward, individuals who would open investment accounts with a portion of their Social Security payments would have to pay fees for the money-managing services of private companies, thus generating an estimated $240 billion in income for the big investment houses over a ten year period. This explains why the powerful financial lobbies, like the Investment Company Institute, which represents the mutual fund industry, had tried to push the scheme on Clinton, then cheered on the Bush administration until just before election time 2002. They will keep pushing for some sort of new "privatization" program, perhaps under a different name. In early 2003, Bush himself was supplying fresh words of enticement as he put forward the idea of government sponsored "personal savings accounts."

Social Security, to Trust or not to Trust

Social Security has been our most reliable federal program for two thirds of a century. Retirement checks arrive reliably and are adjusted to keep up with inflation, while the government expense of running the program is very low. Because of its commitment to paying spouses who survive the original recipients, Social Security also serves as our largest life insurance program, its $12 trillion of insurance being worth more than all the policies of all private insurance companies combined. Its administration is incredibly efficient, costing less than 1% of total revenues because the aim of the Social Security Administration is to distribute the checks, not to turn a profit. This is far superior to the private sector, which keeps 12% to 14% of its premiums as the cost of doing business. Furthermore, Social Security is the most successful poverty program of all time, having reduced the poverty rate for people over 65 from 35.2% in 1959 to less than 10% forty years later. Without Social Security fully half of all senior citizens would fall below the poverty line.[4]

Economists Dean Baker and Mark Weisbrot wrote a book called *Social Security:*

The Phony Crisis in order to relieve the anxieties of many Americans, especially younger working people. Many of Americans in the 18 to 34 age group are worried about Social Security's ability to fund full benefits when they retire, but polls show they also support the idea of strengthening the system. Even when the stock market was at its peak in 1999, they were not prepared to throw away Social Security. They favored guaranteeing future benefits rather than diverting money to private investment accounts, especially if the investment choice involved substantial deductions from the amount put aside for fixed benefits.[5] Although all of the schemes that were proposed by the Bush administration involve such deductions, this fact was masked by propaganda and polls issued by right-wing think tanks like the Cato Institute.[6] Because of the way the Cato poll questions were worded, many respondents never understood that their contributions to regular Social Security would be 15-20% less under the Bush plans, and their guaranteed benefits still lower. The amounts to be diverted to market accounts of one kind or another were, in truth, deductions from guaranteed benefits.

Weisbrot and Baker argue that under normal conditions of economic growth Social Security is in no grave danger at all. And if the economy falters badly, then so would private retirement accounts. The fact is that a steady flow of cash from Social Security withholding will sustain American retirements for at least thirty years to come, a much cheerier prognostication than one can make for any other source of money in the economy. In the future, because we will have a higher proportion of retired people than we have at present, we may have to increase the amount of social security withheld from workers pay in the year 2032. This is exactly what happened in the 1980s to guarantee that funds would be sufficient for the next thirty years. Baker and Weisbrot point out that these costs will not be excruciating, at the most requiring an increase of withholding taxes from 12.4% to 14.4% (the combination of employee and employer payments on wages) about 25 years from now. This would keep the program solvent over the next 75 years.[7] Very few other tax programs and no private business plans can make such predictions with such reliability so far into the future.

This reliability has already been proven in the past. The percentage of withholding was raised when it was predicted that more elderly people would be surviving into their seventies, eighties, or nineties. Because our incomes have been rising over time, but also because we pride ourselves in supporting those who worked hard for many years to build up our nation, Americans have been willing to submit to increased deductions from wages and salaries in the past. If we could afford to increase Social Security withholding to 12.3% in the 1980s, when it had been only about 6% in the 1950s, then we can certainly handle a comparatively small increase to 14.3% in the distant future (for an even better alternative, see Chapter 19).

"Trust Fund"— More Trustworthy Than Tax Cuts

Members of the financial elite (and friends of the Bush Gang) often like to set up their children with trust funds in order make sure they will never suffer for want of money. Most of the rest of us are born and raised without a trust fund, grow into adulthood without a trust fund, and find it perfectly natural to have to work for a liv-

ing for years to come. So when silver-tongued politicians start suggesting that we are the beneficiaries of a "trust fund," perhaps we have a right to be skeptical. But in the case of Social Security, there really is something like a "trust fund," because the government has been collecting more withholding taxes than necessary in recent years (ever since the withholding increases of the 1980s) and then issuing the equivalent of government bonds that guarantee that extra money will be available in years to come.

The rich financiers should be happy that we are emulating them in a small way by having our own "trust fund." But they are not. The Bush Gang screams about Social Security "shortfall" and the potential bankruptcy of the system because they are trying to destroy the last vestige of New Deal economics. The ruthless pirates want to board the cruise ship full of retirees and reintroduce them to "social insecurity," which has been the condition of most working people in their older years from time immemorial until the very recent past.

Three economists writing on behalf of the Center on Budget and Public Policy Priorities, Peter Orszag, Richard Kagan, and Robert Greenstein, compared the so-called "shortfall" in

WHAT IS MORE DANGEROUS TO YOUR FUTURE: BUSH TAX CUTS OR SO-CALLED SOCIAL SECURITY "SHORTFALLS"?	
Cost over 75 years as % of GDP	**In dollars**
Soc. Sec. Shortfall 0.73%	$3.8 trillion
Tax Cut 2.3-2.7%	$12.1 to 14.2 trillion

Source: Center for Budget and Public Policy Priorities: Peter Orszag, Richard Kagan, and Robert Greenstein, "The Administration's Tax Cuts and Long-Term Budget Outlook," March 19, 2003.

Social Security with the 2001 and 2003 tax cuts, which were characterized as very prudent by the Bush administration. They pointed out that the cost of the tax cuts over 75 years, which Bush is exhorting congress to make permanent, will be more than three times greater than the cost of correcting Social Security.

Retirement, "The Fix Is In"— Fixed Benefits vs. "Fixed" Benefits

The biggest tragedy of the Enron scandal was not the immoral behavior of the principal actors, nor the corruption of the political process caused by Enron's connections to the Bush Gang, but the destruction of the life savings of thousands of Enron's employees. They can be excused for their loyalty to the company, for millions of other Americans also suffered from over-the-top idolization of CEOs during the 1990s; they should be pitied for being herded into "defined contribution" pensions and 401(k) plans, which were really not true pensions at all. They were convinced by managers that, just like employees in hundreds of corporations across the country, they were going to be much better off because they were required to invest in their own company's stock.

No one was counseling them about the obvious. The companies were proposing this course of action for different reasons, among them: 1) employee purchases helped drive up the price of the stock; 2) they could pay employees in stock instead of giving raises; and 3) even more important in the long run (at least for corporations that would have a long run), retirement programs characterized by "defined contri-

butions" and 401(k) plans were substantially cheaper than the traditional "defined benefit" pensions. Defined benefits are the result of a contractual agreement between management and workers (usually unionized workers) that specifies exactly how much the pension payouts will be far in the future, during retirement years. Employee benefits are fixed. A "defined contribution" pension—the newer, cheaper alternative—attaches workers to an individual investment vehicle, such as 401(k), that grows with fixed contributions each month. It will go up or down with the market, and could dwindle or disappear altogether. It only became popular with a large number of wage and salary earners during the stock market boom of the 1990s because they were convinced, sometimes with a great deal of encouragement from management, that they were missing out on the gravy train. The point was well taken—until the market bubble burst.

Meanwhile….

A pattern of pension reduction has allowed corporations to cut back on pensions, or reallocate pension funds to top-end employees, at every sign of economic downturn. For instance, in one three-year period of recession, 1989-1992, the portion of pension funds that were devoted to only the top 10% of employees increased from 53 percent to 62 percent of the total.[9]

Defined contribution schemes seemed great at the time they replaced defined benefit

THE PERCENTAGE OF WORKERS WITH "DEFINED BENEFIT" PENSIONS AT LARGE AND MEDIUM-SIZED EMPLOYERS DROPPED DRAMATICALLY		
1979	1989	1997
87%	63%	50%

(Source: Bureau of Labor Standards)[8]

plans in the 1990s, but by 2001 they looked terrible. After the market bust, even those who were not wiped out completely, like the Enron workers, suffered grievous shrinkage of their retirement savings. The value of defined contribution pension funds fell by 13.5 percent from the end of 1999 to the end of 2001, from $2.1 trillion to $1.8 trillion; they most certainly had fallen sharply again along with the market in 2002.[10] It is in this light that one should look at all fixes to Social Security that propose private investment accounts. They are akin to the 401(k) plans that are designed to reduce the amount of money that has to be set aside for working people's retirement. They will not supply fixed income, but "fixed" income, a fraudulent concept of income security relying on market forces far in the future, decades away, that cannot possibly be predicted.

Individual social security accounts, especially in the hands of the Bush Gang, could become yet another means of reducing the social wage in the United States. If we allow wealthy investment bankers frivolous access to the hard-earned savings of working people by paying them exorbitant fees to manage them, the result might be the same as it was for some young workers in 1999. Convinced by the incessant media propaganda that their Social Security would be worthless some day, they threw their savings into the stock market in 1999—and bam! By fall of 2002, nearly 80% of their money had been wiped out if they invested in NASDAQ stocks, 50% in the S&P 500, 40% in the Dow Jones industrials. As for the dot.coms, they could kiss that pig goodbye.

Fooled About Saving

Just as some of the young were fooled, so were many older workers, even though some who built up stock wealth over a long enough time were still ahead when the market crashed. As mentioned in earlier chapters, the gains in income among the upper class were immense over the past 20 years; in the upper-middle class, they were often quite solid. Among middle-income people were those who already had substantial stock and kept investing their money in the market. If they received stock options as part of a company compensation plan, they believed their salaries were going through the roof. The gains in the stock market were so spectacular that people who owned stocks felt much richer and decided they could afford to consume more. The savings rate of all Americans fell to 1.9% by the fourth quarter of 1999, a record low, far less than the historical average of 10%. And in 2000, there was no savings rate, it was less than zero. This is the extreme example of what economists call the "wealth effect." When people feel certain that their assets have increased they spend more: studies have shown that the wealth effect during the stock market boom generated $192 billion to $256 billion in additional consumption each year, an amount equal to 1.9 to 2.6 percent of Gross Domestic Product.[11]

Then the stock market crashed. The illusory savings, the ones that seemed be there in the form of appreciated stock, evaporated. The savings that could have been put away by many higher income citizens had been spent already. Many people in the 55 to 64 age bracket did not fare so well and had to think again about the possibilities of early retirement. Among that group in October of 2002, the percentage who were working had increased by 3% since 1999. This was a clear sign that they had either lost money and returned to work, or were afraid about losing out and were still holding onto their jobs. What did they think about the investment advice they had received in the 1990s?

Did it occur to them that they had been ill-served?

> Responsible economists and economic analysts should have been warning the public about the prospects of a market crash and its implications for both the economy as a whole and their personal finances. However, few economists were issuing such warnings. And if they were, the media was not paying attention, so the public never would have heard an explanation as to why the stock market boom of the late nineties virtually guaranteed a subsequent crash.[12]

So wrote economist Dean Baker in December of 2002 when he scolded the rest of his profession and the investment community in general for falling down on the job. Since our economy is predominantly owned by an elite class of investors who employ a small cadre of highly educated and highly paid professionals to advise them on what to do with society's accumulated wealth and savings, these people should have been alerting the corporate stockholders and the media about the huge bubble that was developing. Consider the amount of waste that could have been avoided, not to mention the severe misdirection of economic resources and human energy. Their failure was unconscionable. Baker and a few others had written detailed analyses of the overheated market before the crash, all clearly based on available information on business conditions and historical statistics. The numbers revealed the immense size of the bubble, in comparison to the historical records of other bubbles that burst and markets that collapsed.[13]

The failure of both private and government oversight may haunt the economy for years to come. Credit Suisse First Boston analysts reported that the businesses comprising Standard and Poor's 500 companies would face a whopping $243 billion shortfall in pension funding by the end of the 2002. CalPERS, the giant California state employees pension fund that serves well over a million people and once had 58% of its funds in the stock market, was worth $172 billion in 2000, but only $128 billion in 2002. These losses are typical of what happened to U.S. savings as the bubble burst. When the Republican Congress was close to passing laws that would have put Social Security funds into the stock market in the late 1990s, it was really not so difficult to see what the result would be. Even a writer who is not a specialist in these matters, such as this author, could recognize that the investment companies were running a con game that could destroy our federal retirement program when the bubble burst. As I wrote in *Sharing the Pie* in 1998, the idea of privatizing Social Security was a recipe for disaster:

> If the mutual fund managers and their allies keep manufacturing evidence concerning Social Security's coming demise, many people will want to abandon ship. If individuals are allowed to detach themselves from a universal program, it cannot possibly survive in its current form. Standards and benefits will erode, leaving lower-income retirees to sink back into poverty. And then, when the stock market finally falls, as it inevitably will, a whole contingent of ex-middle-class escapees from Social Security will be clamoring for help. But at that point, who will be left to guarantee a life-support system for the elderly?[14]

The con-men have not gone away. They currently ride with the Bush Gang. They will be back again, somehow hoping to tap into the hundreds of billions of dollars that stream into Social Security collections each year, money that is already helping to make up for the shortfall in other taxes. As the Bush administration continues to give tax cuts to the rich and corporations, it will be tempted to use Social Security funds to pay for Rumsfeld's new space weapons, Ashcroft's domestic surveillance schemes, and so on. But their confederates in the business world may be even more dangerous. As they dust themselves off from their $9 trillion dollar debacle, pretending that a stock market crash never occurred, they will be very hungry for cash and drooling over the prospect of the steady flow of Social Security from millions and millions of paychecks. One can almost hear them yelling:

"Time to take that pig to market!"

Eight

The Bush Remedy for an Ailing Economy

The Chainsaw and the Ax

The alarming development and aggressiveness of great capitalists and corporations, unless checked, will inevitably lead to the pauperization and hopeless degradation of the toiling masses.

—Constitution of the Knights of Labor, 1869

I t was just one week after the 2002 elections changed the makeup of the Senate and gave George W. Bush a majority in both houses of Congress. The president had to survey the condition of an economy in disarray and consider the plight of overstressed workers as well as the growing ranks of the unemployed. He was determined to send a signal.

November 12, 2002

Our nation's economic recovery has not been strong or sustained, and the survey shows that CEOs do not expect the situation will improve significantly in 2003. Frankly, we are concerned.

—John T. Dillon, CEO of International Paper, and Chairman of The Business Roundtable. The Roundtable reported that 60 percent of its members expected to cut jobs in 2003, only 11 percent expect to hire more workers.

November 13, 2002

Businesses may also have managed to eke out increases in output per hour by employing their existing workforce more intensively. Unlike cutting fat, which permanently elevates the levels of productivity, these gains in output per hour are often temporary, as more demanding workloads eventually begin to tax workers and impede efficiency.

—Federal Reserve Chairman Alan Greenspan testifying to Congress

November 14, 2002

The Bush administration's Office of Management and Budget announced that nearly half of all Federal jobs, or 850,000, would be possible candidates for privatization.

November 15, 2002

At this time of national and economic insecurity for so many Americans ... I don't understand why the president would place 800,000 workers who have good jobs, good pensions and good health care in jeopardy.

—Senator Barbara Boxer (D-CA)[1]

November 19, 2002

Why would the White House pursue such a policy? Simply put, the Bushies hate unions because they are the steadiest opponents of corporate consolidation, the transfer of jobs overseas and the thievery of greedy accountants and CEOs. In other words, strong unions are still anathema on the corporate gravy train that fattened Bush, Dick Cheney and a historic number of fellow administration honchos.

—Robert Scheer, *The Los Angeles Times*

The Chief of the Chief Executives decreed that the federal government would try to save money at the expense of federal workers. This brought back memories of the attacks on labor that began in 1981, when President Reagan decided to single out the air traffic controller's union and fire all its members. Because they were perceived, or at least portrayed in the major media, as a privileged, well-paid bunch that was taking advantage of other citizens, that union received very little public support and was broken easily. This was a signal to American business that the next twelve years would be open season on labor: Reagan and the Bush Gang had begun an unre-

lenting war against workers, attacking wages, regulations, the minimum wage, any kind of labor organization, and almost all laws and government programs that supported a better life for working people.

The return of the Bush Gang in 2001 was a declaration that the war on working Americans should resume in a harsher form, and this was made all the easier once it could be conducted behind the curtain of fear created by Bush's War on Terrorism. The increasing regimentation of life according to corporate standards and the growing authoritarianism required by big business organizations could now be construed as necessary sacrifices that common people must make in order to fight "Evil" and support their "Homeland." In retrospect, we might note that a slightly milder version of this drill had already been conducted in the 1980s, when the American people were asked to support big increases in military spending and shoulder the burden of huge federal deficits, all in the name of defeating the "Evil Empire" of the Soviet Union. This time the Bush Gang was not going to mess around with a few thousand layoffs in the federal government. The executive order of November 14, 2002 declared that almost half of the 1,800,000 federal jobs would be open to privatization. A spokesman from the Office of Management and Budget predicted that the government could save as much as 30% in the bargain, no doubt because the corporate world has been specializing in cutting costs the easy way, by cutting jobs and cutting wages.

By looking at the brief commentary above, from one week in November 2002, one can get a compressed but accurate view of the state of the nation and the economy. The biggest companies in the United States were bewildered by the weak state of business recovery and contemplating more lay-offs, while the head of the Federal Reserve was warning the Business Roundtable that this was not necessarily a good idea. Alan Greenspan, who for many years had been a staunch advocate of keeping labor's wages firmly in place so that profits could rise, was suggesting that the corporate world had finally gone too far. Big business's previous cost-cutting measures were so severe that they were raising productivity in the wrong way, by increasing workloads to the point where working people were becoming exhausted and less productive.

This was a veiled warning: speedups, forced overtime, temp job overloading, and the refusal to replace workers were all dangerous tactics. Why had Greenspan, the ultra-conservative acolyte of Ayn Rand, a man who had always believed that rising wages caused inflation, suddenly become an advocate of treating labor better? Because it was now evident that the United States, as a nation of consumers, was withholding too much money from those who did the work and bought the products of its corporations. He knew that ordinary homeowners had extended themselves mightily with new mortgages at low interest rates; this enabled them to buy new homes or get more cash from the equity of their homes and spend it, thus sustaining an economy in the recession of 2001. But what else could they do? Had the very structure of the economy, the monopolist corporate model embraced by the Bush Gang, become so severely contracted that it would not be able to generate a benign period of growth?

It was apparent that the second Bush regime did not comprehend the message from Greenspan and was determined to follow in the footsteps of Bush Gang I. The new tax cuts for the wealthy would be maintained and deepened, the government would keep tightening the strings on working people's purses, and the Pentagon and the weapons producers would get to go on a spending spree which might be unlimited. No doubt some of the private sector was happy as they contemplated the profits to be gained through taking over federal government tasks and putting ex-federal employees to work for lower wages. But was that the kind of activity that would build the economy?

The previous four chapters have examined the evidence concerning the huge amounts of money that have been transferred so effectively to a small minority of Americans. The next three will illustrate a few ways in which that has been accomplished. For the process was not accidental, that is, it was not due to changes in demographics. Even the very deliberate and very favorable tax treatment of the rich was only of secondary importance. University of Massachusetts economist David Kotz calculates that "declining of taxation on capital contributed about 40 percent as much to the rise in the rate of profit as did the decline in the real wage in the face of rising labor productivity."[2] The primary reason that incomes and wealth were redistributed is that the Bush Gang gave a green light to Corporate America in its war against workers. The "Money Power" reorganized the world of work according to some very frightening models.

The "Chain-Saw Al" Massacre

"Chainsaw Al" Dunlap laid off 11,200 workers in eighteen months and collected a hundred million dollar paycheck at the Scott Paper Company.

Did I earn it? Damn right I did. I'm a superstar in my field, much like Michael Jordan in basketball and Bruce Springsteen in rock'n roll.

—"Chainsaw" Al Dunlap

Al Dunlap liked his nickname and he was one of the most highly celebrated CEOs of the 1990s. He delighted in his reputation for ruthless cost-cutting and chopping labor forces to the bone, so much so that he wrote a book celebrating his own exploits called *Mean Business*. He saw himself as a sort of hired gun who traveled from company to company, driving up the value of corporate stock by doing the kinds of things no one else was willing to do. After he fired the workers at Scott Paper, he merged the firm with Kimberly Clark and moved its headquarters from Philadelphia to Boca Raton.

Although Al Dunlap's style was a bit extreme, he was not really out of the ordinary in the realm of corporate CEOs who were roaming the land in the early to mid-1990s. Frank A. Shrontz, CEO of Boeing, laid off 25,000 workers and received a 73% raise, while Robert F. Daniell, chairman of United Technologies, steadily pushed his salary up to $11.2 million by dumping 30,000 employees over a period of five years. There was no glory in saving jobs or doing anything else other than jacking up share prices; on the contrary, according to Professor Peter Cappelli at the Wharton School of Business, "Today a CEO would be embarrassed to admit he sacrificed profits to protect employees or a community."[3] Sometimes just announcing layoffs was enough to make share prices jump within 24 hours—Xerox stock went up 4% when they said that 10,000 would get the ax; Chase Manhattan and Chemical Bank gained 11% when their merger plan revealed that 3,600 jobs

would disappear.

Al Dunlap clearly convinced the business world that he was a star, though maybe not of the magnitude of Jack Welch, who piloted the General Electric Company to the very pinnacle of Wall Street glory. Welch was dubbed "Neutron Jack" by the adoring business press, the nickname referring to Welch's ability to wipe out people—that is, the people who labored for him—without destroying the business that surrounded them. The physical assets and the corporate paper were saved as he eliminated workers, which made him just as efficient as the nuclear weapon known as the neutron bomb. Investors in the 1990s were fond of violent appellations like "Chainsaw Al" and "Neutron Jack," because they suggested that nothing should stand in the way of the value of shareholders' stock.

In 1996, on the basis of his record at Scott Paper, and his self-promotion as the guy who could "save bad companies and make good companies great" (the sub-title of his 1996 book, *Mean Business*) Al Dunlap went to the Sunbeam Corporation. The stock price of $12 jumped 50% on the day he arrived, then tripled over the next year and a half to $54 per share. The market was hopping, and Dunlap was hopping mad. One division president described his behavior: "He was like a dog barking at you for hours. He just yelled, ranted, and raved." By November of his first year, he had a plan in place: cut the work force by 50% and eliminate 87% of the household products that carried the Sunbeam name.[4]

Since the market was booming, Sunbeam's price kept climbing, too, until it reached its high point in March of 1998. Then, however, it was clear that the numbers to support Dunlap's strategy were not adding up and the stock price suddenly dropped from $53 to $34 per share in April. One billionaire stockholder, Ronald Perelman, owned 13% of the shares and thus could demand to have his own men pry into Sunbeam's books. They uncovered purposeful accounting irregularities in both inventories of goods and sales figures. "Chainsaw Al" was gone by June. Company stock hit $6 per share late in the year, about half of its value when Dunlap arrived. By 2001, the company had sunk into bankruptcy and one share was worth 9 cents or less.

Since the rest of the stock market was still racing upward toward the peak it would reach in the spring of 2000, few stopped to notice Dunlap's record and compare it to the heroics of other hot honchos. If they had, they would have noticed that Dunlap was a trailblazer for many other CEOs. "This was a primer in the techniques of financial fraud, in that they employed such a wide variety of techniques to manage earnings," Securities and Exchange Commission enforcement officer Thomas Newkirk noted, after reviewing Sunbeam's cooked books. Dunlap and his managers, with the help of bookkeeping wizards from the-yet-to-be-notorious Arthur Andersen, were frantically manipulating profits and "stuffing inventory" in an attempt to make Sunbeam attractive as an expensive buyout property. Dunlap hoped to sell quickly and walk off with piles of cash just as he had done two years earlier when he sold Scott Paper. This time, however, he had to face the music in the Sunbeam caper. Dunlap was required to repay millions of dollars out of his own pocket to settle civil suits brought by cheated investors and to pay a fine assessed by the SEC, which not only found him guilty of fraud but also banned him from taking part in any corporate management in the future.

Dunlap ended his career as he started it. It turned out that he had erased debits from the early years of his resume just as he had hidden debts from Sunbeam's corporate books; somehow he managed to rise in the corporate world while hiding the fact that the first paper company he ever managed, Nitec of Niagara Falls, New York, had a remarkably similar history in the 1970s—it enjoyed "impressive profits" in the 1970s with the help of some tricky bookkeeping, then went bankrupt. The owners sued Dunlap for fraud but never collected.[5]

The Ax and the Rack

"Chainsaw Al" was unusually colorful for a chief executive. Nobody else was accused of giving their employees "the chainsaw" treatment. Maybe the imagery was just a little too bloody.

But CEOs have been giving their employees "the ax"—the old term for layoffs, chopping back the payrolls—at an extraordinary rate throughout the Bush-Clinton-Bush era. Most of the time stockholders were positively giddy at the prospect, like the crowds that used to turn out for executions in 18th century London. Al Dunlap may have failed ultimately in his attempts to reshape companies through "leanness and meanness," but his corporate colleagues did not think he was wrong. They, too, saw this way of pursuing profit—maybe in a less flamboyant way, maybe even without the accounting shenanigans—as the ultimate in 21st century business sense. Were they out of their minds?

Lay-offs have always been a part of business—normal seasonal layoffs, cutting back to give a troubled business a chance to survive, or in certain good times, adding labor-saving machinery that increased productivity and the pay of the workers who stayed on the job. In the last case, a vibrant economy would probably find a place for the laid-off workers. In well-run economies, the government or industry would have plans to recycle and retrain such workers, thus helping another industry advance by combining more advanced methods or technology with more skilled production or service. The productivity of society would advance. Wages and leisure time could increase for everyone.

Lately, not enough American business leaders have been contemplating that kind of positive cycle of layoffs and productivity. While there have been progressive productivity advances—computerized equipment, information technology, etcetera—there has also been a very strong, negative mechanism for increasing productivity. Employers have been putting their workers on the rack and squeezing or stretching them until they produce more and more work.

This is exploitation. It may not be exploitation in the classic sense of the19th century Robber Baron who drove his workers into the Satanic mills for a six day week of eighty hours labor in exchange for starvation wages (although this does exist in some parts of the world); but it is definitely exploitation in terms of pushing wage and salary employees until they are exhausted, frustrated, and getting sick. Currently, there is a very slow, jobless recovery taking place in the U.S. economy; even as firms pulled out of the recession they laid off 1.2 million workers in the first ten months of 2002. The workers were not dismissed because there was nothing for them to do; they left because management decided their co-workers could be pushed to take up the slack. Those who remain are called "ghost workers," trying to do the mysterious work of those who left as well as their

own, facing endless tasks, some of them very unfamiliar and strange, that are piling up at their work stations. "Ghost work" can be scary, according to Hamilton Beazley, a management consultant who coined the term, because it "is demoralizing and can cripple the individual as well as the organization."[6]

The business pages of the major media are starting to take notice of this phenomenon, as in a November 2002 issue of *Time* entitled, "Where Did Everyone Go?" and subtitled, "Firms are laying off workers even as business revives. That boosts profits—at the cost of morale."[7] The speed-ups that were isolated to certain industries like meat-packing in the 1980s, and the purposeful understaffing that the nursing profession has suffered under for years, especially at for-profit hospitals, are spreading throughout offices, stores, and workplaces throughout the economy. In blue-collar work, there have been speed-ups combined with mandatory overtime—nice if you need it, but too physically exhausting for some older workers who would rather work a steady forty-hour week and be able to make it to retirement. If exhaustion takes its toll and the worker has to retire early, the company hires a young new worker who will not notice the stress right away. In some cases, where the company has already negotiated contracts that call for two-tiered wages—higher for old union members, lower for new hires—this increases the managers' incentive to run the veterans out of the plant.

In office jobs, salaried workers are extending their hours, taking more work home, and leaving planning work undone. Eventually all this takes a toll: "the larger workload and stress on productivity leave workers less able to focus on the work at hand," says Michael Faenza of the National Mental Health Association, "It can lead to depression, anxiety, and substance abuse."[8] Middle managers are stressed, too, because they have to please senior management's objectives even while they know they are pushing their employees, and maybe themselves, beyond the brink. Productivity, which usually falls in economic slumps, was rising at a 4% annual rate in mid-2002.

Factory workers have known about this kind of pressure for years. This is one of the seldom mentioned, but sound justifications for labor unions. Work rules that are negotiated properly allow experienced, middle-aged workers with skills and knowledge to work at a reasonable speed and keep their jobs. Blue collar workers tend to be more familiar with "speed up" and "stretch out" (on the "rack" of extended hours) than most office workers. They know it is not a good way of increasing productivity because it can take years off your working life—or off your life, period. But in the age of NAFTA and runaway shops, workers are not so likely to stand up to a company that threatens to move to Mexico or Mississippi if the union does not give concessions on work rules or wages.

Even though few workers today are familiar with the concept of surplus labor—the term socialists once used to describe the part of one's labor that goes to the manufacturer or capitalist as profit—they are probably beginning to understand the meaning of exploitation. More work—same wage—means more money for somebody else. Unfortunately, once this process takes hold as a general phenomenon in a whole society, or in many interconnected societies, it is difficult to stop. The logic of capital, always demanding higher returns, does not listen to pleas for social justice.

The Bush Gang does not listen either.

Not content with the threat of privatizing federal jobs, the President announced that he would rescind most of the wage increases that had already been granted to federal workers in earlier agreements and negotiations. He claimed to be doing it because of the demands placed on the nation by the "War on Terrorism," but he made no such demands on the owning class which was gaining by "speeding up" and "stretching out" their workers.

November 25, 2002

Full statutory pay raises in 2003 would interfere with our nation's ability to pursue the war on terrorism.

—George W. Bush

Nine

Back to the Jungle

The Corporate Predators Return

They would speed him up until they had worn him out, and then they would throw him into the gutter.

—Upton Sinclair, *The Jungle*, 1906

They've eliminated the middle man. The corporations don't have to lobby the government any more. They are the government.

—Jim Hightower, former Secretary of Agriculture for the state of Texas

Without adequate government regulation, the worst of the corporate predators will return. Since the Bush Gang has dragged the United States back down to the level of the Robber Barons, where the lives of many working people are steadily degraded, it is only fitting that we look at the industry that epitomized corporate degradation a century ago—the meat industry. In 2003, just as in 1903, the monopolized production of animal flesh has become more inhuman and immoral, both in its treatment of the men and women that slaughter our food and in its contempt for the health of all those who eat that food.

Upton Sinclair became the most famous of the muckrakers, the writers and journalists who did battle with the Robber Barons a century ago, when he wrote his novel, *The Jungle*. The book depicted the life in the meat-packing plants and stockyards of Chicago, where workers endured brutal labor conditions and struggled, often unsuccessfully, to keep their families alive on their pitiful wages. Sinclair's intention was to bring attention to the hundreds of thousands of desperately poor working people, many of them immigrants, whose labor produced obscene profits for the giant firms that controlled the markets in beef, pork, and sausages.

Sinclair won the attention of the American public, including President Theodore Roosevelt. Many people, when reading passages such as "speeding them up, grinding them to pieces, and sending for new ones," looked straight past the metaphor—that is, working people were being treated like so many sausages—and thought about the sausages themselves. They were sickened by compelling passages in *The Jungle* that dealt with the utterly disgusting quality of the food that was produced by the meat monopolies—diseased cows, dead rats, and unspeakable pig parts were dumped into meat grinders and sent off to unsuspecting consumers all around the world. And readers who cooked with lard had to stomach the tales of workers who fell into the fat-cooking vats and dissolved into the lard itself.

The American middle class wanted to know: is that meat, the meat we eat, really so unclean?

So, when Theodore Roosevelt and other progressives took action and investigated the meat-packing companies, their first priority was not the appalling treatment of the workers, but the appalling quality of the food. In short order, Congress succeeded in passing "Pure Food and Drug" legislation that helped protect American consumers. Although some states also began passing worker's compensation laws at that time, the overall conditions of labor were not improved very much. Whenever union organizing efforts succeeded, as in 1904 and 1918 for the packinghouse workers, the big meatpacking companies countered with a variety of violent and underhanded union-busting techniques, including stirring up antagonisms among the most downtrodden workers, the Eastern European immigrants fresh off the boat and the African Americans newly migrated north. Working people in general continued to be exploited by American corporations, even during the booming economy and stock market bubble of the 1920s. Upton Sinclair later joked ruefully that *The Jungle* did not help advance the interests of the working class as much as he had hoped, "I aimed at the public's heart and by accident I hit it in the stomach."

The meatpacking workers, like most of those in the burgeoning ranks of industrial workers, toiled for the people Sinclair called

"plutocrats," the elite class of business owners and bankers who for over six decades successfully foiled the efforts of industrial trade unions to win decent wages. Finally, with the help of the National Labor Relations Act and other legislation passed during Franklin Roosevelt's administration, the United Packinghouse Workers Union was able to organize the entire industry in the 1940s. The law of the jungle was erased in favor of agreements that guaranteed a dignified working life: a forty hour week and much safer conditions on the assembly line. The work was still rough and tough, but the meatpackers and meat-cutters were well-paid, in the 1960s earning about three dollars an hour more than the average manufacturing wage.

Not long after the meatpackers won their dignity in the 1950s and 1960s, the giants of the industry, such as Swift and Armour, were starting to move out of the union neighborhoods that had sprung up around the stockyards of Kansas City, St. Paul, and Chicago. They moved to non-union, rural areas, following upstart companies such as Iowa Beef Producers, or IBP, which had created non-union shops and managed to cut wages by as much as 50% while undermining safety regulations. The rest of the meatpacking industry just needed an extra nudge to follow IBP in that direction, back to the jungle where only the most ruthless companies would survive.

Enter the Bush Gang

At the beginning of 1981, when George H.W. Bush took office as Ronald Reagan's Vice President, he immediately took charge of the Task Force on Regulatory Relief. In February of that year, Bush was granted "line item" authority for deregulation of American business through Executive Order 12291, which established the principle that federal regulations must "be based upon adequate evidence that their potential benefits to society are greater than their potential costs to society." There was a particular bias imbedded in this language: the Bush Gang was suggesting that the cost of existing health and safety standards, as well as other workplace regulations, were too great a burden on American society. In March of 1981, Bush wrote to businessmen and invited them to enumerate the areas of "society" that they wanted to see deregulated. By the end of the year Bush's office bragged about a "significant reduction in the cost of federal regulation."

For the meatpacking industry, deregulation meant that the speed-up of the production lines would not be hampered, permitting companies to save money by eliminating jobs, even though injuries were sure to increase. Meatpacking already had three times as many injuries as other American factories. The Bush Gang ordered the Occupational Safety and Health Administration (OSHA) to cut back on expenses and be less bothersome. Inspections dropped off dramatically over the next eight years. In 1980, OSHA conducted 280 inspections of meat packing plants, but only 176 in 1988. With the door open for potential abuse, Iowa Beef Producers and other companies increasingly made use of immigrant laborers who could be easily intimidated, just as the meat-packing giants in 1900 had done when they took advantage of newly arrived families from Eastern Europe. In the 1980s and 90s, many of the exploited were recruited by company agents and brought to the U.S. from small towns in Mexico, and others came as refugees from wars in Bosnia and Central America.

The owners of the industry believe the

worker is disposable, just as in Sinclair's day: "They had worn him out, with their speeding up and their carelessness, and now they had thrown him away." Well before Henry Ford's auto plants were built, the slaughterhouses had been one of the first American industries to operate on an assembly line system. Or should it be called a "dis-assembly line?" Whole cows and hogs hang from chains and move past each worker, who takes a few quick hacks with his sharp cutting tools before the carcass passes on to the next worker. The faster the company can run the line, or "chain," then the higher are its profits. The typical line-speed in an American slaughterhouse, 175 cattle an hour in 1976, was up to almost 400 an hour in 2001.

America's largest agricultural corporations noticed how much money was being made and moved in on the action. Cargill, a world-wide giant in the grain trade and a notorious union-busting firm besides, took a big cut of the beef market through its subsidiary, Excel. Tyson Foods, which rose to prominence with its low-wage chicken-killing factories based in the low-wage state of Arkansas, noticed the wage-cutting successes of IBP, which had become the largest beef producer in the country. Tyson decided to expand its horizons by acquiring IBP for $4.7 billion in 2001.

Perhaps Tyson executives had been studying news magazines such as US News and World Report, which noted that IBP was able to better the record of the industry as a whole, which had cut average wages by 31.4% over a fifteen year period. Because of the low pay and high rate of injury (leading, in some plants, to a turnover rate in employees of over 100% each year), it became hard to find American citizens who wanted the jobs—in 1996 state officials in Nebraska estimated that 25% of all meatpack-

WAGES IN MEAT INDUSTRY FAR LOWER THAN IN OTHER INDUSTRIES			
U.S. Manufacturing $14.38	Meat Packing Slaughter $10.94	Meat Packing Processing $11.80	Poultry Slaughter Processing $9.45

(Source: U.S. Department of Labor, Bureau of Labor Statistics, 2000)[2]

ing workers were illegal migrants. Although corporations were fined for hiring recruiters who ventured into little towns in Mexico to find new flesh for the factories, the penalties were not sufficient to discourage the practice.[1]

Cheap labor meant big profits. At the beginning of the 21st century wages in the meat industry were about $3 an hour lower than the national average for manufacturing. They had been $3 higher than the hourly average thirty years earlier.

Even worse than the drastic fall in wages was the fact that meat-packing workers labored in the nation's most dangerous occupation according to the Bureau of Labor Statistics.[3] More than one quarter of the nation's meat-packing workers suffered a job-related injury or sickness in 1999, indicating that the rate of serious injury had increased to a level five times higher than the average in manufacturing. The list of accident reports filed with OSHA had titles such as "Employee Killed When Arm Caught in Meat Grinder" and "Caught and Killed in Gut-Cooker Machine" that were reminiscent of the gruesome descriptions of work in *The Jungle*.

Nasty Meat

The meat produced by maimed workers could also maim your stomach. In the summer of 2002, the Sierra Club issued a report based on state and federal records from the 1980s and 1990s. They found that slaughterhouses had produced and sold 134 million pounds of contaminated meat over those two decades and had paid $48 million for health and environmental violations.[4] One reason the meat was so unhealthy was that big corporations have increasingly relied on "factory farms" and "animal factories," the giant feedlots that were springing up from the Carolinas to California in the 1990s. These operations packed an unbelievable number of cows and pigs into a very small number of acres, force-fed them, let them wade around in a sloppy mixture of mud and manure, pumped them up with overdoses of antibiotics to try to reduce the rates of disease, and then slaughtered them in close proximity to one another.

Companies such as ConAgra bought up the famous labels of the old meat monopolists, such as Swift and Armour, and revived the 100-year-old corporate practice of producing really bad meat. A highly respected consumer health advocacy organization, the Center for Science in the Public Interest (CSPI), reported in February 2002 that they had penetrated deep into hidden federal records using the Freedom of Information Act. CSPI discovered, by reviewing government food safety inspections, that nearly half of the turkeys processed at ConAgra's Longmont, Colorado, facility were contaminated with harmful Salmonella bacteria, as were almost one-third of the turkeys produced at four other ConAgra plants.[5]

This kind of information apparently put the U.S. Department of Agriculture's Food

Safety and Inspection Service on notice, for in July 2002 they announced that ConAgra Beef Company was voluntarily recalling approximately 19 million pounds of beef products that may have been contaminated with another especially virulent pathogen, E Coli O157:H7. Eric Schlosser did further reporting on this E Coli bacteria because it originated at the giant feedlot in Greeley, Colorado, one of the places featured in his book, *Fast Food Nation*. The Greeley bacteria had attacked people in June of 2002 and made them "severely ill, mainly small children...vomiting and defecating blood."[6]

After this revelation, more bad news came to light concerning other ConAgra misconduct. David Migoya of *The Denver Post* reported in late July of 2002 that "ConAgra executives knowingly resold about 80 tons of meat in 2000 that South Korean customs agents had quarantined because they said it contained listeria, a potentially lethal bacteria. Rather than destroy the frozen meat or cook it to kill pathogens, executives at one of the world's largest food conglomerates sold it to other countries with lower standards than South Korea's—including selling it in the United States, according to corporate e-mails between ConAgra and executives at its Monfort Inc. subsidiary."[7]

There are obvious lessons to be learned from this story. One, the leaders of U.S. corporations apparently believed they could get away with murder more easily in the United States than in South Korea. Two, the Department of Agriculture did not want American consumers to know about the deadly levels of bacteria that are allowed in local supermarkets. The USDA had allowed ConAgra's voluntary recall to be so tardy that only ten percent of the meat could be located. Elsa Murano, USDA undersecretary for food safety, was anxious to deflect attention

from 18.6 million pounds of bad beef. She decided that the consumers, not the company, might as well take the blame for any illness. She announced, "If people cooked their food correctly, a lot of outbreaks would not take place."[8]

To the Rescue: Food Monopolists and Factory Farms Need Help

At a time when the long-term deregulatory policies of the Bush Gang were leading to serious health risks, the Bush II administration decided to send someone to the rescue. But she was not rescuing American consumers and small farmers. A long-time member of the Gang rode in from the West to add firepower on the side of the corporations that have nearly destroyed family farming in America. Ann Veneman, chosen as the first female Secretary of Agriculture by George Bush II, had already served Father Bush as Undersecretary of Argiculture for Foreign Affairs and Commodities. Veneman was not chosen for her feminist credentials, but for her willingness to serve the interests of the food monopolists. She had performed notable work as attorney/lobbyist for the biggest agricultural and food conglomerates, with special expertise in pushing genetic engineering for plants and animals. She had served on the board of directors of Calgene, the first company to get a USDA permit to field test a genetically modified crop, a tomato. The company and the patent on the tomato were later gobbled up by the company at the top of the chemical food chain, Monsanto.

As partners in crime, Veneman chose such people as Dale Moore as her USDA chief of staff; he had spent his career as chief lobbyist for the National Cattlemen's Beef Association. Her USDA Assistant Secretary for Congressional Relations, Mary Waters, moved to government service after serving as legislative counsel for ConAgra. Not surprisingly, the Center for Responsive Politics reports that the meat and livestock interests gave George W. Bush $600,000 for the 2000 presidential campaign, while only giving Al Gore $23,000.[9] And as we have seen above, underlings such as Elsa Murano, Undersecretary for Food Safety, are guided toward insuring the financial security of corporate food producers rather than the safety of the public.

The Bush ideology has inverted the logic of government intervention that Teddy Roosevelt, the trust-busters, and the food-safety advocates helped initiate one hundred years ago. Rather than forcing the big-business purveyors of food to be responsible corporate citizens, they have encouraged irresponsibility on the side of the new Robber Barons (in every industry, not just meat and food) while letting ordinary citizens fend for themselves.

When the major players in corporate agriculture, or their subsidiary growers and contractors, come under attack by the people—for instance, when they are sued by local communities that want to run them out of town for polluting the soil and the rivers—they import legions of lawyers to fight such lawsuits. They also lobby the government incessantly for ways to avoid paying for the damage, if and when they are convicted. One constant source of funds for the American agricultural industry comes in the form of billions of dollars in farming subsidies that are given out by the U.S. Congress each year. These payments go mostly to large-scale farming interests rather than to small family farms. And since many big farms,

feedlots, and agricultural processing centers are part of large corporations, they can sign on for a big chunk of other kinds of corporate welfare that are available to all of big business (these payments amount to between $100 and $200 billion per year for the entire corporate economy).[10]

One brand new source of money, part of the federal farm bill of 2002, came in a provision designed for the problem alluded to above—what to do when the company is sued for destroying the local environment because it failed to properly treat wastewater at its factory farms. According to this legislation, created through heavy lobbying by the corporations, the government would pay these same farm corporations handsomely if they showed some effort to clean up the animal wastewater and associated environmental damage caused by their operations. This is classic free-market, Republican doctrine: privatize the profits while socializing the costs. As food production is controlled more and more by corporate giants which pay well for the services of conservative political forces, the companies find they can dictate government policy.

There was a time, however, when the U.S. government was willing to oppose the food giants and protect U.S. consumers. A 1916 study, requested by President Woodrow Wilson and performed by the Federal Trade Commission, found that there was no longer competition in the meat packing industry because four firms—Swift, Armour, Cudahy, and Wilson—controlled nearly 40% of the market. In 1921, with the passage of the Packers & Stockyards Act, the Congress ordered an end to monopoly control over the meat slaughtering industry of the United States and made the Big Four divest of many of their interests.

At the beginning of the 21st century, the industry has regressed one hundred years. After two decades of government encouragement for a new round of monopolization, there was once again overwhelming concentration of power in the meat industry. The U.S. Department of Agriculture's study of who controlled the beef packing industry in the late 1990s revealed the following picture: Iowa Beef had 38% of the business; Cargill (through its subsidiary Excel) had 22%; ConAgra 21%; or 81% of the market between them.[11] That is twice the level of monopolization that Woodrow Wilson confronted.

Pigged Out

In addition to the adverse health effects on workers and consumers, the expansion of a "factory farm" system has also brought environmental hazards to anyone who lives in their vicinity. First there is the smell factor, since odors of so much concentrated manure and carnage can spread out over miles of neighboring territory. Sometimes outraged citizens, like Ann Thorne, whose husband operated a cattle farm in St. Joseph, Missouri, have been successful in stopping the threat to rural traditions. "They wanted to slaughter 16,000 hogs a day," said Thorne after leading a successful fight against a pork factory. "Do you have any idea what that would do to our lovely community? .... I didn't want my life ruined by those hogs."[12]

But often public protests are disregarded and corporate developers prevail, especially in poor rural areas that need jobs or increased tax revenues. The smells that waft across the prairie are a health hazard and much more odious than the odors from the cow manure that diary farmers used to spread on their fields. But more frightening and dangerous are the threats to natural drainage and water systems. Most of these giant industrial farms depend on "lagoon" systems (artificial, undrained ponds) to deal with animal waste. In 2002 the Sierra Club added up the damage from flood spills and seepage of millions of gallons of animal feces and urine from these giant manure pits and calculated that they had polluted 35,000 miles of American rivers.[13] The corporate farming sector is occasionally brought to account—for instance, Cargill plead guilty in February of 2002 to violating the Clean Water Act of Missouri because one of its manure spills had killed 50,000 fish in the nearby Loutre River.

The Environmental News Service reports that 10 million hogs live in North Carolina's coastal region and 8 million humans live in the whole state. And according to a University of North Carolina study in 2000, the quality of life in hog farm communities has been deteriorating fast. Karen Priest, an Elizabethtown, North Carolina resident, painted a graphic picture of the problem. "I feel," she said, "like I'm raising my children in one of those third world countries that we see some celebrity on TV trying to raise money for because of the sewage that runs through their village." Since some of these communities are standing up on their feet and fighting back, agricultural giants like Smithfield Foods started having second thoughts about the wisdom of their ways.[14]

Smithfield's thinking led elsewhere. Maybe they did not have to be corporate polluters in the United States. Maybe they could pollute another country.

Like many other American companies that are globalizing their production, Smithfield dreamed of escaping to Mexico. It seems that a factory can crank out pigs as easily as automobiles there and still enjoy the freedom to pollute. Smithfield did not spare any expense on its new facility in the State of Veracruz according to an October 2001 article by Betsy Freese in Successful Farming Online: "In a valley surrounded by extinct volcanoes, Smithfield is building swine units one after another. There are 14,500 sows on the ground now, with another 4,800 near completion, and plans to grow to 56,000 within five years. A new feed mill is under construction to handle the expansion. Jerry Godwin, who heads up all pig production for Smithfield Foods from his office in North Carolina, visited the Veracruz construction in 2002 and concluded, 'It looks as good as any in the U.S., it's a good place to grow.'"

Because very skilled and loyal employees could be hired for one dollar an hour, construction of the facilities is state of the art. For the same reason, Smithfield can hire more farm workers than they would in the U.S., thus allowing them to give extra care to the little piglets. This allows the company to have industry-leading piglet survival rates and thus a higher yield of pork as the end result. Still, all was not well at Smithfield in late 2002, but this was not due to the spanking clean Mexican operations. Prices and profits were down because of the level of worldwide corporate competition, combined with a looming pork glut due to overproduction. Poland, it seems, is a bustling center of factory farming in Europe, often financed by Danish and Dutch multinationals; and Brazil is pushing a lot of pigs out of South America.

* * *

We should be grateful that once again a few journalists are emulating Upton Sinclair and bringing attention to the fact that our government is permitting the meat industry to poi-son us. They are also awakening the public to the disgraceful treatment of meat-packing workers. And fortunately not every public servant has given up the public trust in favor of corporate contributions. There are some prosecutors in the government who are willing to indict corporations for endangering the public's health and others who are going after the companies for endangering the well-being of American workers, including the most recently arrived.

Tyson Foods was indicted on December 19, 2001 and charged with 36 counts of recruiting illegal workers from Mexico and transporting them to several of Tyson's 57 poultry processing plants in the Midwest and South. According to the indictment, Tyson managers arranged with smugglers to pick up workers just inside the U.S. border, and then organized transportation for them from the border to its plants. Tyson managers paid the smugglers $100 to $200 per worker in "recruitment fees." Tyson was stooping to criminal activity to maintain its number one position in the meat industry: in the chicken market, it had 23% of the business; and in the beef market, its acquisition of IBP gave it a 27% share; and in the pork market, at 18%, it stood number two after Smithfield Foods. The company's 120,000 employees constituted more than a quarter of all the workers in the meat and poultry processing industry. Tyson, just like the other major meat processors, had pursued a business plan that continually degraded the conditions of work. Given this kind of competition, which American unions have called "the race to the bottom," Tyson and the rest of the industry have had difficulty finding enough workers. Neither legal immigrants nor American citizens were willing to endure the dangers of the meat chain line for such crummy pay. Rather than make working conditions more humane, the meat companies went after a fresh supply of illegal immigrants.

The United States attorney in Chattanooga, John MacCoon said, "It's much more productive, we think, to attack the source, the companies that recruit these illegals, than to pursue endless prosecutions of illegals at the border." The government brought the indictment only after Tyson refused to pay a $100 million fine for hiring illegal aliens. This penalty was assessed based on the assumption that: 1) Tyson was able to pay lower wages because it hired illegal workers; therefore 2) Tyson should forfeit excess profits earned as a result of hiring illegals. Meat industry pay, which had already been driven down to levels far below that of most manufacturing workers, was being pushed down even farther in many parts of the country. How far could they go in order to inflate profits? Figures for 2000 from the Bureau of Labor Statistics reported that the median wage—not the bottom wage—for cutters and trimmers in Arkansas was a mere $7.70 an hour; for slaughterers and meatpackers, $8.29; in North Carolina, the pay was $8.08 and $7.81 for those two jobs.[15]

As prosecuting attorney MacCoon said about the Tyson case in Chattanooga, "This trial is all about greed."

A century ago, Upton Sinclair described how workers and their families were herded into Chicago like animals—"the people came up in hordes." They were rapidly beaten down and destroyed by an inhuman system of production—"speeding them up, grinding them to pieces, and sending for new ones."

Eric Schlosser, whose book *Fast Food Nation* documents the return of this inhuman system, echoed Sinclair's impression when he wrote about the sanitation workers in the meat processing plants: "The nation's worst job can end in just about the worst way—sometimes these workers are literally ground up and reduced to nothing."

Once again the corporate giants are preying upon animal flesh and upon human flesh. They know what they're doing, and some of their CEOs even joke about it. Former chief executive of ConAgra, Mike Harper, liked to give out wall plaques to his top executives that pictured two vultures sitting in a tree and talking to each other:

"Patience my ass," says one vulture to the other, "I'm gonna go kill somebody."[16]

Ten

Wal-Mart

Save You a Nickel, Steal Your Soul

Man is born free, and everywhere he is in chains.

—Jean Jacques Rousseau

Men and women are born free, and everywhere they are in chain stores.

—Anonymous

The largest fortune in the world:	The Walton Family	$94 billion
The biggest private employer in the world:	Wal-Mart	1,300,000 people
The highest annual sales volume in the world:	Wal-Mart	over $235 billion

(Figures for 2002)

Imagine that you live in the richest country in the world, you work for the world's largest company, and you have just walked outside into the sunshine. You look at your check. You cannot survive on that kind of money. Your husband pulls up in the van to pick you up, he looks at your check and groans, "We can't live on that."

This is the work of the Bush Gang and their corporate supporters. They have made a systematic effort to keep the wages of most Americans low in order to transfer wealth and income to the very richest Americans. Today, too many of the most successful American corporations—and in Wal-Mart's case the nation's biggest employer—have prospered because they have mastered the art of extracting high profits out of poorly compensated workers.

To Barbara Ehrenreich, a social critic with a practical and scientific mind, the implications of this reality were troubling. How can anyone, she wondered, survive at the bottom of the U.S. labor market while earning anything close to the minimum wage? Because she's unusually brave for a writer, Ehrenreich decided to research the question by going to work—first, as a waitress in Key West, Florida; then as a house-cleaner and nursing home aide in Portland, Maine; finally as an "associate" (company public relations parlance meaning an hourly laborer) at Wal-Mart in Minneapolis. With little difficulty she proved her hypothesis: it's impossible for a single person to live in many parts of the United States—that is, to pay for rent, utilities, food, and transportation and hardly anything else—on six or seven or eight dollars an hour for a forty-hour week.

Ehrenreich's valuable book, *Nickel and Dimed*, demonstrates how the underside of our economy operated in the so-called boom times of the late 1990s. The situation, if anything, is worse in bust times. About thirty percent of American workers earned eight and half dollars an hour or less in 2002. Most of them labored in the vast expanse of service industries that now provide most of our jobs. Many work for corporations that have routinized and dehumanized service labor as systematically as the assembly lines that exploited factory labor in the 19th century and the beginning of the 20th century.

It is demoralizing to work all week at the world's biggest employer, Wal-Mart, and still be unable to feed your children. Former Wal-Mart manager Gretchen Adams said the wage-earning mothers she used to supervise "were not paid enough to live on... they would come in crying because they had hard decisions to make: whether to take their child to the doctor or pay the rent."[1] The situation bothered Adams so much she quit her job so she could organize against Wal-Mart and educate the public about its practices. Many mothers (and fathers) who work at Wal-Mart have to face the reality of applying for federal food stamps in order to put macaroni and cheese on the table. But they also have another worry. Within the authoritarian corporate culture of the world's largest employer they are constantly in danger of being humiliated and persecuted for "time theft."

This recently invented crime is one most people learn about only if they take an employee orientation course at Wal-Mart. "Time theft," it seems, is the new name for the age-old prerogative of all employees to take a tiny break in the midst of work—not the official coffee break of ten or fifteen minutes, but the minute or two extra that has kept people sane since the dawn of the punch clock. The bathroom break with a few extra seconds tacked on, so you can sigh at yourself in the mirror and make a silly face. The break from the keyboard of three and

a half minutes (medically necessary to avoid carpal tunnel syndrome), so you can tell the person at the next desk about your sick dog. The slight slowdown as you re-stack sweaters and try to make friends with the new workmate in your department. Wal-Mart tells you that this is "stealing" from them. They pay you for your time and you owe them every second. Wal-Mart has broken the sacred trust that all employers owe to their employees, that all parents give to their kids (at least the parents who can get their kids to do any work)—one must trust them to stop work occasionally, day-dream for a moment about the astounding world that exists outside the dreary confines of their wage labor, even malinger for a while, and then get back to work. This simply recognizes that people are human beings, not machines.

It turns out that Wal-Mart itself is the real thief. Wal-Mart has concocted schemes for stealing from its employees on a grand scale. In June of 2002, *The New York Times* described exactly how one such scheme works: "After finishing her 10 p.m. to 8 a.m. shift, Verette Richardson clocked out and was heading to her car when a Wal-Mart manager ordered her to turn around and straighten up the store's apparel department. Eager not to get on her boss's bad side, she said, she spent the next hour working unpaid, tidying racks of slacks and blouses and picking up hangers and clothes that had fallen to the floor. Other times after clocking out, she was ordered to round up shopping carts scattered in the parking lot. 'They wanted us to do a lot of work for no pay,' said Richardson, who worked from 1995 to 2000 at a Wal-Mart in southeast Kansas City. 'A company that makes billions of dollars doesn't have to do that.'"[2]

This corporation has developed a system of forcing workers to work overtime without paying them, usually by requiring them to prepare or clean-up their work site, or wait on tardy customers, before or after their official working hours. For some employees, this can amount to four or five hours of unpaid labor every week.

What is the world's richest corporation up to? It is company policy to put extreme pressure on managers to turn in "clean" timesheets for their workforce, that is, timesheets that show no overtime. Bookkeepers working at Wal-Mart have admitted that managers ordered them to alter employee time cards and eliminate extra hours. Several of their managers have testified, in response to suits brought by Wal-Mart workers, that they were under pressure from headquarters to yield the highest profit possible on their stores, then were instructed to keep staff levels low while paying no overtime at all. In 2000 in Colorado, Wal-Mart was assessed fines of $50 million for the very real crime of "overtime theft." As of 2003, it faces many similar lawsuits brought by employees in other parts of the country.

Why is it that the heirs to the Wal-Mart dynasty—Jim, John, Alice, Robson and Helen—were worth $94 billion in 2002, collectively more than twice as much as Bill Gates, yet were only paying their employees an average of $7.50 an hour?[3]

Because this is how they got so rich. They put the screws to their employees from the very beginning: intimidating them with talk of "time theft," paying the lowest wages possible, and refusing to honor the basic right to be paid for extra time on the job. According to Wayne Hood, a financial analyst with Prudential, Wal-Mart does keep labor costs lower; they amount to only 16.5% of their operating costs as opposed to the average in the retail industry of 20.7%. Multiply that 4.2% difference times over

one million U.S. employees and it really helps bolster the family fortune. Since Wal-Mart sales are now growing more slowly than in past years, Hood expects the company to crack down even further on its employees in order to maintain its high profit rates.[4]

Sam Walton, the founder of Wal-Mart, was always a self-avowed cheapskate, and adamantly anti-union. Still, he had a homey touch and a reputation, deserved or not, for looking after his workers. He would visit his various stores, ask employees about their concerns, and emphasize the possibility of "associates" (low-level employees) moving up to become managers. This was one way of getting away with the dirt-poor wages. Sam demanded loyalty and paid fierce attention to creating obedient employees in the old days. He could get everybody to shake their butts. Literally. Every Friday morning, the assembled employees in each store would holler out the Wal-Mart cheer: "Give me a W!" "W!"—"Give me an A!" "A!"—"Give me an L!" "L!" "Give me a squiggly!" Everyone bends forward and shakes their butt—a squiggly apparently is the line between the L and the M. Then they finish spelling the company name and yell: "Who's No. 1?" "The customer. Always!"[5]

Fortune writer Mark Gimein claims they still do this at Wal-Mart stores, but the butt shaking does not mean the employees are happy. Dianne Molander told him about working in the Mt. Pleasant, Iowa store, where she earned $6.12 in clothing department until she quit at the height of the 2001 Christmas season. She felt her job was terribly inefficient because management would not trust employees to do anything on their own initiative. "Every manager is at war with us," she said.

And managers were squeezed themselves.

A former assistant manager in Pennsylvania recalled being ordered to do more with less, "Where I had maybe six or seven people, I would be cut down to four. The assistant managers were told, 'You guys will have to work a six-day week, mandatory.' They really didn't care how much of a toll it took on the employees."[6]

Can Workers Fight Back?

Workers have tried to organize unions at Wal-Mart stores, but without much success. Actually, with no success at all. Wal-Mart is the largest private employer in the United States, it is the largest retailer in the world, the largest importer, the largest purchaser of manufactured goods, the largest outlet for almost every major supplier of virtually every consumer product in the United States. It abhors unions and uses every possible means to keep organized labor out, including a tracking system to identify and eliminate union supporters. This system is called UPI—Unresolved People Issues—and the corporate managers who run the system call themselves People Managers.

"It is like something out of George Orwell's *Animal Farm*," said the head of the United Food and Commercial Workers, Doug Dority, when he was speaking to the National Association of Letter Carriers. The UFCW represents workers in grocery stores, meat packing plants, and other retail businesses, and has decided to take on Wal-Mart. The union realizes it is in store for a long, frustrating fight, because Wal-Mart already engages in heavy anti-union propagandizing and will fly in teams of union busters at the first scent of an organizing drive. The need for union representation is clear: workers in 27 states are suing Wal-Mart for violating wage-and-hour laws. In December of 2002, an Oregon jury found Wal-Mart guilty of forcing employees to work overtime without pay.

Union members at other supermarkets and stores that are similar to Wal-Mart make significantly more money, 31% more, than the "associates." But their jobs will be in jeopardy if Wal-Mart and companies modeling themselves on Wal-Mart keep making in-roads on their retail areas. Not only that, but other service workers with good contracts, like the letter carriers, will find themselves faced with similar threats. As noted previously, President Bush has already announced that it is open season on federal workers. He imposed a cut in already negotiated wage increases and announced the government might privatize half of the 1.8 million federal jobs. The Bush Gang must be dreaming of the possibilities: the federal government can save a lot of money that it needs for war if it can break the letter carriers union. Maybe they ought to be called "postal associates."

If the unions fail to put up a fight, it seems certain that Wal-Mart and those who copy Wal-Mart will win "the race to the bottom." (Labor unions are using this expression to describe the intense competition between corporations, especially in anti-union environments such as the United States and many parts of the developing world. Companies are competing to see how low they can push wages and benefits, and how harsh they can make working conditions.)

The UFCW announced an opening strategy in 2002, one designed to educate the general public about Wal-Mart and the condition of low wage jobs in general:

> We are building a campaign that brings together women's organizations, civil rights groups consumer organizations, religious leaders, workers and

neighborhood organizations to challenge Wal-Mart to live up to its responsibility as the largest retailer, employer and corporation in America.

One of the organized groups that signed up for the task was the National Organization of Women. In September 2002 they began their campaign by demonstrating at 600 stores around the country. This development showed great potential: a mostly middle-class organization was showing solidarity across class lines as NOW members took the side of working women who sold them their clothes.

Furthermore, there are serious issues of gender bias that afflict women at Wal-Mart. While 72% percent of the firm's employees are women, only 33% of Wal-Mart managers are women. This may not sound so unusual, since men still tend to dominate in the management of many industries. But not in retail. Over 50% of the managers in companies comparable to Wal-Mart are women; in fact, according to the study done by economist Marc Bendick, those companies had more female managers way back in 1975 than Wal-Mart had in 2002. Many women across the country have come forward with stories of sex-discrimination and have successfully filed suit against the company. [7] As of 2003 a giant class action suit, *Dukes v. Wal-Mart*, was being brought on behalf of 700,000 workers to prove that there has been systematic pattern of favoring males for promotion, better pay, and better assignments. While this lawsuit is on behalf of all women working at Wal-Mart, its primary plaintiffs are women who were blocked from going higher in management.

In November of 2002, there were other anti-Wal-Mart actions. Union and concerned community groups staged a National Day of Action and gathered in 100 different localities to demonstrate at Wal-Mart stores. Their purpose was to educate the public about working conditions, and educate workers about unions. Rather than call for boycotts, many groups staged "shop-ins" at Wal-Mart which allowed protestors to spread their message, via T-shirts and conversation, while they shopped with other working Americans. The point is to get people's attention about the future of work in America. Will the public be interested in hearing about the kind of employment that may lie ahead for them?

- Wal-Mart pays $2 to $3 an hour less than union stores.
- Wal-Mart leaves more than two-thirds of its employees without company health insurance, and those who get insurance pay sizable amounts out of pocket.
- Wal-Mart has no employee pension plan.
- Turnover at Wal-Mart exceeds half a million people every year.

Clearly, with turnover this high, most Wal-Mart employees are not loyal, nor enamored of the treatment meted out by the ghost of old Sam Walton. They are being treated like the lowest of temp workers, disposable and replaceable. A person living alone will definitely struggle to survive on the paltry wages, but what about the woman or man trying to support and care for others?

The mother of one or two small children cannot possibly survive on Wal-Mart wages. She will need food stamps, subsidized daycare, and a government rental housing voucher, if she's going to keep her family together on $7.00 to $8.00 an hour. Since the world's largest corporation, residing in the world's richest country, is not going to pay her enough to pay her bills, the rest of us have to pitch in. Charity? Not exactly. We are already paying her bills. All of us, as taxpayers, are picking up the tab. Our taxes are supporting the various government subsidies—for food, housing, child care—that a hard-working mother needs to survive, plus paying for the tax rebates (Earned Income Tax Credit) that are given to the poor or near-poor.

Should we resent the fact that we are helping them out? Not at all. But we should recognize that their problem is not lack of work or lack of effort, but the lack of decent jobs. We ought to resent the fact that we, as tax-paying citizens, are augmenting the profits and subsidizing the stockholders of every corporation that fails to pay a living wage.

Where are the outraged, middle-class tax protesters when we really need them? They ought to be picketing the huge discount chains, and especially Wal-Mart, for coming into our neighborhoods and towns and relying on our tax money to defray the size of their payrolls. While they are out picketing, the tax protesters could also stop by their parents' nursing homes, often owned by large for-profit chains that utilize many of the low-wage, coercive strategies that Wal-Mart does, and tell the companies to give their nursing aides a big raise, too. Many full-time workers all over the United States must rely on some type of government assistance to help them survive on their pitiful wages.

The Race to the Bottom

The race-to-the-bottom strategy that is spreading throughout U.S. corporations could become a losing proposition for everyone. The ideology of the Bush Gang, which has permeated American political and business culture for over two decades, has effectively forced corporations to make this race. Bush I and Bush II have encouraged business with every kind of deregulation while simultaneously erecting various barriers that impede working people's organized opposition. The corporate participants now have little choice in the matter. If they do not leap into the race, some competitor—like Wal-Mart—will get to the bottom faster, grow bigger, and swallow them.

The race is international. Wal-Mart is opening stores all over the world, in Mexico, China, England, and even in Germany, a country that American corporations dread. Germany is a frightening place because it has a standard of living more or less as high as that of the United States, but with fewer poor people and much better wages for most working people. Generally, as economic productivity goes up in Germany, pay goes up proportionally. This record of rewarding productivity is why the average German manufacturing worker, who earned 86% of the American hourly wage in 1979, earned much more than his American counterpart, 127% of the U.S. wage, in 2000.[8]

Wal-Mart decided to begin its invasion by buying up chains of already-existing German stores, with a plan to follow with 50 of its own new super-stores. By the year 2000, it was a flop. Plans to build the super-stores were being scrapped because Wal-Mart was continually losing money in Germany. Its fame in cost cutting through better networking of supply, crisper management of inventory, better deals with suppliers, all appears to be an illusion (or delusion). Its German competitors in the low-cost retail sector are better at all those things, and they pay their workers better because German unions demand good contracts. Wal-Mart, despite various attempts to slip around contracts and employment codes, has not succeeded in arbitrarily pushing wages down to the American level at its 95 German stores because they are unionized, too. In July 2002, workers at 46 stores went on strike because Wal-Mart would not agree to a 6.5% wage increase. To top it off, German workers do not like the American management style. Being among the most productive in the world, they would deeply resent a manager who accused them of "time theft." Plus, being independent minded, they are not interested in jumping up and down in front of the managers once a week. German workers, according to Jürgen Glaubitz, "do not like to be regarded as cheerleaders, but as personalities with their own ideas and rights."[9]

Clearly there is a struggle between capital and labor going on, which is par for the course in any capitalist society. Some of the great capitalists of the past, such as Andrew Carnegie and Henry Ford, had intense antipathy for unions and hired private armies to police and undermine organized labor, and even shoot at them. Yet their breakthroughs in steel and auto production led them to pay their workers more, not less than other competing industrial enterprises. They did this out of a sort of paternalistic pride, feeling that they should demonstrate to society, and to their fellow Robber Barons and corporate leaders, that their successful enterprises provided well for their employees.

Wal-Mart, as the biggest monopolist of our day, does precisely the opposite, and this has tremendous repercussions around the world, and not just on the employees of its stores. Wal-Mart is the largest importer of Chinese goods, spending $10 billion per year on products from several thousand Chinese factories. American imports are often touted as proof that globalization works. The trade is important for foreign workers, pro-

ponents say, providing jobs, income and a rising standard of living, elements that would be missing without our presence in the global market. But certainly in the case of Wal-Mart, it is impossible to paint such a rosy picture. Charlie Kernaghan of the National Labor Committee reports, "In country after country, factories that produce for Wal-Mart are the worst," adding that the bottom-feeding labor policy of this one corporation "is actually lowering standards in China, slashing wages and benefits, imposing long mandatory-overtime shifts, while tolerating the arbitrary firing of workers who even dare to discuss factory conditions."[10] Furthermore, unlike some other corporations, Wal-Mart blocks human rights groups seeking to monitor its behavior in the factories it does business with in China. In fact, it even refuses to divulge the list of the companies with which it does business.

Wal-Mart, with its overwhelming market position, could easily add a few cents to the price of each product and then inform its Chinese subcontractors that wages must be raised. It could inform its American customers, with some degree of pride, that it was bettering the situation of Chinese workers. All fine and good, except that then Wal-Mart would have face up to the task of helping its own employees.

Then, too, Wal-Mart would be obligated to do something about the meat packers and meat cutters that were sent back to work in the jungle, including the low-paid chicken handlers at Tyson Foods. Wal-Mart's supermarket sections are Tyson Food's biggest customers. Like Wal-Mart, Tyson is native to Arkansas, that lowest-wage state that breeds various sorts of bottom feeders.

But is better pay enough? Every American ought to look around at our towns and our landscape and wonder why they are being destroyed by the huge parking lots and the ugly giant boxes that belong to the multinational retailers. This chapter has concentrated on corporate deregulation, a favorite theme of the Bush Gang, and its link to higher profits and the corporate degradation of labor. If there were more time, we could move on to the corporate degradation of American life—since there are other ways that the American upper class has been increasing their return on capital while decreasing the livability of American society. Because their thirst for higher returns is insatiable and they cannot leave any market unturned, Wal-Mart and similar giant corporations want to suck the life out of every community in the country. Bill Quinn, in his book *How Wal-Mart is Destroying America (and the World)*, explains how the consequences have been immense: for instance, the destruction of thousands of small town businesses and downtowns, as profits are sucked out of small cities and towns and into the pockets of the Walton family, their shareholders, and their investment banks.

Bottom-feeders will devour anything. The big corporate fish have sunk to the lowest possible level—low ethics and low wages are just too tempting. But more than temptation is involved. Most companies are under pressure to adopt low wage policies as a mandatory feature of an American economy that had been made over to Bush Gang specifications. If they are going to control their markets and expand their businesses they have to continue to satisfy investors' hunger for profits. Yes, they scooped up the smaller fish and some tidy profits for a while, but in the process they deprived their workers of the income necessary to keep the economy chugging along. Capital thinks it has triumphed over labor, but in so doing it is running itself into the ground.

Eleven

Negligent Homicide

Stealing Our Health Care, Killing Our Health

"All because they couldn't afford health insurance."
—*Rex Morgan, M.D.*
The good doctor from the comic strip was saddened by the family's tragedy.
But he had the prescription for others: national health insurance.

9 out of 10 nursing homes had inadequate staffing levels in the year 2002.

25% of the people in Texas had no health insurance in the year 2000.

Now that the governor of Texas is the Chief Executive Officer of the United States, there is every indication that the Bush Gang will make health care even worse for the whole country. If they can achieve the same results as they did in Texas, then about 75 million Americans will lack health insurance, instead of the 42 million that lacked coverage of any kind in 2002. In addition to the uninsured, there are a great many people who have inadequate coverage and forego treatment for themselves and their children. Millions more get into serious financial difficulty trying to pay off the bills that insurance companies and HMOs will not pay. Among the senior population, all of whom are covered by Medicare, there are many who run up big bills for things that are not covered by their insurance, especially drug purchases, and

then have to give up something else—such as food. The American Association of Retired People, AARP, reported to the U.S. Senate Select Committee that the percentage of health costs senior citizens had to pay out of their pockets rose from 12% in 1977 to fully one quarter, or 25%, by 2000.

Health Reform: Bungled and Burgled

Long ago, during the election of 1992, Bill Clinton won many votes by promising to reform the U.S. health system so that all Americans could receive quality care. He pointed out that the Reagan/Bush administrations had sadly neglected the nation's health because they had allowed the number of uninsured Americans to rise from 23 million to 33 million. He tried to get Congress to enact a comprehensive plan in 1993-94, but failed, partly because of the stupid way in which his administration proceeded.

The Clinton health care team started off with the notion, fostered within the Democratic Leadership Council, that they must please the entrenched business interests that were responsible for making American health care expensive and inefficient. They patched together an awkward and unworkable "reform" mixture called "managed competition" and sought to rely on the already fragmented private system with only minor redirection from government. This Rube Goldberg contraption did not impress anyone as a vehicle for bringing moderately priced, universal medical care to the American public. It became another round of ammunition for the Republican Party and most of the corporations who dealt in health and insurance, for they then mounted a ferocious campaign against any plan that would try to meet the needs of the uninsured.

Corporate privatization of American health care was already well under way in the early 1990s and those who were profiting did not want any changes, either in the form of rational government intervention or even through the weak Clinton proposals. The insurance industry produced a scurrilous series of TV ads featuring "Harry and Louise," fictional characters who were worried about having continued access to their existing health plans. These two were particularly upset about the impending crisis of "rationed care." Harry and Louise worried that new health maintenance organizations might withhold their services because someone else, quite possibly poorer and less white than themselves, might be in line ahead of them.

This highly effective propaganda, along with an onslaught of newspaper editorials and other right-wing hollering, convinced many middle-class Americans that their society could

not afford universal health care. As a result, very little was accomplished at the federal level, and the health care system was turned over to giant corporations. Ten years later, the number of uninsured people had grown from 33 million to 42 million, certainly a sign of drastic health care rationing. But this kind of rationing did not save money, because by the end of 2002, corporations were raising their insurance costs quickly and dumping much of the burden on their employees (or retired former employees who still retained coverage).

The irony for the "Harrys" and "Louises" and the rest of middle-class America was that they could not avoid the rationing of health care. A right-wing Congress made the choice, under heavy lobbying pressure from those who profit from the delivery of health care, to let more and more of our population go without health care. They also gave the green light to the private sector to profit by rationing the medical care of working-class and middle-class citizens who still kept their insurance. Restricting health options and paying less for care for "Harry and Louise" became a fundamental requirement of business plans devised by privatized health maintenance organizations (HMOs) and other forms of for-profit managed care. As HMOs took control of the health care market, most people, whether they were Republicans or Democrats, hated the results. A Wall Street Journal/NBC poll in 1998 showed that 41% of Americans thought that HMOs had made the quality of health care in the United States worse, while only 16% thought they had made it better.

Throughout the nineties, nearly everyone had a story about family or close friends who had been denied coverage for a necessary procedure by their HMO or insurance carrier, or had been asked to accept what they realized was an inferior kind of treatment. Many physicians complained that the new system of restricted care forced them into a pattern of giving patients inadequate time. This limited their ability to make informed diagnoses and offer adequate advice during patient visits. Patients certainly knew that their doctors were giving them less care. Hospitals pushed people out of their sick beds much more quickly and hired fewer qualified nurses to take care of the very sick people who remained behind on the wards. Some for-profit hospitals reduced the ratio of registered nurses to patients by as much as 25 percent, but then only partially replaced them with less qualified nursing assistants. By 1997, studies showed that investor-owned facilities were far more ruthless than public and non-profit hospitals, employing 17 percent fewer staff members per 100 patients.[1] No one had any doubts about the motivation involved. According to Claire M. Fagin, former dean of the University of Pennsylvania's School of Nursing, corporations, not patients or nurses, were the only winners: "The cutbacks," she said, "are improving the bottom line of managed-care organizations."[2]

The aggressive posture of management, which eliminated the jobs of some registered nurses and increased the workload of those who remained, drove many nurses out of the profession. The job was too discouraging for experienced care-givers who knew they could no longer provide the best of care for their patients. "These changes," said Kathryn Hall of the Maryland Nurses Association, as she explained why a nursing shortage had developed, "have occurred at the same time that the patient acuity has increased, the use of sophisticated technology has increased, and the length of stay has decreased. Therefore, fewer nurses are being asked to care for an increased number of sicker patients with greater health care needs."[3] In many hospitals, particularly those bought up by for-profit companies, the persistent under-staffing was leading to a greater mortality rate for patients.

There was a parallel decline in the quality of care in the more privatized sector of health care, the nursing home industry. Nine out of ten nursing homes were so understaffed that they could not guarantee "minimally necessary" care according to a report released to Congress in April 2002, by the Centers for Medicare and Medicaid Services (this is the federal agency that was giving out $40 billion per year to help pay for three out of four nursing home residents in the United States). Nursing homes were failing to fill 12 percent of all certified nursing home aide positions, and they had an annual employee turnover of over 80 percent. "The pay is so poor that it provides a median income of just $13,287 per year," said Steven L. Dawson, President of the Paraprofessional Healthcare Institute of the South Bronx, "Nearly 18 percent of all nursing-home aides return home to families living in poverty, while 13 percent must rely on food stamps. And in a bitter irony, even though these aides serve our nation's health-care system, more than one in four has no access to health insurance."[4]

Changes Compatible With the Values of the Bush Gang— Privatize! Piratize!

The Bush Gang was big on privatization and deregulation in health care, as in every other field, and did a lot to encourage the rise of private hospitals in the 1980s. There was big money to be sucked out of health care. By 1992, Thomas Frist, Jr., the head of a Nashville-based family firm called Hospital Corporation of America or HCA, was earning $127 million annually, the highest compensation of all of America's overpaid CEOs. Dr. Tom Jr. and his father, Dr. Tom Sr., had started the company in 1977 as one of the very first private companies to start spreading the corporate net, hauling in a bunch of non-profit hospitals and operating them for profit. The big money at HCA helped bankroll Frist's brother, Dr. Bill, when he gave up his practice as a heart surgeon in 1994 and won a seat as the Republican Senator from Tennesee. He instantly became the Senate expert on the finer points of delivering medical care to the whole nation, and was still promoting the extension of corporate control of the U.S. health system eight years later. When he became majority leader in the Senate in 2002, Bill Frist was in a unique position to keep overseeing a process that had been predicted thirty years earlier.

> Change in the health industry... would have some of the classical aspects of the industrial revolution... and profitability as the mandatory condition of survival.
>
> —Dr. Paul Ellwood

In 1971, health analyst Paul Ellwood coined the term, Health Maintenance Organization, or HMO. He was also the leader of the Jackson Hole health reform group that led the Clintons into the private healthcare morass in 1993. He had worked as a physician early in his career, but gained most of his knowledge of big business as president and CEO of Jackson Hole Ski Corporation in Wyoming

from 1972 to 1987. He had recognized that capital, organized through corporate America, was going to change health care into an "industry," and would organize it into a system that was profitable in one way or another. By 1999 he was not happy with the result of the process he had helped initiate. This was partly because he felt that the Clinton administration had bungled the operation, but also because he came to realize that the market did not work as a vehicle for making good health care decisions. He was singing a different tune—"Market forces will never work to improve quality, nor will voluntary efforts by doctors and health plans...Ultimately this thing is going to require government intervention."[5]

The HMO and managed care "revolution" in health care had yielded results consistent with the early stages of "industrialization"—that is, simplification of labor, cuts in labor costs, harsher working conditions, and less care per patient were leading to higher profits. There was one accomplishment of note: the runaway inflation in health care bills was temporarily reduced in the mid-1990s, so that costs rose by just 3% annually in 1997, about the same rate as in other sectors of the economy. But was this efficiency? Part of the savings had been achieved by serving a smaller percentage of the population. And other features of the expanding private system were simply encouraging robbery.

Giant companies had dreams of making money hand over fist. One was the notorious Columbia/HCA corporation that planned to own 10% of the nation's hospitals by the year 2000. Columbia, which bought out the Frist operation, was a venture backed by financier Richard Rainwater, the Texas billionaire who had put up the cash for George W. Bush to play ball with the

Texas Rangers. His CEO was Richard Scott, pioneer in the kind of accounting fraud that became so popular in other kinds of corporations at the end of the 1990s. Scott had to leave Columbia/HCA in 1996 after Kurt Eichenwald broke a story at *The New York Times* explaining how the CEO had encouraged his managers at 348 hospitals to falsify data in order to get higher reimbursements from Medicare.

The firm did continue to reside in reliable Republican hands, however, because Tom Frist, Jr.—the co-founder of the original HCA and brother of Senator Bill Frist—was called back to be the new CEO of Columbia/HCA. Frist soon turned over the management of the company to another CEO and its name was changed back to Hospital Corporation of America again, but this did not put an end to the longest running fraud case ever brought against a health care company. On December 17, 2002, the Justice Department announced it had reached an agreement with HCA to pay a $880 million settlement. When this was combined with its previous settlements for fraud—including pleading guilty to 14 felony counts in the year 2000—the total came to "more than $1.7 billion in civil and criminal penalties, the most ever secured by federal prosecutors in a health care fraud case."[6]

The unanswered question, a full 10 years after this memorable corporate crime was first uncovered, was why the Frist family and Senator Frist were considered reliable experts on American health care. The whistle-blowing employees at HCA had started exposing various kinds of management fraud at HCA in 1993, even before it merged with Columbia. That is, the crimes were likely to have been taking place the year before in 1992 when Thomas Frist, Jr. was still in charge and bringing home that $127

million paycheck. Frist may have not have taken part in the fraud at all, but it certainly must have contributed to the profits of the corporation and therefore to that incredible level of compensation. It seems that the Frist family ought to owe the nation some apologies for their part in wrecking the American health care system. Instead, by late 2002, the Frist family was revered. Bill Frist was one of the most respected Republicans in the U.S. Senate and easily pushed the disgraced Trent Lott out of the Senate leadership. Frist's father and brother were not offering any mea culpas either. For their extraordinary success in wringing profits out of the practice of medicine, Tom Frist, Jr. and Tom Frist, Sr. were honored by Healthcare Financial Management Systems. This corporation announced that it gave them its 2002 achievement award because "Dr. Frist Jr. and Sr. are generally credited with the development and significant growth of the investor-owned sector of the healthcare delivery system."

Poor People, Poor Risks

For-profit hospitals not only ripped people off, they also became notorious for the way they did not deliver medical care. They withheld care from indigent people and other very ill people who did not appear to have adequate insurance. They sent them to public hospitals, thus overloading their already overextended emergency rooms. What kind of efficiency is it when you save money by not giving any care to sick people who show up at your door? In any case, this false efficiency did not last for long. As the 1990s ended, the crazy quilt-work of private insurance, HMOs, and private and public hospitals could no longer keep costs anywhere near the rate of inflation. A Dow Jones/AP dispatch gave a grim prognosis: "Costs in 2003 for health plans at big companies ought to be at least 15.4% higher than in 2002 when they increased by almost 14%. The average cost for one employee will be over $6,000 per year—corporations have two strategies for keeping their own expenses down—making employees pay more out their own pockets and switching to health care providers which offer fewer benefits."[7] This cumulative increase of 31.2% in just two years was enough to put the whole country's health system at risk. "The Painful Truth," an article that appeared in *Business Week* at the same time, suggested the increase in insurance costs would be even higher, over 40%.

At a time of severe economic downturn, the health insurance corporations had found that they could keep profiting from working people by forcing them to pay higher premiums and making them pay much higher deductibles at the same time. Smaller workplaces with less than 200 workers were hit with such overwhelming rates that the percentage of their workers with health insurance coverage dropped suddenly, from 67% in 2001 to 61% in 2002. Most other people gritted their teeth and paid up, because rising unemployment made it imperative to hold onto their jobs. Their fear was justified: they knew that the surest way to personal bankruptcy, aside from losing employment entirely, was to encounter an uninsured medical catastrophe.

Just when the administration should have been looking for a way to stem the tide of corporate abuse in the health care markets, one of the new members of the Bush Gang, Janet Rehnquist, daughter of the Chief Justice of the Supreme Court, decided it was her job to let health corporations off the hook. She took the law into her own hands as inspector general of the U.S. Health and Human Services and began easing up on the "corporate integrity agreements" that had been imposed on the private health providers. She and the Administration were not interested in implementing these anti-fraud measures that were supposed to keep hospital companies—the scandal-prone Tenet Corporation of California was one prominent example—from cheating on Medicare and other government disbursements.

Paging Dr. Morgan

"All because they couldn't afford health insurance," sighed Dr. Rex Morgan. The handsome, greying physician who has not aged in 54 years, was describing a tragedy that began with the death of a father from undiagnosed colon cancer and led to the breakdown of the whole family. His prescription for future cases: national health insurance in the United States.

Rex Morgan, M.D., hasn't aged because he is a comic strip character. He had been treating America for over fifty years when he finally decided it was time to shed the compassionate conservative image and speak out. He wanted the government to provide everyone with medical care. And so did his illustrator and writer, Woody Wilson, a 55-year-old registered Republican from Tempe, Arizona, who had voted for George W. Bush in the 2000 elections. "I believe the country that is supposedly the richest and most powerful in the world shouldn't be forcing its citizens to choose between paying their mortgage or saving their lives. Yet that is what is happening with millions of Americans right now," Mr. Wilson said in an interview with the *Toronto Globe and Mail*, "What's needed is health care for everyone instead of dividends for stockholders in pharmaceutical companies."[8]

There are real doctors thinking about a single-payer, universal medical care system, too, including the 9,000-strong Physicians for a National Health Program. Others, such as Dr. Michael T. Kennedy, past president of the Orange County Medical Association and described as "predominantly a political conservative," are also getting involved. He wrote an editorial piece for the *Orange County Register*, a staunchly Republican newspaper, entitled "National Health Care May Be Our Only Solution." Kennedy described the waste and confusion of a local system that cannot treat people adequately, much to the aggravation of doctors who want to provide decent care, then he moved toward the solution: "It may be that a universal system, covering everyone regardless of ability to pay, could be funded out of the total current expenditures of the present system, which has so many distortions."[9]

Doctors were waking up to popular sentiment. For over thirty years, about two thirds of the American people have supported national health insurance. Young doctors-in-training and their teachers did not ignore this preference. In 1999, a nationwide poll of medical students, interns, residents, medical school deans and faculty showed that 57% of them favored a single-payer national health system.[10]

Princeton Professor Uwe E. Reinhardt, an expert on health care delivery, probably sympathized with the fictional and real doctors, but was pessimistic about the commitment of the Bush administration in 2002. "I can infer clearly," he said, "the preferences of the nation's politically dominant elite. If that elite could not find it in its heart and mind to extend health insurance to uninsured Americans when the nation was awash in budget surpluses, it is

unlikely to do so as the government once again faces red ink as far as the eye can see."[11]

Some Corporations Actually Like the Idea of National Health Care

Luckily, there are times when the corporate world does not act consistently as a team. The interests of one business sector may be opposed to another—one industry, for instance, may approve of tariffs because it produces for the home market, another likes free trade because it profits come primarily from foreign sales. In times of recession or economic slowdown, when the country is not awash in profits, the competition for capital can get more intense, and the resentment of the productive sector of the economy can escalate. For example, the last time the Bush Gang presided over a severe economic downturn, in 1989-1992, the manufacturing sector grew concerned about the amount of money being siphoned off by less productive areas of the economy. The automotive industry, because it is so attuned to competition from other countries and its own industrial costs in other parts of the world, can easily assess the cost of its workers' health insurance and then determine how much it adds to the cost of each car it sells.

In 1991, Walter B. Maher, head of Chrysler Corporation's health policy office in Washington, offered his assessment of health costs to *The New York Times*, which was bold enough at the time to entitle the article, "Potential Savings of National Care." Maher's central premise was simple enough: if U.S. health care cost more than twice as much as Japanese health care, and almost exactly twice as much as German health care, then U.S. factories were going to operate at a big disadvantage. The high cost of health care had to be added into the price of each automobile.

WHY SOME IN BIG BUSINESS LIKE NATIONAL HEALTHCARE

Cost of Health Care per Capita in 1991

Japan	Germany	France	United States
$1,113	$1,287	$1,421	$2,566

Health Care Costs per Automobile

$246	$337	$375	$700

(Source: Chrysler Corporation, 1991)

Then, as now, all three of the other countries, and the rest of the advanced industrialized countries, for that matter, were providing their people with good health care—that is, health care that matches what most Americans who are well-insured receive—at about half the cost, or less, of the United States. Even more astounding, they were providing better medical service to their populations as well:

- There were hardly any citizens without health coverage.
- They made more visits to their doctors per year.
- The average citizen lived longer.
- The infant mortality rates were lower.

The Chrysler Corporation actually endorsed the idea of a national health service in 1991, but it never caught on with Bush Gang I. They were too enmeshed with the owners of capital, whether they were Texas billionaires like Rainwater or the giant insurance companies of Connecticut, who wanted to finance the expansion of a corporate-owned health care system. And the prospect of a national health service never had a chance of being adopted as part of the "health reform" package proposed by

Clinton two years later, because the Democrats were afraid of snubbing big business and appearing "socialistic."

More than a decade later, the great American industrial enterprises witnessed the flagrant waste of capital in the stock market debacle, and were worried about their collapsing assets. As the automobile companies, even more beleaguered by foreign competition than they were in 1991, examined their costs of production, they were more appalled than ever about health care. And the stock market was worried as well. "Automakers' Health Care Costs Scaring Investors," said *Bloomberg News* in November 2002, because GM, Chrysler, and Ford had very high insurance obligations to their employees, both active workers and the retired. If the United States had introduced a rational and comprehensive health care policy for working people in the early 1990s, the auto companies could have saved billions of dollars in the ensuing decade.

The extremely inefficient mix of privatization, health management, and managed competition, even with all their cuts in health benefits, had not helped contain health spending, which reached a record 14.7% of the Gross Domestic Product in 2002. Other countries were spending 7% to 9% of their GDP and insuring their entire populations. Even in 1998, before the U.S. suffered its most recent big increase in health costs, the comparison in costs per person were terribly unfavorable, as can be seen on the following page.

The other outcome, the overall health of the citizens of each society, had not changed much either, except that it looked like the U.S. position, which had deteriorated a lot since 1960, was till slipping. Statistics comparing infant mortality and longevity showed that the

INTERNATIONAL COMPARISONS: PER CAPITA HEALTH CARE COSTS, 1998

USA	Germany	Canada	Sweden	France	Japan	Italy
$4,270	$2,400	$2,250	$2,120	$1,820	$1,780	$1,660

(Source: Health Affairs 2000; *Bleeding the Patient*)

United States had continued to slide when compared to other nations between 1990 and 1997.

U.S. automobile companies are still paying attention to these kinds of statistics. One particularly revealing reaction on their part concerns their appraisal of medical care in Canada (one of many countries ranking ahead of the U.S. in health outcomes), where they have had a significant manufacturing presence. Perhaps they knew it was futile to tell Bush Gang II that it was time to consider national health care again, because they decided to join with the Canadian Auto Workers Union (CAW) in strongly endorsing the Canadian approach to health care. General Motors, Ford and Daimler-Chrysler all signed letters together with the CAW urging that Canada's national health care system be "preserved and renewed." The letters read, in part:

> Workers in the auto industry, and in the many manufacturing and service industries which supply automakers, benefit directly from access to public health care services. Thanks to this system, they are healthier and more productive. Employers in the auto industry, meanwhile, enjoy significant total labour cost savings because most health care services are supplied through public programs (rather than through private insurance plans). The public health care system significantly reduces total labour costs for automobile manufacturing firms, compared to the cost of equivalent private insurance services purchased by U.S.-based automakers; these health insurance savings can amount to several dollars per hour of labour worked. Publicly funded health care thus accounts for a significant portion of Canada's overall labour cost advantage in auto assembly, versus the U.S., which in turn has been a significant factor in maintaining and attracting new auto investment to Canada.

HEALTH CARE OUTCOME: MORTALITY AND LONGEVITY

	1960	1990	1997
U.S. rank in infant mortality	12th	21st	24th
U.S. rank in longevity of males	17th	21st	22nd
U.S. rank in longevity of females	13th	17th	20th

(Compiled by OECD, 1999—Please note that the rankings do not indicate that the rate of infant mortality in the U.S. has gone up, for it has kept decreasing; nor has adult longevity decreased among Americans. The rankings do indicate, however, that many countries keep passing us by in terms of these statistics which are the most widely used in demonstrating the overall health of nations. Clearly they are spending much less per capita on health care than we do and delivering medical service to a much higher percentage of their populations.)

This statement is so clear that it probably indicates the automakers were trying to send a message to the United States, or more accurately, to the rest of the U.S. business community. Other industries were getting the message, too. For example, Peter Buzzarell and Associates, a business consulting firm in Reston, Virginia, was offering advice to the U.S. Confectionery Industry in April of 2002. They cited their own analysis of the savings a company might achieve by relocating to Canada: health insurance costs per employee would be $605 per year as opposed to almost four times that much in the United States, $2,256 per annum.[12]

If the U.S. is going to compete with the rest of the industrialized world in manufacturing without impoverishing its own workers, then it will have to notice what is working elsewhere.

National Health Care: Impossible?

The United States has some of the best medical facilities in the world, as well as many excellently trained medical professionals. On the other hand, its medical delivery system is so complicated and overlaid with layers of waste that it does not produce very good overall results as measured by health comparisons with other nations. Within almost every component of our system lie aggregates of capital investment that are begging to be fed and nourished whether they are productive or not. Money passing through insurance companies, health care facilities and hospitals, surgeries and clinics, drug companies, home care services, management companies, ad infinitum, is supposed to provide a nice return on investment for the stockholders involved at each stop on the journey. This money not only has to provide profits

at each stop, it has to pay for administration and paperwork, too.

Believe it or not, a bigger bureaucracy can mean less bureaucracy.

Canada has a national health service, a comprehensive bureaucracy covering most health care, while the United States has so many bureaucracies no one can possibly count them. We have thousands of private and public hospital administrations, doctors' offices, HMOs, state authorities, insurance companies, and so on, and they are totally uncoordinated. Administration and billing at hospitals cost $68 per person in Canada in the year 2000 versus $372 per person in the United States. Physicians' office accounting costs $430 per person in U.S. versus $102 in Canada.[13]

The biggest single savings in Canada is due to single payer insurance. National Health serves as one big insurer, much as Social Security and Medicare function in the United States. The provincial health services in Canada, which collect and disperse the money, need only 1% of all payments to pay for their costs of operation. Private insurance companies in the United States, on the other hand, keep 14% of premiums for overhead and profits.[14]

Government interference, usually seen as detrimental in the U.S., has a very positive function in Canada. For example, a government appointed board negotiates drug purchases from big pharmaceutical companies so that hospital patients will get discounts—the cost of government program is $2 million, the savings almost one thousand times as much, $1.5 billion. As for the cost of drugs at a pharmacy, there can also be huge savings: the breast cancer drug Tamoxifin costs about $90 a dose in the U.S.A. and $15 in Canada. These kinds of savings can be found in other countries, too. Claritin was costing about

15 cents in Britain when it cost 2 dollars in the United States, and prices in Mexico are about half of what they are in the U.S. for the top selling 10 drugs, according to the U.S. General Accounting Office. A headline from the Canadian Press service in October 2002 indicated that some American citizens were making the best of their bad situation by shopping up north: "U.S. patients streaming into Canada...."[15]

For years doctors Steffie Woolhandler and David Himmelstein have been providing a convincing analysis of the U.S. system and comparing it to Canada's single payer system. They are quite frank about where Canada has fallen short or has been driven backwards by its own right-wing forces, but contend that we could do much better by emulating features of medicine as it is practiced in Canada and the rest of the world. In their latest book, *Bleeding the Patient: The Consequences of Corporate Health Care*, these two practicing physicians, who also teach at Harvard Medical School, offer an eye-opening observation concerning our health system. They contend that we already have "national health care," albeit in a very perverted form, because most of our medical costs are already paid for, directly or indirectly, by government. This means that taxpayers are supplying an immense subsidy to medical corporations in return for exceptionally inefficient care.

They calculated that in 1998 the funds for meeting medical needs that were supplied by various government entities amounted to $737 billion, almost two-thirds of the total cost for the nation of $1.15 trillion. They started by adding up the most obvious programs, Medicare, Medicaid, CHIP for children, Veterans Administration and other military coverage, etcetera. Then they added in the cost of insurance coverage paid by all federal, state, and local

governments on their own employees. To top it off they added in all the ways the government subsidizes private health care, including the monstrous tax breaks given to corporations, their employees, and other individuals because health care insurance costs and payments out of pocket can be deducted from taxes. Most people probably thought Medicare for the elderly was the biggest federal subsidy. Not so in 1998, according to the diagnosis of the good doctors—the Federal tax subsidy that allows health plans supplied by employers to be tax exempt totaled $111 billion. And this government handout was certainly not for the poor—relatively well-to-do employees, those earning over $100,000 per year in 1998, received 24% of the benefit.[16]

Americans Have No Problem with National Health Care

Even during the stock market euphoria of 1998, average American citizens were not at all averse to the idea of their government taking the lead in meeting their medical needs. A USA Today/Harris Poll posed the following declaration:

"THE US GOVERNMENT SHOULD PROVIDE QUALITY HEALTH CARE TO ALL ADULTS..."

The percentage that agreed among different groups

77% general public	53% employers	52% state legislators	47% Congressional aides

Not surprisingly, employers were not as enthusiastic as the great majority of the population, but they were slightly in favor, more than can be said of the Congressional aides. The denizens of Congress and their bosses are, after all, the primary recipients of corporate lobbying efforts from drug companies, hospital corporations, insurance companies, and HMOs. (These lobbyists paid Congress $300 million in 2000.)

In addition, the public's general discontent with health issues is shared by most doctors, who are no longer so enamored of their profession. As mentioned earlier, doctors in training already favor a national health program. As for older doctors, the Kaiser Foundation reports that 87% of physicians say that morale has fallen within their ranks, and 76% say that managed care has negatively affected their practices. Applications to medical schools are down sharply, by about a third compared to twenty or thirty years ago. It is not clear whether this is because young people are worried about the money, or because the prestige of doctors has diminished because they are increasingly seen as gatekeepers for the health industry rather than care givers. The cost of a medical education is inordinately high and the U.S. educational establishment does not seem to have caught on to the idea favored in many other industrialized countries—educate doctors for free.

Bush League Care

With Bill Frist running the U.S. Senate at the beginning of 2003, the Bush administration pressed ahead with more privatization initiatives. They floated the idea of individualized Medicare accounts for the elderly, something that sounded suspiciously like individualized Social Security accounts, and proposed a Medicare drug plan that appeared as if it were written by the pharmaceutical industry. Their obvious intention was to start limiting the options of senior citizens so that the government could start cutting Medicare coverage and

costs. Rather than deal with the severe inefficiencies of private insurance companies, HMOs, and private hospitals, they were more interested in finding ways for these corporate entities to develop new ways to profit at the expense of senior citizens.

In May of 2003, Republicans in Congress accepted Bush's proposal to develop "preferred provider organizations" for Medicare patients. This would be a boon to health corporations, according to a study by the Medicare payment advisory commission, because "private health plan fees are about 15% higher than Medicare fees."[17]

Meanwhile, in order to distract the public from the real causes of inefficient health care service, Republicans around the country were exaggerating a crisis in medical malpractice insurance. In his 2003 State of the Union speech, George W. Bush blamed medical malpractice suits and trial lawyers for just about everything that ailed the American people. This was part of a Republican campaign to convince the public that medical malpractice suits brought by injured patients and their lawyers were increasing exponentially and driving malpractice premiums through the roof.

This was simply not true. The cost of all malpractice awards equaled only one-half of 1% of national health costs in 2002. Malpractice awards in most states were increasing only slightly, at about the rate of inflation. The rising cost of malpractice insurance was due to something else entirely: the nation's major insurance companies had been pursuing very bad investment strategies. Most of them had suffered big losses in the stock and bond markets of 2000-2002 and were trying to recover by overcharging physicians and hospitals (they were also doing this in others fields, foisting big increases on individuals and businesses that bought home, auto, and other kinds of insurance).

The former insurance commissioner for the State of Texas, J. Robert Hunter, produced an actuarial study that explained how this was a cyclical phenomenon. During boom times when insurance company investments were performing well, they lowered their premiums to compete with each other and attract new business. Then in bust times, as in previous instances in the mid-1970s and the mid-1980s when their investments also crashed, the insurance companies proclaimed a "malpractice crisis" and jacked up their physicians' rates excessively.[18] A report on the front page of *The Wall Street Journal* in the summer of 2002 indicated just how badly the insurance industry had miscalculated during the run-up in the stock market, and how much they had to recover by jacking up premiums in a hurry: "a decade of short-sighted price slashing," said *The Journal*, "led to industry losses of $3 billion last year."[19]

Medical associations in some states, such as Pennsylvania and West Virginia, somehow missed all this evidence. Instead they raised a hue and cry about the spectre of lawsuits driving doctors out of business. The consumer organization Public Citizen advised them that their diagnosis of the problem was completely unrealistic, and produced analyses of the malpractice situation that demonstrated that the major underlying problem was the sickness of the insurance companies themselves. They also pointed out to the medical profession that the states that had the worst problems getting malpractice insurance for doctors were usually the ones where state medical societies had the worst record of reviewing physicians' performance, and thus had failed to weed out incompetent doctors.

George Bush, Bill Frist, and their compatriots had little or nothing to say about insurance company malfeasance. Malpractice was their smokescreen. They exaggerated the importance of malpractice suits against doctors and other civil suits against hospitals and HMOs because they wanted to blame someone else for the failure of the American health system. They wanted to distract attention from rapidly escalating medical costs that are primarily due to the way that medicine is now practiced in the United States. America's disorganized for-profit health community is largely responsible for delivering the world's most expensive medical care and doing a poor job of it. Profit-making medicine is withholding treatment from a very significant number of the Americans and giving insufficient attention to many more.

In the world's richest nation, this amounts to negligent homicide.

In their rush to protect the perpetrators of such crimes, the Bush Gang extended a hand to the giant drug companies, too. The Eli Lilly pharmaceutical corporation had produced a preservative for vaccines called Thimerosal, which was alleged to have caused autism in thousands of children. After the 2002 elections, the Republicans inserted a provision in the Homeland Defense Bill that protected Eli Lilly from any future lawsuits brought on behalf of autistic children and their parents. When the legislation passed, none of the Republicans wanted to claim credit for writing an amendment that helped Lilly, a major Republican campaign donor. But there was one senator who had introduced the same amendment to another piece of legislation earlier in the year, the senator most knowledgeable about how to make big profits from the health system.

That senator was Bill Frist.

CORPORATE CULTURE

M. WUERKER

Twelve

The Law of Insatiable Capital

The Bush Gang Will Do Anything For Money

> With adequate profit, capital is very bold. A certain 10 percent will ensure its employment elsewhere; 20 percent will produce eagerness; 50 percent audacity; 100 percent will make it ready to trample on all human laws; 300 percent, and there is not a crime which it will not scruple, nor a risk it will not run, even to the chance of its owner being hanged.
>
> —Karl Marx

In the summer of 2002 on page one of *The New York Times'* "Week in Review," the lead article ran under a half page photo of the New York Stock Exchange draped in a giant American flag, and it was entitled "Could Capitalists Actually Bring Down Capitalism?"[1] The reporter, Kurt Eichenwald, who had been writing a particularly fine series of articles covering the most outrageous crimes and improprieties of corporate executives, was giving American business a well-deserved tongue lashing for its immoral and wasteful performance. The problem, according to Eichenwald, was that corporate practices in the United States had strayed so far from the way capitalist enterprises were supposed to work: "Capitalism, at its most basic," he wrote, "dictates that the company producing the best product at the lowest price wins."

Eichenwald probably conceived of this last argument as a reasonable way to get the attention of investors and businessmen who read *The New York Times*. But as a description of how capitalism works, at least at the highest levels over the last century or so, it is not remotely close to the truth. Capitalism does not necessarily require that a company produce anything at all, let alone "the best product at the lowest price." J.P. Morgan, the quintessential capitalist, formed the Steel Trust, the Coal Trust, and General Electric, but not because he wanted to create products. He dealt in creating monopolies. Even among the heroic figures of American capitalism who actually did produce or sell something—Rockefeller in oil, Gates in software for personal computers, Walton in discount stores—the question of selling the "best product at the lowest price" was not the primary issue. Establishing special advantages or monopolies in a burgeoning market, regardless of the quality of one's products, was the important element of success for most of the richest capitalists. Hard and ruthless business practices were more likely to win than the highest quality. And success has been measured by one thing, the basic requirement of all capitalist enterprises: capital has to multiply itself as rapidly as possible. Biggest profit. Highest rate of return.

Whatever one thinks of Karl Marx, it is difficult for anyone to dispute his contention that at the very heart of capitalism is capital itself. Capital wants to be rewarded. It goes into enterprises; it comes out larger and more robust, ready for bigger and better things. If the capitalist enterprise does not provide a sufficiently high return—in the form of an interest rate, a rising stock price, the cost of real estate, or some other profitable distribution within a finite period of time—then capital will demand the services of a new, and often more ruthless capitalist. While it is tempting to focus on the most daring entrepreneurs and the craftiest investors, these capitalists will come and go as long as the system of capitalism keeps relying on one thing: capital, emboldened by "adequate profit."

How much is "adequate?" How high is the ultimate rate of return? There is no limit. Or else it is that number known as "infinity minus one." As the return on investment, or profit rate, rises to ever more dizzying heights, the lure of infinite riches summons up the most desperate human behavior. The humans who respond directly to the demands of capital may behave in different and not necessarily rational ways. The entrepreneurs, who may or may not begin the venture with their own money, must push the business to its extremes in order to deliver the promised profits to their investors. The investment capitalists, who passively enjoy the steady income generated by their capital, may be tempted to sell out and invest in other, high-

er yielding propositions, especially if they suspect their present investment is stagnating or even in danger.

For these reasons, we may be able to generate a tiny bit of sympathy for the much maligned corporate CEO, even the crooked one. Let us presume that he, like Bernie Ebbers at WorldCom and "Kenny Boy" Lay of Enron, had spent years toiling away at building up the company's prestige and assets and watched as large stockholders doubled, tripled, or quadrupled their holdings—without ever lifting a finger. Let's recall that the main proponents of "stockholders' rights" were often billionaire investors such as T. Boone Pickens and John Malone who were pushing top managers to do anything, even divest of valuable company assets, if it would generate robust quarterly reports and raise stock prices in the short term. The stock market often responded positively to massive layoffs, interpreting them as proof of leanness and meanness and overall efficiency, while the nation's business press showered adulation upon the corporate officers who downsized most ruthlessly.

When the market got shaky, the executives who once graced the covers of the news magazines began to contemplate bailing out. Some had their golden parachutes in place and had already built up huge fortunes. Others did desperate things to cash out quickly and match the exponential increases in capital that they had achieved for their shareholders. In some cases, the intrepid leader convinced himself that the corporation was really not doomed to fail. Being afflicted with that pathological optimism that is sometimes necessary to push a company to the top, the CEO may have believed that by cheating on quarterly or annual reports and showing non-existent profits, he was simply giving himself time to turn things around.

In such situations, at the highest levels, it is always the cool head of capital that prevails. Hot-headed active capitalists are pushed aside when they do not perform. Unresponsive investing capitalists who do not make a move are simply disregarded as so much dead wood. But capital—having no emotions, loyalties, nor human frailties—will win out. Honesty, quality, and other measures of good work are inconsequential. The point is to win, no matter how. "100 hundred percent profits," as Marx noted, makes capital willing to "trample on all human laws."

Modern Capitalism Began with Blatant Plundering

The classic and extreme example of the pursuit of profit at any cost occurred at the beginning of the European capitalist era when Columbus set forth sailing west to find the riches of the East. A short review of the arrangements for this exploration reveals an example that is being emulated 500 years later. The King and Queen of Spain put up the capital, Columbus promised them amazing treasures in return, and they guaranteed him 10% of the profits. His first voyage found interesting possibilities, but it was on his second trip in 1495 that Columbus and his brother Bartholomew found ways to extract riches from the new world. They demanded gold from the native Americans who inhabited Hispaniola and they slaughtered them if they did not produce it. Those who did not report regularly to the Spanish soldiers with the required ransom of gold nuggets had their hands chopped off. The large island was quickly stripped of its indige-

nous population and its meager supplies of gold, which immediately made it ripe for the next stage of exploitation—the importation of slaves from Africa in 1502 and the beginning of sugar cane production on plantations.

Columbus died in 1506, moderately well off but very disgruntled because he thought the King of Spain had reneged on their agreement and paid him far less than the 10% of profits that were supposedly guaranteed. Obviously, the King controlled the accounting business in those days and his books, fairly or unfairly, showed large losses incurred in the early days of conquest. In the coming century, however, the gold and silver plundered out of Mexico and Peru, followed by the sugar produced by slaves in the Caribbean and Brazil, produced the huge profits that would set a global system of business in motion.

> The profits of the sugar plantation are much greater than any other cultivation that is known either in Europe or America
>
> —Adam Smith, *The Wealth of Nations*

Bankers from Italy, Germany, and Holland disseminated the riches of Spain to the rest of Europe. Meanwhile the British pirate ships under the direction of Sir Francis Drake and Sir Walter Raleigh (both in partnership with Queen Elizabeth I) were just as efficient in their own way—they spread the wealth after plundering the Spanish treasure galleons. This was the moment when capitalism took off and assumed its non-stop expansion throughout the rest of the world. French historian Michel Beaud explained why our present economic system was born at the end of the 15th century:

What was new was the incredible pillage of the Americas.

Plunder, Pillage, and Piracy

The brief discussion of pillage and plunder above serves to remind us that the complete deregulation of business activity and an accompanying disregard for the rule of law can lead us to that intense level of money-making activity known as piracy. The ethic is as simple and compelling as it is destructive: if we don't steal it, someone else will, and as they gain strength from their theft, they will come after us next.

The Bush Gang and their many collaborators have not yet stooped to the barbarous level of Columbus and his brother, at least not as far as domestic labor is concerned. But they definitely have used milder forms of "labor discipline" (as illustrated in the previous four chapters), such as the systematic use of worker lay-offs and willful disregard for the requirements of labor law, in order to increase profits. They have also supported all kinds of deregulation of business activities—especially in regard to environmental hazards, accounting practices, and workplace safety—that cause corporations to compete on the basis of how much they can exploit the worker, the environment, and the law itself. In both cases, they are not very concerned about legal niceties—they usually keep pursuing these illegal courses of action until lawsuits are brought in civil courts, and even then they often write this off as a cost of doing business. Their single-minded purpose: always keep lowering the costs of production. The class nature of the Bush "pirates" is evident in the fact that they see no problem if increased profitability for the owners is gained at the expense of the people who produce the goods and services.

The lesson of early America is extreme, but instructive about the ultimate amorality of capital: outside the rule of law, or within a system of increasingly inhumane laws, some people can profit when others are worked to death. The current methods of profiting from the pain of others, while not so bloodthirsty, still requires laboring people to suffer. As we have seen, whether you work at Wal-Mart, ConAgra, the Health Corporation of America, or any number of other U.S. corporations, you can expect to put up with lower wages and unpaid work, increased stress and work speed-ups, dangerous and unhealthy conditions in the workplace. Since most people in the United States already live pretty well compared to workers in the Third World, in the eyes of the upper class they are ripe for a fleecing. Astute representatives of the people have been trying to warn us about this for the past two hundred years, just as the young Abraham Lincoln did in the Illinois legislature in 1837:

> These capitalists generally act harmoniously and in concert to fleece the people.

Working people can be, and have been, shorn of a large share of their increasing productivity by business leaders who want to increase the level of corporate profits. The CEOs reason, quite accurately, that most of us can stay alive on much less, just as our ancestors did.

One problem with such logic—the logic of capital itself—is that humane behavior and the progressive course of human development are sacrificed for the sake of accumulating money for a few. There is also the inconvenient reality that many capitalists do not comprehend how successful 20th century capitalism actually worked. The concept of advanced capitalism continues to be a puzzling paradox to those who believe they must continually drive the cost of labor down. Successful capitalism in the 20th century (which was also highly regulated in comparison to the Bush Gang's version) featured the broad dispersal of goods and services to most citizens, which in turn depended on the widespread dispersal of income. The more equitable circulation of wealth was necessary to promote the high levels of popular consumption that fueled the American economy.

While capitalist firms can function within such an environment—one where they are disciplined by democratic public opinion—the alluring and never-ending enticements of capital are so hard to ignore. Why settle for 6% profits, or 10% profits, when the sky's the limit? Unlimited profitability is particularly alluring when the new enterprise in also a foreign adventure, because then the owners' ability to disregard human decency and the law is magnified—it will simply expand with the rate of profit. "Free trade" in the past meant that strong nations were "free" to fight wars to seize the resources of weak nations or force their products on other people. They even protected the right of private investors to trade in drugs, most notably in the Opium Wars of the 19th century.

Britain waged two wars against China so that its trading companies, especially the East India Company, could sell vast quantities of opium that were transported from Turkey or English plantations in India. Some Americans, such as John Quincy Adams and his wealthy constituents in New England, were sympathetic to the British, no doubt because the drug trade was bringing very substantial profits to the New England privateering companies which contracted with the British to ship the opium (see Chapter 14, for discussion of the origins of Skull and Bones and Bush family piracy.) Adams, the

sixth President of the United States and generally a man of sound judgment, turned into a rabid proponent of "free trade" in his later years, especially when it affected the fortunes of Massachusetts' richest families (he returned to Congress from that state after serving as president). He came to believe that the Chinese were lacking in certain Western virtues and was disdainful of a Chinese society which tried to resist the creation of millions of drug addicts among its citizenry. In a lecture on the subject, he explained that the "churlish" Chinese were just asking for trouble at the hands of the English:

> The moral obligation of commercial intercourse between nations is founded entirely, exclusively, upon the Christian precept to love your neighbor as yourself...but China, not being a Christian nation, its inhabitants do not see themselves bound by the Christian concept, to love their neighbor as themselves...this is a churlish and unsocial system...the fundamental principle of the Chinese system is anti-commercial... It is time that this enormous outrage upon the rights of human nature, and upon the first principles of the rights of nations, should cease.[2]

Capital—Financialization and the Real Cause of Criminal Activity

Kurt Eichenwald's definition of sound business—"capitalism at its most basic dictates that the company producing the best product at the lowest price wins"—is only true of idealized capitalism or very highly regulated capitalism that prevents both the excesses of exploitation and the inherent march toward monopolization. If we ever see such capitalism, it will be when the investment of capital is so restricted by law and so fine-tuned by regulations and rules that it will bear no resemblance to the wild creature that has stalked the stock markets in recent years.

In the meantime, real capitalism demands down and dirty behavior. Beating the other capitalist to the punch. Using the sucker punch if necessary. Restricting the market, monopolizing distribution, paying off those in government so they do not intervene, or so that they intervene on your side. Survival of the fittest, law of the jungle, go for the jugular, and all that.

This was especially true over the past twenty years, when the rules of fair play were abrogated or ignored. Capitalists were overjoyed. Profits jumped, nearly doubling from the 1970s to the mid-1990s. Capital controls—such as the distinction between investment banks and commercial banks, usury laws against excessive interest charged on consumer loans, progressive taxation of investment income—were relaxed or eliminated. Capital, the ultimate arbitrator in such matters, was set free.

Karl Marx's famous book is not called *Capitalist*. This is because the individual capitalist is not the star of the show. The big banana, the sina qua non, the marquee idol, is *Capital* itself. One need not be a Marxist, or a socialist, or radical of any sort to appreciate this. *Capital* seeks to extract as much value as possible from human labor and the natural world. *Capital* that can do this, that can multiply its value most rapidly and most consistently, is the hero of the story, and successful capitalists follow behind, noting where capital in its various forms—money, gold, exploitable land, accumulated and desirable merchandise, saleable natural resources—can deliver the highest return on investment. Certain individual capitalists and

entrepreneurs do have their moments of glory, as they show *Capital* the true path to its highest redemption, but they will eventually settle on the sidelines as new sources of profit or hungry new capitalists overtake them.

Capital lets its followers calculate numbers predicated on which human activities will or will not generate more fresh capital. When these choices are correctly made, capital can keep replicating and expanding its activities. In the abstract, but also in the real world over the past five hundred years, the realm of things and activities that have been commodified and sold for profit has expanded enormously. Many pursuits that were once the province of small business professionals or non-profit institutions—such as the practice of medicine or the production and preparation of food—are increasingly controlled by big business corporations. Many forms of recreation—whether children's play or adults' casual exercise—were until recently never bought and sold at all, but now they are marketed on an international level. Today there are very few things or activities left on earth that cannot be pursued with an eye to profit.

The serious devotees of *Capital* are those with sufficient holdings, members of a group sometimes identified as the capitalist class or the rich, to do two things, sometimes simultaneously. First they must have enough liquid financial resources, either alone or in the company of other well-situated individuals, to pour into quickly materializing investments that might transform an industry or corner a market in raw materials or finished goods. Secondly, and this may be even more important, they must have access to so much extra capital that they can afford to wait patiently—holding on to a contract, a resource, large land holdings, an industrial patent, or large sums for loans—until the optimal moment that these holdings can be redeemed or employed at the highest rate of return. When Capital successfully multiplies itself in such activities, it rewards the capitalists—not for their work, their ideas, or anything else relating to their personal qualities or skills—merely for the fact that they held the *Capital* in the first place.

While the capitalists do not have to be active, but merely willing to employ people who want to activate their capital, they naturally gravitate toward arrangements that make the success of these endeavors as easy as possible. Hence, they are often happy to invest limited amounts of money on developing political power and political loyalty among those who run the government. And they favor showering gifts—in our present era, campaign contributions—on those who grease the wheels of commerce. Naturally they favor laws and practices that accelerate the movement of their capital and, if possible, insure its success against other recalcitrant human forces. Going beyond that, many will not scruple to bend or break the laws if this can be done with very little inconvenience, especially if lawyers can delay their punishment interminably or minimize it to the point of inconsequence. Some of the biggest conglomerations of capital attempt to regularly break the law—as in the cases mentioned in previous chapters, such as Wal-Mart's intentional cheating on wages, ConAgra's disregard for food safety or worker safety, or Columbia/HCA's manipulation of medical records—because they have calculated that they can make more money even if they have to pay large fines.

This system in which humans worship and wait upon capital might seem ideal, at least from the point of view of the capitalists, except for one major flaw. Capital is insatiable. It never stops wishing for a higher return. Accordingly, the large capitalist business that once yielded a perfectly acceptable 10% annual return must compete with other capitalists and capitalist enterprises if they start delivering returns on investment of 20% with any consistency. They are forced to keep up with their class. If they don't, those who get stronger will eat their lunch. If their efforts to accumulate are unhindered and their pile of wealth gets higher and higher, there is a point at which their capital will sit idle, for there will be no longer enough productive activities to keep it busy. In a modern industrial economy particularly, there will be fewer opportunities to invest in the production of items for mass consumption, because the buying power of the non-capitalists is not increasing at nearly the pace of the capitalist class—maybe it's not increasing at all. Then the idle capital gets restless and begins looking for other activities—the fun and games that were once sideline distractions become the center of attention.

Degenerate, unemployable capital, incapable of turning out useful goods or services, is sidetracked in two directions. Down one path lie the pleasures of sheer excess, the luxury purchases of rich people who already have more than enough luxuries. The other way offers fresh speculative investments, which all too often are absolutely silly, downright destructive, or both. Capital burns itself up.

Crash and Burn

Hedge fund—This now famous term literally means funds to cover contingencies or arbitrage operations, but in the Orwellian world of finance, they would be more accurately described as funds for speculation. Hedge funds cover a wide variety of enterprises, chiefly investment companies which engage in "ultra-sophisticated" speculation management for wealthy private individuals (able to invest amounts in excess of several hundred thousand dollars) or institutional investors.[3]

—Ibrahim Warde, University of California at Berkeley

In 1997, the Nobel Prize committee for economics was so intrigued by the mysteries of the bubbling, worldwide investment markets that it gave the prize to Myron Scholes and Robert C. Merton. These two professors had developed an elegant formula to plot the reactions of various derivative investments based on the movements, up or down, of stocks, bonds, and more exotic financial instruments. What made the prize even more intriguing was that the winners had, a few years previously, been asked by John Meriwether, the founder of the Long-Term Capital Management, an investment company, to join his hedge fund as principal investors and help run the show. Long-Term Capital actually tested their theorems as they served the super rich. To join in the profits and invest in the fund, clients had to be able and willing to bet at least $10 million, while asking no questions of managing principal partners, who took 27% of all earnings off the top. In its second and third years of operation, the yields on these wagers were fantastic, even after paying for fund management—42.8% in 1995, 40.8% in 1996. Perhaps this was what caught the eye of the Nobel committee, and what moved economist Zvi Bodie to say that the impact of Scholes and Merton work was going to be as dramatic as the discovery of the structure of DNA.

The drama ended, however, in the disaster that came six months after the Nobel Prize was awarded. Long-Term Capital Management had used its capital, estimated at between $2.2 and $4.8 billion, as collateral to buy between $125 and $200 billion in securities. It then used those securities as collateral to enter into exotic financial transactions worth $1.25 trillion. But in 1998, the mathematical formulas and the furious electronic trading in all kinds of countervailing market forces were no longer coping with reality. Several international occurrences, such as financial crises in Russia and East Asia, were far outside the predictive powers of their mathematics. Their model, unfortunately, was predicated on the same ahistorical assumption that most of Wall Street had followed in regard to stock prices. Because things had been booming, and most everyone believed they would keep booming, the geniuses did not believe that the markets could turn bad or that credit could tighten. But, of course, they did.[4] The investors' capital was going up in smoke and the Federal Reserve asked fourteen major financial institutions to immediately step in to bail out Long-Term Capital with $3.5 billion. A lot of money, but not nearly as much as would be lost if the company failed.

"The LTCM faced bankruptcy," said *The New York Times* in October of 1998, "but if the company went down, it would also take with it the total value of the positions it held across the globe—by some accounts $1.25 trillion, the same amount as the annual budget of the U.S. government."[5]

University of California professor Ibrahim Warde, writing in *Le Monde Diplomatique,* explained that the Nobel laureates, and all the physicists and mathematicians they had hired to chase money around the globe, had simply made the wrong bet. "In September," he wrote, "after mistakenly gambling on a convergence in interest rates, it found itself on the verge of bankruptcy. It seems their formula made no accommodation for the possible effects of economic downturn."[6] Not all capitalists were happy when the big bettors were bailed out by the Federal Reserve Bank. Michael Thomas, a former partner at the Lehman Brothers investment house, wrote that "capitalists now all want it one way. They want to do whatever the hell they feel like, but let someone else pay. It's called privatizing the profits and socializing the risks." Russell Mokhiber and Robert Weissman, the authors of *Corporate Predators,* suggest that gambling is not just the sin of the rich and should be treated even-handedly: "The gamblers in Atlantic City don't get this kind of treatment. Neither should those on Wall Street."[7]

Hedge funds retreated for a while after the Long-Term Management bailout and the stock market soared for another year and a half. There was no shortage of idle capital or of those who promised to make it multiply. Throughout 2001, the stock market bets were having such a run of bad luck that the hedge funds were making a comeback. There were about 5,000 hedge funds managing upward of $500 billion in capital worldwide. Rich individuals accounted for more than 80 percent of hedge fund investment, with rich people's banks and institutional investors making up most of the rest. [8] By 2003, there was $600 billion sunk into hedge funds, primarily because the stock market kept performing so

badly and the hedge funds' meager 5.3% annual return was looking good. Very wealthy investors still dominated the market, but wily investment houses were coming up with new investment vehicles for middle class investors who were disappointed in their mutual funds and willing to gamble $20,000 or $40,000 on those who hedge their bets.[9]

This brings us back to the beginning of this chapter and an interesting question from Kurt Eichenwald's article: "But now, a staggering rush of corporate debacles is raising a disturbing question; can capitalism survive the capitalists themselves?" Probably not, since they need each other to stay alive. But it brings up the question of the two core components of capitalism, capital and human beings. Capital, an artificial concept built on the circulation of money, will survive no matter what. But what about us, the people? How long will our society survive if we have to keep bailing out the capitalists?

They get in trouble, exploit our fellow citizens, cheat each other, and increasingly waste a good share of the capital produced by all of our labor. Then we the people are the only ones left to clean up the mess.

> These capitalists generally act harmoniously and in concert to fleece the people, and now that they have got into a quarrel with themselves, we are called upon to appropriate the people's money to settle the quarrel.
>
> —Abraham Lincoln, speech to the Illinois legislature, 1837

Thirteen

Laws for the Lawless

Why Corporations Rule

I hope we shall crush in its birth the aristocracy of our monied corporations which dare already to challenge our government to a trial of strength, and bid defiance to the laws our country.

—Thomas Jefferson, 1816

Corporations have been enthroned and an era of corruption in high places will follow.

—Abraham Lincoln,1864

For too many of us the political equality we once had won was meaningless in the face of economic inequality. A small group had concentrated into their own hands an almost complete control over other people's property, other people's money, other people's labor—other people's lives.

—Franklin Delano Roosevelt, acceptance speech for the Democratic nomination for president, June 27, 1936

Since we did not heed the advice of Jefferson, the founding father of the Democratic Party, corporations ended up crushing us under their staggering weight. Since we ignored the warning of Lincoln, founding father of the Republican Party, the corruption of the corporations contaminated the leadership of both political parties as well as almost every nook and cranny of our democracy.

The result, according to Franklin Roosevelt, was a degree of economic inequality so great that it overwhelmed the legal guarantees of political equality that had been gradually extended to all citizens since the founding of the United States. With this is mind, it is worth remembering that the American Revolution began with popular rebellion against the corporation as well as against the King of England. When the patriots who launched the Boston

Tea Party threw 342 chests of tea into the Boston harbor, part of a half million pound shipment that had just arrived from England, they were not only protesting "taxation without representation," but they were also punishing the corporation that had successfully lobbied the English government to avoid taxation. The East India Company, hoping to extend its monopoly of tea sales throughout the thirteen colonies, was expressly exempted from the tea tax that was imposed on every other merchant and shipper in America. The 1773 Tea Act was judged to be "a legislative maneuver by the ministry of Lord North to make English tea marketable in America" with the intention to "sell 17 million pounds of tea stored in England."[1]

Thus the American Revolution began with outright acts of rebellion and sabotage against the leading corporation of the era, which under cover of law was receiving preferable and profitable treatment at the expense of English commoners. George Monbiot, author of *The Captive State: The Corporate Takeover of Britain*, documents how British democracy has declined (just like American democracy) because the government has slipped under the control of corporate interests over the last few decades.[2] He also points out that British corporations were originally charitable organizations under license to the crown. Because of their socially useful services, they were exempted from certain taxes or death duties, thus allowing their activities to continue in perpetuity even though individual donors and directors might pass away. Profit-making and competition with merchants were prohibited for these corporations. This changed at the end of 16th century when "charters of incorporation" were granted to trade associations such as the East India Company, which were partly inspired by the lucrative international trade and extraordinary profits generated by similar conglomerations of capital in the Netherlands, particularly the Dutch East India Company.

The rest of the inspiration came from Queen Elizabeth's investment in the wild schemes of Sir Francis Drake, who in 1577 proposed to make a voyage around the world on *The Golden Hinde* and return with new-found wealth for England. This charming pirate found all kinds of things to pillage and loot, then returned to share the booty with his partners. Their take was a huge amount for the time, six hundred thousand pounds, with the return on investment for Drake and the other small investors calculated at 5,000%; the deal was equally lucrative for the Queen, who supplied 50% of the capital and received 50% of the profit.[3]

The success of this adventure not only allowed the Queen to accumulate the funds required to outfit a fleet that would defeat the Spanish Armada, but it also led England to compete with the Dutch and challenge their dominance of the world spice trade. In 1600 Queen Elizabeth and over two hundred rich merchants and noblemen formed the East India Company. The Company served as a model for the modern English corporation, known as a "limited liability corporation." The Queen insisted on this arrangement, which meant that each investor was liable for losses only to the extent of his or her original investment. She could not be sued for the death of the crew that went down with their unsafe ship. Nor could she be charged for the crimes that might be committed against Catholic rivals, heathen infidels, or peaceful villagers who just happened to get in the way of efficient pillaging. A limited liability corporation is the perfect vehicle for putting pirates to work so that they will steal from others rather than from you. At the same time, if you are willing to give your pirate-in-chief a cut of the loot, he will probably be willing to come back the following year, strategize with you about the perfect new target, and bring back the bloody treasure once again. And if you, as Marx suggested, promise his capital a return of "300 percent, there is not a crime which it will not scruple, nor a risk it will not run, even to the chance of its owner being hanged."

Most importantly, you as the Queen, do not have to expose the rest of your fortune if the corporation somehow incurs enormous debts and obligations, such as to the suppliers and shipbuilders who risked their own money and materials to outfit the ships for the voyage. For the Queen and other extremely wealthy participants in the venture, this was a felicitous solution to the hazards of risky business undertakings. If she committed 100,000 pounds in an entrepreneurial scheme that failed by accruing excessive debts, then she could lose that original 100,000, but could not be pursued for payment of more extensive losses by the company. Her exposure to loss was limited by the corporate rules and she would be free to employ the rest of her fortune in new endeavors.

American and British profit-making corporations have followed this model ever since. From the beginning the English corporation was a global enterprise that entertained the prospect of doing business wherever profitable opportunities presented themselves. Because the liabilities were strictly limited, participation in a variety of simultaneous ventures was always a possibility for the biggest investors. The corporate boards of the East India Company and the Virginia Company that founded Jamestown in 1607 were interlocking. In fact, the American operations of both were coordinated by the same man, Sir Thomas Smythe.[4] The settlement of Jamestown and Virginia was defined by the guidelines put down by the corporation, as were the plans for producing income by recruiting indentured laborers who were hauled to the New World from the slums and failing farmland of England, Scotland, and Ireland.

When the colonists fought the British Empire in the 1770s, they were striking out at two kinds of familiar hierarchical and authoritarian control, one embodied in privileges accorded to the King and the other being the corporative prerogatives demanded by the East India Company and other allied corporations. When the Americans threw off British rule, they may have thought that they were rid of the rule of the British corporation, too.

But the influence of the latter stayed behind, since the Anglo-American corporation was multinational from the beginning, capable of operating anywhere in the world where sufficient profit was offered. The corporate influence lingered through the heritage of men like Elihu Yale, who were born in America but went to work for the East India Company as it was becoming the world's largest corporation. Yale became fabulously wealthy as the company's governor in Madras, India, and upon his return home to Connecticut he endowed the school he had attended as a boy with a good part of his fortune. In gratitude, the school changed its name to Yale College. A hundred years later, another Connecticut adventurer, Samuel Russell, would find employ as a sub-contractor in the East India Company's operations. Russell made a large fortune hauling opium from Turkey to China for the English and flew the skull and bones flag on his privateering ships. Part of that fortune ended up endowing a peculiar club at Yale, the Skull and Bones, which would later produce hundreds of Wall Street pirates and privateers, plus three future presidents, two of them named George Bush (the third was William Howard Taft.)

Did They Teach You This at Law School?

[There] is looming up a dark power...the enterprises of the country are aggregating vast combinations of unexampled capital, boldly marching, not for economical conquests only, but for political power... Which shall rule—wealth or man? ... Which shall lead—money or intellect? Which shall fill public stations—educated and patriotic freemen, or the feudal serfs of corporate capital?[5]

When this speech was given to the graduating class of the University of Wisconsin Law

School in 1873, the speaker was not a socialist, nor a radical member of the Knights of Labor, not even a fired-up farmer from the Grange (and Karl Marx, as far as anyone knows, never managed to slip into the United States to give a subversive lecture). The distinguished orator was Edward G. Ryan, who was about to assume his job as Chief Justice of the Wisconsin Supreme Court. Like many concerned mainstream politicians of the time, Ryan had been watching the railroad companies and the banks run roughshod over the farmers and small businessmen of his state as they tried to buy up legislative influence. He wanted to utilize the courts and laws of the State of Wisconsin to slow down the onslaught of corporate money. This seemed only fair, since the States had been accustomed since the founding of the Republic to grant charters under certain specified conditions to corporations that wanted to do business within their borders.

Another wary politician of the mid-19th century was none other than Abraham Lincoln, who had helped the process of corporate expansion because he needed full cooperation from the railroads, weapons manufacturers, and financiers in the prosecution of the Civil War. In November of 1864, when the North's victory was already assured, Lincoln wrote a letter to a friend and explained his great fear for the future of the United States:

> As a result of the war, corporations have been enthroned and an era of corruption in high places will follow, and the money power of the country will endeavor to prolong its reign by working upon the prejudices of the people until all wealth is aggregated in a few hands and the Republic is destroyed. I feel at this moment more anxiety than ever before, even in the midst of war. God grant that my suspicions may prove groundless.[6]

Unfortunately Lincoln's suspicions were only too accurate. When the war ended and the populace was exhausted by the slaughter and emotional distress, the rising corporations were barreling down the tracks of the railroad boom, intent on increasing the economic advantages that had accrued to them during the war. Their economic momentum fueled their legal and political power, and quickly involved them in a crucial constitutional struggle.

As is well-known, corporations, ever since 17th century English lawyers attempted to justify and control their activities, have been considered "artificial persons" under the law. This meant they could own and dispose of property, enter into contracts, etcetera, but were not to be considered "natural persons" with the full range of rights granted to real human beings. Under this long legal precedent, national, state and local governments had been free to enact laws that restricted the activities of corporations, particularly when they thought the encroachments of these "artificial persons" were endangering the rights and general welfare of "natural persons," that is, the real living, breathing citizens of the nation.

After 1865, American corporations were determined to change this state of affairs and win the enhanced status of "natural persons" before the law. They seized upon a unique opportunity in 1868, the passage of the 14th Amendment to the Constitution, which granted full citizenship and legal rights to former slaves and "all persons born or naturalized in the United States." For the next eighteen years, corporate lawyers and railroad attorneys besieged the courts of the nation with claims that the "artificial persons" they represented were meant to be included among the "all persons born and naturalized" stipulated in the 14th amendment.

In the beginning, the corporate lobbyists were usually laughed out of the state courtrooms. When they received more serious consideration, as in a 1873 case that reached the U.S. Supreme Court, they were firmly reminded that this amendment was not written for corporations at all. On the contrary, its "one pervading purpose was the freedom of the slave race," wrote Justice Samuel F. Miller.

By 1886, big business pressure was winning out and the U.S. Supreme Court declared 231 state laws invalid because they violated the rights of corporations. One of the most obscure of these cases, the *Santa Clara* decision, declared victory for the Union Pacific Railroad against the state of California. A small clause in the court commentary on the case referred to the rights that corporations had as "persons," and this has been used ever since to justify the freedom of corporations to do almost anything they please. Thom Hartmann, in his book *Unequal Protection: The Rise of Corporate Dominance and the Theft of Human Rights*[7] argues that the Supreme Court was actually trying to avoid any clear-cut decision about the "personhood" of the corporation, because it was never clearly affirmed in the judges' decision itself. Hartmann makes a good case for the possibility that one member of the court or the official court recorder, each with his own pro-railroad bias, may have inserted the reference to *person* as opposed to *artificial person* into the court commentary after the case was closed.

The outcome of all this was that the 14th Amendment was hijacked from the human world and placed at the service of the corporate world. A grave injustice was committed against the cause of desegregation in the process, for according to Justice Hugo Black, writing in 1939:

Of the cases in this Court in which the Fourteenth Amendment was applied during the first fifty years after its adoption, less than one-half of one percent invoked it in protection of the Negro race, and more than fifty percent asked that its benefits be extended to corporations.[8]

From the time of the Civil War to the tenure of Franklin Roosevelt, the majority of justices, men from upper-class backgrounds and corporate law practices, were sympathetic toward this interpretation of the constitution. Justice David J. Brewer clarified the defining issue lurking behind this sympathy, when he invoked a "law" that will never be found in the Constitution during a speech to the American Bar Association in 1893: "It is the unvarying law that the wealth of the community will be in the hands of the few."[9]

Supreme Court justices have generally been sympathetic to the wealthy since the founding of the American republic. What was new after the Civil War was the need for the Court to adjust this preferential treatment to the changing nature of ownership and control of the nation's productive resources. Ownership was passing from individual proprietorship—which was not necessarily democratic or humane, especially in the case of slavery—to more sophisticated forms of upper-class control. According to Professor Martin J. Sklar, by establishing "new trends in legal doctrine and political-economic theory" allowing "the corporate reorganization of the property-production system," the Supreme Court helped to sabotage popular social protest movements against corporate power.[10]

The Bush Gang is a Corporate Gang

The corporate ability to change the law and hide behind the law was generally enhanced by Congress and the courts from the Civil War to the present. Exceptions to this trend can be found in the labor legislation of the 1930s, which gave working people the right to organize unions that could stand up to corporate domination, and the consumer protection, health, and environmental measures that were legislated in the 1960s and 1970s. Since then, Republican administrations have attacked those prerogatives with a vengeance, and reconstituted the Supreme Court with a pro-corporate majority. Although the Sherman Anti-Trust Act had a brief moment of glory during the Clinton administration's suit against Microsoft, the Bush administrations virtually stopped anti-trust enforcement, just as Coolidge did in the 1920s.

One of the few methods of popular control left to the people is their participation in jury trials concerning corporate misbehavior. They occasionally award huge amounts of compensation to workers and consumers who are injured or killed by defective products or negligent corporate practices. While right-wing commentators decry the high fees earned by flashy trial lawyers, they sidestep the major issue: ordinary citizens are willing to use the law to limit the arrogant power wielded by corporations. While these awards are large in dollar terms, they do not necessarily do what they are supposed to do: deter repeat behavior.

Some multi-billion dollar corporations, such as tobacco companies which repeatedly lied about the medical consequences of smoking, were able to weather multi-billion dollar lawsuits because they market a very addictive product. In other cases, such as the lawsuits that Ralph Nader brought against the major auto companies, the public embarrassment of corporations (a form of negative advertising) probably had more to do with persuading them to build safer cars than the size of the fines levied against them. After all, corporate accountants had already anticipated a certain number of lawsuits in advance, and estimated that they would not cost as much as changing the design of the cars. One of the priorities of the second Bush Gang is to patch this small breach in the corporate armor by putting severe limits on civil lawsuits. As mentioned earlier (Chapter 11), when he gave his 2003 State of the Union address, George W. Bush made the thoroughly misleading suggestion that putting an end to medical malpractice suits would enable people to get the health care they need.

With the elections of 2002, which gave control of both houses of Congress to the Republicans, George Bush II was awarded the ability to stack the courts of the nation with more right-wing appointees. Many of them are likely to adhere to the views of the reactionary Federalist Society, an ultra-conservative, pro-corporate legal group that started under the tutelage of Antonin Scalia and Anthony M. Kennedy before they were members of the Supreme Court. Lawrence Walsh, the Republican Wall Street lawyer who battled the Bush Gang I during the Iran/Contra hearings, was very leery of this new kind of Republican judicial thinking and predicted that there would be "a cleavage between the Federalist Society members and non-members."[11] Many of these new conservatives have taught or were educated in the various "Law and Economics" programs that have proliferated at the law schools of our major universities, courtesy of big grants from the Olin Foundation and other conservative groups that want American law to be pro-business law. Closely associated with the movement is Chief Justice Rehnquist, who has pushed a "new Federalism" for many years in a effort to gradually transfer power to the state courts.

In 1975, Rehnquist wrote about "a concept of constitutional federalism which should ... limit federal power under the Commerce Clause." The following year, immediately after his appointment as an associate justice on the Supreme Court, he sided with the lawyers leading the attack on the Commerce Clause. He and the majority of the judges made a ruling in *National League of Cities v. Usery* that simultaneously limited congressional control over wages and restricted the rights of workers. They ruled that the federal system permitted state governments to disregard the provisions of the Fair Labor Standards Act.

Theodore Roosevelt noted a century ago that the appeal to states' rights was a common defense of corporations which wanted to escape control of more aggressive law enforcement at the federal government level. Corporate appeals to the judiciary often foiled his efforts to bust the trusts. "The effective fight against adequate Government control and supervision of individual, and especially corporate, wealth engaged in interstate business," Roosevelt pointed out, "is chiefly done under cover of an appeal to states' rights."

Presidential advisor Karl Rove tried to compare George W. Bush to Theodore Roosevelt in January 2003, saying that "I would suspect that Theodore Roosevelt would be standing up and applauding the president's initiatives" on the environment, and Bush himself said T.R. was his third-favorite politician after Ronald Reagan and Winston Churchill.[12] There might be similarities in terms of foreign policy: they both like big sticks. But on matters of corporate governance, they are poles apart. Bush does not oppose the powerful team of the corporations and the Supreme Court, since the former paid for his election and the latter gave it their blessing. The Bush Gang works hand in hand with them both to consolidate their power and limit the possibilities of democratic movements ever gaining control over the elite.

If Theodore Roosevelt were present in Washington today he would be hounding the "artificial persons" and trying to chase them out of town. The Supreme Court, as the ultimate guarantor of corporate power, was Roosevelt's enemy. His attempt to outlaw all corporate political contributions in 1906 was shot down by the Supreme Court, which ruled that such a law would deprive those "persons" of their First Amendment rights. Still, he persisted in saying to Congress, "I again recommend prohibiting all corporations from making contributions for any political purpose, directly or indirectly." Not to be thwarted entirely, he had another weapon at his disposal, the Sherman Anti-Trust Law, and used it to attack more than 40 monopolistic corporations during his presidency, including the American Tobacco Company and Rockefeller's Standard Oil.

Handy as this law was in restraining corporate power for a while, the power which corporations wield over real "natural persons" is nearly unstoppable a century later. The corporations have purchased the Bush Gang and purchased our system of justice. This is why many decades ago Supreme Court Justice Felix Frankfurter made the observation that "the history of American constitutional law in no small measure is the history of the impact of the modern corporation upon the American scene."

M.WUERKER

Fourteen

Skull and Bones

Degenerate Genes and the Decline in Bush Family Values

> Competition is the law of nature... liberty, inequality, survival of the fittest; non-liberty, equality, survival of the unfittest. The former carries society forward and favors all its best members; the latter carries society downwards and favors all its worst members.
>
> —William Graham Sumner, 1879

Sumner was one of the foremost spokesmen for Social Darwinism in the United States and professor of political and social science at Yale from 1872 to 1909. As a Yale student in 1863, he became a member of the exclusive club, Skull and Bones.

In 1911, Stanford University president David Starr Jordan gave this definition of eugenics. He called it "the art and science of being well-born."

Jordan was not giving this definition in jest, for he was one of the leading eugenicists of his time; he served as the first chairman of the eugenics committee of the American Breeders' Association, which was dedicated to breeding superior humans, not racehorses.[1]

Yale's Professor Sumner, considered one of the founders of modern American political science, joined Englishman Herbert Spencer in developing Social Darwinism, a remarkably un-

scientific theory that was based on a distorted reading of Charles Darwin's *Origin of Species*. (Darwin's theory had nothing to do with individuals succeeding within one lifetime or within their own species; it was about the natural selection of one species over others due to evolutionary changes over many, many generations.) Social Darwinism was combined with another new pseudo-science, eugenics, which was probably even more popular at the time. Eugenics emphasized the superiority of some breeds, or races, of humans over others; it advocated breeding improved stocks of young people who were to be separated from lesser mortals; and it encouraged society to consider sterilizing and eliminating "waste" people who were decidedly inferior. Professor Irving Fisher was a nationally renowned economist and leading light in the economics department at Yale for over forty years and the first president of the American Eugenics Society. In his widely read 1910 textbook,

Elementary Principles of Economics, Fisher wrote about "Population in Relation to Wealth," and warned white readers that "race suicide" was a danger to capitalists and their capital: "If the vitality or vital capital is impaired by a breeding of the worst and a cessation of the breeding of the best, no greater calamity could be imagined."[2]

The reasoning of these famous academics may have been faulty, but their timing was perfect. The rich industrialists of the time loved this doctrine because it justified the idea that they were the "fittest" individuals, and therefore deserved all the loot they had amassed. The large doses of clap-trap served up by Social Darwinists and eugenicists sold very well at such places as Harvard, Yale, and Princeton, where the founding Congregationalists and Presbyterians already believed that God looked favorably upon people like themselves. According to Calvin's doctrine, there were a limited number of people predestined to be God's "elect," and the Calvinists were those people. In the hands of the reigning professors, the idea of the "elect" degenerated a bit: in their eyes only a few people were supposed to be rich, otherwise God and Nature would not have allowed them to take everyone else's money.

Many rich parents in the late 19th and early 20th centuries exposed their children to the ideas of William Graham Sumner, David Starr Jordan, Irving Fisher and a host of other similarly-minded educators at elite institutions. Social Darwinism, when linked with the "science" of eugenics, provided the perfect upper-class doctrine for maintaining class and race purity. In their intense preoccupation with preserving their ethnic heritage and breeding the right kind of offspring, wealthy people sheltered their kids from the everyday realities and hardships faced by other children. By so doing, they perpetuated the "survival" of a class system, not the "survival of the fittest."

The rich played it safe and avoided the "laws of nature," preferring to isolate and "nurture" their boys in the most protective settings they could imagine. They hid them away, as far as possible from the soot and smoke of the cities and the powerful influence of "the great unwashed," the immigrants. In the hothouse atmosphere of elite preparatory schools and colleges, they created environments where their sons' adolescence could be extended as long as possible, where they would very slowly grow to manhood while making friendships with other young Anglo-Saxon men who shared the same social attitudes and prejudices. They also learned that they were, as a class of young men, entitled to special treatment, often immune to the usual laws of punishment, and far from the prying moralistic eyes of parents. As they awaited their release into the "real world," the students would join in special societies and clubs that fostered juvenile fraternal attachments and encouraged them to think that they should make their own rules of conduct.

When this long training session was over, the lucky rich young men were very well prepared for surviving in life. They had developed a web of valuable social and business contacts for the future and, quite possibly, further access to large sources of investment money. This social cocoon explains, much more clearly than theories of natural selection, why so many of their peers—as opposed to say, shoeshine boys—embarked on careers at investment banks and Wall Street law firms. Of all the most elite and rarefied organizations on American campuses, none was so successful at sending its sons out to capture other people's money as a small society at Yale. It selected only fifteen members each year. It flew the black flag with the white skull and cross-bones.

The Basis of the Skull and Bones Gang: Dealing in Drugs

In 1832, William Huntington Russell and Alphonso Taft founded a secret society for rich Anglo-Saxon boys at Yale that came to be called Skull and Bones. Over the years the club recruited so many sons of the Robber Barons that its pirate banner seemed entirely appropriate. Had some clever students chosen the flag to poke fun at the ideas of eugenics and suggest that degenerate genes were passed down to them by their piratical parents? Did they think that, owing to the criminal make-up they had inherited, that they were destined to keep stealing very large sums of money from the American people?

Actually the Skull and Bones flag was not a student joke. The club had been endowed by a family fortune, The Russell Trust. The money originated with Russell and Company, which was the premier American opium smuggling operation in the first half of the 19th century. All its ships flew the Skull and Bones flag. Russell and Company worked directly for the British East India Company, transporting vast quantities of opium from Turkey and India to China. The origins of the Yale club have fueled any number of wild conspiratorial theories about its members. What about the countless connections between the international drug trade and the CIA, many of whose important members came from Yale? How about the British and American banking families who were said to have joined with the legendary Illuminati in order to dominate the world's financial institutions? Why the inordinate amount of help that Skull and Bonesmen gave to the German corporations that supported Hitler?

All in all, the stories of implausible intrigue are not any more compelling than the non-conspiratorial and unvarnished truth. Although there are bits and pieces of real information connected to many of the conspiracy theories, there is a much more revealing, but not so secret, reality about the power of Skull and Bones members. They were simply young men who benefited from a special association with other wealthy students; consequently they were able to play a major role in the course of American politics and finance over the past century.

A Few Members of Skull and Bones

The "Mr. Republican" family
- Alphonso Taft—one of the founders; U.S. Attorney General 1877, father of ...
- William Howard Taft—President of the U.S., 1908-1912, father of...
- Robert A. Taft—Senator from Ohio, almost President, father of ...
- Robert Taft Jr.—Senator from Ohio, father of ...
  (Bob Taft, went to Yale, not a Bonesman—governor of Ohio, 1998)

The Bush Gang
- Prescott Bush—Senator from Connecticut, financier, father of...
- George Herbert Walker Bush—President of the U.S., 1988-1992, father of...
- George Walker Bush—President of the U.S., 2001-200?
- George Herbert Walker, Jr., uncle of George H.W. Bush.

- Jonathan Bush, uncle of George W. Bush.
  (Jeb Bush—Governor of Florida, not a Yale guy, but might be President some day)

and many others, including:
- Averell Harriman—Financier, Governor of New York, the major moneybags of the Democratic Party for more than half a century, and his brother...
- Roland Harriman—Financier
- Henry Luce—Publisher of *Time*, *Life*, *Fortune*
- Henry Stimson—Financier; Secretary of War for Taft and Franklin Roosevelt, Secretary of State for Hoover.
- Morris Waite—Chief Justice of the Supreme Court 1874-1888, presided over the case in which corporations assumed the rights of natural people.
- John Forbes Kerry—U.S. Senator from Massachusetts who has declared his candidacy for the Democratic nomination for president in 2004.

Membership in a rich and influential family can be a great advantage in politics, just as a Wall Street pedigree helps one's business career. But these are not the only requirements for success. Association with Ivy League colleges is a plus, too, hence there are 20th century Presidents from Harvard (the two Roosevelts, who were distant cousins, and Kennedy), Princeton (Wilson), and Yale (the two Bushes and Taft). For the presidents with more plebeian roots, there have been cabinet members of great stature who added the proper elite component—for example the Dulles brothers (corpo-

rate law and Princeton), were Secretary of State and head of the CIA for Eisenhower; Acheson (corporate law and Yale), was Secretary of State for Truman; James Baker (corporate law and Princeton), Secretary of the Treasury for Reagan.

There has always been plenty of room for such fellows at the top. Presidents or presidents-elect, whether they come from elite backgrounds or not, have learned that to get things done efficiently in Washington they must surround themselves with people who can interact smoothly with the business and social elite. So they usually appoint rich Ivy League types or rich corporate types to their cabinets, and preferably a combination of the two.

205 INDIVIDUALS SERVED IN PRESIDENTIAL CABINETS FROM 1897—1972[3]

60%—were members of the upper-class social elite
78%—were worked in corporate law firms or served on corporate boards
50%—were both of the above
12%—were neither of the above

Skulldiggery

The privileged sense of entitlement associated with wealthy families and elite social environments often leads children to believe their actions are above the law. But sometimes their fraternity pranks do not end up being humorous at all, as when Prescott Bush, grandfather of George W, embarked on a post-college caper with his Bonesmen buddies. They decided in 1918 to steal the skull of Geronimo, the great

Apache hero, from its burial place at Fort Sill, Oklahoma. Bush had transported the skull back to Yale so it could be displayed in a case in the Tomb, the windowless meeting place of Skull and Bones. When George Bush I was running for President in 1988, a tribal chairman of the Apaches, Ned Anderson, was notified about the skull. He tried to recover it because the tribe wanted to bury it properly in an Apache ceremony. George H.W. Bush's brother, Jonathan, who was also a member of Skull and Bones, arranged to meet secretly with Anderson, and asked him to take what appeared to be the skull of a small child. Anderson, knowing this was a sham, refused the remains and pursued a variety of legal avenues to recover the authentic skull. But he never succeeded.[4]

Bush Financial Skullduggery and the Rise of Nazism

This sense of special privilege often stays with the Skull and Bones members and leads them into activities that others would not even contemplate. A much more serious case involves the behavior of investment bankers, including Prescott Bush, George Herbert Walker, and Averell Harriman, when they promoted the rise of the industrialists who supported the Nazis in Germany in the 1920s and 1930s.

Averell and his brother Roland were heirs to one of America's biggest fortunes, left to them by their father, E.H. Harriman. The elder Harriman was one of the most ruthless Robber Barons of the late 1800s and presided over the largest railroad empire in America, the Union Pacific. After World War I, the Harriman sons put their capital into one of the country's largest private investment companies, the W.A. Harriman Co., which was organized and managed by George Herbert Walker. Prescott Bush married Walker's daughter Dorothy and became vice-president of the bank in 1926. Prescott had been inducted into Skull and Bones in 1917 with Roland Harriman, and Averell had become a member a few years earlier. In 1931, the Harrimans merged their bank with Brown Brothers of England to create what would become the world's largest privately held investment bank; in the process they brought more Bonesmen on board, until a total of eight of them were partners at Brown Brothers Harriman. (Bonesmen of this era were very fond of investment banks; nine of them joined the ranks of another private financial powerhouse when they became partners at Guaranty Trust, the J.P. Morgan investment bank).

In the wake of World War I, the specialty of the Harrimans' banks was international finance, in particular buying up the pieces of European economies that had been destroyed in the conflict. Averell Harriman traveled to Germany, Italy, and Russia in search of profitable returns for American investment in the 1920s. This led both G.H. Walker and Prescott Bush into one of their more infamous financial adventures, the Union Banking Company, a financial vehicle they managed for the Harrimans and Fritz Thyssen of the German Steel Trust. The Union Banking Co., along with other Harriman interests, was a primary conduit for rebuilding German industry and shipping and eventually financing the German war machine. Thyssen and his major manufacturing ally in the Steel Trust, Friedrich Frick, became the biggest financial supporters of Hitler during the 1920s. By the early 1930s their funds were arming the private army of 300,000 Nazi brownshirts and stormtroopers that were disrupting the elected government and creating the social chaos that would bring Hitler to power in 1933.[5]

Prescott Bush managed to derive a nice fortune from his German investments during the 1930s, but these sources of income were lost to him and his father-in-law George Herbert Walker in 1942. The Bush/Walker/Harriman companies were seized under the Trading with the Enemy Act and taken without compensation, because they were of direct material aid to the German war machine. The Union Banking Corporation, the Holland-American Trading Corporation, the Seamless Steel Equipment Corporation and the Silesian-American Corporation were then dissolved by government order. Some people accused Bush and Walker of being direct Nazi supporters, while others have pointed to their partiality to the people-breeding ideas of the eugenics movement (Prescott had been director of the Connecticut chapter of the Mental Hygiene Society, which recommended the sterilization of mental defectives. It was closely related to the American Eugenics Society; both organizations had been headquartered at Yale since the early 1900s.)

The direct Nazi connection is difficult to prove, but in a way, unimportant.

The bankers' highest priority was to make money, and they could disregard, up to a point just short of treason, the politics of the unsavory people they assisted. Averell Harriman was most of all devoted to the free movement and biggest possible return on his capital, so that he was as likely to invest it in Russian oil as German steel. In fact, he did have large investments in both even as those two countries were battling it out on the Eastern Front during World War II. And by no means was the Harriman/Bush cartel alone among American corporate interests in

dealing with the enemy. The Rockefeller banks and Standard Oil were deeply involved with German industrialists and invested in Nazi industry; and the Wall Street law firm of Cromwell and Sullivan, home to the Dulles brothers, arranged many of the major business connections between American and German corporate and banking groups. Major corporations, such as General Motors, IBM, Standard Oil, and ITT kept doing business with the Nazis throughout the war through their foreign subsidiaries.[6]

As mentioned above, the Bush family connection to the criminal world of upper class banking and political intrigue goes back to George Walker Bush's great-grandfather Walker. On the other side of the family, great-grandfather Bush was making his way up the ladder to the highest rungs of the upper class; he sent his son, Prescott, off to Yale and Skull and Bones. Although he did not work for the Harriman banks, Samuel P. Bush owned a steel mill in Ohio, Buckeye Steel Castings Co., that made parts and equipment for the Harriman railroads. Bush became director of small armaments and ammunition on the War Industries Board during World War I and in that capacity assisted Percy Rockefeller (also a Skull and Bones man and a friend of the Harrimans) in his takeover of major weapons manufacturers such as Remington Arms.

The Maintenance of Privilege

Clearly the rules for the elite, as well as for the banks and businesses they own, are very flexible. The Harriman/Bush connection is a fascinating one, because both families escaped opprobrium for their less-than-patriotic business dealings before and during World War II. They then went on to be a major influence in American politics for the remainder of the 20th century. It is ironic that the same private banking fortune, and the same Skull and Bones connections, would end up promoting the political dreams of both the Democratic and Republican parties. Prescott Bush became U.S. Senator from Connecticut, President Eisenhower's favorite golf companion, and the president of the United States Golf Association. His son and grandson used family influence and Skull and Bones connections to rise higher, to the Presidency (but they are said to be terrible and impatient golfers).

Averell Harriman used his Establishment advantages to profoundly affect the implementation of the Cold War through his close friend, Dean Acheson, and the coterie of other "Wise Men" from Yale that surrounded Harry Truman and determined his foreign policy.[7] Although he failed in two attempts to secure the Democratic nomination for president in the 1950s, Harriman continued to serve various administrations as a roving, freelance ambassador who went on special missions to such sensitive places as the Soviet Union and Iran.[8]

At the Democratic National Convention of 1988, there was a key moment that illustrated the staying power of the upper class, and Harriman money in particular. When Michael Dukakis finished his speech accepting the presidential nomination, few Americans were aware that they were witnessing a rare, open demonstration of deference to the power that lurks behind the "democratic" facade of American political life. The first person allowed to come out and share the podium, holding up Dukakis's hand in victory, was none other than Mrs. Pamela Churchill Harriman, the widow of Averell (he had died two years earlier.) She

gained this honor because under the Harrimans' leadership rich Democrats had started to push the party rightward. Their small but influential organization, "Democrats for the '80s," was instrumental in picking Dukakis as the top dog in 1988. The group renamed itself "Democrats for the '90s," and latched onto the moderately conservative Democratic Leadership Council and its chairman, Bill Clinton. Even though Averell Harriman was no longer on the scene, his residual power and money kept influencing Democratic choices in the 1990s, thus helping to elect Clinton in 1992 and 1996.

Skull and Bones was not finished, for in 1996 there was an interesting development at the Republican convention. Running the whole show as master of ceremonies was a political newcomer, recently elected to his first office, but inducted into Skull and Bones almost thirty years earlier. He was George W. Bush, the Governor of Texas. There was no Bonesman pulling the strings on the stage of the Democratic convention in 1996 or 2000, but there is one waiting in the wings for 2004. John Forbes Kerry from Massachusetts, said to be the richest man in the U.S. Senate, came out of Yale and Skull and Bones in 1966, two years before Bush. In December of 2002, he launched his candidacy for the Democratic nomination, thus opening up the possibility of the ultimate elite/insider battle in 2004.

George Bush I and George Bush II never would have been noticed in national politics without connections. They were launched on the road to success by family associations and enthusiastic backing from their blue-blooded friends (Bush II received campaign donations from 48 men who were either members of Skull and Bones or the sons of members). While upper class associations confer advantages, they can be stumbling blocks to political progress, too. Reagan supporters with anti-Eastern Establishment sentiments used George Bush I's elite connections against him in 1980; for instance, the right-wing Florida Conservative Union mounted an ad campaign claiming: "The people who gave you Jimmy Carter want to give you George Bush." Their argument was that if David Rockefeller had placed both Carter and Bush on his Trilateral Commission and backed them both for president, then there was a conspiracy afoot.

George Bush I ended up feeling that the real conspiracy was against him, since his social and economic assets had been used against him. Journalist Alexandra Robbins wrote that "when Fay Vincent made a consolation call to Bush after his 1980 loss of the Republican presidential nomination to Ronald Reagan, the weary candidate said, 'Fay, let me tell you something. If you ever decide to run for office, don't forget that coming from Andover, Yale, Skull and Bones, and the Trilateral Commission is a big handicap. People don't know what they are, so they don't know where you're coming from. It's really a big, big problem.'"[9] This may be why his son, George Bush II, has cultivated the down-home Texan image and distanced himself from the days he spent as head cheerleader at Phillips Academy in Andover, the elite prep school, and as fraternity president, party animal, and Bonesman at Yale.

Franklin Delano Roosevelt was also reviled on account of his upper-class connections, but for much different reasons. Many wealthy, upper-class Americans thought he had betrayed them. Although his manner and some of his friendships clearly portrayed a man from a very privileged background, most of the Eastern Establishment elite in the 1930s felt he was act-ing against his (and their) class interests. Especially upsetting was Roosevelt's proposal that all individual income that exceeded $200,000 per year should be taxed at a rate of 100%. They called him a "traitor to his class" because of his commitment to help working Americans, and some wealthy conservatives refused to even use his name, simply referring to the pariah as "that man." When he first ran for president, a straw vote held by the Harvard *Crimson* showed a three-to-one preference for Herbert Hoover. Four years later a *Crimson* editorial called the president, himself a former editor of the college's paper, "a traitor to his fine education."[10]

Does this portend anything for today's politics? Roosevelt was able to overcome his early training, which destined him to become a Republican pirate.[11] So it may be possible that another man branded with the curse of Skull and Bones can become president—as a Democrat! If there is a chance for Kerry to redeem himself and gain the confidence of the American people, it might well depend on whether he, like Roosevelt, has the courage to be a "traitor to his class" and "his fine education."

Cons-Piracy?—With Pirates?

The origin of the word "conspiracy" has nothing to do with pirates, or Skull and Bones for that matter. "Con-spirare" meant to breathe or whisper together, as in whispering and plotting behind the king's back. Clearly there have been many conspirators throughout history, and some of the most successful have been rich aristocrats, but this does not mean they were all part of one giant, never-ending conspiracy that controls the fate of the world. It would be a mistake to look at a young men's club at Yale as the secret key to understanding every important political and economic event of the past century.[12] Skull and Bones is important, not as a suspected den of perfidy, but as an example of how social privilege, money, and familiarity can combine to advance the fortunes of men. If William Graham Sumner, or any other political scientist, really wanted to create the "fittest" children to lead the nation, why would he choose to educate the spoiled offspring of the rich? The real mission of elite institutions was, and is, to maintain the status of rich young men so that later they can be more likely to take the places of their fathers in positions of power. One can go elsewhere looking for conspiracies: how about Harvard, home to the Roosevelts and the Kennedys? Or Princeton University? It not only produced Woodrow Wilson and the international lawyers who helped run the Eisenhower administration, the Dulles brothers, but it also spawned the ambitions of Donald Rumsfeld, the most powerful Secretary of War of all time, and his close friend, Frank Carlucci. Carlucci, a former Secretary of Defense and a highly regarded operator in the CIA, until recently headed the Carlyle Group, the giant private investment operation that frequently incorporates the talents and the fortunes of James A. Baker III (Ivy Club, Princeton) and his close friend, George H.W. Bush (Skull and Bones, Yale).

The point is this: it is not a particular conspiratorial atmosphere, but rather the narrow confines of upper class institutions, where family wealth and corporate ownership are so concentrated, that have made it possible for politically active families, such as the Bushes, Roosevelts, Rockefellers, Kennedys, and Tafts, to figure so prominently in American life. This has a purpose, according to a sociologist of upper class behavior, E. Digby Bartzell, who was himself a product and defender of the class system:

> The main function of an upper class is the perpetuation of its power in the world of affairs, whether in the bank, the factory, or in the halls of the legislature... Whenever an upper-class way of life becomes an end in itself, rather than a means of consolidating its power and influence, the upper class has outlived its usefulness. [13]

Most who are born into this class are reluctant to leave its comforts. It is easier for them to trust in the motivations of their fellows among the rich than to rely on the workings of democracy. We can talk about their proclivity to crime, their ability to live above the law, and their tendency to go unpunished, but the rich and powerful often see it differently, as if they are the only ones in America who can be trusted.

Stewart Alsop and his brother Joseph were two of the most influential syndicated newspaper columnists in the United States from the 1930s to the 1970s. They were very rich cousins of Franklin Delano Roosevelt and were educated at the Groton prep school and Harvard. Stewart put it this way:

> I suspect that a great power needs an elite, a class of self-confident and more or less disinterested people who are accustomed to running things.

The Elite and "Corporatism"

If there is another term of office ahead for George W, and possibly one or two terms for his brother Jeb, the Bush Gang will wear out a lot of White House furniture and entrench a plutocratic power-base that will be very difficult to dislodge.

Not all who serve the interests of the wealthy have to have four generations of inherited wealth behind them, nor do they have to be rich themselves. There is plenty of room for talented nouveau rich and ambitious middle-class politicos because most truly rich people have very little interest in politics, except when they write generous checks to the party that will do the most to keep their taxes down. G. William Domhoff, the nation's foremost expert on the "power elite," once concluded that wealthy campaign donors "spent far more on their dogs and horses than they did on politics."[14] George W. Bush has gone outside the ranks of the old Establishment rich to find operatives who have cultivated political skills and ideas that serve the corporate class; some of them are more interested in ideological power than money, but others appreciate both. Often he brought them into his administration the same way he arrived, through the binding ties of nepotism and heredity.

Consequently, in the first two years of the Bush II administration, jobs were found for children from families who had used their long-term government association with the military/industrial complex to climb into the ranks of the very rich. Dick and Lynn Cheney's daughter, Elizabeth, was given a new desk in the State Department as Deputy Assistant Secretary of State and her husband was named chief counsel of the Office of Management and Budget where he was busy at work finding ways for the Bush Gang to renege on their obligations to federal workers. Michael Powell, son of Secretary of State Colin Powell, was quickly chosen to head up the Federal Communications Commission, where he is a friend to every corporate merger and an enemy to regulations that would hamper the monopolization of the media.

In addition there was room for kids from not-as-rich families as long they were committed to right-wing policies. Janet Rehnquist, daughter of the Chief Justice of the Supreme Court, was appointed inspector general within the Health and Human Services Department. As the chief attorney there, she immediately started favoring the industries that she was supposed to keep an eye on. According to syndicated columnist Molly Ivins, Rehnquist was one of "the weasels sneaking into the henhouse." She "quickly put her stamp on the office, easing anti-fraud measures and instead emphasizing voluntary compliance. She scaled back the use of 'corporate integrity agreements' in which health-care companies found to have defrauded the government acquiesce to strict reporting conditions, saying she was 'concerned about [their] financial impact on providers.'"[15]

Rehnquist's predecessor at Health and Human Services, June Gibbs Brown, said these changes had "weakened the system... It's really giving in to industry." In the 15 months after she took office, Attorney Rehnquist carried out a wholesale purge of her department, the largest of the 57 inspector general offices within the federal government. Nineteen career officials, including five of the six deputies in the department, were either removed through retirement, forced to resign or transfer.[16]

Eugene Scalia, son of Antonin, Bush's favorite ultra-conservative justice on the Supreme Court, was chosen as the top lawyer in the Labor Department because he has such a splendid anti-labor record. Senator Edward Kennedy, who opposed the appointment, noted that "Mr. Scalia is well-known for his long-standing opposition to workers' rights and protections."

The intensely pro-corporate ideas of the

Rehnquist, Scalia, and Cheney families were not born in Skull and Bones. They were fostered by the growing influence of right-wing think tanks and university programs, then pushed to prominence by ultra-conservative media companies such as those of Rupert Murdoch. Corporate and upper-class dominance of the major media is nothing new, nor is its preference for right wing views. Henry Luce, another alumnus of Skull and Bones at Yale, was the owner of the dominant American magazine empire in the first half of the 20th century—he published *Time*, *Life*, and *Fortune*—and he was also an enthusiastic backer of fascism. In 1934, he spoke to the Chamber of Commerce of Scranton, Pennsylvania and told them, "The moral force of fascism, appearing in totally different forms in different nations, may be the inspiration for the next general march of mankind."

Does this mean Luce and his buddies from Skull and Bones were all fascists? Not exactly. Nor was Prescott Bush necessarily a Nazi just because he worked closely with the industrialists who bankrolled the Nazi movement. There are no pictures of Henry Luce and Prescott Bush goose-stepping in Mussolini black shirts or Hitler brown shirts. Since World War II the word "fascist" has degenerated into an insult that is vastly overused, and perhaps best avoided when describing contemporary right-wing movements. But back in the 1930s Luce was clearly sympathetic to fascism and his words are pertinent because they suggest how this powerful social and ideological movement was helped along by support from the corporate upper class. Ever since corporations began to display clear dominance in American society a century and a half ago, the institutions of the corporate elite have repeatedly given a voice to those who jus-

tified the monopolization of wealth and power, and frequently backed an agenda with authoritarian and anti-democratic overtones.

The support for Social Darwinism and eugenics was in part a loony diversion for upper class academics, but it was by no means harmless. Since these ideas masqueraded as social and political science, they were used to infuse elite students with a sense of their superiority. They gave legitimacy to racist ideas that were already present in the United States and were later used to justify the most horrible crimes against humanity in Europe.

The Skull and Bones club, which served as an important transmitter of both capital and upper class mores, was implicated in all this. Irving Fisher, the leading Yale economist and eugenicist cited at the beginning of the chapter, was also a member of Skull and Bones, class of 1888. Averell Harriman's mother bankrolled his influential group, the American Eugenics Society. And Fisher's close friend, Madison Grant, who graduated from Yale the year before he did, became a wealthy New York City lawyer and a leader in the eugenics movement. His 1916 book, *The Passing of the Great Race: The Racial Basis of European History*[17], was an outright appeal to white, Aryan ideals and was widely read in the U.S. and abroad. After the book was translated into German in 1925, Grant received a fan letter from a German reader. "The book is my Bible," wrote Adolf Hitler.[18]

In his latest version of *Who Rules America*, G. William Domhoff describes the people who congregate in the institutions that serve both "the corporate community and the upper class." Organizations such as Skull and Bones not only serve as practical ways for the rich to associate with each other, but they also prepare them psychologically to wield power in a very non-egalitarian society. "Involvement in these institutions," writes Domhoff, "usually instills a class awareness that includes feelings of superiority, pride, and justified privilege. Deep down, most members of the upper class think they are better than other people, and therefore fully deserving of their station in life."[19]

With their great funds of money and their influence over elite educational institutions, the corporate upper class is uniquely situated to control events at the highest levels of business and government. The relation of this class and the Bush family to the right-wing authoritarianism of the early 20th century has largely been forgotten. But since American citizens of the early 21st century must now listen to a conservative/authoritarian message coming from the Bush Gang, from apologists for the military-industrial complex, and from the screaming commentators on right-wing talk-radio and talk-TV, there is the temptation to give a name to this phenomenon. Mussolini himself came up with the perfect word, "corporatism," which meant a fusion of government/business control at the highest levels of society. "Fascism," he said, "should more properly be called corporatism, since it is the merger of state and corporate power."

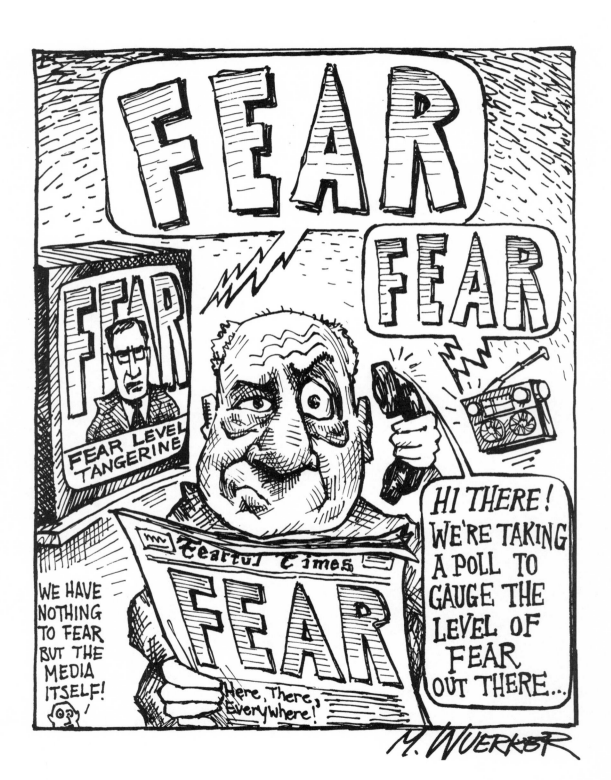

Fifteen

Murdocracy in America

Big Money, Big Media, Very Little Democracy

...private capitalists inevitably control, directly or indirectly, the main sources of information (press, radio, education). It is thus extremely difficult and in most cases quite impossible, for the individual citizen to come to objective conclusions.

—Albert Einstein, 1949[1]

There is only one thing in this world, and that is to keep acquiring money and more money, power and more power. All the rest is meaningless.

—Napoleon Bonaparte

George W. Bush's cousin, John Ellis, has been his close friend since childhood. He was hired by Fox News to be a head honcho on their "Decision Desk," sitting at the center of election night coverage in November 2000. During the broadcast he periodically took a break from his desk and telephoned George W and Jeb Bush about the progress of the vote counting. He made his fifth call at 2 a.m. and told his cousins, "Our projection shows that it is statistically impossible for Gore to win Florida." He then returned to his desk and made "The Decision" at 2:16 a.m. He went on the air and named his cousin "the winner." Ellis later bragged to a reporter, Jane Mayer of *The New Yorker*, "It was just the three of us guys handing the phone back and forth—me

with the numbers, one of them a governor, the other the president-elect. Now, that was cool."[2]

Ellis was the first television announcer to declare George W. Bush the winner of the presidency. Then all the other networks followed suit. Even though the victory declarations at Fox and every other network were later rescinded, many television viewers were left with the impression that having a recount in Florida was unfair to Bush. How could the vote be determined to be too close to call? Hadn't Bush already been declared "Winner in Florida?"

Some time later Ellis admitted, "I am loyal to my cousin.... I put that loyalty ahead of my loyalty to anyone else."

This explains why John Ellis called the election for the Bush Gang. But the real question is: Why was Fox able to install Ellis as the man in charge of election night reporting—manning the main desk just like Dan Rather at CBS—without revealing to the public that he was the cousin and very close friend of one of the candidates? John Ellis had not been signed on to give occasional right-wing opinions, nor to give political commentary as a family friend—in short, he was hired to report the news. Why didn't the other news media scream to high heaven before, during, and after the election night broadcasts? And who placed Ellis in that position on TV and how could they get away with it?

The puzzle fits together quickly. Ellis had been hired on a 30-day contract and worked for Roger Ailes, the director of Fox News and Republican media genius who brought Richard Nixon back into politics in 1968. Ailes was responsible for revving up the campaign of George Bush I in 1988, and later produced the Rush Limbaugh radio show for a while. Ailes was at Fox News because Rupert Murdoch, the Australian-born, multi-billionaire media baron, asked him to run the network.

Fox News is but one part of Murdoch's world-wide empire, which began when he inherited his father's newpapers in Australia. There he controls more than 60% of the country's metro, regional, and suburban press, which range from a sophisticated national paper, *The Australian*, to mass-market daily tabloids. The pattern of Murdoch's scheme for global conquest under the flag of the News Limited, or the News Corporation, became apparent when he went to Great Britain. In the 1970s and '80s he accumulated 40% of the English newspaper readership. According to Russ Baker of the Columbia School of Journalism, "During the regimes of Prime Ministers Margaret Thatcher and John Major in Britain, Murdoch ventures—especially his purchase of newspapers and the launch of his BskyB service—were repeatedly favored with easing of regulations and with government

failure to invoke monopoly oversight. Murdoch's papers, in turn, played a central role in bolstering Thatcher's career and virulently attacked her opponents."[3]

Murdoch finished circumnavigating the English-speaking world by landing in the United States, where he later assumed American citizenship. He took over print media such as HarperCollins publishers, *TV Guide*, *The New York Post*, and *The Weekly Standard*, as well as 20th Century Fox films. Most of his money and energy, however, went into buying and expanding his American and international TV holdings.

Murdoch has corporate subsidiaries in over 50 countries, but his primary interest has been in dominating the press, TV, and politics of the Anglo-American world. His political preferences are right-wing, even ultra-conservative. Murdoch "is far more right-wing than is generally thought," according to Andrew Neil, who used to edit Murdoch's *London Sunday Times*. "In the 1988 American presidential election his favorite for the Republican nomination was Pat Robertson," Neil wrote in his book *Full Disclosure*. "Dole is far too moderate a conservative for his tastes."[4]

While Murdoch was living in Britain, he was the major backer of Margaret Thatcher's Conservative government, and then gave her a $5.4 million book contract when she left office. Once settled in the U.S., Murdoch became one of the biggest contributors to the Republican Party, giving them about $1 million in 1996. The year before, while he was trying to get Congress to deregulate media laws that restricted his business expansion, he needed the help of Republican House speaker Newt Gingrich. He offered Gingrich a $4.5 million advance for his book, *To Renew America*. The Speaker was ready to accept, but the House Ethics Committee forced him to give up the contract because it was such a blatant conflict of interest.

Rupert Murdoch is not averse to political flexibility, however, when it serves his business interests. His newspapers have tended to be quite tolerant of China, sometimes publishing very favorable articles, especially at those times when his companies were negotiating for major access to the Chinese television market, the largest in the world. To sweeten the deals, he arranged for HarperCollins, his big publishing house, to print a book by Deng "Maomao" Rong, the daughter of the Chinese leader Deng Xiaoping. The advance, for a volume *The New Yorker* called "a turgid, barely literate piece of propaganda," was rumored to be $1 million.

Murdoch has also sided with Labor Party governments in Australia and Britain when he thought he could push them rightward on a range of issues. This was the case with Tony Blair, who traveled to Australia to confer with Murdoch and gain his favor before his first election as Prime Minister. The rightward shift of liberals and labor parties has suited two of Murdoch's business objectives, namely to ease controls over monopoly ownership and to lower corporate taxes.

Murdoch's giant umbrella corporation, the News Corporation, has been a real pioneer in international tax evasion and the invention of new tax havens. It has woven a web of more than 800 subsidiaries which continually transfers profits from different operations in different countries until they find the safest—that is, tax free or nearly tax free—home. *The Economist* reported in 1999 that "The most profitable of News Corporation's British operations in the 1990s was ... News Publishers, a company incorporated in Bermuda. News Publishers has, in

the seven years to June 30th 1996, made around £1.6 billion in net profits. This is a remarkable feat for a company that seems not to have any employees, nor any obvious source of income from outside Mr. Murdoch's companies."[5]

While the Bermuda angle is a great scam for Murdoch, just as it is for U.S. multinational firms, there was a better place for Murdoch to set up shop. As far as the interests of the News Corporation are concerned, it had to be a country where rampant deregulation and a favorable tax atmosphere allowed corporations to overwhelm democracy in a big way. Murdoch decided that the United States fit the bill, especially once the first Bush Gang let the deregulators loose and opened up the country for merger mania in the 1980s.

In 1981, forty six corporations controlled most of the book, magazine, newspaper, movie, and television industries in the United States. By 1986, this number had shrunk to twenty nine, and by 1989 to twenty five. Then, in the early 1990s, the process of conglomeration in the media was so rapid that one could scarcely follow the players. Disney bought ABC, Viacom took over bought CBS, and General Electric grabbed NBC. Murdoch kept expanding on his global base, while Time Warner not only controlled magazines, movies, and books, but took over Turner Broadcasting, CNN, a wide swath of the cable TV distribution network, and finally merged with AOL.

Five huge players—Viacom, Disney, News Corp, GE/NBC, and AOL/Time Warner—now dominate a wide range of information, broadcasting, and entertainment industries. Two widespread newspapers chains—Gannett and Knight Ridder—have hundreds of city presses under their control, while Newhouse Publishing, Bertelsmann, and Filipacchi have taken over more and more of the book and mag-azine market. Similar consolidation of local radio and television stations has taken place, too, and there seems to be no stopping the trend. Clear Channel, controlled by Bush's close allies in Texas, now owns over 1,200 radio stations throughout the U.S. It dedicated itself to pro-war cheerleading (and banning play time for the Dixie Chicks) once Bush began the war on Iraq.

Michael Powell, the lawyer son of Colin Powell, was appointed head of the Federal Communications Commission by Bush and gave every indication he wanted to speed up the process of media mergers rather than slow them down. What others saw as monopolization, he saw as the operation of the free market—big fish will swallow up small fish. (In 2000, when Michael was a member of the FCC, but had not yet been made chairman, he voted to approve the merger of AOL/Time Warner. He was criti-cized for not recusing himself from the decision because his father, a board member at AOL, held options for $13.3 million worth of AOL stock before the merger.) The younger Powell was not at all worried about a few huge corpora-tions dominating the media business or oppress-ing the public. "The oppressor here is regula-tion," Powell was quoted the day after he took over the chairmanship of the FCC.[6] In June of 2003 the FCC tried to open the way for even more concentrated ownership by the biggest media companies.

As Murdoch and the other oligarchs relentlessly extinguish the free press and media, American people are increasingly the object of a steady barrage of news that tends to justify whatever the government is doing. During the War on Terrorism coverage that built up the Middle Eastern war with Iraq, the TV networks and Bush Gang worked closely to bombard the public with many reports that could only gener-ously be labeled news and more accurately should be called military propaganda. Actual reporter-on-the-scene coverage of warfare in Afghanistan was limited by the U.S. Armed Forces, just as it had been in the Gulf War of 1990-91. Many hours of each day's telecasts were filled with what seemed like Army, Navy, and Air Force recruitment films, with planes landing and taking off from aircraft carriers and airstrips. Generals and colonels continually paraded before the cameras to tout a new weapon program or point at a map, as did grow-ing legions of "terror experts" and military ana-lysts, a disturbing proportion of whom came from right-wing think tanks.

As war news degenerated into cheerleading for war, there was an especially close working relationship between Fox TV operatives, the ultra-right representatives of the Bush adminis-tration, and ultra-right political experts that were drawn in from think tanks and periodicals sponsored by the likes of Murdoch. Rarely has such a tight circle of influence with such an intense and open political agenda—pro-War, pro-Israeli, anti-Muslim, and pro-Anglo-American Empire—been seen on American tel-evision. When the Fox anchor people invited guests of other political persuasions—liberal, left-wing, Middle Eastern, etcetera—their modus operandi was either to scream at the guests unmercifully or to help a second guest do the haranguing. This is the only network news that must keep telling the viewer—"Fair and balanced coverage"—because just the opposite is true. This is right-wing tabloid TV.

Neo-Conservatives and the Fox/Bush Connection

Rupert Murdoch did not directly choose George W. Bush to be President of the United States. In fact, he was astute enough to let some of his newspaper editors in Australia go their own way and praise Al Gore during the campaign—for Murdoch clearly wanted to leave the door open to do business with Gore if he were elected.

On the other hand, Murdoch had been cultivating the right-wing public advocacy apparatus that helped Bush at election time and afterwards. The most stunning example of this is the neo-conservative, or neo-con, axis that runs directly through the White House, Murdoch's Fox TV, his *The Weekly Standard* political journal, the American Enterprise Institute, and other conservative foundations.

The neo-conservatives are a small group of highly active political operatives—William Kristol, John Podhoretz, and Fred Barnes are three directly employed by Murdoch—who want U.S. conservatism to be an activist agent for international change. They are not too concerned with lowering taxes or keeping government out of the average citizen's life, which are two of the more standard conservative values, but are very interested in promoting conservative Judeo-Christian values and American style capitalism around the world. They see activist government as a plus, but are not so interested in the traditional government activism of the liberals. The neo-conservatives are the most aggressive practitioners of a long-standing American policy: fusing the strength of the U.S. government with American economic culture to overwhelm other nations, then requiring them to play by our free-trade capitalist rules

and abandon their other economic and social priorities.

A key intellectual reference point to the neo-conservative thrust within the Bush administration is *The Weekly Standard*, a small, sprightly journal of political advocacy run by William Kristol, who was chief of staff for Dan Quayle during the Bush I years. *The Weekly Standard* was founded in 1995 by Rupert Murdoch for the express purpose of developing a new, more aggressive conservative voice. The editorialists and writers maintain very close relationships with the White House, *The Wall Street Journal*, *The National Review*, the Heritage Foundation, the American Enterprise Institute, and other conservative foundations. Often *The Weekly Standard* will produce an essay or editorial about a proposed government course of action, only to have it followed up by a policy statement at the White House or a longer, expository article in *The Wall Street Journal*. This is especially true of foreign policy issues.

For example, *The Weekly Standard*, at the very same time it was virulently attacking President Clinton about his sex life, was relentlessly prodding him to attack Iraq. With help from various scholarly-looking representatives from the right-wing think tanks, they kept a myth alive for the last five years of the Clinton presidency and into the 21st century—they insisted that there was a madman in the Middle East, Saddam Hussein, who was intent on destroying the United States. They linked the threat of the "Demon Iraq" neatly to the need to support Israel. They said that Israel was entitled to deal very harshly with the Palestinians, who, according to the editors, did not necessarily deserve their own land and nation. This new Israeli aggressiveness would require a similar display of determined force by the United States according to the neo-cons. The logical course of action then, was for the United States to arm itself sufficiently to assume its rightful place at the top of a new imperial order. In the neo-con view of the world, American hegemony would be benign, but wielded with a stern hand, and would assure that world oil supplies were stable and world markets open for business.

Neo-conservatives are so expansionist that they believe the government and the military can be hyper-aggressive agents of promoting American power all over the world, but especially in the Middle East. Godfather of the movement, Norman Podhoretz, wrote in the September 2002 issue of his journal *Commentary* that the list of the regimes "that richly deserve to be overthrown and replaced should extend to Syria and Lebanon and Libya... the Saudi royal family and Egypt's Hosni Mubarak, along with the Palestinian Authority....provided that the United States has the will to fight World War IV, 'the war against militant Islam' to a successful conclusion, and provided too, that we then have the stomach to impose a new political culture on the defeated parties." (Norman is the father of John Podhoretz, who was editor of *The Weekly Standard* before Murdoch moved him to the position of editorial page editor at *The New York Post*.)

Murdoch's band of neo-cons developed some of the highest profiles of anyone in the media business because they had the distribution power of the mighty News Corporation behind them. In the 1990s Fox News became a favorite of right-wing heavyweights on Capitol Hill because it linked *The Weekly Standard* with the ultra-conservative publications such as *The Wall Street Journal*, *The National Review*, *Commentary*, and *The Washington Times*. Among

themselves, Rush Limbaugh, and a never ending stream of conservative pundits who appeared on the screen and on the printed page, they helped the right wing of the Republican Party attain a dominant public voice that it used to harass the Clintons unmercifully while simultaneously pushing the Democratic polity to the center-right.

Plutocracy Supports Murdocracy—Breeding and Bribing the Intellectuals

Who needs a vast right-wing conspiracy when you've got a vast right-wing network?

So wrote columnist Eric Boehlert of *Salon* in November 2000, as he deftly pointed a finger at the Murdoch network's use of John Ellis on election night. He was making a good point: why should the right wing do its dirty work in secret if the Fox network can do it more effectively in public.

There is, however, a much larger issue, and a much larger network that lies behind Murdoch's astute positioning in the media markets. His methods would not work nearly so well in the United States, which is so much bigger than the British and Australian markets that he previously dominated, without the vast web of right wing institutions that were already functioning when he decided to move to the U.S. and become an American citizen. Rich, ultra-conservative gentlemen like Murdoch have financed this collection of think tanks, university programs, and policy foundations for thirty years. They supply the intellectual voices that not only shout at the public on Fox TV, but also get plenty of time to quietly persuade the more moderate viewers of PBS and parade experts onto news programming at ABC, CBS, and NBC.

The formation of a vast and relatively open right-wing network began with a few very rich, ultra-conservative families in the 1950s. For instance, William F. Buckley, a Skull and Bones member at Yale in the 1940s, was so upset that left-leaning professors were allowed to teach there that he used the family oil fortune to found *The National Review*, the granddaddy of the ultra-right publications. Out in Indiana, Dan Quayle's grandfather, the billionaire Eugene C. Pulliam, built a right-wing newspaper empire centered in Indianapolis, then extended it to Arizona where he became an early backer of Barry Goldwater in the 1950s. At the time, however, these efforts did not generate widespread support for right-wing causes among the business community. This meant that "true believers," such as Dan Quayle's father, Jim, had to operate on the radical-right fringe in groups such as the John Birch Society.

A key moment for the ascendancy of much broader right-wing influence came in the 1970s. Big business was becoming quite disgruntled with the political behavior of the American public, and a Republican president was frustrated with the amount of public dissent that assailed him because of his conduct of the Vietnam War. In 1971, shortly before he was appointed to the U.S. Supreme Court by Richard Nixon, Lewis Powell wrote an article for the U.S. Chamber of Commerce entitled "Attack on the American Free Enterprise System." The Chamber stamped it with the label "Powell Memorandum" and circulated it with their newsletter/magazine, *Washington Report*, which they sent out to influential leaders in business and politics. Powell warned that the country was being infected with an anti-corporate, anti-American mood, and that big business was being criticized by a variety of "perfectly responsible elements of society who shaped opinion: from the college campus, the pulpit, the media, the intellectual community." Powell urged the business world "to stop suffering in impotent silence, and launch a counterattack" so that it could persuade the public of the value of the "free enterprise system."[7]

The "Powell Memorandum" succeeded in getting immediate results. Joseph Coors, ultra-right scion of the Coors Brewing Company, reported that he was "stirred up," and "convinced" that he and other leaders of corporate America had been "ignoring a crisis." Determined to fix the situation, he joined with Richard Mellon Scaife, the ultra-conservative heir of the Mellon clan, to fund the 1971-1972 start-up of the Analysis and Research Association in Washington, DC. This organization soon became the most influential of the right-wing think tanks and renamed itself the Heritage Foundation.[8] The Heritage Foundation differs from other non-profit, public policy foundations because it spends a larger portion of its budget, about 60 percent, on putting out an explicitly political message. According to *The Wall Street Journal*, the Heritage Foundation, "more than other think tanks, has extended its political influence by spending more money on raising funds and promoting its thoughts than on researching them."[9]

The Heritage Foundation has been joined by a raft of far-right vehicles designed to change public opinion, such as the American Enterprise Institute, the Cato Institute, the Hudson Institute, and the Manhattan Institute. They distinguish themselves from older, middle-of-the-road foundations, such as Ford and

Rockefeller, which are certainly not anti-business, by devoting a large proportion of their funds to openly conservative political causes. All are very well-funded by corporate money and big fortunes that favor ultra-right politics, such as the Sarah Mellon Scaife Foundation, the Smith Richardson Foundation, the Coors' Castle Rock Foundation, the Olin Foundation, and the J. Howard Pew Freedom Trust. The right-wing think tanks have been fantastically successful, for by the year 2000 their spokespeople were be found everywhere on television news and opinion shows, proudly holding forth and dominating coverage as the designated experts on almost any topic.

Occasionally conservative foundations have supported new Social Darwinist research such as Charles Murray's influential book, *The Bell Curve* (lavishly funded by the Bradley Foundation and the Pioneer Fund). In this way they were emulating the race research funded by the old Robber Barons and Skull and Bones crowd a century earlier, when they were infatuated with eugenics and the good breeding techniques required to reproduce the upper class. But mostly they steered clear of the old racist claims to power, and instead chose to support new fields such as "Law and Economics". According to political and economic analyst Robert Kuttner, "these ideas are reinforcing of the laissez faire ideal and thus very congenial to society's most powerful."[10]

The Olin Foundation, in particular, distinguishes itself by funding academic programs in "law and economics", thus following the advice that Justice Powell gave in his memorandum to the Chamber of Commerce in the early 1970s— "buy the top academic reputations of the country to add credibility to corporate studies and give business a stronger voice on the campus."[11]

Olin Foundation money has flowed to the best universities, in particular to fund programs in "Law and Economics" at places such as Harvard, Yale, Stanford, Chicago, Duke, MIT, Penn, and the University of Virginia, where they are "intended to strengthen the economic, political, and cultural institutions upon which ... private enterprise is based." The core values of Law and Economics reduce all human activity to the pursuit of individual self-interest in the marketplace, so that the law itself adheres to market and corporate values.

Because the Olin Foundation was interested in promoting more depth in political scholarship than the other conservative think tanks, it heavily backed significant conservatives in other academic programs, too—for example, in the humanities, Allan Bloom at the University of Chicago; and in politics and government, Samuel Huntington at Harvard. Huntington, who was a graduate school classmate of Henry Kissinger's and a fellow instructor with Zbigniew Brzezinski at Harvard in the early 1950s, shared with them an appreciation for the ways nations can gain hegemony through the exertion of military and diplomatic power. He was later picked to serve on the elite policy group, the Trilateral Commission, for whom he wrote one of his most famous comments in the 1970s: "Some of the problems of governance in the United States stem from an excess of democracy... needed instead is a greater degree of moderation in democracy." The problem was that Huntington's ideal of "moderation" was not democratic at all. "Truman," he wrote, "had been able to govern the country with the cooperation of a relatively small number of Wall Street lawyers and bankers."[12] Always one with an ear for how the powerful wanted to exert their power, he anticipated the conflict between the United States and Islamic countries in his 1990s book, *The Clash of Civilizations*, and cautioned the U.S. not to trust in conciliation and peaceful co-existence with these potential enemies.

Another major player on the far right is the American Enterprise Institute (AEI), which was a small, obscure policy institution until it was launched into prominence at the Pentagon during the Vietnam War. President Nixon's Secretary of Defense, Melvin Laird, decided AEI's conservative opinions could be helpful to the administration, so he hosted a $25 million fund-raising dinner for the organization in his private Pentagon dining room in 1971. The AEI was off and running, so that by 1980 its annual budget was higher than the moderate and centrist think-tank, The Brookings Institution, which had previously dominated Washington policy studies. Besides defending the Vietnam War and an aggressive American foreign policy, AEI backed corporations who were fighting government regulatory agencies and organized labor.

By 1981, when Reagan/Bush took office, several hundred corporations were contributing 40 percent of AEI's budget. John B. Judis, in his book, *The Paradox of American Democracy*, points out that top CEOs were recruited to fund-raising posts, "including Walter Wriston of Citibank, Willard Butcher of Chase Manhattan, David Packard of Hewlett-Packard, Thomas Murphy of General Motors, and Reginald Jones of General Electric." A host of foundations connected to rich conservative families also contributed mightily because, like the corporations, they felt it was necessary to inculcate a fresh view of the world in the American people. According to Judis, "This version of reality pivoted on a simple formula: government rather than business was responsible for America's ills—from inflation and high energy prices to the slowdown in growth and the rise in unemployment."[13]

The American people had come through the Vietnam War and the Watergate scandals with a deep distrust of the motives of American foreign policy and American business. Because the right-wing foundations endeavored to change these perceptions, they gradually won the trust of business leaders. The corporate executives had organized themselves, too, with encouragement from the Nixon White House in 1972, into a very powerful group, The Business Roundtable. The Roundtable had its origins in the "Construction Users Anti-Inflation Roundtable," a corporate group that was trying to lower construction costs by eliminating construction unions and forcing down the wages of skilled craftsmen. It turned into a lobbying group for 200 of the largest American corporations when the chairmen of GE and Alcoa met with Nixon's Treasury Secretary John Connally, his deputy Charls Walker, and Federal Reserve Board Chairman Arthur Burns to discuss a much larger business counteroffensive.

The government men urged the executives to bypass lesser powers, such as the broad-based Chamber of Commerce and the fragmented business and industry associations, and address their concerns directly to Washington. The idea was for big business CEOs to become powerful policy spokesmen themselves, appearing in person to tell Washington what they wanted. The stated purpose of the Business Roundtable was that "chief executives of major corporations should take an increased role in the continuing debates about public policy."[14] In December of 2002, when George W. Bush and the rest of the gang became exasperated with Secretary of Treasury Paul O'Neill because of his opposition to some of the proposed tax cuts, they replaced him with John Snow, the CEO of CSX Corporation. Snow had acted as chairman of The Business Roundtable in 1996 and 1997.

21st Century America—the Convergence of Murdocracy, Plutocracy, and the Aristocracy of Business

The reason that Rupert Murdoch and his News Corp could step so boldly into the middle of the American scene, then let George W. Bush's cousin brazenly announce a Bush victory in 2000, was that the media mogul arrived at the right time. Oligarchy reigned. Monopolies of power and wealth had taken over politics, the media, the most influential of the think-tanks, and other rapidly merging sectors of corporate business.

Most of these entities had become deeply ingrained with right-wing political thinking during the last quarter of the 20th century. Circumstances created by the Bush Gang favored Murdoch's success in America; but, as already noted, Murdoch began his ascent in similar circumstances in Britain and Australia, so is representative of a global trend in monopolization that can jump from country to country. When combined with right-wing politics and television ownership, this trend has created other anti-democratic "Murdochs" in other languages. Silvio Berlusconi of Italy, with his ownership of the major private television networks and his control of public television through his position as Italian prime minister, is

the extreme example. Gustavo Cisneros, said to be the richest man in South America, controls much of the television media in Venezuela plus the giant, multinational Spanish speaking TV network, Univision, that has become a major media outlet in the United States and most of Latin America. Cisneros is an old friend of George Bush, Senior, and has been an enthusiastic backer of the right-wing coup efforts against President Chávez in Venezuela.[15]

Consolidated corporate power and media dominance are overwhelming democracy. Nearly 170 years ago, Alexis de Tocqueville predicted that the major threat to democracy might well come through the fledgling industrial system being organized by capital. If this system kept growing, he feared that new authoritarian conglomerations of power and wealth would be capable wiping out the equality and liberty enjoyed by the American people.

> The manufacturing aristocracy which is growing up before our eyes is one of the harshest that ever existed in the world....If ever a permanent inequality of conditions and aristocracy again penetrate the world, it may be predicted that this is the gate by which they will enter.

The harsh aristocracy of the early 21st century is ruled by hierarchical, anti-democratic corporations that control transnational manufacturing and much more—worldwide finance, services, and, through the major media, the kinds of news and information that are available to most people. This new aristocracy is more powerful and wide-ranging than anything de Tocqueville could have imagined, and it is definitely intent on replacing democracy.

If the Bush Gang's consolidation of power

facilitates the final formation of a plutocracy of giant corporations and multi-billionaires, this will be a congenial outcome for Rupert Murdoch and the other media barons. Their stranglehold on information and public expression represents the deathknell of the free press, the institution that de Tocqueville felt was most central to the democratic experience. On his visit to America in the 1830s, he was struck by the proliferation of newspapers, published in every town and city by individuals and small groups with distinct voices. In *Democracy in America*, he wrote:

> The more I consider the independence of the press in its principal consequences, the more am I convinced that in the modern world it is the chief, and, so to speak, the constitutive element of liberty.

Sixteen

International Thuggery

The Resurrection of the Bush Sub-Gang

We will export death and violence to the four corners of the Earth in defense of
our great nation.

—George W. Bush, 2001[1]

Only one nation has ever been found guilty of terrorism by the International Court of Justice—the United States in 1986. Some of the men who ran this secret terror operation—North, Abrams, and Poindexter—were convicted of lying to Congress about their activities.

Two of the above were invited to rejoin the rejuvenated Bush Gang in Washington in 2001, along with two other men—Negroponte and Reich—who helped them plan their past terroristic activities. The third criminal, Oliver North, was too busy with his Fox TV show, "War Stories," to rejoin the others.

In 1986, the Reagan administration disregarded international law and ignored the order from the International Court of Justice, part of the World Court in The Hague, Netherlands, to desist from its hostile activities. The U.S. continued sponsoring, training, and supplying arms to the Contras, the army it had created to carry out illegal attacks on the nation of Nicaragua. Several years earlier the Nicaraguan people had launched a left-leaning, democratic revolution and freed themselves from the long, brutal, dictatorship of the Somoza family. The United States government had supported the Somozas for decades, just as it had backed a string of right-wing dictatorships throughout Central America, the Caribbean, and Latin America.

The Reagan administration also disregarded the laws of the United States of America, in particular those that the U.S. Congress had passed earlier in the 1980s forbidding U.S. assistance to the Contra forces. Nicaragua, a poor nation with only three million people, was badly hurt by the repeated terrorist acts—its main harbor was mined to discourage civilian shipping, its medical personnel were massacred at rural clinics, and its citizens were tortured and murdered by the U.S. sponsored terrorists.

When Oliver North, Elliot Abrams, and John Poindexter—all operatives in the President's National Security clique—were called before Congressional Committees, they lied about their involvement in the subterfuge in Nicaragua. Their crazy plot involved selling arms illegally to the mullahs of Iran so that they could raise secret funds to buy weapons for the Contras. As their activities were gradually uncovered, President Reagan denied all knowledge. This may have been true, for during his second term the President was sleeping through many meetings and not always attentive when he was awake.

The Vice-President, Bush I, claimed he was "out of the loop," too, and denied any involvement. But this was much more difficult to believe, since he was not getting senile and had been in regular contact with all of the perpetrators. Much later, long after his underlings were convicted, then freed, George H.W. Bush's diary entry concerning Iran/Contra became public. The entry for November 5, 1986 read: "I'm one of the few people that know fully the details.... This is one operation that has been held very, very tight, and I hope it will not leak."[2]

George Bush I, the only president of the United States who was ever the Director of the Central Intelligence Agency, has continued to keep his involvement in the Iran/Contra operation secret. Clearly he and his henchmen, the first Bush Gang, had been in control of much of the nation's foreign policy ever since Bush assumed leadership of the White House Special Situation Group in March of 1981. But whether he was the mastermind of Iran/Contra or merely was giving the go-ahead signal from the periphery, the whole episode became an extreme embarrassment to the United States. First of all, it was a very clumsy affair. Secondly, it was a totally un-Constitutional breach of the legal powers invested in the national government, since the Reagan/Bush administration was not only waging a war by proxy without a Congressional declaration of war (something several other presidents had done), but was doing so after Congress explicitly told them to stop such activities. Finally, and most importantly, the United States was putting its com-

mitment to democracy abroad in a very bad light. In creating undemocratic subterfuge in the form of the Contras, the U.S. relied on the same Nicaraguan officers who had been brutal enforcers for the old Somoza dictatorship. This added to our growing reputation for supporting repressive, anti-democratic governments, particularly throughout Central America.

Our war against Nicaragua was accompanied by even worse bloodshed, tortures, and massacres in Guatemala and El Salvador. In those countries, right-wing militaries trained and armed by the United States, and sometimes assisted by the CIA, slaughtered many thousands of people in order to suppress popular rebellions. For these small nations the toll was very heavy: an estimated 70,000 killed in El Salvador, 20,000 dead in the contra war in Nicaragua, 200 "disappearances" in Honduras, 200,000 people eliminated in Guatemala, most of them in the indigenous villages in rural areas. The Historical Clarification Committee, which met in the 1990s to review the human rights crimes committed in Guatemala, catalogued "626 massacres against Mayan villages."[3]

The Reagan/Bush administration tried to claim it was backing the forces of democracy, but few believed this. One former Contra leader described their activities:

> It is a gross fabrication to claim that the contras are composed of democratic groups.... As I can attest, the 'contra' military force is directed and controlled by officers of Somoza's National Guard.... During my four years as a contra director, it was premeditated policy to terrorize civilian noncombatants to prevent them from cooperating with the Government. Hundreds of civilian murders, tortures and rapes were committed

in pursuit of this policy, of which the 'contra' leaders and their CIA superiors were well aware.

—Edgar Chamorro, former member of the directorate of the main contra organization, the Nicaraguan Democratic Force.[4]

The United States was not fighting terror in our hemisphere in the 1980s, it was the exponent and exporter of terror. The death and destruction in Central America was expedited by a small sub-gang of Bush operatives. It seems ironical in the extreme that these men, who were tarred and feathered with a fair amount of ignomy for their participation in this disgraceful chapter of American history, have been recalled to the center of power. Now they are being asked to help prosecute a war against terror. On the other hand, their recall can be seen as a sign of their rehabilitation.

For Abrams, Poindexter, Negroponte, and Reich, this return to power also constituted an endorsement of their past actions. As illegal as their actions were, they were effective in the end. The countries in Central America were subdued and pacified, and are not a source of irritation to the United States any longer. Their current governments are feeble attempts at democracy and their social structures and economies so shattered by war that they are worse off now, in Guatemala and Nicaragua especially, than they were before Bush Gang I began its intrigues twenty years ago. If this result is viewed as a success for U.S. foreign policy then the Middle East and other troubled parts of the world had better beware.

For some in the United States, the devastation of the Central American wars was always seen as a triumph. For them Iran/Contra was a heady mix of pure adventure, of secret operations by clandestine warriors who threaded their way between fanatical Muslims, sly communists, and the namby-pamby Congressmen who did not appreciate the exertions of real patriots. The insular world of right-wing Washington, combined with the geopolitical imperatives of manning military installations and gathering information in all parts of the world, has over many decades produced men who live and breathe a covert version of "manifest destiny." They feel committed to advancing U.S. power no matter what obstacles they may face. In order to get the "bad guys," they think, it may be necessary to tear up the fabric of democracy. For such people, Admiral John Poindexter, Elliot Abrams, and Lieutenant Colonel Oliver North were not misguided zealots, nor criminal soldiers, but true heroes who were not appreciated by their countrymen.

Poindexter told Congress why he never let Reagan know about the secret operations: "I made a very deliberate decision not to tell the president so that I could insulate him from the decision and provide some future deniability for the president if it ever leaked out." This meant that people other than the president had taken over U.S. foreign policy. And they were all loyal to George Bush I, whose diary had implicated him in the conspiracy and demonstrated that the Bush Gang truly was running the country during the Reagan/Bush era.

To the extent that North, Poindexter, and Abrams finally testified about their activities, it was to shield those above them. North's and Poindexter's convictions were later overturned on a technicality when it was ruled that their testimony to Congress, even though it revealed real criminal activity on their part, should not have been used to incriminate them because they had been granted immunity.

George Bush I pardoned Abrams and Casper Weinberger, the Secretary of Defense, when he left office in 1992. This ensured that Bush would not be called to testify and that Weinberger's notes concerning Bush's activities would not be read at a trial. Iran/Contra prosecutor Lawrence Walsh said that Weinberger's notes "contain evidence of a conspiracy among the highest-ranking Reagan administration officials to lie to Congress and American public," and thus he was "gravely concerned" about the Weinberger pardon "in light of President Bush's own misconduct." Ultimately, Walsh admitted, his investigation was foiled—"the Iran-Contra cover-up, which has continued for more than six years, has now been completed."[5]

The Bush Gang's Enforcers

Let me be clear here. Until this point, I have used the "Bush Gang" as an extended metaphor that is both convenient and fun, plus totally justified in the context of American political discourse. The "Bush Gang" is representative of the elite economic and political forces that are intentionally robbing most Americans of their income and wealth as well as the liberty and equality that are essential to a democracy. We are entitled to call them "criminals" in order to wake up the populace and motivate them to fight back. Since there is always a tendency for the aroused citizen to look for a short cut to understanding the economic, political, and social forces that empower such an elite, I have cautioned repeatedly in this book against looking for conspiracies. In the long run, it is much more productive to dig into the evidence that lies right out in the open, if we are going to mount a democratic counteroffensive.

However, the Bush Gang that operated in Central America and Washington in the 1980s and early 1990s was not a metaphorical construct. It was clearly conspiratorial and the gang members were convicted of felony crimes,

including conspiracy, or threatened with prosecution in order to elicit their testimony in the Iran/Contra case. Perhaps some future administration (but more likely intrepid reporters using the Freedom of Information Act) will dig into vast secret archives of the CIA, the NSA, and the Defense Department and learn more about the foreign crimes that are hidden from the citizens of our democracy because they are labeled "Secrets of State" or "National Security." The Bush II administration, of course does not want anyone to investigate. One of George W's first acts as president was to keep his father's papers, which were due to be released, locked away in secrecy. He claimed to be protecting "national security" rather than hiding the illegal operations of his Dad and his friends, not to mention the activities of the Gang's enforcers. Every gang needs muscle men and dirty tricksters as they expand their territory and set up protection rackets. The enforcers literally force new victims to toe the line, while reminding old victims why it is necessary to buckle under to gang rule.

The return of these criminal conspirators is extraordinary because they should have left public service in disgrace, never to return. The rehabilitation of the sub-Gang of Abrams, Poindexter, Reich, and Negroponte was a clear indication that the Bush Gang II was prepared to commit another set of outrages in foreign affairs. A brief review of the careers of these four returned alumni can shed light on the potential for trouble.

Elliot Abrams

In the Reagan and Bush I administrations, Elliot Abrams served as assistant secretary of state for human rights and humanitarian affairs and later as assistant secretary of state for inter-American affairs, supervising U.S. policy in

Latin America and the Caribbean. In that capacity he constantly covered up the realities of Iran/Contra, oversaw much of the conspiracy, and lied about it to the press and Congress. Jim Lobe, of Foreign Policy in Focus, writes that "he clashed frequently and angrily with mainstream church groups and human rights organizations, including Human Rights Watch and Amnesty International, who often accused him of covering up horrendous abuses committed by U.S.-backed governments."[6]

Journalist and film-maker Saul Landau reports that: "In his testimony to Congress, the scrappy Abrams made witness history when he declared: 'I never said I had no idea about most of the things you said I had no idea about.' The now 54 year old Abrams also explained in his autobiography that he had to inform his young children about the headline announcing his indictment, so he told them he had 'to lie to Congress to protect the national interest.'"[7] He did not tell Congress about the horrific massacre in El Mazote, El Salvador, that he covered up for the Reagan administration by denigrating the work of very accurate reporters.[8] Nor did he explain that U.S.-trained death squads had carried out 85% of the 22,000 "extra legal" killings in the country. Instead, Abrams defiantly told Congress how proud he was of the United States record in El Salvador: "The Administration's record on El Salvador is one of fabulous achievement."

During his forced absence from government, Abrams resided within the right-wing Ethics and Public Policy Center where he devoted a great deal of this energy to bolstering the arguments and political connections that kept elevating the right-wing, militarist agenda of Likud and its allies in Israel and the United States. Jim Lobe reported that "In *Present*

Dangers, a book produced by the Project for the New American Century (PNAC) in 2000, Abrams outlined a new U.S. Mideast policy that called for 'regime change' in Iraq and for cracking down on the Palestinian Authority. Foreshadowing the current U.S. policy based on superior military power, Abrams recommended that in the Middle East 'our military strength and willingness to use it' should be the 'key factor in our ability to promote peace.'"[9]

Elliot Abrams was rehired by Bush Gang II in 2001 as National Security Council senior director for democracy, human rights and international operations, and then, in the first week of December 2002, he was transferred within the NSC to the position of director of Middle Eastern affairs. Given his extremely aggressive posture in all his foreign policy dealings, this can be seen as a preparation for tenacious warfare, expediting the removal of Saddam Hussein in Iraq, threatening Syria and Iran, and reassuring Israel about its superior position vis a vis the Muslim countries that surround it.

Otto Reich

In the 1980s, Otto Reich was chief of a department in the State Department that was called the Office of Public Diplomacy and staffed with CIA and Pentagon "psychological warfare" specialists. The function of the operation was to fool the American public about the nature of the conflicts in Central America by disseminating false information, discrediting reporters whose work the Reagan administration did not like, and using other means of misleading propaganda. In short, the Office of Public Diplomacy was in the business of producing disinformation of the kind that is generally used to mislead an enemy during conventional warfare, except that during the unconventional and illegal Contra war it was being used to lie to journalists, Congressional committees, and the U.S. people. Reich "helped plant stories and opinion pieces praising the Contras in U.S. newspapers. It wasn't just the stories that were phony, so were the authors. Reich's office wrote them all."[10] Congress, once it uncovered the illegal operations of this office, closed it down and Otto Reich barely avoided indictment.

Otto Reich was sent off as Ambassador to Venezuela after the Contra war, where he was able to secure the release of the jailed Cuban-exile terrorist, Orlando Bosch. This man had been jailed for eleven years for his role in the worst instance of airline terrorism in the Western Hemisphere (up until September 11, 2001, that is). This was the bombing of a Cuban plane which killed all 73 civilians on board in 1976. The U.S. Justice Department had evidence of Bosch's involvement in more than 30 other terrorist acts, some of them committed within the United States, including a rocket attack on a Polish ship in Miami. With the help of Otto Reich and Jeb Bush, who was busy ingratiating himself with right-wing Cuban Americans in Florida, Bosch was pardoned by George Bush I in 1992.[11]

In 2001, Reich rejoined the Bush Gang by taking over the Latin American desk at the State Department for just one year. The Administration used a special loophole that allowed for his temporary appointment without getting the approval of the Senate. This was because many Senators, such as Senator Christopher Dodd of Connecticut, would have grilled him about his past activities and opposed his formal nomination. When the one year term expired, Reich was immediately appointed as a

special Latin American envoy to the National Security Agency, another post that does not require congressional approval. This allowed him to keep pursuing his major preoccupation, which was the same as Abrams'—to overthrow regimes and control oil. The only difference was that Reich was assigned to raid and plunder in the Western Hemisphere (not the Middle East), where he was overseeing the destabilization of the government of Venezuela, the biggest American oil producer. He was also seeking to oust President Chavez, the democratically elected leader who was detested by the Bush Gang for his obstinacy and independent thinking, particularly on the issue of using Venezuela's vast oil revenues. Chavez had stated that he wanted to use the country's oil wealth to serve and educate the poor, who form the vast majority of the country's population.

Reich regularly met with Chavez's upper-class opponents in Washington to contemplate strategies, one of which was a constant barrage of attacks from the Venezuela's press and television, almost all of which are controlled by a right-wing business oligarchy. A military coup was engineered by the oligarchy in April 2002 after repeated consultations with Washington, but it failed. Then, in December of 2002, a large scale petroleum strike was engineered by state oil company executives in concert with a commercial business shutdown planned by the oligarchs and the rest of the upper class. Both actions failed to dislodge President Chavez. As of the spring of 2003, the Venezuelan upper class had failed in their coup attempts. The plots that Reich had helped initiate were as ill-conceived as the Iran/Contra scandal and ended up as fiascos. The business shutdown in December hurt the middle class more than the poor, while the sabotage of the oil industry nearly wrecked the economy and cost the country many billions of dollars. The oil shutdown also helped push the price of oil sky-high as the U.S.A. and the world braced for war in the Middle East.

John Negroponte

John Negroponte was never pursued by Congress for his old role as the ambassador to Honduras in the 1980s, even though he was one of those responsible for coordinating aid to the Nicaraguan Contras and holding together the dictatorship of an assortment of Honduran generals. Although the level of brutality toward the people of Honduras was lower than in the war zones on either side of them, there were hundreds of assassinations and disappearances perpetrated by the ruling Honduran military's notorious Battalion 3-16, a U.S. trained unit; one of their victims was Joseph Carney, a Jesuit priest from the U.S. Negroponte's job was to keep silent about their atrocities and help cover them up.

The Bush Gang brought Negroponte back in 2001 as Ambassador to the United Nations, where he had the tricky task of feigning to work at diplomacy with the other member states while trying to make it possible for the United States to pursue its aggressive objectives without being constrained by the UN. Journalist Conn Hallinan wrote about the occasion, "When the U.S.'s new United Nations Ambassador John Negroponte rose to praise that body's Sept. 28 resolution on terrorism, reminding delegates that the action 'obligates all member states to deny financing, support, and safe haven for terrorists,' his remarks were greeted with studied silence by Latin American delegates. It is hard to cheer when you're gritting your teeth."[12]

John Poindexter

Admiral John Poindexter was the National Security Advisor in the Reagan/Bush White House and the man who brought in a brash Marine, Oliver North, to assist him in schemes to attack and undermine the Sandinista government in Nicaragua. After being convicted of conspiracy, lying to Congress, defrauding the government, and destroying evidence in the Iran-Contra scandal, Poindexter went off to work in civilian life. Trained as a physicist, he was able to immerse himself in computer applications concerning secrecy and spying and became vice-president of a software company that contracted to work with the Pentagon agency known as Defense Advanced Research Projects, or DARPA. In 2002, Poindexter was rehired by Bush II to head the Total Information Awareness Office of DARPA, which immediately developed at plan for super-computer surveillance of the nation's internet, phone, and fax lines, enabling it (among other things) to tap into computer databases to collect the credit, financial, medical and travel records of individual citizens. In 2003, when the U.S. Congress barred the program from spying on Americans, the Pentagon changed the name of the office to Terrorism Information Awareness and permitted it to keep exploring similar operations. At the end of July 2003, two Democratic Senators—Dorgan of North Dakota and Wyden of Oregon—exposed the next item in Poindexter's bag of tricks, a futures market for predicting terrorist acts called "Policy Analysis Market." Under the plan, Wall Street traders were about to sign up at a website that the Pentagon was operating with private partners; they were scheduled to begin trading futures on Middle East developments as of October 2003. This bizarre scheme was so embarrassing to Republican Senators and the Pentagon that Poindexter was immediately forced to resign.

John Bolton

Another Bush appointee, John Bolton, Undersecretary of State for Arms Control and International Security Affairs, had been on the periphery of Iran/Contra, but proved to be of great help to the sub-Gang as they began a new round of criminal endeavors. Bolton, formerly a vice president at the American Enterprise Institute, is a fervent right-wing opponent of the United Nations and almost any other international agreement or treaty that might limit the options and behavior of the United States. He was named to the Arms Control post by George W. Bush specifically because he opposes all arms controls. Part of his job is to refuse to limit any restrictions on weapons, including the biological and chemical varieties, that might someday be useful to the United States. Bolton signed the letter sent to Kofi Annan at the United Nations in May 2002, reneging on the Clinton administration's agreement to the treaty that created the International Criminal Court. Bolton told *The Wall Street Journal* that signing the letter that renounced the Rome Statute creating the International Criminal Court "was the happiest moment of my government service."[13]

Obviously, a government that is contemplating any number of military actions, including "pre-emptive attacks" against those who might be thinking evil things about the United States, does not want its hands tied by accusations of unlawful conduct outside of U.S. borders. Bolton is a spokesman for the ideological position of Bush, Cheney, and Rumsfeld—that no international body shall ever be allowed to sit in judgment of the United States.

In addition to defying the International Criminal Court, the Bush administration has indicated its profound disrespect for international law of all kinds by canceling its obligations under the Kyoto Protocol on Global Warming; not ratifying the Rio Pact on biodiversity; withdrawing from the Anti-Ballistic Missile Treaty so the U.S. can build a missile defense system; declaring it will use nuclear weapons; refusing to comply with the ban on land mines; disregarding the UN convention against torture, sabotaging the small-arms treaty; resisting new aspects of the biological-warfare convention; and refusing chemical-weapons inspectors access to its own laboratories. To top it off, Bush went to the United Nations to announce that if it did not agree to go to war with Iraq, then the United States would proceed with a war anyway. He carried through on his threat.

Outside the Law, or Answering to a "Higher Law"

The idea of being above the law is common to those born of privilege, and to those who have come to believe that they are truly superior to others in wisdom and strength. This kind of inordinate pride is dangerous, whether encouraged in adolescent Skull and Bones activities, generated in the corporate board room where the owners' liability is limited, or heated up in the fanatical pursuit of foreign policy objectives. And when such hubris is wedded to religious certainty that one's country is God's chosen country, then all hell breaks loose.

Most criminals, for all their moral failings, at least know they are criminals. They work outside the law because the attraction of free loot is more than they can resist. The Bush Gang members who were responsible for Iran/Contra do not know they are criminals. They thought of themselves in the 1980s as unappreciated heroes who were stepping outside the law to do battle with "bad guys" vaguely connected to the "Evil Empire" of the Soviet Union. By their way of thinking they were loyal to the Bush family and the country, "the homeland," and deserved a second chance. Not a second chance to make up for their transgressions, but a second chance to prove how good and righteous they were the first time around.

So, what better place to go than to the Holy Land.

The lure of Palestine, Israel, Mecca, Babylon, and the Garden of Eden is as old as recorded history, and it has inspired and beckoned people from various empires—Egyptian, Roman, Holy Roman, British, American—across the millennia. Since we are beginning yet another millennium and another empire, it is, perhaps, fitting that the United States cannot seem to stay away from the place. Those who cheer the loudest for the "good" intentions of the U.S. in the fight against the "evil" that still lurks in the Middle East are the right-wing Judeo-Christian forces who provide the ideology of the Bush Gang and the Republican Party and fill most of the places within the dominant public policy foundations and the conservative media. These people see American culture, including its business culture, as a superior form of human endeavor that is destined to take over the world. The foremost spokesmen are the neo-conservatives that dominate the Murdoch media and its imitators, as well as such think tanks as Heritage, Hudson, Cato, and American Enterprise.

A great many of the commentators and experts who have been educating the American people about the Middle East and the War on Terrorism are allied with the most aggressive right-wing leaders of the Zionist movement in Israel, which includes Sharon and Netanyahu. Jim Lobe reported on how the Bush administration was following their "Rightwing Blueprint for the Middle East" in the spring of 2002. Nearly a year later he analyzed the significance of George W. Bush appearing at the American Enterprise Institute (AEI) to give a speech about the impending attack on Iraq. "AEI's foreign policy 'scholars' are closely identified with the most unilateralist and pro-Likud elements in the Bush administration. The institute serves as the hub of a tightly knit network of neo-conservative activists and groups, including the Project for the New American Century (PNAC), the Center for Security Policy (CSP), the Jewish Institute for National Security Affairs (JINSA)."[14]

This network accounts, in part, for an overwhelming right-wing bias in information presented to the public concerning Muslim culture and religion, the roots of terrorism, weapons of mass destruction, and the workings of Arab, Iranian, and Turkish politics. James Zogby, an advocate for Arab-Americans and a mainstream Democrat, has described the successful collaboration between the "neo-conservative movement, a small but extremely influential group of writers, media commentators, political operatives and academics," and the Christian Right, the broad coalition of conservative Christians that form such an effective mass constituency for George W. Bush. Zogby acknowledges that many of the neo-conservatives are Jewish Americans, often more secular than religious, but makes a point of agreeing with political science professor Steven Spiegel of UCLA: "If you just focus on the power of the...Jewish groups, you're missing the boat.

The Christian right has had a real influence in shaping the view of the Republican Party toward Israel."[15]

The key element is that both groups have a religious zeal about fighting pure "evil" in the world; it used to be directed against the Soviet Union, now it is focused on Arabs and Muslims. Conservative scholar Samuel Huntington once gave advice to the Reagan/Bush administration that was very useful for promoting U.S. policy in Central America in the 1980s: "you may have to sell [intervention or other military action] in such a way as to create the misimpression that it is the Soviet Union that you are fighting. That is what the United States has done ever since the Truman Doctrine."[16] Following this advice, the new Bush administration simply substituted the words "Arab terrorism" for the "Soviet Union" as it launched its offensive in the Middle East.

American right-wing evangelical fundamentalists share a common bond with the right-wing Israelis that goes back to the English Puritans and their reading of the Old Testament. Both groups believe that they are the "Chosen People," destined by the grace of God to inhabit the "chosen land" (either in Israel or America). Lately the Christian Right has been able to monopolize the old Protestant certainty that America's destiny is manifest in God's plan for the world. Some conservative Catholics have joined the evangelicals in the formation of the "New Religious Right;" they have been very effective organizers and spokesmen, among them Paul Weyrich, Michael S. Joyce, and William Bennett. The fact that conservative Christians and Jews are now able to join together in believing that America is the "city on the hill," a place that must be the guiding light to the rest of the world, suggests that their particular religious beliefs are coalescing around an "uber-belief."

This super-faith has the potential to transform a large and powerful country, the United States of America, into a super-nation and a super-culture, an imperial nation that feels entitled by its greatness to rule the world.

In the mid-1990s, when it was uncertain whether the United States was capable of playing such a global role, Susan Rose, Paul Gifford, and I co-authored *Exporting the American Gospel: Global Christian Fundamentalism*. This book studied the development of the Christian Right as an expanding force that is having a tremendous impact, not just within the United States, but throughout much of the world. One of our observations was that fundamentalist Christians were joining with ultra-conservatives in the United States in order to promote and monopolize a set of powerful, nationalistic, and self-righteous beliefs that we called "fundamentalist Americanism." After gaining legitimacy within the Republican Party throughout the 1980s, the right-wing Christian movement was the repository of enormous amounts of pent-up political energy during the Clinton years. There was a storm of righteousness gathering, as well as a passionate longing to project the manifest destiny of the United States onto the entire world. But since the movement was not directly encouraged by Clinton's presidency, it was unclear that fundamentalist Americanism could find sufficient support, especially at the highest levels of politics, to be able to dedicate itself to a jumbo-jihad.

Now things have changed. Bush, Rumsfeld, and Cheney, as well as those who surround them, believe in this agenda. They believe that God smiles on America and sanctions the global imposition of American values. This particular God approves of Crusades and disapproves of Muslims.

Franklin Graham, son of the famed evangelist Billy Graham (the man who turned George W into a "born again" Christian), gave the blessing at George W. Bush's inauguration in 2001. Later, Franklin declared that Islam was a "very wicked and evil" religion. When the victory in Iraq was nearly won in April of 2003, Graham was invited to the Pentagon on Good Friday where he proclaimed that "there's no other way to God except through Christ" while a Christian singer provided the back-up: "There is one God and one faith." Muslim employees at the Pentagon refused Graham's request to be photographed with them, perhaps because they knew that the evangelist had a Christian relief group waiting in Jordan, ready to move into Iraq as soon as the fighting ended. Franklin Graham said that he and his agency, called Samaritan's Purse, had a mission: "We are there to reach out and love them and save them."[17]

The Bush Gang feels that the United States is entitled to assert its imperial will by almost any means necessary, including religious means. The fact that our economy is failing and many of our multinational corporations are in disarray makes their globalist projection of righteous force even more attractive to them. While war provides a convenient distraction from domestic troubles, it also offers a way to keep asserting American power at a time when other economies and political forces around the world—"old Europe," China, India, and various countries in South America—are beginning to feel strong enough to resist American economic and political hegemony.

The Bush Gang is launching the nation wholeheartedly in the direction of a crusade that looks beyond the Muslim world. This global military crusade is one that Rose, Gifford, and I described in 1996, but at the time we thought this kind of politico/religious inclination toward

total war was a rather remote possibility. We did not know that George W. Bush would step in as president in 2000, achieve immediate acceptance as the legitimate "born-again" leader of the Christian Right, and raise the prospect of a war against infidels in 2001—"this crusade, this war on terrorism, is going to take awhile," said Bush after September 11.[18] But we did anticipate some of the circumstances that are currently fusing fundamentalist Christianity and Americanism into a powerful political force. In *Exporting the American Gospel*, we raised the possibility that an aggressive, self-righteous regime could arise in the United States—a regime that might not be able to resist the urge to transform "spiritual warfare" into the outright exercise of unilateral military force throughout the world.

> The United States may remain the major military power in the world, the master trainer of armies, and the leading merchant of weapons for many decades to come. If this role is elevated as U.S. economic interests are humbled, and global political disturbances keep erupting in places where the new Christians have some influence, then 'spiritual warfare' may portend more frightening things. Currently in the mid-1990s, the impressive influence of the highly motivated Christian Coalition and the elevation of charismatic Christian leaders such as Oliver North and Pat Robertson demonstrate that there are growing legions of disgruntled American citizens. Americanism is treasured by many millions of angry people, fundamentalists and social conservatives alike, and they clearly favor a deepening of authoritarian values at home while wanting the United States to keep dominating the world scene as a Christian superpower nation.[19]

Seventeen

Tasks of Empire

Kill for Oil, Lie for the Homeland

I went down on my knees and prayed Almighty God...and one night late it came to me this way...there was nothing left for us to do but to take them all...and Christianize them.
—President William McKinley explaining to the ladies of Methodist Missionary Society how he decided that the United States should conquer the Philippines in 1900. (Most Filipinos, by the way, were already Catholics.)

Benevolent Assimilation…is the pious new name of the musket.

—Mark Twain

There's no telling how many wars it will take to secure freedom in the homeland.
—George W. Bush, August 5, 2002

We once had freedom in the United States, before we started calling our nation "The Homeland." Why would anyone want to call our country "The Homeland?" The word does not sit well with democracy because it has an imperial ring to it. In the 20th century, the word was more fitting to the fascist countries that dreamed of expanding outwards into Europe and beyond. It suggests that soldiers and citizens should be able to venture out into the world, acquire the riches of any land they like, wreak vengeance upon those who dare to oppose them, and return home to "The Homeland" where their safety, and the safety and comfort of their loved ones, is guaranteed. Only empires have "homelands," to distinguish their base territory from all the lands they have conquered.

We are now two years into a different century and the Bush Gang has changed the rules. In the 21st century, if they have their way, the United States of America will become something different—the United Empire of America perhaps—an openly aggressive, super-duper power that makes the rest of the world conform to American standards, American culture, and American demands. Long-time anti-imperialist critic Noam Chomsky summed up the situation when he spoke to the World Social Forum in early 2003: "the most powerful state in history has proclaimed, loud and clear, that it intends to rule the world by force, the dimension in which it reigns supreme."

It used to be that only outright anti-capitalists spoke about American imperialism and empire, as part of a deep critique of the direction the United States was heading. But in 2002, rather suddenly, one could find arguments in favor of "American Empire" throughout the mainstream media, written by those who are very close associates of the Bush Gang and their vision of the world. *The New York Times* quoted conservative columnist Charles Krauthammer as saying,

> People are now coming out of the closet on the word 'empire.' The fact is, no country has been as dominant culturally, economically, technologically and militarily in the history of the world since the Roman Empire.

The Weekly Standard published "The Case for American Empire," by former editorial features editor at *The Wall Street Journal* Max Boot. He wrote: "We are an attractive empire;" and "Afghanistan and other troubled lands today cry out for the sort of enlightened foreign administration once provided by self-confident Englishmen in jodphurs and pith helmets." Robert D. Kaplan, the author of *Warrior Politics: Why Leadership Demands a Pagan Ethos*, said, "There's a positive side to empire. It's in some ways the most benign form of order."[1]

Even those who were not enthusiastic supporters of Bush's imperial ambitions were ruminating on the situation. Paul Kennedy of Yale, author of *The Rise and Fall of the Great Powers*, wrote in the *Financial Times* of London, "From the time the first settlers arrived in Virginia from England and started moving westward, this was an imperial nation, a conquering nation." As Kennedy well knows, the ambitions of the Anglo-Americans did not end with the annihilation of the American Indian nations and the extension of the republic to the edge of the Pacific. The Robber Barons had their imperial urges, which Henry Cabot Lodge described so eloquently in the 1890s, "The great nations are rapidly absorbing for their future expansion all the waste nations of the earth. It is a movement

that makes for civilization and the advancement of the race." The aristocratic Lodge did not think the Anglo-Saxon elite could contain their lust for other lands, such as Cuba and the Philippines: "We have a record of conquest, colonisation and expansion unequaled by any people in the 19th century," he bragged. "We are not about to be curbed now."

Imperialism requires war. And on this issue, George W. Bush was able to find common ground with Theodore Roosevelt, who on domestic issues was an enemy of the Robber Baron mentality. Roosevelt wrote to a friend one year before the United States embarked upon the Spanish American War and its conquest of Cuba and the Philippines, "I should welcome almost any war, for I think this country needs one."

Karl Rove, who astutely charts the course of George W. Bush's political pronouncements, instructed Bush to promote the image of a wartime leader preoccupied with homeland defense, for this served as an effective distraction from the domestic collapse of the economy during the 2002 elections. But even though this election strategy proved successful, it would be a mistake to think that the primary reason that the Bush Gang wanted war with Iraq was to fool the populace and defeat the Democrats. Likewise, it is a delusion to put too much stock in the family psycho-drama story that Bush II was motivated by an immature psychological urge to prove himself by bettering his father's record against the evil Saddam. For the truth was...

The Bush Gang Had Been Gearing Up for War Against Iraq for a Long Time

There are at least three serious reasons that compelled the United States to go to war against Iraq. None of them has much to do with "weapons of mass destruction," and all involved the extension of Empire. One reason is to promote the survival and expansion of Israel along the lines of the conservative Likud ideology held by both Sharon and Netanyahu. In so doing the United States can aggressively shape the political destiny of the Muslim countries of the Middle East. Muslims of all political stripes see the prospect of a Middle East war as a Judeo-Christian invasion. Most of the rest of the world, with the exception of China and Japan, went through this experience centuries ago—the colonization and subjugation of their cultures by white, European settlers who had an alien religion.

The second reason is simpler and probably more important: oil. The Bush Gang says we are fighting for freedom, which on one level means the freedom to use all the hydrocarbons that lie beneath the feet of a billion Islamic people. The Bush pirates have their eyes on the prize—an Ocean of Oil—stretching from North Africa to the Middle East, through the Persian Gulf, around the Caspian Sea, and down to Indonesia—that corresponds roughly to the grand sweep of Islamic culture across the middle of the world. According to Daniel Yergin's authoritative book on petroleum, this is "The Prize," by far the biggest economic and natural resource ever to sit before the greedy eyes of Homo sapiens. [2]

Finally, there is a third objective that gets to the heart of the matter. At a time of eco-nomic uncertainty, but a time when U.S. military might is unparalleled, the United States wants to serve notice to the rest of the world that it is in charge. That is, although oil is a very precious resource, it is not the only reason the U.S. has decided to expand its global hegemony and start dictating unilateralist policies to the rest of the world. Our nation has decided—or better said, a small group has decided for the nation—that the time is ripe to act like an empire.

This third objective is so large—for it encompasses all sorts of economic possibilities and chances for pure geopolitical dominance—that it naturally includes the first two. By pursuing these objectives simultaneously and exaggerating the component of potential terror attacks—with an almost unbelievable level of hysteria and contrivance concocted by the American media—the administration was able to drum up sufficient domestic support for war against Saddam Hussein.

International support was another matter. Bulldozing through the opposition of other nations seemed like an easy task to Bush at first, for he himself announced at the United Nations in September of 2002 that the United States would go ahead with its adventure by forming a "coalition of the willing" if the UN did not grant its blessing. But clearly the Bush Gang had miscalculated the recalcitrance of France, Russia, and China, which later threatened to veto a formal approval of war by the Security Council. Just as important, the administration had failed to realize it could not browbeat and bribe lesser nations such as Mexico and Chile into giving symbolic assent to American aggression. Above all, by the end of the year 2002, massive resistance to the war was being voiced by tens of millions of people around the world who began protesting in the streets against the impending attack on Iraq by the United States. Even the British and Spanish governments, whose prime ministers had been such eager cheerleaders for war, were waffling because their populations were clearly opposed to an invasion without UN approval. In Spain, where millions protested in the larger cities, eighty to ninety percent of the people were opposed to the collusion of conservative Prime Minister Aznar.

With ever-expanding protests being coordinated simultaneously in the United States and many foreign countries from January to March of 2003, the Bush Gang decided to press ahead, seize the prize, and claim that democracy had won. It is important to recall that opponents of war had never claimed that Saddam Hussein was anything other than a brutal tyrant. They were, however, deeply troubled about two things—their fears of unilateral declarations of "pre-emptive" war by the world's only superpower, and their doubts that such action would promote democracy when it was clearly meant to serve U.S. strategic and economic interests.

One of the most vexing questions in the aftermath of war was what the future held for Iraq and the other Islamic nations of the Middle East. Palestine, which had its nationhood revoked many decades earlier, was in danger of disappearing altogether. Conservative parties in Israel had long talked about "removal" of the Palestinian people from the West Bank and Gaza and they had achieved strong majority control in the Israeli parliament. The Likud Party formed an alliance with two ultra-right parties in 2003, the National Religious Party and the National Unity Party, that openly advocated the murder of the Palestinian leadership and the forcible ejection of Palestinians to some

far corner of Syria or Jordan.

This was the culmination of a problem that Arabs inhabitants of the country had anticipated a full century earlier when they were still part of the Ottoman Empire. The number of Jewish inhabitants of Palestine had increased from 3% of the population in 1878 to approximately 9% at the beginning of World War I in 1914. This occurred largely because of the immigration promoted by the Zionists, especially among those Jewish peasants forced out of Russia by the Czar's pograms. More or less simultaneously, Palestinian Arabs were pressing for their freedom from four centuries of Turkish domination. In 1905, Arab writer Negib Azoury, in his book *Le Reveil de la Nation Arabe*, called for a revolution against the Ottomans and the establishment of an independent Arab state that included Palestine, Sinai, Lebanon, Syria and all of the Arabian peninsula; he cautioned fellow Arabs that the designs of Zionists to acquire Arab land would be an obstacle to their national liberation.

This historical experience has direct implications for the peoples of the Middle East in the 21st century. Behind the conflict between Arabs and Jews lies an even larger problem, which is the British and American desire to control the future of Eastern and Central Asia. This imperial project overshadows the issues of self-determination for these peoples and is far more important than the resolution of Israeli/Palestinian borders. When looking at the question of liberty and self-determination for the Islamic countries that surround Israel and Iraq, it is hard to imagine that political freedom and democracy-building will be allowed now that the Anglo-American forces have succeeded with their invasion. The United States and Britain have done their best to discourage any genuine democratic movements in the Middle East ever since World War I, when the English first described their conquest as if it were going to be a delightful experience for the Iraqis.

> Our armies do not come into your cities and lands as conquerors or enemies, but as liberators. Your wealth has been stripped of you by unjust men...the people of Baghdad shall flourish under institutions which are in consonance with their sacred laws.
> —General F.S. Maude, commander of British forces that occupied Iraq in 1917.[3]

Britain had raced to Bagdhad during World War I to make sure it would control the whole Arabian peninsula before an armistice was signed. This gave the British Empire de facto control over important geopolitical assets—Palestine, Jordan, and Iraq—that lay at the crossroads of Europe, Asia, and Africa. It also abrogated claims on future oil development by Turkey and Germany, for the newly created nation of Iraq had borders that neatly, and just barely, encompassed Kirkuk and Mosul. These areas had already been identified as very promising by petroleum engineers and the giant oil companies which had been negotiating with the Turkish Sultan before the First World War. Britain promptly legalized its control of the country through its League of Nations mandate, then installed a puppet monarch.

In 1920, there was a fierce rebellion against British occupation by over 100,000 Iraqi tribesmen. This situation, decided the occupiers, called for the invention of a new kind of mass destruction utilizing methods that had not been employed during World War I. The Queen's Royal Air Force began experimenting with massive aerial bombardment against the towns and villages of the rebels. The process was horribly efficient—nearly 9,000 Iraqis were slaughtered during the summer of 1920 while only nine English airmen died. One of the participants in the English efforts, Arthur Harris, is generally credited with the development and refinement of both "heavy bomber" and night-time "terror" raids; he was later to become Air Commodore Harris, one of those most responsible for planning and executing the massive fire-bombings that annihilated large parts of Dresden and Hamburg during World War II. When he was a squadron leader in Iraq, Harris reported on the demoralizing significance of air terrorism:

> The Arab and Kurd now know what real bombing means. Within 45 minutes a full-sized village can be practically wiped out, and a third of its inhabitants killed or injured, by four or five machines which offer them no real target, no opportunity for glory as warriors, no effective means of escape.[4]

Winston Churchill, as secretary of state for war at the time, totally approved of the suppression of the Iraqis, and he was especially interested in trying out another weapon of mass destruction, poison chemicals. He suggested that the British troops use them "against recalcitrant Arabs as an experiment," and dismissed the misgivings of others, saying "I am strongly in favour of using poisoned gas against uncivilized tribes [in order to] spread a lively terror."[5] In fact, chemical weapons were only used occasionally by the British, since the bombing raids with high explosives were proven to be a far more effective method of terror.

British exerted brutal military control over Iraq until the end of World War II. Iraqi defiance of British rule continued apace (Arabs in

Palestine and Jordan also resisted British rule and the growth of Jewish settlements throughout this same time period). At the same time British oil companies had assumed leadership in developing the huge Iraqi oil fields, with the Anglo-Persian Oil Company playing a key role. This company had been established in Iran in 1913 when Britain intervened to develop that country's newly discovered oil resources and install the Pahlavi family as governing monarchs. Within a few years, the determination of the British government and British capitalists to capture the lion's share of the world's petroleum had proved successful. In 1920 London's *Financial News* openly gloated about the extent of the plundering: "present command of the world's oil resources runs to no less than seventy-five percent of the entirety, compared with two percent when the country entered the war."

The United States, which was challenging Great Britain's status as the ultimate capitalist power after World War I, was sure to press for a share of this extraordinary booty. First and foremost, this meant access to the levers of economic and political power in the Middle East. Standard Oil demanded and received a one-quarter share of ownership of the Iraq Petroleum Company on behalf of a consortium of U.S. companies in 1928; it also moved into Saudi Arabia in the 1930s and struck very lucrative deals with the reactionary, feudalistic Wahhabi kingdom under King Saud. This government, the most backward and anti-democratic of any in the Middle East, continued to enjoy the whole-hearted support of the U.S. for the rest of the century. It would eventually play a key role in helping the U.S. and Pakistan support the fundamentalist Islamic forces that took over Afghanistan.

After World War II, the United States assumed unquestioned leadership of the world's capitalist countries because Britain had been severely wounded, both at home and throughout its empire, by the ravages of the global conflict. The US consequently took over the British role of trying to direct the course of political and economic development in the Middle East. In Iran, American interest in the Iranian oil industry came into conflict with the country's newly formed democratic parliament, which had decided to nationalize the Iranian oil companies. In a classic bit of 1950s intrigue (events in Vietnam and Guatemala were unfolding in similar ways), the United States helped stage the military coup that restored the rule of the country to the Pahlavi family under Shah Reza (his father had been deposed by the British for getting too friendly with the Germans before World War II). The United States maintained a close relationship with the new Shah, cared for his money at Chase Manhattan and other large American banks, and even helped train his hated secret police, SAVAK. By the 1970s, the Shah and SAVAK had eliminated much of the internal, secular opposition to their dictatorial rule and moved to the top of Amnesty International's list of human rights violators.

But Iraq was not forgotten. The secret services of the U.S. and Great Britain also helped suppress and derail democratic movements in Iraq until 1958, when a nationalist rebellion among Iraqi military officers overthrew the monarchy that Britain had created forty years earlier. At this time, writes retired Colonel David Hackworth, a syndicated columnist who follows U.S. military affairs, "CIA director Allen Dulles declared Iraq 'the most dangerous spot in the world,'" and began immediate American efforts to subvert Iraqi independence.[6] As a result of CIA support, a nationalist group known as the Ba'ath Party gained ascendancy, and, according to Hackworth, a "made-in-the-USA monster" was created in the form of a lowly officer named Saddam Hussein.

During the 1960s Hussein and his colleagues received covert assistance from the United States as they staged a violent takeover of the Iraqi government, then proceeded to slaughter a large left-leaning, secular movement that was thought to be too friendly with the Soviet Union. Saddam Hussein and the Ba'ath Party proved to be unreliable puppets of the U.S., however, and later pursued their own agenda. The most troubling aspect of their behavior, as far as the capitalist powers were concerned, was their nationalization of all Iraqi oil production in 1975 and their strong role in establishing and maintaining OPEC, the Organization of Petroleum Exporting Countries. OPEC gathered together the world's most important oil producers—Saudi Arabia, Iraq, Iran, Libya, Venezuela—and successfully challenged U.S. dominance of world oil reserves in the 1970s.

The U.S. victory over Iraq in 2003 is a defeat for OPEC and the independence of major oil producers around the world. In retrospect, it is clear that the dominant capitalist powers were not about to let lowly nations reverse the historical pattern of conquest that began a century ago. Why in God's name (that is, their own God's name) would the United States and Britain want to grant the countries of the Middle East real democratic freedom? The most likely result of democracy would be the creation of highly motivated republics that would resist Western imperatives even more strongly than they did in the past. Such governments, whether they were influenced by Islamic doctrines or a secular/Islamic mix of ideas, would definitely be highly nationalistic and intent on pursuing their own course in the world. Their first acts of national sovereignty would be to immediately relieve the United States and Britain of their control over both the oil industry and the proceeds of that industry which move through Anglo-American financial institutions.

This was not going to happen. Just two months after the United States invaded Iraq, *The Washington Post*, a newspaper that wholeheartedly supported the military operation, published an article entitled "U.S. Adviser Says Iraq May Break With OPEC." This advisor was none other than the former head of Royal Dutch Shell operations in the United States, Peter J. Carroll. Shell Oil was one of the four multinational companies (Anglo-Persian, Compaignee Francaise, and Standard Oil were the other three) that originally divided up the Iraqi oil assets between themselves 75 years earlier in 1928. Reporter Peter S. Goodman wrote that "the U.S. executive selected by the Pentagon to advise Iraq's Ministry of Oil suggested today that the country might best be served by exporting as much oil as it can and disregarding quotas set by the Organization of Petroleum Exporting Countries. His comments offered the strongest indication to date that the future Iraqi government may break ranks with the international petroleum cartel."

The article went on to remind readers that political analysts in other nations had predicted this development well before the war began: "commentators—particularly in Europe—have contended that the real purpose of Bush's war in Iraq was to put in place a government that would break OPEC." From Carroll's comments it was clear that Bush and Powell's promise to "punish" France was about to be implemented, and that Russia would receive similar treatment for its reluctance to join the "coalition of the willing." These two countries had signed huge contracts for developing and marketing Iraqi oil long before the war began; the chances of these legal agreements being honored afterward looked very doubtful, because "Carroll also signaled that oil contracts signed under the old regime are now potentially void or subject to renegotiation." A final comment from Goodman's article revealed that Carroll, even though he did not work for Halliburton, fits in perfectly with the ethically challenged oil men in the Bush Gang. Carroll said that he expected private companies to play a role in the future of Iraqi petroleum and "confirmed a report in *Los Angeles Times* that he continues to own substantial stock in Fluor, which has already announced intentions to bid on contracts to reconstruct Iraq's oil industry."[7]

Project for the New American Century

Real freedom in the Middle East is the last thing the Anglo-Americans, now led by the Bush Gang, want to see. It is as unlikely for them to promote democracy and self-determination among the Arab, Iranians, Afghans, and Kurds in 2003 as it would have been for the Spanish government to restore the good fortunes of the indigenous, non-Christian civilizations of the Western hemisphere in 1603. At that historical moment, nearly a century after Spain started looting the gold and silver from the temples and mines of Mexico, Peru, and Bolivia, the conquistadors had not nearly finished the job. Should we expect anything less from the dominant empire of the 21st century when there are still trillions of barrels of "black gold" to be extracted from the earth? And when 65% of those reserves lie beneath Iraq, Iran, Saudi Arabia, Kuwait, and the United Arab Emirate?

The United States, Great Britain, and Israel are extending their control over the Middle East because it benefits all three of them at the expense of the rest of the world. Long before George W. Bush announced his candidacy for president, the Bush Gang was formulating a plan which would harness the right-wing Likudnik lobby, the right-wing segment of the military-industrial complex, and the right-wing Christian lobby to one imperial wagon.

In 1997, a small group of potentially powerful people, just twenty five of them, announced the formation of a new organization dedicated to building up the power of the United States to unparalleled levels. They were clearly looking forward to the presidential election of 2000 and the beginning of a new millennium, because they called their organization "The Project for the New American Century" (PNAC). Among the principal signers of the Statement of Principles were Dick Cheney and Donald Rumsfeld, as well as a number of people whom they recruited to join them in the Bush administration, including Cheney's National Security Adviser, I. Lewis Libby, Deputy Defense Secretary Paul Wolfowitz, former Middle East envoy Zalmay Khalilzad, and new special Middle East envoy Elliot Abrams. A few right-wing Republican politicians, Jeb Bush, Dan Quayle, and Steve Forbes signed on; two influential representatives of the Christian Right, William Bennett and Gary Bauer; and some influential neo-conservative intellectuals and writers, such as Francis Fukuyama, Norman Podhoretz, Midge Decter, and Eliot Cohen. This was a pretty tight group; according to their declaration of principles they were committed:

to accept responsibility for America's unique role in preserving and *extending an international order* friendly to our security, our prosperity, and our principles [my emphasis].

Intimately connected to those who signed the declaration of principles were other people who had drafted much of the language of the organization and would later make the recommendations of the Project for a New American Century (PNAC) into the foundation of a new, definitive U.S. policy—for example, Richard Perle, Chairman of the Defense Policy Board that reports to the Pentagon; William Kristol of *The Weekly Standard*; John Bolton, at the State Department as chief arms control negotiator; and Douglas Feith, chief assistant to Rumsfeld.

The Project for a New American Century from the beginning saw itself as an agent of bold change, one that could strengthen Israel as well as the United States. Just a year before its founding, in 1996, Israeli Prime Minister Benjamin Netanyahu was presented with a report that recommended repudiation of the Oslo Accords and the whole idea of "land for peace," and instead called for the seizure of the West Bank and Gaza Strip as well as encouraging an outright invasion of Iraq by the United States. It then suggested the next items that should be on the agenda: toppling the governments of Syria, Lebanon, Saudi Arabia, and Iran. This report, entitled "A Clean Break: A New Strategy for Securing the Realm," was co-authored by Perle, Feith, and David Wurmser, who now works at the State Department under Bolton. A few days later these ideas, which would later become key policies of both Netanyahu and Sharon, were endorsed by the editorial page of *The Wall Street Journal*.[8]

In the next few years, John Bolton and

others wrote essays for the PNAC and for the neo-conservative press that expounded upon these three themes: expanding Israel, taking out Iraq, and subduing the rest of the Middle East in one way or another.[9] By the fall of 2002, advocates of this position were sharing their enthusiasm with the mainstream media. Interviewed in *The Boston Globe*, Meyrav Wurmser, wife of David Wurmser and director of the Center for Middle East Policy at the ultra-right Hudson Institute, was enthusiastic about the extended effects of the U.S. establishing "democracy" in Iraq: "Everyone will flip out, starting with the Saudis. It will send shock waves throughout the Arab world... After a war with Iraq, then you really shape the region."[10]

This position was bolstered by support from various other neo-conservative allies and the right-wing foundations. Writing in the *London Telegraph* on the first anniversary of 9/11 was Michael Ledeen, who holds a special position as "freedom analyst" at the American Enterprise Institute. He once worked as a foreign policy propagandist for the Reagan/Bush administration in the 1980s and formulated much of the misleading anti-Communist rhetoric that led to the Central American wars. Ledeen described a "war of vast dimensions" coming in the Middle East, one that would topple "tyrannies and replace them with freer societies, as was done after the Second World War ....A war on such a scale has hardly been mentioned by commentators and politicians, yet it is implicit in everything President Bush has said and done ... America's enemies will soon be the subject of revolutionary change at its hands."

James Woolsey, the former CIA director under Clinton who later joined the neo-conservative effort at PNAC, seconded Ledeen's arguments at a NATO conference in Prague in

November of 2002 and announced that "Iraq can be seen as the first battle of the fourth world war."[11]

Within this context, the program for building up the right wing in Israel and conducting a widespread war to "liberate" Iraq was not an end in itself, but part of an even bigger geo-political transformation, the new role that was being assumed by the United States. In September of 2000, just before the presidential election, the Project for a New American Century came out with a detailed blueprint for the military and foreign policy of the future Bush administration, a report called "Rebuilding America's Defenses: Strategies, Forces And Resources For A New Century." The ninety page report bluntly suggested the direction that the U.S. would end up pursuing a year later after the attacks of September 11, 2001: "The United States has for decades sought to play a more permanent role in Gulf regional security. While the unresolved conflict with Iraq provides the immediate justification, the need for a substantial American force presence in the Gulf transcends the issue of the regime of Saddam Hussein."

The rest of the document outlined most of the detailed program that Bush presented two years later in the fall of 2002. "The National Security of the United States" was the Bush Gang's plan for nothing less than a total change in the declared foreign policy of the United States. Whereas in the past the U.S. had claimed to be resisting hostile regimes such as the Soviet Union through containment and pledged itself to work within a variety of global organizations and treaties that promoted peace, the new policy was clearly imperial in tone. It stated that the United State would not be constrained by membership in multinational peace-keeping organizations—"we will be prepared to act apart when our interests and unique responsibilities require"—and when necessary would construct "coalitions of the willing" to follow its bidding.

The new National Security Doctrine suggested that the U.S. had the right to discourage others nations from building up their military power and could act "to dissuade potential adversaries from pursuing a military buildup in hopes of surpassing, or equaling, the power of the United States." This included the new explicit policy of "pre-emptive" war whenever the U.S. feels threatened: "America will act against such emerging threats before they are fully formed." What is more, the new American edict told other nations that the conservative economic objectives of the Republican Party were policies that should be implemented throughout the whole world. The list included the following requirements: "pro-growth legal and regulatory policies to encourage business investment, innovation, and entrepreneurial activity; tax policies—particularly lower marginal tax rates—that improve incentives for work and investment... strong financial systems that allow capital to be put to its most efficient use; sound fiscal policies to support business activity... and free trade that provides new avenues for growth and fosters the diffusion of technologies and ideas that increase productivity and opportunity."[12]

This new foreign policy was the basis for the speech that Bush made to the United Nations in September of 2002. He told them that the United States was ready to go it alone in the world if the U.N. did not join his pre-emptive war. The U.S. would take any action that it deemed necessary, against Iraq or anyone else. His administration was making preparations to act quickly and decisively by shedding its various multilateral constraints. The United States was now strutting on the world stage.

Empires Look for Reasons to Go to War

It might be useful to think of the United States in light of the Roman Empire, which was briefly ruled by a triumvirate as it was transformed from a republic into its imperial form. In the last week of August of 2002, two powerful members of an emerging American triumvirate, Cheney and Rumsfeld, spoke in front of large audiences of American soldiers and war veterans three times and urged them to support a war of aggression in the Middle East. The words they used were euphemistic and bombastic in the extreme. They used "regime change" when they meant an unprovoked attack on another country. They railed against the imminent threat of "weapons of mass destruction," not the ones that the United States possesses in almost infinite capacity, but the ones that Saddam Hussein might have been able to produce in the future. The essence of their message was—we must attack Iraq because we must.

At the end of 2002 and the beginning of 2003, there was a brief respite in the drive to war as U.N. weapons inspectors were sent back into Iraq to assess the destructive capability of Saddam's army. When chief U.N. weapons inspector, Hans Blix, embarked upon a serious attempt to identify and dismantle Iraqi weaponry, the U.S. began to get seriously annoyed as its invasion was postponed. The delay gave ordinary citizens an opportunity to do something unprecedented—people in cities and towns around the world expressed their displeasure with the whole idea of this "pre-emptive" war,

something all the more remarkable because they were protesting before the war actually began. This caused the American triumvirate to announce it was skeptical of the inspection mission, while actively disparaging the efforts of the United Nations. Bush, Cheney and Rumsfeld then proceeded with plans for their transparently aggressive war.

Most of the Bush Gang were oil men. They knew where the oil was, and they had proceeded to surround it with arms and soldiers. Once the armed forces were in place, it seemed impossible for the Bush Gang to refrain from using them.

As for motivating the American public, there were sufficient stores of moral outrage built up, generated by September 11th, that it allowed the Bush administration to redirect that anger by constantly demonizing Saddam Hussein. Immediately after September 11th, Richard Perle had convened a meeting of the Defense Policy Board, and James Woolsey, the former CIA chief, was dispatched to Europe to find evidence of Saddam's connection to Osama Bin Laden. Weeks later he emerged with a story: "that an un-named informant had told Czech intelligence that he had seen the leader of the September 11th skyjackers meet with an Iraqi agent in Prague in the April before the attack. Even though the report was dismissed as not credible by U.S., British, French and Israeli intelligence agencies, it became the basis...of a major propaganda campaign against Iraq."[13]

The Bush administration also managed to make people feel that they were continually threatened by sounding regular alarms, from the fall of 2001 to the spring of 2003, about impending acts of terrorism that never materialized. Even though they were completely unsuccessful at showing that the terrorism of September 11th had any connection to Iraq, the White House, Fox TV, and others continued to broadcast a tremendous volume of innuendo and misinformation about Al Qaeda/Iraqi connections. Thus most Americans, 65% of them, according to a public opinion poll by Knight Ridder in January 2003, thought that Iraq was plotting terrorist attacks in conjunction with Al Qaeda. By a startling margin of 50% to 17%, most of them also believed that Iraqi terrorists had been on board the hijacked airliners on 9/11 (33% simply did not know).[14] In addition, because of the constant talk about weapons of mass destruction, many Americans also believed that Iraq must have been behind the anthrax attacks in the United States in 2001 even though the FBI and scientific observers insisted that all the evidence was pointing to an American perpetrator with connections to the U.S. government's own bio-weapons laboratories. Clearly the propaganda turned out by the right-wing think tanks and media was doing its part, along with not so carefully programmed intelligence information that was generated by the Department of Defense after September 11th.

All the questionable accusations against Iraq were distracting the public from the reality of the situation. The truth was that the Bush administration, having planned its strategy in the Project for a New American Century, had wanted to topple Saddam Hussein ever since they took office in 2001. There was plenty of support for this on the Republican Right, according to Marc Thiessen, spokesman for Republicans on the Senate Foreign Relations committee chaired by Sen. Jesse Helms. Thiessen explained why there was an effort to back the weak exile group known as the Iraqi National Congress (INC) : "The goal of our policy has to be the overthrow of Hussein.... Our strategy in Iraq must be the same as in Nicaragua, which was to provide the means and training necessary for the Contras to take back their country. Every argument used against the INC was used against the Contras. Until the U.S. got serious about helping, the Contras also weren't any more organized than the INC."[15]

The Iraqi National Congress did not look ready to fight or rule Iraq, however, for it had gained notoriety over the years for political infighting and dishonesty. There were numerous concerns about money that had disappeared or been mishandled in the past. Ahmed Chalabi, the INC leader, was the man brought to Baghdad at the conclusion of the Iraqi war as the American candidate to lead Iraq in the future. Chalabi, a long-time friend of Richard Perle, James Woolsey, and the PNAC, had not lived in Iraq for 40 years and had once been under indictment in Jordan for embezzlement. In 1987, Chalabi left Jordan with millions stolen from Petra Bank. He was tried in absentia, convicted, and slapped with a $46 million fine and a 22-year jail sentence. The governor of the Jordanian central bank called Chalabi "one of the most notorious crooks in the history of the Middle East." Chalabi clearly knew the way the Bush Gang liked to do business. In the fall of 2002, when major media sources started talking openly about the usefulness of all that Iraqi oil, *The Washington Post* wrote that Chalabi "favored the creation of a U.S.-led consortium to develop Iraq's oil fields, which have deteriorated under more than a decade of sanctions. 'American companies will have a big shot at Iraqi oil,' Chalabi said."[16]

When the Administration and Defense Department intelligence units tried to reinterpret data about Iraq that the CIA did not find particularly threatening, they had difficulty coming up with any hard evidence of any plots that could please the media. So, in the interests of pushing the public and the press along, and trying to counteract the growing antiwar sentiment in the U.S. and Europe, the U.S. government created yet another propaganda effort called the Committee for the Liberation of Iraq (CLI); it was initiated in November 2002 under the leadership of National Security Adviser, Condoleezza Rice. Its purpose: "education and advocacy efforts to mobilize U.S. and international support" for "freeing the Iraqi people from tyranny." In reality this committee was going to renew their "advocacy efforts" for war, because many of the members had been pushing for "liberation" in the Middle East ever since the Project of a New American Century (PNAC) was created in 1997. The chairman of CLI, Bruce Jackson, the secretary, Gary Schmitt, and the president, Randy Scheunemann, all held important positions within PNAC. Because of the PNAC's direct ties to the likes of Cheney, Rumsfeld, and Wolfowitz in the Bush government, and to the reliable press advocates who could spread the propaganda (such as William Kristol at *The Weekly Standard* and John Podhoretz at *The New York Post*), the Liberation Committee successfully added to the drumbeat of war. This kind of apparatus is always part of the repertoire of countries which are intent on invading others, and is most fully developed among countries that do it frequently—that is, empires. The British Empire liked to provoke such convenient battles with weak adversaries, and Rome, according to Joseph Schumpeter's classic essay, "The Sociology of Imperialism," was a master at arranging wars:

> There was no corner of the known
> world where some interest was not

alleged to be in danger or under actual attack. If the interests were not Roman, they were those of Rome's allies: and if Rome had no allies, then allies would be invented... The fight was always invested with an aura of legality. Rome was always being attacked by evil-minded neighbors, always fighting for a breathing space. The whole world was pervaded by a host of enemies, and it was manifestly Rome's duty to guard against their indubitably aggressive designs.[17]

Suffering From the Worst Complex of All—The Military Industrial Complex

The Cheney, Rumsfeld, and Bush triumvirate were anxious to put the gears of empire into motion. Are these men the true patriots? Or, are these men crazy? In either case, they are the embodiment of that specter that Eisenhower saw gathering years ago, the military-industrial complex.

> In the councils of government, we must guard against the acquisition of unwarranted influence, whether sought or unsought, by the military industrial complex. The potential for the disastrous rise of misplaced power exists and will persist. We must never let the weight of this combination endanger our liberties or democratic processes. We should take nothing for granted. Only an alert and knowledgeable citizenry can compel the proper meshing of the huge industrial and military machinery of defense with our peaceful methods and goals, so that security and liberty may prosper together.

Rumsfeld and Cheney are the products of the military industrial complex. They have been running back and forth from the Department of

Defense to private industry for decades, and so have their closest associates and deputies. Rumsfeld had been the youngest Secretary of Defense ever during the Ford administration when he was 43, and even then he did not flinch from making hard choices about extending U.S. power. In 1975-76 he kept aiding the Argentine military in its efforts to maintain a barbaric dictatorship, and he undermined Henry Kissinger's attempts to negotiate arms agreements with the Soviet Union through the Salt II talks. At the time, George Bush Senior, then the acting Director of the CIA, joined Rumsfeld in introducing the Committee on the Present Danger, a group of dedicated super-hawks, to the White House. The Committee had created a "Plan B" for American defense, a grandiose armament plan, based on a series of exaggerated appraisals of Soviet military strength. Though it was not adopted in the 1970s, it was developed further and used to convince Ronald Reagan, the Republican Party, and some Democrats that the United States had to invest heavily in defense appropriations during the 1980s.

Among those Democratic operatives who wanted to invest in war were some aides working for Henry "Scoop" Jackson, the Senator from the state of Washington and the beneficiary of great support from the aeronautics and defense industries. From their ranks came people, such as Richard Perle, who formed the core of the neo-conservatives that joined the Republican Party because they were not happy with the pro-peace factions that had grown up within the Democratic Party in the 1960s and 1970s.

Back in the 1950s, President Eisenhower dealt with people of this ultra-conservative persuasion throughout his eight years in office.

They frightened him because they believed the U.S. could fight, and win, a nuclear war with the Soviet Union. But he may not have suspected the level of chicanery and stupidity that these military-industrial types would display more than two decades later, when they decided to expedite the chemical warfare that was being waged by Saddam Hussein.

It all began in the 1980s when the United States actively encouraged Saddam Hussein in his war against the revolutionary government of Iran (at the time the major U.S. enemy in the Middle East.) The Iran/Iraq conflict was a very brutal war that lasted most of the decade, killing over a million soldiers on both sides. At a certain point the Iranians, with their superior numbers, seemed about to overwhelm Iraq. The United States and Great Britain, anxious to have Iraq prevail, responded with help in the form of loans and technology transfers that would help Iraq produce deadly chemical weapons.

In addition, the Department of Defense and the CIA supplied Iraq with surveillance photos of Iranian troops and other military information at the very moment that Iraqi soldiers began to make use of the poison gas. This did not seem to trouble U.S. military advisors. "The use of gas on the battlefield by the Iraqis was not a matter of deep strategic concern," said Walter Lang, a former senior U.S. defense intelligence officer. Long after the gas attacks, the United States and Britain also supplied the materials Iraq might need for biological warfare. According to reporter Maggie Burns: "The U.S. Department of Commerce licensed 70 biological exports to Iraq between 1985 and 1989, including at least 21 batches of lethal strains of anthrax, sent by the American Type Culture Collection Shipments."[18]

When Iraq used chemical weapons against the Iranian troops and the Kurds, no one was calling them "weapons of mass destruction." Instead, the United States chose to ignore their use. In 1983 and 1984, Donald Rumsfeld was sent on missions to Iraq by the Reagan/Bush administration to talk about the various ways the United States could help Saddam Hussein with economic and military assistance so that he would prevail in the war against Iran. Rumsfeld's March 1984 visit came at precisely the time that the U.N. first reported the use of poison gas by the Iraqis against the Iranians and its Kurdish allies on Iraq's northern border. Rumsfeld did not make a peep about this transgression of international law; nor did he or any other representative of the civilized West talk about "mass destruction," since the U.S. was in the midst of a massive armaments build-up of its own which in turn had prompted very large peace protests under the banner of The Nuclear Freeze. ("Weapons of Mass Destruction" is a loaded phrase that falsely suggests that biological and chemical weapons are in the same class as the real tools of mass annihilation, nuclear weapons. The use of the phrase began in the 1990s as part of the U.S./Israeli propaganda barrage leveled at Iraq.)

At the time that Rumsfeld's visit was helping to normalize relations, U.S. companies sold 45 helicopters to Iraq that were suitable for military use. Rumsfeld later told *The New York Times,* "It struck us as useful to have a relationship, given that we were interested in solving the Mideast problems." When Hussein used the helicopters to attack the Kurds of Northern Iraq with poison gas in 1988, the U.S. Senate passed a sanction to deny most weapons' technology to Iraq, but the White House vetoed the proposal.[19]

This incident demonstrates that the military-industrial complex is seldom denied its share of U.S. booty, and that the Bush I regime was especially attentive to the needs of military contractors in Iraq even when Saddam Hussein was in power.

The Bush II administration is now demonstrating that kicking Saddam out of power is an even more lucrative proposition. Given Dick Cheney's years of practice playing both sides of the game, it is not surprising that his former company, Halliburton, cruised right in for a killing when contracts were given out on Iraq. At the end of April 2003, Congressman Henry Waxman of California revealed that an open-ended deal was structured to channel up to $7 billion to Halliburton over a two-year period. When he brought pressure upon the Army Corps of Engineers to explain what was included in the no-bid, freebie contract, it became clear that it went far beyond emergency contingencies such as "extinguishing fires" in the oil fields during the immediate aftermath of the invasion. The Corps wrote that Halliburton also had the lucrative and very broad assignment of "operation of facilities and distribution products" for the entire Iraqi oil business.

Of course, other military contracting hogs were pushing their way to the trough, too, and some of them had a Bush pedigree. Bechtel, the largest construction firm in the U.S., latched onto its own no-bid contract for $700 million and was sure to win some more. George Schultz, a former Secretary of State during the Reagan/Bush years, once headed up the Bechtel firm (Caspar Weinberger, the convicted criminal who served as Secretary of Defense in the 1980s, was a vice president and general counsel for Bechtel). Schultz was chosen chairman of the advisory board of the Committee for the Liberation of Iraq (CLI) when it was hastily cobbled together in late 2002. One of CLI's stated purposes was "to work beyond the liberation of Iraq to the reconstruction of the economy." Jack Sheehen, retired general from the Marine Corps who served as senior vice president at Bechtel, got a close look at this reconstruction bonanza when he was appointed to the Defense Policy Board by Douglas Feith and Donald Rumsfeld.

The Center for Public Integrity, the watchdog group that follows the money trail in American politics, disclosed in early 2003 that at least 9 of the 30 members of the Board were "linked to companies that won more than $76 billion in defense contracts in 2001 and 2002."[20] The chairman of the Defense Policy Board, and one of the chief architects of the entire U.S. plan to subdue the Middle East, was none other than Richard Perle, one of the chief ideologists for the Pentagon along with his friend, Paul Wolfowitz. Because of public revelations in early 2003 about his own conflicts of interest and lucrative dealings in the war business, Perle was asked to step down from the chairmanship but the Bush Gang kept him on as a member of the advisory group.

Bob Herbert, columnist at *The New York Times*, linked two important realities lurking behind the Iraq war. First, "this iron web of relationships among powerful individuals inside and outside government" had succeeded at "achieving what they wanted all along, control of the nation of Iraq and its bounty." Secondly, the postwar gains of the military-industrial pirates in the Middle East were very much related to the structures of class piracy that the Bush Gang utilized at home: "There aren't a lot of rich kids in that desert. The U.S. military is largely working-class. The power brokers homing in on $100 billion worth of postwar reconstruction contracts are not."[21]

Lying Our Way Toward Empire With WMDs (Words of Mass Deception)

The groundwork for Empire was being laid by the U.S. (and the more covert sectors of its military/industrial complex) long before the Bush Gang came to power. Ever since World War II, the United States had been meddling in the Middle East. More often than not, U.S. intervention was accomplished through subterfuge rather than direct military means. Anti-U.S. sentiment in Iran was generated in large part by the ruthless way the U.S. undermined a democratic government in the early 1950s. We installed the Shah in order to solidify the dominant position of American oil interests, and then let him rule as a brutal dictator. The opposition that toppled the Shah in 1979 was destined to be a radical religious movement because the U.S. had previously encouraged the Shah's secret police to wipe out the secular leftist opposition.

In Iraq, the U.S. decided to give covert support to Saddam Hussein's Ba'ath Party nearly twenty years before they encouraged him to use his army to punish Iran. While they were granting various loans and credits to Iraq to support this war effort in the 1980s, the Bush sub-gang cooked up its plot to sell weapons to the Iranian mullahs in order to supply the Nicaraguan Contras with cash. Then, when Hussein's very bloody war against Iran was over, the U.S. immediately turned on him because he invaded Kuwait. Had U.S. diplomats and agents lured Saddam into war by not warning him of the consequences of his actions? Possibly yes, since we were up to our necks in intrigue already.

We never can get a completely accurate picture of the motives of the United States government when it operates on several conspiratorial levels at once without any requirement to come clean to the American people. The degree of secrecy with which we operate abroad is a severe blow to the operation of democracy and the rule of law. The number of criminal activities perpetrated by the CIA and the Defense Intelligence networks—ranging from drug dealing to assassination to toppling democratic regimes—is staggering. William Blum's books on the subject, *Killing Hope: U.S. Interventions in the Third World* and *Rogue State: A Guide to the World's Only Superpower*, provide a very lengthy list of "extremely serious interventions" in over 70 countries since World War II. Ex-CIA operations agents and intelligence analysts have recounted these episodes of imperial meddling in a slew of books; they are horrified by the work they once supported. Why does it happen? Blum summed it up in *Z Magazine* in 1999:

> The engine of American foreign policy has been fueled not by a devotion to any kind of morality, but rather by the necessity to serve other imperatives, which can be summarized as follows: making the world safe for American corporations; enhancing the financial statements of defense contractors at home who have contributed generously to members of congress; preventing the rise of any society that might serve as a successful example of an alternative to the capitalist model; extending political and economic hegemony over as wide an area as possible, as befits a "great power."[22]

These are the purposes of an empire, not of a democracy that wants to foster the development of other democracies. For a long time after World War II, the word "imperialism" could not be uttered in polite company in the U.S., unless it referred to the much more limited Eurasian realm of the Soviet Union. The U.S. struggle to win over the world was always couched in terms of spreading U.S.-style democracy, which was always pure and good. George Black wrote an informative book, *Garrison Guatemala*, concerning the U.S.-supported terror in Guatemala in the 1980s, and he placed a quotation from John Foster Dulles, U.S. Secretary of State in the 1950s, on his title page. It read: "The world is divided into two groups of people, the Christian anti-Communists and the others."

Now that there is no Communist Soviet Union to threaten U.S. interests, we find that the level of U.S. interventions has not diminished, but is higher than ever under the Bush administration. Cheney, Rumsfeld, and Bush are demonstrating every possible feature of imperialism. They are embarking full throttle on the activity that made Western Civilization superior to all others centuries ago—they are arming themselves to the teeth and plundering the rest of the world. We can expect them to lie, cheat, and steal in order to enrich themselves, since the Bush Gang's record of foreign intervention already proves that they are disposed to that kind of behavior. That said, we cannot necessarily know which of their objectives they have achieved by criminal conspiracy, especially without access to their secret files and sensitive documents. Mostly we have to take what we do know and fit it into the historical patterns.

To take one example: many people around the globe have amused themselves, or terrified themselves, with speculation about whether the United States purposely attacked itself with exploding jet airliners on September 11, 2001, thus giving itself an excuse to attack Al Qaeda and the Muslim world. It is possible, but very unlikely.

Much more likely is a different scenario. Let us recall that empires such as Rome and the British Empire always liked to provoke weaker countries into offensive activities, or even merely insulting activities, that could then be used as an excuse for invasion and conquest. As of late 2002, for instance, the Pentagon announced it was initiating new operations designed to draw terrorists in various parts of the world out from their lairs. A study recommended setting up P2OG, "Pro-Active, Preemptive Operations Groups," which would "launch secret operations aimed at 'stimulating reactions' among terrorists and states possessing weapons of mass destruction," wrote William M. Arkin, a military analyst, in *The Los Angeles Times*.[23] The idea was to "Develop an entirely new capability to proactively, preemptively evoke responses from adversary/terrorist groups," according to the Defense Science Board, a Pentagon advisory group. In English, this means to try to provoke the enemy into committing acts of terrorism and then squash them like bugs.

This Pentagon project suggests how wars and conflicts get started in the first place. Our struggles with Al Qaeda and Iraq have their origins with antagonisms created in large part by U.S. meddling in the world. While we did not force Al Qaeda to attack us, we did create the conditions under which Muslim fundamentalists ran rampant in Central Asia. As the books of Ahmed Rashid so carefully point out,[24] Al Qaeda and the Taliban would never have come into being or gained any terrorist expertise if they had not been trained and funded by the United States, Pakistan, and Saudi Arabia. The idea was to use them to unmercifully harass the Soviet Union and provoke a war in Afghanistan in the 1980s. The operation was very successful from the U.S. point of view for it helped lead to

the demise of the Soviet Union. The problems arose later when we ignored the terrorist fundamentalists we had created.

The Bush Gang, like the Clinton administration, was annoyed with Al Qaeda's activities, but they had bigger things on their mind, which they had already mapped out in their Project for the New American Century. They wanted to control the natural resources of the world, most especially hydrocarbons, and they wanted to control the Central Asian and Middle Eastern countries surrounding that oil and natural gas. They not only wanted strategic control over the energy products themselves, but they also wanted to set up military bases in various small countries and control energy distribution lines and routes going out to the rest of the world. Thus, by the summer of 2001, the Bush administration was surrounding the Taliban and Al Qaeda, organizing neighboring countries to help coerce Afghanistan into agreeing to oil pipeline deals with American companies, and threatening to invade the country if they did not comply.

All of this helped provoke the devastating attacks on the World Trade Towers and the Pentagon. They constitute a horrific example of "blowback," the word coined by the CIA for the unintentional repercussions of covert operations and subversion practiced by those who are trying to manipulate geopolitical events around the world.[25] Did the Bush triumvirate expect that by antagonizing Al Qaeda they would elicit such a terrible attack?

I think not. But once the acts of infamy were committed, the United States had more than enough excuse to retaliate en masse in Afghanistan, move into military bases in the surrounding countries to the north, and then pursue, unrelentingly, its course of war with Iraq. Rumsfeld was ready, as he revealed on

September 11th with his instructions to his subordinates. Less than three hours after the airliners crashed into the World Trade Towers and the Pentagon, the CIA began reporting to Rumsfeld that signs clearly pointed to Bin Laden. Rumsfeld accordingly ordered the military to begin preparing strike plans. Notes made at the time revealed his intentions, "Best info fast. Judge whether good enough hit S.H. at same time. Not only UBL." The last initials refer to Usama (or Osama) Bin Laden. The first set refer to Saddam Hussein. Rumsfeld did not care if he had evidence against Saddam or not. He had already determined to get him and Iraq's oil. The notes quote him as saying, "Go massive. Sweep it all up. Things related and not."26

Nothing was going to stop Rumsfeld, Cheney, and the rest of the Gang from stepping into the middle of the Middle East. Certainly lack of evidence was not stopping them. By September 15, 2001, according to Bob Woodward's *Bush at War*, Rumsfeld's right hand man, Paul Wolfowitz, "put forth military arguments to justify a U. S. attack on Iraq instead of Afghanistan." This is a familiar imperial pattern that frightened the rest of the world. Although no one felt very sorry for Saddam Hussein personally, other countries did not like watching a country and its people be steadily impoverished and beaten down as Fox TV and CNN pounded out the rhythm on their war drums. Aside from the incessant media propaganda, there was the continuous pattern of outright lies—one could call them WMDs, or "words of mass deception"—that were peddled by George Bush, Dick Cheney, Donald Rumsfeld, Colin Powell, Tony Blair, and a host of lesser minions.

This was not just ordinary lying, an effort to conceal the facts, but "bald-faced lying," the practice of repeating accusations that have already been demonstrated to be false. Well before the war began, President Bush and his helpers claimed that Iraq's possession of so-called "weapons of mass destruction" was the primary reason for invading the country. Bush claimed that "the Iraqi regime continues to possess and conceal some of the most lethal weapons ever devised." Cheney frightened a convention of the Veterans of Foreign Wars seven months before the invasion by painting an ominous scene: "The Iraqi regime has in fact been very busy enhancing its capabilities in the field of chemical and biological agents, and they continue to pursue the nuclear program they began so many years before." Along the way the Gang listed the awful weaponry that had to be taken out of the hands of tyrant of Baghdad: 500 tons of mustard and nerve gas, 25,000 liters of anthrax, 38,000 liters of botulinum toxin, 29,984 prohibited chemical munitions devices, dozens of SCUD missiles, 18 mobile weapons factories. Ari Fleischer, White House press secretary, summed it up when he stated flatly on April 10, 2003: "this is what the war is all about."

On February 6, 2003, the day after Colin Powell presented the United Nations with a laundry list of Iraq's terroristic weapons and activities, the Iraqi ambassador to the U.N., Mohammed Aldouri, said Powell's speech was "utterly unrelated to the truth."

Three months later, Aldouri was proven correct. "Frustrated, U.S. Arms Team to Leave Iraq: Task Force Unable To Find Any Weapons," announced the headline on May 11, 2003 in *The Washington Post*. Reporter Barton Gellman wrote about the feeling of the soldiers of the special unit he traveled with: "They said they expected to find what Secretary of State

Colin L. Powell described at the U.N. Security Council on Feb. 5—hundreds of tons of biological and chemical agents, missiles and rockets to deliver the agents, and evidence of an ongoing program to build a nuclear bomb. Scores of fruitless missions broke that confidence, many task force members said in interviews."

In June 2003 *U.S. News and World Report* revealed that when Powell practiced his mendacious delivery at CIA headquarters on February 1, he "tossed several pages in the air. 'I'm not reading this,' he declared. 'This is bullshit'." The Defense Intelligence Agency had long before concluded that "there is no reliable information on whether Iraq is producing and stockpiling chemical weapons." Their report was issued in September of 2002, at the very time Donald Rumsfeld was lying to Congress and claiming that Saddam's "regime has amassed large, clandestine stockpiles of chemical weapons, including VX, sarin, cyclosarin and mustard gas."[27]

The weapons did not exist. Nor had any proof come to light that Saddam had conspired to harm the U.S.A. through connections to Al Qaeda or by sharing nuclear weapons material with other terrorists. Even before the war began Mohammed El Baradei, Director General of the International Atomic Energy Commission, dismissed the U.S. evidence of a nuclear weapons program in Iraq as a fabrication based on a forged document from the African country of Niger. Subsequent reporting by Seymour Hersh in *The New Yorker* showed that State Department officials knew that this was a patently false document for a year before Colin Powell presented it as part of his misleading testimony to the United Nations in January of 2003.[28]

On April 22, 2003, the day that Hans Blix requested that the U.N. Security Council to send his team back to Iraq, he told the BBC, "I think it's been one of the disturbing elements that so much of the intelligence on which the capitals built their case seemed to have been so shaky." Blix also said it was "conspicuous" that nothing was turning up so long after the invasion, and that he did not want his inspectors treated like "dogs on a leash" by the American military. In any case, the U.S. was adamant that they did not need any further contribution from the U.N. weapons teams.

And why should they want assistance from the U.N.? Blix was likely to keep contradicting the false intelligence information that had been so carefully crafted in Washington. When Rumsfeld's Defense Department did not like the intelligence data produced by the CIA or by its own DIA (the Defense Intelligence Agency), it simply turned to small groups like the Office of Special Plans which it had created to turn out reports that justified U.S. actions. "They didn't like the intelligence they were getting," one former intelligence officer told investigative reporter Hersh, "and so they brought in people to write the stuff. They were so crazed and so far out and so difficult to reason with—to the point of being bizarre. Dogmatic, as if they were on a mission from God." Patrick Lang, the former chief of Middle East intelligence at the DIA., summed it up for Hersh, 'The Pentagon has banded together to dominate the government's foreign policy, and they've pulled it off.'"[29]

This overly aggressive stance by the United States is bound to make the rest of the world distrustful of American motives. The U.S. was implicitly threatening to destabilize any countries which stray slightly from the imperial plan, whether or not they are ruled by democracies or dictators. The behavior of the Bush

Gang suggests that there were more interventions to come, for Rumsfeld and the State Department are exerting great pressure on Iran and Syria and trotting out the same WMD accusations that triggered the Iraqi invasion. "It's bait and switch," a former high-level intelligence official told Seymour Hersh. "Bait them into Iraq with weapons of mass destruction. And, when they aren't found, there's this whole bullshit about the weapons being in Syria."[30]

This kind of gunboat diplomacy followed the course of action that the neo-conservatives such as Perle, Wolfowitz and Woolsey had charted for dominance of the Middle East; it also fit the classic pattern of Anglo-American imperialist strategy that was established more than a century earlier. Great powers have often used military and economic intimidation to get their way without necessarily resorting to outright invasion and occupation.

This kind of efficient imperial influence has been wielded by both Britain and the United States in Latin America for nearly two centuries. One can expect that the U.S. will soon turn more of its attention to its traditional backyard in the Western Hemisphere even as it continues to apply pressure on other Islamic countries in the East. If the Bush Gang remains in power after 2004, they will have the opportunity to renew or intensify destabilization efforts against Cuba and Venezuela; they also may decide that Luis da Silva's democratic, left-leaning government in Brazil needs to be disciplined and brought into line. If so, U.S. imperial intervention would be following the Anglo-Ameirican pattern that was played out in Chile in both the 19th and 20th centuries, and then again in Venezuela in 2002.

The Cost of Imperial Displeasure

In 1888 Balmaceda, the reformist President of Chile, unveiled a plan to nationalize the nitrate industries by buying out the British. The investment community in Britain provoked an uproar in the London press, where Balmaceda was called a "butcher" and a "dictator of the worst sort." The English proceeded to stage a fake "civil war" on Chile's border with Peru and insist that the unstable Chilean government was endangering their investments. British warships were brought in to blockade Chile's ports. President Balmaceda was despondent over the failure of his reforms and his lack of a political network that could resist the British, and he committed suicide. By 1890, three quarters of all Chilean exports went through Great Britain.

Less than a hundred years later in 1970, Salvador Allende, a democratic socialist, was elected President of Chile after running for the office for twenty years. He promised to nationalize the copper mines, which had become Chile's major export industry, and compensate the American owners. The American ambassador to Chile sent a message back to Washington even before Allende took office, saying "we shall do everything in our power to condemn Chile and all Chileans to utmost deprivation and poverty." Allende survived all kinds of destabilization attempts funded by the CIA, including a trucking company strike that caused work stoppages and economic hardship. Upper-middle class Chileans, accustomed to live much better than the working classes, were incited by U.S.-funded, right-wing newspapers to come out in the streets and bang on their pots and pans in protest. Still Allende held on without violating democratic freedoms and was on the verge of picking up even more support in the Chilean Congress. At this point the United States became desperate, with Secretary of State Henry Kissinger sputtering, "I don't see why we have to stand by and watch a country go Communist due to the irresponsibility of its own people." The CIA then began working with its friends in the Chilean army on a final solution to Chilean independence, because, as Kissinger said, "the issues are much too important for the Chilean voters to be left to decide for themselves."

Since the CIA had already assisted in the assassination of the Army chief of staff who was loyal to Allende, right-wing military forces under General Pinochet were able to stage a violent coup while an offshore U.S. Navy ship communicated with them. President Allende died at the presidential palace while under attack by his own army. Many supporters were tortured and murdered and ten percent of the Chilean population fled into exile, while Pinochet brought the "free market" and dictatorship to Chile for the next sixteen years.

A very similar script was followed thirty years later in Venezuela in 2002; President Chavez was attempting to reorganize the nation's very profitable state-owned oil business in order to bring prosperity, better education, and health care to the majority of the population. As mentioned in the previous chapter, Eliot Abrams had returned to work for the Bush Gang on the other side of the world while Otto Reich was back doing what he did best. On his advice and with the backing of other American friends, the upper classes of Venezuela tried to stage a coup but failed when the military would not follow a few corrupt senior officers.

Six months later, right-wing business leaders, who controlled all the media in the country, tried another tack. They had their allies, the oil executives, stage a lock-out and shut-down of the entire oil industry, cutting off all exports. Meanwhile the conservative media oligarchy called for daily demonstrations in the wealthy areas of Caracas, the capital city. All day long the TV stations showed middle class demonstrators who were banging loudly on their pots and pans, just like their counterparts in Chile years before. Stories and images of the strike by the rich were carried out to newspapers and television stations all over the world, portraying a whole country in rebellion and in great distress.

In reality, the majority of the population were not affected and went on with daily life in the streets and markets, while the armed forces tried to help load the oil tankers that were scheduled to make deliveries around the world. In Venezuela, the divide between rich and poor was immense, and it mimicked, in one country, the split that exists in the whole world. The twenty percent (or less) of the population that was middle class and rich was predominantly white and Spanish. The eighty percent that struggled to get by on very little were a more brown-skinned mix of indigenous Americans, descendants of African slaves, and poor whites. Their president was the first in Venezuelan history who was brown-skinned himself.

The rich were calling on the U.S. for help, not because they were being abused, but because they did not want to share Venezuela's wealth with their fellow citizens. At Christmas time 2002 the upper-class strike began to fizzle, and some non-rich Venezuelans joked that the wealthy could not sustain their rebellion because they always did their shopping in Miami at that time of year. More significantly, the Organization of American States would not relent to pressure from Washington and condemn President Chavez. Instead they called for the continuation of democratic rule at the same time that the left-leaning President-elect of Brazil, Luis da Silva, conveyed his support to Chavez.

The question remained: was it possible for a democratic government that had resisted the wishes of Washington to survive the standard de-stabilization plan? At the very moment that the Bush Gang was mobilizing its forces to control the oil of the Middle East, its imperial will was being challenged by democratically elected elements in its own backyard. Just as mainstream conservative forces were openly praising the idea of an American Empire and launching the half-baked idea that it would bring democracy and freedom to large parts of the Muslim world and Asia, the United States was being embarrassed by its clumsy attempts to subvert freedom and re-privatize the oil resources of Venezuela.

Perhaps the Bush administration had launched too many initiatives (or acts of piracy) at the same time. In its anxiety to plunder the world and plunder its own citizens, the U.S. appeared to be overstepping the bounds of the possible. Would the world wake up and throw roadblocks in front of the marauders? Would the American people wake up to the fact that they might have to pay for an imperial army for many years to come?

Eighteen

They Stole Our Democracy

Can We Take It Back?

When corporate criminals invade our workplaces and our markets to steal our jobs and our savings, we must react every bit as decisively as when thieves enter our homes and try to bring harm to our loved ones. And we must respond just as strongly when co-conspirators of those criminals occupy and take control of our government, our legislative bodies and our regulatory agencies.

—John Sweeney, president of the AFL-CIO, July 2002

ail to the Thief! Hail to the Thief!"—20,000 protesters were shouting this greeting to George W. Bush on his inauguration day, January 20, 2001. The newly selected president decided not to walk the last four blocks through the crowd to the inauguration ceremony, as presidents had done for the last forty years, and rode in his limousine instead.

Loss of Nerve

There are always sore losers in an election. And then there are those who did not lose. When Democrats saw Bush lose the popular election by over half a million votes, only to have the Supreme Court award the presidency to him by a single vote, they were understandably upset. On the other hand, the rules are the rules, and the American system has an antiquated structure that dates back to a time when most people were not allowed to vote. Electoral votes count, not popular votes, thus the narrow victories in a handful of small states, plus the disputed vote in Florida, pushed Bush over the top.

A month-long battle was waged to see how those Florida votes should be counted and the Republicans won the fight. Because the Democrats were less tenacious, they lost their chance to influence the recount process and persuade the American people that the election was being hijacked. Certainly the Supreme Court tipped the balance with its 5-4 vote, but that was to be expected because of the partisan divisions already present on the Court. Rupert Murdoch's clever ploy, hiring a Bush cousin who announced his victory prematurely, was a nasty little trick but it did not cost Al Gore the election.

The story of the real crime was published first outside the United States. Greg Palast, an

American journalist, told the secret of Bush's Florida advantage in *The London Observer*, on November 26, 2000, sixteen days before the Supreme Court decided to award Bush the presidency. Before the election, 56,000 African Americans had been wiped off the voting rolls in the state of Florida for being ex-felons. Supposedly, they were not allowed to vote according to Florida law because they had been convicted of serious crimes. Katharine Harris, the Secretary of State of Florida and George W. Bush's state campaign director during the election, had hired DataBase Technologies (DBT) to check over the state's voter lists. The company worked with such zeal that they eliminated a great many voters, particularly African Americans, who were not ex-felons at all. Because 90% or more of African Americans voted Democratic in Florida, Gore's victory would have been assured if they had been permitted to vote.

Michael Moore picked up on Palast's story and fashioned the opening of his entertaining and informative book, *Stupid White Men*, around the electoral fraud in Florida and the denial of voting rights to African Americans. Greg Palast enlarged on the theme in his own book, *The Best Democracy Money Can Buy*, and added details in a *Harper's* article.[1] For instance, one Florida county, without instruction from the state capital, checked every one of 694 names on the list of excluded voters that was sent by Harris and DataBase Technologies and found that only 34 were really ex-felons. Most counties did not check. DataBase was not really the primary villain because it did send a letter to Harris suggesting that all local election officials should check addresses and bank accounts to make sure they were excluding the right people. A handwritten note was later found attached to

this written suggestion in the state election department's files; it said "Don't need." In this way Katharine Harris, daughter of one of the richest men in Texas, helped fix the election beforehand; afterwards she would limit the recount process in such a way that it limited Al Gore's chances to win. In 2002, she decided to go to Washington, too, and was elected to Congress from a safe Republican district.

The tragedy for the Democratic Party and the democratic form of government was not the commission of this crime, for humans are always capable of immoral activity, but the fact that this story was not uncovered or seized upon during the recount process in November of 2000 by the Democrats themselves. Many top Democrats lost their nerve. Republicans came running to Florida ready to duke it out, led by James Baker, the tough, old, upper-class warrior who was the brains behind the first Bush Gang. Jesse Jackson arrived the day after the election to join a variety of black, white, Haitian, and Hispanic voters who had been discouraged from voting, harassed by police, or confused by funny-looking ballots. These Democrats were mounting rousing, but polite street demonstrations, but they received scant encouragement from Al Gore and Democratic leaders, who must have thought the protest was lacking in decorum.

Republicans, on the other hand, were ready to get downright ferocious. On Nov. 22, 2000, four days before Greg Palast's original *Observer* article appeared, Republicans called in their forces, including many activists from outside the state, to stage a variety of protests in counties that were performing recounts that might be favorable to Gore. In what was later called "Brooks Brothers riot" they converged on a Miami canvassing board that was starting to examine ballots and caused such a fuss that they eventually intimidated and discouraged the poll workers and helped stop the recount.

This fit a long-standing pattern. The Democrats have been letting the Bush Gang walk all over them since the 1980s. George W. Bush's first in-depth experience with presidential electioneering was working on his father's campaign in 1988 in close daily contact with Lee Atwater, the unscrupulous political genius who ran the Bush campaign under the guidance of Roger Ailes. The low point of the campaign was the racist "Willie Horton" ad, which featured a scary-looking picture of an African American convict who had been released from jail in Massachusetts and had raped a white woman. This was good 'ol Southern lynching propaganda, and it was aimed at Michael Dukakis, the Democratic governor of Massachusetts and Bush's opponent. The Republicans obviously thought they could get away with the crudest appeals to anti-black, right-wing populism among white voters, by suggesting that Dukakis was going to let such criminals run free across all America.

Atwater later admitted, when he was dying of a brain tumor, that he was ashamed of this kind of work. Said Atwater, "In 1988, fighting Dukakis, I said that I 'would strip the bark off the little bastard' and 'make Willie Horton his running mate.' I am sorry for both statements: the first for its naked cruelty, the second because it makes me sound racist, which I am not. Mostly I am sorry for the way I thought of other people. Like a good general, I had treated everyone who wasn't with me as against me."[2]

Earlier, shortly after that 1988 election, Atwater explained to political analyst William Greider why it worked. "I think the Dukakis campaign badly miscalculated thinking that they could get away with an issueless campaign. I'm very glad that they did not develop the populist theme that they began in the last two weeks...there is constantly a war going on between the parties for the populist vote, the swing vote in every election. The Democrats have always got to nail the Republicans as the party of the fat cats, the party of upper class and privilege. And the Democrats will maintain they are the party of the common man."[3] (The other young party operative, who was learning from Atwater and became friends with George W. Bush during that 1988 campaign, was Karl Rove. He had already studied electoral crime at the feet of Donald Segretti, Nixon's "dirty tricks" expert in the 1972 election who was later convicted for distributing false campaign literature.)

The Democrats Need Some Pride

The Democratic Party has caved in on two of the issues that should have made it most proud, its traditional alliance with working people and its efforts to promote racial equality. Ever since Republicans adopted the Southern Strategy in Nixon's election campaign of 1968 and used George Wallace's populist appeal to racism, they shifted their base of strength from the North to the South. In the hands of emerging leaders like Senator Trent Lott of Mississippi, the Party of Lincoln became the Party of Jefferson Davis. Lott finally embarrassed himself in 2002 by the way he praised the good ol' days of Strom Thurmond, the ancient and racist Senator who once ran for president on the slogan of "Segregation Forever!"

Lott had been able to climb to the position of Senate Majority leader without having to hide his own racist tendencies. While campaigning for Reagan in 1984, he spoke to the Sons of Confederate Veterans and said, "The spirit of Jefferson Davis lives in the 1984 Republican platform." This was demonstrably true, for nineteen years after the Democratic Party had pushed through the Voting Rights Act and ended one hundred years of Jim Crow laws in the South, the Reagan/Bush administration, under the direction of Attorney General Edwin Meese, was trying to stop the progress of civil rights in the United States. Lott's long-term associations with the Conservative Citizens Council, a successor to the overtly racist White Citizens Council, were revealed when he became Senate majority leader by alternative news groups such as FAIR, but were ignored by the mainstream media.

This failure may have reflected the unspoken racism inherent in moderate/liberal news organizations, but another factor was more important—the racist strategy worked for the Republicans because so many in the Democratic Party were retreating on issues of race. Why hadn't they pilloried Lott for his role in keeping black students out of his Sigma Nu fraternity in the early 1960s? At the time his racism was not aimed at keeping people of color out of Sigma Nu at Ol' Miss because none of the African-American students were crazy enough to apply for membership. Trent wanted the race ban maintained nationally, and he fervently argued that the whole Sigma Nu organization would have to be disbanded if chapters in the North were allowed to pledge black members. The Northern representatives of Sigma Nu backed down, and Trent Lott and racism won their first

battle; but at least the frat boys from the North came back in the late '60s and forced a vote for integration.

White Democrats should have countered with well-planned political offensives when the Republicans played the race card. They should have dared to put their beliefs on the line in the 1970s, '80s, and '90s, and contrasted Lott's, and the whole Republican Party's, immoral stance on race with their own positive contributions. A well-conceived anti-racist campaign could have won over most of the media and isolated the prejudiced Republicans in the South. As we know, the opposite happened: the Democratic Party embraced moderate candidates from the South, who then tried, not always successfully, to win over white Southerners. While these Democrats won some states for themselves in presidential elections, the entire South turned into a Republican swamp that sent some of its worst critters to take over both the House and Senate.

The Democratic record of standing up for the working classes was even worse. Party leaders abandoned their main constituency. At least on the issue of race, Clinton came across as a president who clearly enjoyed the company and the assistance of many African Americans. On the issue of how to communicate to the large majority of Americans who earn wages and moderate salaries for a living, a whole string of Democrats—Gore, Clinton, Dukakis, Carter— had little clue of how to win the support of working people and promote their interests. Instead of bolstering the efforts of unions, too many Democrats avoided them, and could no longer articulate why rising profits should be accompanied by rising wages. They had come to disregard the successes of the New Deal that had depended upon the Democratic Party portraying itself as a universal party that could advance the interests of all citizens at once.

The single most effective thing the Democratic Party could have done over the past twenty years was to remind all working people which party was on their side. They needed to speak to the white working man in particular, and tell him that the Republican Party was playing him for a chump. Ever since Nixon's victory in 1968 the Republicans had been successful in winning over the votes of white males by appealing to the patriotism of disgruntled "middle America." They told "Joe Lunch-Bucket" that Democrats cared about everyone but him. They did this at the same time that it was easily demonstrable that working people's wages and salaries were falling, especially during the rule of Reagan and Bush Gang I. So who was stealing the money out of his wallet?

The thieves were the very guys he'd been voting for, the guys whose wars he'd been cheering on, the guys who got tough on crime and threw everyone behind bars except themselves (because they had a giant economy to loot and they hadn't finished the job). The Republicans not only kept the average white male's wage and salary from going up, they pushed it down—hard. These Republicans, or more precisely the movers and shakers behind the Republican Party, the owners and executives of big business and big banks, were the ones most responsible for deciding that capital would enjoy higher returns if they lowered the average worker's pay. One of the keys to this approach was the anti-labor policy that pushed the percentage of unionized workers in private industry (who had been predominantly males) down from 35% to 9% over a forty year period. The opposite was true in the public sphere, where less discrimination on racial and gender grounds was allowed,

and where the employer could not threaten to send good government jobs to Mexico or Bangladesh. In 2002, 37.4% of government workers were unionized, almost exactly the same as the peak reached in the private sector in the 1950s. (As previously discussed, this is likely to drop: immediately after the 2002 election the Bush Gang II took aim at the unionized public sector and announced that it was ready to privatize up to one-half of all federal jobs.)

The Democratic leaders from the South, coming from the anti-union states where so many businesses were relocating because they could pay lower wages and benefits, were not prepared to argue on behalf of labor organizations or persuade working class and middle class citizens that collective bargaining would most assuredly increase their incomes and job security. They were not prepared to tell voters, poor and middle class alike, that there was a sure way to drastically diminish the welfare rolls of the United States and that was to provide jobs at decent wages for everyone who wanted to work. Democrats were not willing to say, flat out, that a country as rich as ours would simply have to supply good health care to all its citizens.

Democrats Once Spoke Up For Working People

All of the above were promises that Franklin Roosevelt and Harry Truman were making in the 1940s, not as pie-in-the-sky dreams for the future, but as the next concrete steps that the world's most productive society was capable of taking on behalf of its people. In his "Fireside Chat" radio program of January 11, 1944, Roosevelt explicitly told the American people they deserved "a second Bill of Rights" which would encompass the economic rights of all citizens to fair employment, good education, adequate medical care, and security in their old age. The new economic rights that Roosevelt listed for his audience sounded pretty substantial:

> The right to a useful and remunerative job in the industries or shops or farms or mines of the nation; the right to earn enough to provide adequate food and clothing and recreation; the right of farmers to raise and sell their products at a return which will give them and their families a decent living; the right of every businessman, large and small, to trade in an atmosphere of freedom from unfair competition and domination by monopolies at home or abroad; the right of every family to a decent home; the right to adequate medical care and the opportunity to achieve and enjoy good health; the right to adequate protection from the economic fears of old age and sickness and accident and unemployment; and finally, the right to a good education.[4]

Some might question whether Roosevelt was really promising to deliver all of these "rights" to the American people, or whether, had he lived past early 1945, he would have been able to deliver on such promises. Was he a progressive anti-capitalist? Certainly not. Was he progressive enough to map out a viable alternative to the Republicans on many issues? Yes. The reason the New Deal and Truman's Fair Deal were so attractive to most Americans was that they proposed universal economic programs that would benefit everyone, just as Social Security did. There was no practical reason that these programs could not have been successfully realized fifty years ago. And there was only one reason that they were not provided then—the resistance of big business.

Throughout the late 1940s and the 1950s, conservative Republicans allied themselves with corporate America and used the rhetoric of the Cold War to attack labor organizations and the egalitarian proposals of the Democrats as "socialistic." Roosevelt realized that keeping the New Deal coalition together after World War II would not be easy and he anticipated that reactionary forces within the United States would try to make a comeback; in the same 1944 "Fireside Chat" that proposed the "second Bill of Rights," he explicitly mentioned the prospect of a "rightist reaction." He warned:

> If such a reaction should develop—if history were to repeat itself and we were to return to the so-called normalcy of the 1920s—then it is certain that even though we shall have conquered our enemies on the battlefields abroad, we shall have yielded to the spirit of Fascism here at home.[5]

The Right did make a comeback in the late 1940s and early 1950s, culminating in rhetoric during the McCarthy era that had a distinctly fascistic ring. In spite of this reaction, significant remnants of the broad-based populist coalition built by Roosevelt and progressive Democrats held up, primarily because they had offered universal provisions for social and economic security to the American people. Many of the compromises governing the interactions of business and labor unions kept working throughout the 1950s and 1960s. While the corporate world clearly had the upper hand, some measure of equilibrium had been gained through the New Deal in the 1930s by putting limits on capital and guaranteeing certain powers and legal rights to labor.

Much to the consternation of right-wing capitalists, these measures ended up being very conducive to overall economic growth in the United States, Europe, and Japan. In fact, their economies functioned more efficiently than ever before, and capitalist manufacturing was more productive precisely because limits were put on the kinds of speculation and the levels of exploitation that were allowed. This could hardly be called socialism since the great firms and enterprises were definitely capitalist in formation, yet there were some elements of "social democracy" present, more so in Europe than in the United States. Governments used the direct, democratic assertion of power to institute some social controls over the use and outcomes of capital. They demanded that a share of the profits or surplus be put aside, utilizing the straight forward method of taxing the high incomes of both the wealthy and the corporations. Then, that surplus was used for a variety of useful social purposes ranging from good public schools and inexpensive public universities to the interstate highway system.

It is precisely since these controls on capital worked, and the constrained capitalist industries functioned so well, that the notion of "capital" comes up again and again in this book. The Republicans talk about capital all the time: capital gains, capital formation, capital stock. The Republican Party is the party of unrestrained capital, and has been for a hundred and thirty years, for all its basic values pay homage to the elitist notion that those who can amass the money are entitled to be the leaders of American government. This follows in the tradition of Hamilton and the Federalist Party, including John Jay, the president of the Continental Congress and the first chief justice of the U.S. Supreme Court, who was fond of a particular, elitist guideline for ruling the nation:

The people who own the country ought to govern it.

If the Democrats or any other party, such as the Greens, hope to distinguish themselves from this conservative tradition, they must, like Lincoln, clearly state a preference for labor over capital. If Abraham Lincoln, hardly a socialist, could argue on moral grounds that "labor is the superior of capital, and deserves much the higher consideration," then so can a 21st century opposition party. It is sad that the Democrats are so shy about this, because they have the right to utter the word "capital," too, and ought to be able to demonstrate the ways in which the wise employment of capital, moderated by such laws as the Glass-Steagall Act and the Wagner Act, led to prosperity in the past. Perhaps they are still afraid of being called socialists, communists, or Bolsheviks, epithets that the Republicans have used for a century or more in their fight to guarantee that capital gets much the higher consideration than labor.

If Lincoln could talk about labor and capital in the same sentence, so can the Democrats. If they want to say that "people should come before money" (a variation on "labor is the superior of capital"), this is exactly the kind of populist message that Lee Atwater said the Democrats need if they are going to overcome right-wing populism. In fact, by invoking Lincoln's respect for toil and labor, the Democrats have all the more reason to assume the "Party of Lincoln" label from the Republicans and leave them under the shameful cloud of Trent Lott and the "Party of Jefferson Davis." A political party that could demonstrate it was both the "Party of Lincoln" and "the Party of Roosevelt" would be difficult to defeat.

A Democratic Strategy?

In assessing the failure of the Democrats to defeat George W. Bush in 2000, there is no shortage of blame to go around. The Democrats spent eight years in the presidency and never distinguished themselves as a force for equality and progress because they were too dependent on corporate lobbyists and the largesse of wealthy donors. Centrist politics, that is, moderately conservative politics of the sort that characterized the Republican Eisenhower administration, were the forte of Bill Clinton and Al Gore. They were pushed around by rabid right-wing bullies in the Republican Party because they were not willing to present a forthright, democratic, egalitarian program to the American people.

They should have said, "We are the party of white, black and brown people. We are the party of working class and middle class people, and a few rich people, too. We are the party of women and men. We are the party of every ethnic group in the world that has decided to settle in the United States. We are the party of every religious believer and every believer in freedom. We believe in economic equality, racial equality, gender equality, and equal access to education and health care. We believe you have an equal right to speak your mind."

"The other guys," Clinton and Gore could have said, "Do not believe in these things. They are white, sexist, anti-egalitarian, anti-democratic, fundamentalist Christian, authoritarian, and they are either rich or willing to be the humble servants of the rich. They believe inequality of all kinds is necessary and right, and that God approves of a world that is ruled by the few. Sure, there are some nice guys among the Republicans, but they have been completely overwhelmed by those who are preaching inequality and intolerance."

Because they could not bring themselves to say most of those things, Clinton and Gore were pummeled into submission during their years in office, and Gore ran a weak campaign for President and lost. In contrast, Ralph Nader ran a pretty fine campaign for president and won two to three percent of the national vote. The reaction of many Democrats was to blame Nader for Gore's defeat, an understandable sentiment in such a close election. Had Nader not run, Gore would have received enough votes to win in spite of the Republican thievery in Florida. Yet to direct the blame at Nader is to mask the very weakness in the Democratic Party that must be addressed if they hope to regain power.

The Democratic Party spent decades unraveling and failing to rebuild its party base. Some of the unraveling was fine and necessary because it allowed the racist white, conservative components to exit in the Southern states and realign themselves with the conservative Republicans. Some of conservative Democratic city bosses in the north retired as their old constituents moved out to the suburbs. These factors of change disrupted the party for several years in the 1970s, but also gave it the potential of becoming a truly progressive party that could honor all or most of the egalitarian possibilities listed above. What is more, this path was not based on utopian ideas that would only appeal to a minority, for every kind of demographic shift was favoring the Democrats, and especially so by the 1990s. Increased minority populations and immigration would eventually favor a party that was tolerant of racial, ethnic, and linguistic diversity. Dual-earner households in which men and women both worked and cared for children would encourage gender equality and a market for good daycare and schools. An aging population would require more attention to government programs that could sustain older people in dignity and in good health without using up the savings of the elderly and their middle-aged children.

Furthermore, all polls of the American people over a thirty-year period that focused on various issues favored by the Democrats—providing good health care and education to all, taking strong action to protect the environment, providing jobs to the unemployed, reducing expenditures on the military and armaments—showed that the overwhelming majority agreed with the Democrats, even at the height of Ronald Reagan's personal popularity in the 1980s.[6] The Party was not getting stronger as an organization, however, in part because it did not have the confidence to recreate itself as a dynamic, progressive organization. The number of committed party regulars, the folks who do the work and handle phone calls and help the candidates, dwindled to such a point that active Republican regulars were said to outnumber their Democratic counterparts by a ratio as high as ten to one. Republicans, meanwhile, had been drafting party workers like crazy, many of them evangelical and fundamentalist Christians brought in by their enthusiasm for Pat Robertson and others on the Christian Right. Republicans not only had the big money donations that they traditionally received from their friends in banking and business, but they also enjoyed the constant flow of small donations from the millions of new party hopefuls who were building up the base.

Here was the anomaly. At a time when demographics and public opinion should have favored the Democrats, the Democratic leadership relied overwhelmingly on big money donations to cover for poor Party organization. Clinton and Gore relied on Big Money that looked an awful lot like Republican Big Money; much of it was coordinated through organizations like the Democratic Leadership Council and the Harriman groups, such as "Democrats for the '80s" and "Democrats for the '90s," that had no grassroots base at all. That is, they were simple political shells for attracting either corporate money or large donations from rich individuals. The party base was irrelevant. The big donors had very little in common with the views of ordinary voters. Nowhere was this better illustrated than in a political poll conducted before the 1996 election and analyzed by Ruy Teixeira and Robert Borosage. The viewpoints of one thousand citizens were compared to the viewpoints of two hundred big-money political donors, half of them Republicans and half of them Democrats.

- 83 percent of ordinary citizens believed that most American families had less security because of the greedy attitudes of corporations; most of the donors disagreed.
- 66 percent of the big donors believed that "big government" was the enemy and interfered too much with businesses and individuals. A majority of citizens disagreed.
- Most Americans, by 59 percent to 25 percent, thought NAFTA was costing Americans jobs. The big pockets were sure, Democratic donors even more so than Republican donors, that NAFTA helped American industries, by 65 to 24 percent. (According to almost all academic studies, and demonstrated by the rapid decline in U.S. manufacturing

jobs, the citizens—not the campaign investors—were the ones who knew what they were talking about.)

- Citizens, by 53% to 38%, said government regulations should be tougher. For the moneybags, that one was automatic: 55% to 31% the other way.[7]

When candidates take in millions upon millions of dollars from people who are really more sympathetic to the economic and regulatory ideas of the Republicans, it sort of takes their breath away. It takes the Democrats' ethical voice and moral compass away at the same time. Why would ordinary citizens want to join a political party that is not representing their views? Why would they even bother to vote?

Well, they don't vote. Not very much, even in presidential elections. 61-63% of Americans voted in the 1960s; 53-55% in the 1970s; 50-53% in the 1980s; 55% turned out because Ross Perot was an interesting third choice in 1992; only 49% in 1996. There was a slight upturn to 51% in 2000, most of that, presumably, due to Nader increasing the turnout. And in Congressional off-year elections the percentage of people voting is pitiful, under 40%. For this reason it was almost a certainty that Democrats would lose seats to the Republicans in 2002, who because of their superior organization were more likely to vote, and all the more so with a "war president" egging them on. Democrats, even with the economy in tatters, failed again to present a strong rebuttal of Bush's economic and tax policies.

Joel Rogers and Ruy Teixeira, in their book *The Forgotten Majority: Why the White Working Class Still Matters*,[8] identified a huge voting block of whites as "working class." With white Americans making up approximately 75% of the

population, those defined as working class were the ones who had not completed a four year college education, forming roughly 55% of the whole population. The authors suggested that the Democratic Party could have benefited greatly if it had adopted (or re-adopted) a platform of economic populism over the previous twenty-five years. True enough. But Teixeira and Rogers would have done better to dispense with whiteness and instead emphasize the need for unifying a racially diverse working class that would comprise at least 75% of the American people.

A better definition of working class could have been obtained by definitions based on income rather than education, for eighty percent of American households were earning less than $75,000 a year. Voting data have generally demonstrated that income divisions are more decisive in predicting voting behavior than the cultural class bias and professional status that are presumed to go along with educational attainment. In addition, a focus on income offers the key for changing the electoral outcome: lower-income people, especially the third of the electorate with household incomes of under $30,000 a year, vote overwhelmingly Democratic. The upper twenty-five percent of households, who make over $70,000 a year, have always favored the Republicans. Voter turnout in presidential elections is about 35 percent of the former, versus 70 percent of the latter.

If Democrats can get the lower half of the working class to register and vote, they will win handily. If they convince the upper half of the working class to vote for their own interests instead of for the interests of the wealthy, they'll win by an extraordinary margin. If a sizable portion of the middle class and upper middle class can be convinced that a more equitable country will be a freer and more enjoyable place for everyone, and if they realize they did not benefit much from their alliance with the rich in any case, the Republican Party as now constituted will go out of existence.

One key part of such an effort is to educate the population about their situation and increase voter turnout from its present fifty percent of the eligible adult population. There are some stumbling blocks no doubt, because some people will not easily give up racial prejudices in favor of new-found class identification. In 2000, there was only one large sub-group of voters that voted overwhelmingly for George W. Bush no matter what their income levels—63% of those who identified themselves as white Protestants voted for Bush, 34% for Gore, according to the exit polls conducted by the Voters News Service; 14% of all voters self-identified themselves as White Religious Right, and they voted for Bush by an 80%-18% margin.[9] These neo-Puritans were still dreaming of God's City on the Hill—a white, gated community—after three hundred years. Most evangelical Protestant Christians, though solidly stuck in the working class or lower-middle class by any objective measure of education and income, seemed quite content to sit at the base of the Hill and form an angry wall of armed gatekeepers for the wealthy who sit above them.

The key to getting the attention of white Protestants, as well as everyone else's attention, is not strictly an economic argument. The larger, broader argument for a more equitable society is a moral one that strongly emphasizes inclusiveness, caring, and sharing. These are values that Christians can readily accept if they are put in the right rhetorical context; and if they are reminded that a great many of the most fervent opponents of the Robber Barons a century ago were evangelical preachers like William Jennings Bryan.

And What About Those Greens?

Clearly the Democratic Party is so enfeebled that it must take most of the responsibility for Bush's victory in 2000, and let Ralph Nader and the Greens off the hook. The Greens, despite their image as an environmental party, were putting most of their emphasis on the corruption and anti-democratic influence of corporate America, and this was well before most of the criminal conduct of major CEOs came to light. Their instincts and analysis were much truer to the vision of a progressive Democratic Party than anything the national Democratic leadership was able to piece together.

With that said, there is a problem with the Green Party which has little to do with Ralph Nader and much to do with the political and legal structure of the American political system. Third parties are ineffectual, especially in nationwide races for the Presidency, and have not been able to dent the two-party system in almost one hundred and fifty years. For all the corruption, lack of imagination, and fealty to the corporate rich displayed by both traditional parties, the problem with the third party is that it seldom has any usefulness except in an indirect way. Third parties in the 20th century have weakened one of the two other parties, but have not come close to superceding one of them. If the party is on the left or right fringe, it might possibly contribute to the victory of the party it disagrees with the most. Thus we have the anger of the Democrats that was directed against the Greens.

On the other hand, it is perfectly reasonable for the Greens to keep running for office. How else would a third party justify its existence and its efforts to win in the future, except by continuing to challenge in each new election and eventually displacing the party that it had already weakened? The Green Party is something more than a vehicle for one person, and will quite likely outlive Ralph Nader. While the Party is small, it has two indispensable qualities the Democrats lack: a youthful, energetic membership and a clear commitment to progressive politics. In the election for governor in California in 2002, the very dull incumbent Democratic candidate, Gray Davis, only won his race by a modest margin even though California is a heavily Democratic state. But Peter Camejo, the Green candidate and ex-member of the Socialist Workers' Party, won over 5% of the vote and more than 7% of the Hispanic vote.

If Democrats don't move forward with a populist agenda, others will. The progressive wing of the Democrats is, unfortunately, in the minority. There are a number of progressive members of the House of Representatives, many of them members of the Congressional Black Caucus and/or the Progressive Caucus; at the local and state levels there are thousands of elected officials whose views are not substantially different than the Greens. Democrats do have two distinct advantages that bolster their record of economic, racial, and gender equality. One is that many of their most committed members come from minority and ethnic groups that have the potential to rally and register masses of non-voters if a national coalition (or the Democratic National Committee) ever comes out with a strong platform. Secondly, a great number of the progressive, hard-working members of the Democratic Party of all races, genders, and social backgrounds have been toiling for decades and seldom faltering despite the failings of their party at the national level.

These Democrats deserve credit for hanging in there, for they have generally been devoted to issues that many young Greens just discovered a few years ago. This agenda includes commitments to: supporting civil rights and affirmative action, women's rights and reproductive freedom; pressing for social justice for the poor at home and abroad; backing the rights and aspirations of working people while opposing excessive corporate power; pushing for strong curbs on pollution and environmental responsibility; protesting for peace and against militarism and imperialist posturing in the world; supporting economic equality and the progressive taxation of large fortunes; and endorsing universal health care for all citizens. In short, they believe in a broad range of liberties and democratic ideals that clearly distinguish them from ultra-conservative Republicans and the Bush Gang.

The Felons who Stole the Election Want to Take Our Freedoms, Too

Progressives must mount a counterattack, but not just because the Republicans stole the last election. The Bush Gang have continued to invalidate the democratic process and the protections of the Bill of Rights in order to keep themselves in power. For example, the Florida "felons" caper—the vote fraud that accounted for Bush's election in 2000—was still an available option for the Republicans in 2002 and would have worked again for the Bush Gang if they had needed it.

Somehow the vote-trimming restrictions on "former felons" remained in place when Jeb Bush, the Governor of Florida (and the man who could be Bush III sometime in the future), ran for re-election in the state in 2002. Data-

Base Technologies, the company that had supplied the names that were scrubbed from the voters' list in 2000, thereby disenfranchising so many African American voters, conceded that if "strict criteria" were used to fix the errors on that list of felons, then fewer than one in thirty would have been excluded. The company was repentant, but the Florida contingent of the Bush Gang was not. They claimed they never had the opportunity to change the old list and proceeded to exclude the same voters all over again. In the end, the stolen votes did not effect the 2002 Florida tally—although a tight election was predicted, Jeb Bush enjoyed a late surge courtesy of his big brother's campaign efforts, and he recaptured the governorship by a margin larger than the number of missing voters.[10]

Speaking of Big Brother, the powers of government repression were becoming ubiquitous in their attempts to deny democratic rights. In Florida and elsewhere, a spooky new concept had come into being even before the events of September 11, 2001—the government decided it had the right to remove protesters from political events. At one Republican event on June 4, 2001, three rather lonely people were arrested for holding up small protest signs in the middle of a huge crowd of Bush supporters. A Republican event organizer had pointed them out to the Tampa, Florida police so that they could swoop in and grab them. Apparently they had not reported to the proper "First Amendment Zones" to hold up their signs. That case was thrown out of court for lack of cause, but more public events for Republicans kept featuring the "First Amendment Zones," which are small fenced-off areas which are designated as the only places where protesters are allowed to hold up their signs or chant. Typically, event organizers locate the zones hundreds of yards from the main event. When George W appeared at the giant Sun Bowl stadium to campaign for brother Jeb in 2002, all protesters were penned in so far from the entrance that no one entering the event could hear their words or read their signs.[11]

The "First Amendment Zones" represented the more benign side of the attack on free speech and expression that the Bush Gang was mounting. All around the United States personal freedoms guaranteed by the Bill of Rights were being abridged, mostly under the pretense of fighting a war on terror. Just as scary as these police-state actions was the attitude of a good part of the American public who were clearly quite comfortable with authoritarian rules. Almost a full year after the September 11 attacks, the First Amendment Center released poll results that showed that 49 percent of Americans thought that "the First Amendment goes too far." Their idea of free and dangerous speech did not seem to be confined to fiery demagogues, because almost half of the sample thought the news media had been too aggressive in its questions about the war on terrorism. This was a startling conclusion. A disinterested observer would have found it difficult to recall any tough grilling of the president or his cabinet concerning their conduct of military operations.

No one asked pointedly whether there really was a war or not, at least within the United States. There had been, to be sure, one terrible act of terrorism, but once "war" was declared by our president, there were no further attacks by foreign terrorists on anyone inside the United States. The nation was put into a pure panic by an anthrax incident in October 2001 that was almost surely committed by Americans using our own biological weaponry; the purpose seemed to be heightening the fear of everyone in the country, rather than murdering as many people as possible. It was a lethal crime and a horrible precedent, but had nothing to do with the business of apprehending Al Qaeda criminals abroad. The only media that kept trying to pin the anthrax crime on the Iraqis were those closely tied into the White House propaganda loop, such as *The Weekly Standard* and *The Wall Street Journal*, and their stories were generally perceived by the rest of the media to be clearly transparent efforts to blame Saddam Hussein for everything.

For more than a year and a half after September 11, there was no "war" taking place in the United States; that is, there were no attacks or counterattacks waged by terrorists and the U.S. government inside our borders. Despite periodic warnings from the FBI in the form of "Yellow Alerts" and "Orange Alerts" indicating possible attacks, none materialized, while the attacks on our constitutional liberties were very steady. The Bush administration is fond of giving questionable concepts official names, so it called the war on terror "Operation Enduring Freedom." In some ways this proved to be a cruelly ironical concept, just like the "First Amendment Zones" that stifle free speech. In its domestic operations, at least, "Operation Enduring Freedom" took on the character of Orwellian propaganda, an exercise in "Newspeak," for it was immediately used to attack our enduring constitutional freedoms.

Attorney General Ashcroft, for example, could not keep himself from abusing the powers given to him by the Patriot Act. In May of 2002, judges on a secret court that reviewed FBI requests for secret snooping told Ashcroft that the FBI was breaking the law by falsifying data about individuals and their cases in order to obtain permission for wiretaps and searches. But Ashcroft did not give up, appealing to an even more secret appellate court in September, a court so secret that it had never met since it was set up in 1978, which concluded that Ashcroft could do what he wanted. David Cole, a professor at Georgetown University Law Center, explained that this was an attack on the Fourth Amendment. "The Fourth Amendment requires probable cause of a crime before a phone can be tapped or a home searched," he wrote. "The special court decided that, under the Foreign Intelligence Surveillance Act (FISA), law enforcement officials need not comply with that constitutional requirement, even where their primary purpose is criminal law enforcement."[12]

In the year after 9/11, over 1,100 "suspected terrorists" were detained and held without trial. Hundreds of them were foreigners who were only suspected of minor infractions such as overstaying their visas, yet prosecutors were allowed to lock them away for many months in hidden locations, unable to contact lawyers or their families.[13] Their court hearings, if there were any, were not open to the public. In response, a federal district judge in Washington ruled that the names of detainees suspected of immigration violations had to be made public. "Secret arrests," wrote Judge Gladys Kessler, "are a concept odious to a democratic society."[14] The law of the land was getting vague and secret, and it was being applied in capricious ways. Some American citizens were called "enemy combatants" by Donald Rumsfeld and entitled to trial, while others were charged with the same offense and held in limbo. The Secretary of Defense had sudden whims about establishing military tribunals, then seemed to drop such ideas. The Bush administration was making up the rules as it went along, feeling free to step outside the law when it felt like it.

As discussed in a previous chapter, they even brought one of the old Bush Gang, Admiral John Poindexter, back into the defense department to run an extremely advanced computer snooping system called Genoa for the Information Awareness Office of DARPA (Defense Advanced Research Projects Agency). Poindexter had worked at a private company called Syntec that did research for the Pentagon and developed the surveillance system that could provide all sorts of information about private citizens by spying on citizens' e-mails, and otherwise making use of electronic and communications data. While the administration had little luck sniffing out more terrorist activity within the United States, it had much more success placing repressive machinery in place, tools which could possibly be used to control the general public. The technicians in Poindexter's laboratory can now identify many thousands of subversive Americans as their giant computer surveys the thoughts of the nation.

Would the computers uncover the ideas that Poindexter's faithful subordinate, Oliver North, came up with in the 1980s? North, when he was working in the White House for the National Security Agency, helped draw up a secret plan known as "Operation Rex." It called for creating internment camps and declaring martial law in order to deal with those Americans who were opposed to the Reagan administration's illegal interventions in Central America.

The scope of Homeland Security is almost boundless: a gigantic and extremely expensive new federal department was created to control a wave of terrorism that as yet has not arrived. The Bush Gang did not seem to realize that there are limits to what the American people would accept. Among Republicans as well as Democrats, there were many who have an abiding concern for American civil liberties. Dick Armey, retiring House Majority Leader, was very disturbed at how lightly the Administration seemed to dismiss the protections of the Constitution. The Department of Homeland Security was constantly stepping over the line, but its worst offense was declaring that it would set up a quasi-organization called TIPS, which was designed to have 11 million loyal Americans assigned to snoop and snitch on their neighbors and any suspected bad guys in their midst. Armey's outrage about a potential army of TIPSters helped discourage Bush from implementing the plan. But Armey still was upset enough about the general attack on basic freedoms that he met with the editors of *USA Today* in October of 2002 and scolded the Justice Department for its "lack of regard for personal civil liberties in America." Armey said, "I told the president I thought his Justice Department was out of control. Are we going to save ourselves from international terrorism in order to deny fundamental liberties to ourselves? It doesn't make sense to me."[15]

Armey was upset because the Justice Department, the Defense Department, and the CIA were being invited to intrude on the private lives of Americans and his fellow Republicans were urging them on. Many members of Congress did not object, such as the head of the Senate Armed Services Committee, Republican John Warner. He said it was time to "break down the barriers" that keep the military out of civilian life.

While those in government were tearing down the constitutional barriers that protect citizens from unwarranted intrusion, they were erecting various blockades to keep the public from obtaining information that is vital to a functioning democracy. Vice President Cheney seemed to prevail in his long battle to keep the American people from knowing what he had promised to Enron and the giant oil corporations when he was setting federal energy policy in early 2001. Judge John D. Bates took the side of Cheney and Bush on December 9, 2002, when he ruled that Cheney did not have to turn over the notes of his energy meetings to the General Accounting Office of Congress. In a number of other areas, even before the September 11 attacks, the Bush administration had instructed federal agencies not to comply with Freedom of Information requests. According to Adam Clymer, a reporter for *The New York Times*, "the Ashcroft directive encouraged federal agencies to reject requests for documents if there was any legal basis to do so."[16]

In early 2003, some people in Ashcroft's employ were frightened enough by the authoritarian orientation of the Justice Department that they leaked a copy of a draft proposal for a "Patriot Act II" to the press. This long document, officially dubbed the "The Domestic Security Enhancement Act," recommended more constraints on American freedoms, even stripping U.S. citizens of their citizenship. ABC News reported, "It would also make it a crime for people subpoenaed in connection with an investigation being carried out under the Patriot Act to alert Congress to any possible abuses committed by federal agents." This kind of threat to constitutional rights prompted groups like the American Conservative Union to join with liberals in the American Civil Liberties Union in warning against the direction that Bush and Ashcroft were taking the country. Michael Hammond of the Gun Owners of America explained why many conservatives were waking up, "All of a sudden it became apparent that a lot of people could be made noncitizens."[17]

Progressive political forces, already saddled with the task of rejuvenating or replacing the sorry leadership of the Democratic Party, also had to work under the increasing threat of antidemocratic measures instituted by the Bush Gang. The administration discovered the usefulness of constantly telling the American people that they were under the threat of attack. When coupled with the exaggeration of Saddam Hussein's "weapons of mass destruction," the fear factor helped promote an aggressive war against Iraq. This in turn distracted many citizens from the enormous problems of the U.S. economy and prolonged the general unease over "homeland security." In sum, the Bush administration put itself in a position to take punitive action against those who keep dissenting against its policies, especially if and when the war in the Middle East is expanded to other countries.

Chief Justice William Rehnquist offered a brief, but scary warning to that effect: "In time of war, the laws are silent."

And the laws are particularly quiet when the powerful want to prevent the people from knowing the truth. The Bush Gang did an unconvincing job of lying about the facts of terrorism and weapons of mass destruction as it prepared to attack Iraq. Unfortunately, many Americans did not seem to care about veracity and liberty once the war began. As Hiram Johnson, the Republican progressive from California, said to his fellow senators in 1917, "The first casualty when war comes is truth."

Nineteen

Throw the Money Changers Out of the Temple

The moneychangers have fled from their high seats in the temple of our civilization. We may now restore that temple to the ancient truths.

—Franklin D. Roosevelt

Raise less corn and more hell!

—Mary Ellen Lease, Kansas populist, 1890

There are only two kinds of rich—the criminal rich and the foolish rich.

—Theodore Roosevelt

Sometimes the criminal rich and the foolish rich are the same people. And sometimes, like the Bush Gang, they sneak into the temple of democracy, set up their tables for peddling influence and exchanging tax favors, portray themselves as patriots, and declare that the business of America is business. Once the rich thieves settle into their seats of power, bound to each through the oligarchy of corporations and the plutocracy formed by very wealthy families, it is difficult to remove them. The people face two major questions: Who is going to throw the money changers out of the temple? And how are they going to do it?

When Franklin D. Roosevelt borrowed the New Testament imagery of an angry Jesus in the temple, he was not trying to prove he was more Christian than his opposition. He was simply employing the rhetoric of moral outrage that average people would readily understand. He was saying that the political coalition that backed the New Deal in the 1930s had the ethical duty to chase the money-men out of the halls of Congress. Only then would the people have the opportunity to rebuild their democracy in ways more compatible with the American principles of liberty and equality.

Theodore Roosevelt, like Franklin, knew a lot about rich people and their families because he had spent a lifetime among them. When he called them "criminal" and "foolish" he probably did not mean to include himself or his friends, for he, too, was making a rhetorical statement. The underlying message was: we cannot trust rich people to do the right thing; some of them will be ruthless in their single-minded passion to accumulate all possible wealth; a great many others are so lazy and silly that they will waste most of their capital; and a few, too few, will devote themselves and their resources to the common good.

The two Roosevelts were not the leaders of the popular rebellion against the rule of the Robber Barons, but they were astute politicians who understood the radicalized mood of the public, perceived the deep sense of moral outrage, and helped advance an agenda of meaningful reform. The people who really made change possible were the thousands of persistent educators and agitators like Mary Ellen Lease—a mix of rowdy populists, earnest Christians, outspoken socialists, methodical progressives, and many others—who convinced the American public that they really could benefit from strong doses of economic equality and democratic participation. This kind of energetic, progressive populism was difficult to find in the Democratic Party as of 2002, especially after Paul Wellstone's death, and many of the Democratic faithful knew this only too well. Robert Reich, a loyal Democrat frustrated by his years in the Clinton cabinet, warned about "The Death of Opposition in America," and wrote that "if political opposition in the U.S. is not to atrophy, then real change is needed within the Democratic Party and American democratic culture more generally."[1]

Robert Reich is not the only one to worry, for there is a new sense of urgency bubbling up on the left-leaning half of the Democratic Party, and among the Greens. Minority and women's groups are still frustrated by discrimination and the union movement is increasingly marginalized. Even the white males who were played for chumps by the Bush Gang are getting angry as they realize how little their labor is valued these days. The big tent of the Democrats is still open to them all, but there's no message to fill all that space. The Party has been accused of practicing "identity politics" and trying to cater to too many constituencies, but that is not really the problem. Politics is a messy job and the United States is particularly big, messy country, so it is not necessarily a mistake to have to meet various demands from different groups. The true mistake is not having an overriding message that binds everyone together, meets the universal needs of the population, and also inspires their universal aspirations for fairness, equality, and liberty.

Symbolic Politics Are Real Politics—Get Rid of the Embarrassments

When George W. Bush and friends in the Senate decided to throw Trent Lott out of the Senate leadership position because of his embarrassing racist record, they were making an attempt to reverse the Republican Party's forty-year pattern of winking at the attitudes of racist whites. Trent Lott and his fellow Republican Southerners swept to power in the South in 1980, the year Ronald Reagan arranged a campaign stop in Philadelphia, Mississippi, the scene of the grisly murder of three civil rights workers in the 1960s. When Reagan declared that he was "a supporter of states' rights" in that town, Southern whites knew he was also saying that the era of civil rights enforcement would end if he was elected. It was not surprising that the locus of power in the Republican Party then moved decisively to the side of the Deep South. As of 2002, this racial formula was no longer an effective tool for the Republicans and they were struggling to disown it.

Democrats have a different kind of housecleaning problem. Their shift toward picking Southern, non-progressive leaders for the Party was accompanied by an increasing subservience to big money donors and a steady distancing from the interests of working Americans. As Carter, Clinton, and Gore struggled to please major financial interests, they abandoned any pretense of speaking for laboring people or limiting the aspirations of capital. As the 21st century began, the Chairman of the Democratic National Committee (DNC), Terry McAuliffe, remained on the job, an embarrassing symbol of how low the Democrats had sunk. He had mimicked the Republican attitude of taking the easy money and compromised the last bits of integrity remaining to his party. McAuliffe was the golfing buddy of Gary Winnick, the CEO who made $600 million by selling his stock in Global Crossing before it collapsed. Winnick hired McAuliffe as company political consultant for $100,000 when he was Clinton's fund-raising champ in 1996 (but not yet chair of the DNC) and paid him his fee in company start-up stock. McAuliffe, like Winnick, knew enough to sell out early in 2000 and he made a cool $18 million.[2] Mark Racicot, the Chairman of the Republican National Committee, told Fox News that he saw no problem with McAuliffe's behavior. Could that be because George Bush I also received Global Crossing stock? Bush gave a speech to a Global Crossing meeting in Tokyo in 1998, passed up the $80,000 cash fee in favor of stock, and watched it climb to $14 million in value. The Bush Gang will not reveal exactly when he sold it, but presumably he bailed out early and made a killing.[3] Although this is the kind of moral equivalency that the Democratic Party does not need, McAuliffe did not comprehend the problem. When he was questioned about the propriety of this kind of calculated politicking, he defended himself stoutly and told his accusers where they could get off: "This

is capitalism. You invest in stock, it goes up, it goes down. You know, if you don't like capitalism, you don't like making money with stock, move to Cuba or China."[4]

Is this what a Democrat should be saying? Can this guy be representing the Party that is full of fifty and sixty year-old people who were once scolded by Republicans for protesting the morality of the Vietnam War and the meaningless deaths of American soldiers? "Love it or leave it!" they were told, "Go back to Russia! Go to Red China!" McAuliffe forgets that he lives in the world's first democracy. And democracy and capitalism are not the same thing, at least not for those Democrats who care to distinguish themselves from the Republicans. In the United States, if you don't like the way capitalism is working, you don't have to leave. You have the right to democratically change the rules to curtail or eliminate the abuses of "The Money Power." There was a time that Democrats were capable of such an effort, as when they showed their mettle in the 1930s and overcame the overwhelming advantages that were wielded by the children of the Robber Barons and their well-paid political shills.

My intention here is not to over-romanticize the past accomplishments or the future possibilities of the Democratic Party. It was never an anti-capitalist party, nor has it avoided the imperialist attitudes that seem to come naturally to politicians who rule great powers. But it often has been, for better or worse, the only electoral vehicle available for positive change. The political awareness of populists and leftists ended up seeping into the Democratic Party in the early 20th century, led to limited progressive victories in the 1930s and early 1940s, and achieved some very practical gains for most working-class and middle-class citizens by mid-century.

Now that these gains have been decimated by the Bush Gang, the question is not whether Franklin Roosevelt was a true champion of the people or was merely pushed in that direction by the events and sentiments of his day. The relevant matter is that he did come to symbolize progressive Democratic politics and ended up as a president who was willing to fight the Republicans on a wide range of important issues. Is any current Democratic candidate willing to do the same? Certainly there were doubts about Al Gore on that score during the 2000 campaign. Did he divest himself of his fairly conservative past, or did he merely dabble in populist ideas at the very end because he realized the political winds were shifting and he needed to appeal to the progressive voters in the country? Unseemly as the notion might be, that is sometimes the job of politicians, for they must either change to reflect the feelings of the people or make way for others.

The Al Gore who emerged from hiding in the fall of 2002 was testing the winds again. This time he bore little resemblance to the man who had once fronted for the pro-business Democratic Leadership Conference, echoed the concerns of the upper middle-class, and hawkishly supported Israeli interests. Instead he delivered an anti-war rebuttal to Bush's foreign policy, made a sweeping endorsement of single-payer health insurance, and spoke up heartily for the interests of working Americans. Gore was trying on the suit of the true left-leaning populist. Whether or not people would believe in this transformation was of no consequence in the end, because Gore quickly announced that he would not run for the Democratic nomination in 2004. The deciding vote had been cast, not by the people but by Gore's old financial supporters on the right wing of the Democratic

Party—they were not about to shell out big-time cash for someone who was turning into an uncouth populist.

This had been Ralph Nader's point: that the corporate investing class, the engine that drives the Bush Gang and so many prominent CEOs in their criminal pursuits, had also corrupted an important segment of the Democratic Party—the people who pay for political campaigns or solicit campaign funds. If the Democrats want Nader and the Greens to step aside in 2004 presidential race, then they had better find another populist to take the place of the unwanted Gore. By March of 2003, Bill Moyers was wondering aloud if it was already too late: "Now Democrats in Congress are so deeply divided and impotent that Ralph Nader is thinking of running again."[5]

Big Problems Require Big Solutions

If the left-liberal coalition is to have a broad-based impact and start convincing moderate Democrats and independent voters, they need more than a morally sound attitude, they need a program. This program does not have to be called a "New New Deal," but it should be based, as were the efforts of the 1930s, on the premise that there are several things that Americans need and want that have universal appeal. Republicans are clear about their message—they are the Party of Money—and they have a program which appeals to the people who happen to have money, the people that want to help the people who have money, and the Christians who think they are more holy than the rest of us. Money, or "The Money Power" as it was called a century ago, would prefer to own both parties. The Democrats are always vulnerable to being bought out. When it happens, the Party loses its focus, as in 1996 when *The Wall Street Journal* said that Bill Clinton was running the "the most conservative Democratic campaign since Grover Cleveland."

A major reason for the conservative shift was that campaigns take big money and big money donors tend to have more conservative views than average Democratic voters. In fact, in 1996 the "fat cats" had more conservative views on economic matters than all American voters from both parties combined, according to the poll data analyzed by Teixeira and Borosage (see previous chapter).

In the fall of 2002, Marcy Kaptur, a ten-term Congresswoman from Ohio, made a challenge for the job of Democratic House leader. Although frontrunner Nancy Pelosi, a liberal from California won the job, Kaptur wanted to remind Democrats that chasing after the Republican money machine was a fruitless pursuit. Kaptur represents both farmers and manufacturing workers in a rural area around Toledo and calls herself a "moderate populist." She tried to set the Democrats straight:

> To win, our party must adopt a reform paradigm. We will never raise more money than the Republicans. Never. We must elevate the non-money wing of the Democratic Party and create populist symbols to convey our message.

Given the blatant thievery that is either planned or condoned by the Bush Gang, the time is ripe for the Democrats to abandon their weak subservience to big money because it prevents them from articulating a consistent philosophy. They need a program that clearly differentiates their Party from the Republicans. The basics of a meaningful progressive program are not difficult to lay out:

1) full employment at good wages, with a flexible work week, and a higher minimum wage.
2) quality day care and quality nursing home care for all who need it
3) federally funded health care that serves everyone.
4) good public schools, inexpensive higher education and training programs for all.
5) comprehensive environmental programs that safeguard our health and the natural world.
6) public works spending that restores roads, bridges, and other parts of the nation's infrastructure.

Measures such as these are not cheap but are well within the reach of the world's biggest economy. As mentioned in the previous chapter, these are the kind of priorities that a large majority of Americans have favored for many years, even at the height of Ronald Reagan's popularity. The big question is: where will the money come from that can sustain a program that provides a dignified life for all our citizens?

Let us recall the mega-crime that was described at the beginning of this book—10% to 15% of all personal income has been redistributed to the rich over the past twenty years. This amounts to a trillion dollars or more—every year—that should be directed to the needs of working people and other socially useful purposes.

Progressive, Egalitarian Solutions

- Raise taxes on the rich. Re-establish hefty upper-bracket federal income tax rates, even if they are not quite comparable to the 70-90% rates imposed during the prosperous decades of the

1950s and 1960s. The top rate on the richest 1% should be at least 50%, and should yield an effective rate of 40% on all income, including capital gains and dividends.[6]

- Re-establish corporate profit taxes at 50%, the approximate rate of the 1950s.

- Raise the minimum wage to $7.50 or $8.00 per hour. (This only seems high because it has been held down so long. If the minimum wage had increased proportionately to productivity gains since 1979, it would now be about $10 per hour.)

- Do not let Bush get away with abolishing the estate tax on great fortunes. Re-establish and increase the effective amount of estate tax collected on rich inheritances of $5 million and above.

- Institute an annual wealth tax on the biggest American fortunes at a rate of between 1% and 3%.

- Cut military spending on new weaponry by $100 to $200 billion to stay in line with the diminished military budgets of the rest of the world, and immediately begin a staged program of demilitarization, disarmament, and weapons inspections throughout the world.

- Extend Social Security taxation to the highest salaries, and to most forms of investment income. This would keep the overall withholding percentage at the current rate of 12.3%; and it would contribute extra funds for a universal health program.

- Introduce federal Health Security, a universal government health program that will provide health care for all Americans. It will be paid through a combination of revenues, such as progressive income taxes levied on the rich and the corporations and the extended withholding tax. The reduction in administrative costs, overhead, and profit will save at least 12% to 14% of costs (see Chapter 11); this savings can be applied to the care of all 42 million Americans who are not now covered by insurance. A range of fees will be set for hospitals and doctors; many drugs will be purchased at discount rates by state or federal agencies. The government will provide malpractice coverage and set up strict boards of review for medical competency, but doctors will be free to practice alone or in clinical groups as they see fit. All patients will be free to choose their physicians, nurse practitioners, and other professionals. Medical school education will be totally free for all doctors, nurses, and other health workers.

The Results of a Return to Progressive Taxation

These proposals may outrage the corporations and the rich, as well as the politicians whom they have so carefully cultivated, yet they will hardly impoverish the well-to-do. Increased taxes levied upon the wealthy will simply help restore the more equitable (but hardly equal) distribution of income and wealth that existed in the United States three decades ago. The exact combination of fiscal measures used to achieve more egalitarian economic outcomes is not so important; they could be modified and achieve the same results.

The effect of such measures on working people will be liberating. A national health security insurance will increase employees' ability to negotiate shorter or more flexible work weeks; it will give them more freedom to pursue new careers or more training, thus making society more productive than ever. An indirect, but particularly positive effect will be felt by those who are self-employed or operate small businesses; they will escape the current onus of paying prohibitively high private health insurance premiums. A universal insurance plan that is based on taxing all sources of national income, not just payroll deductions, can help small businesses and farmers withstand the onslaught of the chain stores and the factory farms. A significantly higher minimum wage, when combined with national health insurance, will not harm small businesses. An independent owner may gain some comparative advantages, especially vis a vis the monopolizing sectors that thrive on ultra-low wages.

Increasing taxation on high incomes will have an immediate effect if it is imposed uniformly. It will help reverse the lopsided increase in CEO salaries and it will also decrease excessive speculative investment in stocks, derivatives, and hedge funds. If high taxes are reimposed on corporate profits and high CEO incomes, this does not really threaten independent, middle-class businesspeople and professionals—their work will increasingly look like an attractive alternative to regimented corporate life. High taxes and high wages can allow other forms of more constructive capital formation to take on a stronger role. As working-class and middle-class incomes increase because of higher wages and steady productivity gains, average citizens will have more to contribute to stable pension funds. (They already contribute mightily to corporate investment. They owned 23% of all stocks and mutual funds in early 2003.) Increased pension fund investment under the direction of administrators who care about their fellow citizens will lead to more productive, well-paid jobs in the United States.

The above measures represent a momentous undertaking, for they must undo the effects of more than twenty years of class piracy committed by the Bush Gang and their allies. The size of their economic transgressions were so great, and so damaging to the social fabric of the United States, that only a strong combination of these recommended fiscal changes will enable us to redress the imbalance of power. These measures are not excessive, but proportionate to the inequality that was imposed as the upper class went on a redistributive binge.

The money is there, or will be shortly, as American working people dig us out of the rubble of Wall Street's latest collapse. This redistribution of money to working people is not utopian, for it will simply establish a fairer balance, one closer to the arrangement that exists in most other highly industrialized countries.[7]

Certainly there are those who will object to high taxes on the rich on the grounds that this will cause a shortage of capital for investment. The obvious question for them is: why, when trillions of dollars of capital were pouring in and out of the pockets of the rich over the past twenty years, did so little constructive investment take place? If anything there was too much speculative capital available. In the 1980s and again in the 1990s, most political conservatives were not conservative at all when it came to how America employed its savings. In the name of free enterprise and free markets they encouraged wild and aimless spending. Orgies of undisciplined, unproductive investment and financial gambling burned up trillions of dollars. The lost opportunities were immense and the performance of the rich and their investment advisors, who were trusted with these assets, was truly appalling.[8]

Because the Bush Gang returned in 2001, wealthy investors were not punished for their incompetence. In fact, they were rewarded with two enormous tax cuts that lifted their fortunes, but gave little help to the rest of the population or the economy in general. Two years later, the nation's economic prospects had still not improved, for the Census Bureau reported that the incomes of 95% of Americans, all except the top 5%, were falling. Businesses were con-

tinuing to lay off employees and were afraid to make investments in expansion or new production. The Federal Reserve announced in May of 2003 that it feared "price deflation" more than anything else, which was a nice way of saying that it hoped the United States and the world would not slip inexorably toward an economic depression. The Federal Reserve Bank set its federal funds rate 1.25%, the lowest rate in 41 years, yet few corporations wanted to borrow money because they saw no prospects for growing sales. Homeowners kept scrambling to get mortgage refinancing at rates lower than 5%, often because they needed funds to deal with mounting credit card debt or a family financial emergency.

The Bush people had only one answer to such problems—more for the rich.

Twenty

Buying the Temple and Throwing Away the Key

Bush II, Tax Cut II

We can have a democratic society or we can have great concentrated wealth in the hands of a few. We cannot have both.

> —Louis Brandeis, Supreme Court Justice (1916-1939)

Supporters of making dividends tax-free like to paint critics as promoters of class warfare. The fact is, however, that their proposal promotes class welfare. For my class.

> —Warren Buffett, second richest man in the United States, May 20, 2003[1]

The real intent is a continuation of the old struggle to enrich the wealthy at the expense of ordinary people, including future generations.

> —Robert Solow and Franco Modigliani, winners of the Nobel Prize in Economics, commenting on Tax Cut II, May 2003[2]

George W. Bush apparently did not notice, or did not care, that the rich had laid waste to our national savings in the wave of excessive speculation that concluded the 20th century. His priorities were exactly the opposite of the progressive agenda sketched out in the previous chapter. The Bush Gang wanted to limit access to the Temple of Democracy and secure the influence of the wealthy money-changers for a very long time to come. In 2003, just two months after winning control of Congress in 2002, they moved quickly toward completing the primary mission that they had undertaken in the 1980s and resumed in 2001— lightening the burdens of the rich. Their first effort of the 21st century—Bush II, Tax Cut I— followed immediately upon George W's disputed presidential win and was the second largest tax reduction in American history after the Reagan/Bush tax cut of 1981. The Bush II, Tax Cut I provided tax breaks of $1.37 trillion over ten years, from 2001 to 2011.

The second big tax reduction of the new century—Bush II, Tax Cut II—was proposed in January of 2003 and originally pegged at $726 billion over ten years, from 2003 to 2013. The Bush administration pretended they were concerned about stimulating the ailing economy and helping average citizens, just as they had claimed in 2001. Accordingly, they did not call their effort a "tax cut." Instead they labeled it "The Jobs and Growth Program." As in 2001, they really wanted to deliver massive favors to the rich, but this time the deception seemed weaker, since the substantial proposals were a more blatant combination of immediate and long-term gifts to the wealthy and the corporations. But then a curious thing happened. The Bush Gang seemed to stumble even though it had an increasingly right-wing Congress at its side. Perhaps the reckless nature of the pirate leaders and their blind greed had caused them to awkwardly overstep and grab too quickly at the remaining resources of working Americans.

The featured item of the Tax Cut II proposal was the complete elimination of income taxes levied on corporate stock dividends. Administration spokespeople claimed that such tax cuts would be an "economic stimulus" that would help pull the country out of recession. Since the very rich, the top one percent, own almost half of all privately held stock in America, this dividend exemption was clearly devised with their well-being in mind. Once again capital income was afforded priority over labor income. According to Citizens for Tax Justice, the dividend tax exemption was going to result in an average tax savings of $13,483 for the wealthiest one percent of households in 2003, while yielding a parsimonious savings of $27 to the median income households.[3] The biggest winners would be Americans with incomes over $1 million per year; they were destined to receive more than 21% of the benefit, or an average of $75,463 per household.[4]

Furthermore, it was clear that any overall "stimulus" from such measures was directed at the particular interests of the upper class— restoring the bank accounts of wealthy people who had lost money in the stock market, expanding the holdings of those who had taken their profits at the right moment before the crash, and reviving the fortunes of brokers by artificially inflating the values of stocks. While some Wall Street analysts were excited by the idea that fresh investment would flow back into the depressed market, the reaction in many sectors of society was negative. A Washington Post/ABC poll showed that Americans favored more domestic spending over tax cuts by a margin of 67% to 29%. A full-page ad in *The New York Times*, signed by 10 Nobel prize winners in economics and 450 other economists, said the tax cut was not likely to stimulate the economy at all: "... the tax cut proposed by President Bush is not the answer to these problems. Regardless of how one views the specifics of the Bush plan, there is widespread agreement that its purpose is a permanent change in the tax structure and not the creation of jobs and growth in the near-term."[5]

It appeared that the economic critique might awaken the public and spur the response that George W. Bush and his father had always dreaded: "Class Warfare," the open struggle for political rights and economic power. After he unveiled his new tax plan in January 2003, Bush tried a preemptory strike against his critics. He started complaining in words that sounded just like his father, suggesting that he was the victim. "You hear a lot of talk in Washington, of course," he said, "that this benefits so-and-so or this benefits this, the kind of class warfare of politics." This allowed Charles B. Rangel, the veteran Democratic Congressman from New York, to take advantage of the opening and respond, "Here the president kicks hell out of the poor and tells us we're guilty of class warfare."[6]

More tortured logic followed from the White House. "There's a principle involved," said Bush. Then he let Ari Fleischer, his White House spokesman, elaborate, "The president does not think it is right to tax the savings and ....to penalize the people who plan for their future." Finally Republican pollster and spin-meister Frank Lutz dared suggest that "Bush is responding to Americans where they were hit hardest. Usually when you think of the economy getting worse, you think of unemployment, but this time it's stock market driven." Somehow the Bush Administration had forgotten that during their first 28 months in office, two million American workers had lost their jobs and many of them had run out of unemployment compensation.

The Bush proposal included other treats for the rich besides the dividends exclusion, such as measures accelerating the series of tax rate reductions for the higher income brackets that had already been passed in the 2001 tax bill. There were, of course, a few favors thrown into the mix to please some middle class taxpayers, such as increasing the tax credit for each dependent child in a household from $600 to $1000. All in all, however, the result of effect of Bush's Tax Cut II was a big fat bonus, an average of $30,127 per household per year, that was slated to go to the richest 1% of Americans. The average benefit for the median family was going to be $289 (most of that due to those families who were eligible for the child credit).[7]

Giveaways for the Rich, Takeaways for Working People

According to The New York Times reporter Elisabeth Bumiller, "the idea of eliminating taxes on dividends dates from at least 20 years ago, from the Reagan administration." The first Bush administration liked this concept so much that they commissioned a study by Treasury official R. Glenn Hubbard that suggested doing away with taxation of dividend income. Hubbard was another alumnus of Bush Gang I who resurfaced in the new administration. When he took the job as the chairman of Bush II's Council of Economic Advisers it was natural that the dividend exemption was revived and incorporated into the tax cut proposal.[8]

There was another side to the taxation equation that was not getting as much publicity in late 2002 and early 2003. Even though the Bush Gang had no qualms about creating big federal deficits again, they still had to bring some money into the federal coffers. Glenn Hubbard joined with other conservatives (such as the Americans for Tax Reform and the American Enterprise Institute) to consider ways to increase revenue without impinging on their wealthy clientele. One idea was to tax the poor.

At first sight, when The Wall Street Journal floated the idea in November of 2002, the concept appeared to be one of those satirical attacks on low-income Americans that the right wing enjoys. "Workers who pay little or no taxes can hardly be expected to care about tax relief for everybody else," the paper's editorial stated. Is it possible that the editors of The Journal do not know that the lowest 20% of American households earn such a small percentage of the national income, slightly more than 3% according to the IRS, that they have a difficult time putting food on the table? The Journal may not realize that our country has already impoverished our low-income citizens to an extent unmatched in all the other advanced industrialized nations, which pay their workers at the low end of the income scale a much fairer wage. The ratio of the high wage, at the 90th percentile, to the low wage, at the 10th percentile, falls within the range of 2 to 1 or 3 to 1 range in Japan and most of Europe. The rate is over 5 to 1 in the United States.[9] (As I have pointed out earlier in the book—for instance, in Chapter 4—this is not a problem caused by salary earners at the 90th percentile earning too much. The particularly low incomes of the poorer members of U.S. society are primarily due to corporate pressure to keep wages down while permitting those at the very top, the 100th percentile, to take an inordinate share of all income.)

Since you can't squeeze taxes out of people

who are earning next to nothing, it was clear that the editors at *The Wall Street Journal* were not really aiming at the poor, but were preparing the way for something else. They were firing the first salvo on behalf of Republican and conservative thinkers who were arguing that the rich were still too heavily taxed. Now that Republicans had gained control of Congress, they were making noises about "simplifying" the tax system, which is the code word for shifting the tax load onto working-class and middle-class citizens. Their experts claimed that complex tax laws created an onerous tax burden borne by the affluent. Glenn Hubbard explained the problem to a receptive audience at a tax forum at the right-wing American Enterprise Institute in 2002, "The increasing reliance on taxing higher-income households and targeted social preferences at lower incomes stands in the way of moving to a simpler, flatter tax system."[10]

The Republicans were taking a big risk by even talking about a regressive flat tax at the same time they were pushing for dividend exemptions and other rewards for the rich. If middle-income working Americans, the ones who would really get stuck with the bill in the end, overheard these discussions they might be jarred out of their somnambulant state (caused by working too many hours to pay the bills). They might decide that the rich had already pressed their advantage too far. Robert S. McIntyre of Citizens for Tax Justice prepared a detailed analysis of the flat tax schemes in December of 2002 and concluded, "the administration has finally admitted that its maniacal zeal to cut taxes for the very wealthy will be paid for by much higher taxes on the vast majority of Americans. Now that the cat is out of the bag, it's time for the public to wake up—before it's too late."[11]

If and when the public does arouse itself and looks for a set of accurate figures, it will have to take a look at the claims of the anti-tax lobby. The ultra-right opponents of progressive taxation claim that the federal income tax has become onerous and unfair. As emphasized earlier in this book (Chapters 3 through 6), the richest 1% received about 9 to 10 percent of all personal income in the United States over a long period of time, from the 1940s through the 1970s. Since then the tax rates of the richest 1% have been cut repeatedly while their income share soared, finally reaching 19 to 21 percent of all personal income from 1999 through 2001.[12] In 2000, the tiniest minority, the richest one-tenth of 1%, pocketed an astonishing 10.6% of all American income, a bigger

---

A SIMPLE ILLUSTRATION:

The Taxes Paid by the Rich Went Up, but the Rich Were Not Hurting

Year	Income of the average rich guy, top 1%	Tax Bill at the Effective Rate of 34%	After-Tax Income
1979	$500,000	$170,000	$330,000

Year	Income of the average rich guy, top 1%	Tax Bill at the Effective Rate of 25%	After-Tax Income
2001	$1,000,000	$250,000	$750,000

Source: IRS, Citizens for Tax Justice[13]

share than all of the top 1% collected twenty or thirty years earlier. So why do the conservatives in power insist that there was a problem?

Because it was true that the wealthiest 1% did pay a bigger share of all federal income taxes in 2001 than they did in the late 1970s. Their tax bill went up even though their tax rates were lowered.

The preceding figures demonstrate that the average rich guy doubled his income in real terms. Why should he complain? It is clear that an after-tax income $750,000 per year handily beats $330,000. Not bad for a year's "work." True, the amount deducted for his tax bill went up, but in these circumstances, why would any-one mind paying $250,000 in taxes instead of $170,000? If federal income taxes had remained as progressive as they were at the end of the 1970s, then the rich guy would have had to pay 34% of his income toward his 2001 tax bill, or $340,000.

It is unseemly for the rich, or their right-wing advocates at Americans for Tax Reform, to bemoan their good fortune. In fact it may be unwise, since too much whining might wake up the public. The rich guy's taxes could have gone up considerably in 2001, to an effective rate of 50%, and he still would have been doing very well, taking home $500,000, a lot more than his after-tax haul in 1979. This compares very favorably to the meager income of the median household, which made $34,300 before federal taxes in 2001, and only about $28,000 after fed-eral income and payroll taxes were deducted.

If middle-income Americans reflected upon their history, they would realize that the wealthier claasses are supposed to make finan-cial sacrifices during time of war. The richest Americans were taxed at a minimum rate of 67% to pay for World War I (a dramatic increase from the 6% rate of 1913), 88% during World War II, 91% during the Korean War, and 70% during the war in Vietnam. So maybe the average rich guy should be paying 62.5% of his income in taxes, not 25%, and accepting $375,000 in take home pay. This would still be more than he took home twenty-some years ago. If he pays $625,000 in taxes, this could be considered a wise investment in his govern-ment. After all, shouldn't he be paying the Bush Gang to look after the security of his stocks in the oil and defense industries?

It seems that making the wealthy pay up in time of war, an American tradition, is an idea that never occurred to Glenn Hubbard, chief number scrambler for the Bush Gang, nor to the others who were putting together tax cut options in late 2002. They were thinking about the very opposite for the decade ahead. Hubbard liked the idea of a flat tax of 15.6%,[14] a proposal that Dick Armey and others have pushed futilely in the 1990s; it would mean $156,000 in federal income taxes for the million dollar earner, substantially lightening his load from the $250,000 paid in 2001.

The Bush Gang's insistence on lowering taxes for the rich meant that their economic team was quietly looking for options for raising revenue after the 2003 tax cut was enacted. They had to decide who would pay off some of the federal deficit, which was increasing by leaps and bounds, and who would bear the cost of the stunning shortfalls in state and city rev-enues that were crippling localities in every part of the nation. There was only one recourse. The money would have to come from working peo-ple with incomes under $100,000 per year (about 92% of the American populace accord-ing to the IRS in 2001), who were paying less, on average, than 15.6% in federal income taxes.[15] A new flat income tax would mean a tax increase for the great majority of Americans.

It was clear, however, that even a 15.6% flat tax would not provide sufficient funds for the federal government. So Jim DeMint, a Republican congressman from South Carolina, came up with an alternative even worse than Hubbard's flat tax. He proposed a national sales tax to replace the income tax at the same time that "conservative thinkers at the Heritage Foundation and other think tanks have begun expressing similar opinions," reported Jonathan Weisman of *The Washington Post* in late 2002. Sales taxes are notorious for being regressive, meaning that they take a much higher percentage of income from the poor than from the affluent. Congressman DeMint concluded that the working poor would not mind paying higher taxes if they did not have the burden of filling out tax returns. He even had a patriotic justification for his scam. He felt that people who were earning $6 or $7 per hour, but not paying income tax, were missing out on a key part of the democratic experience. He decided that paying the national sales tax would make better citizens out of the poor, reasoning that: "You can't maintain a democracy if the people who are voting don't care what their government costs."[16]

Meanwhile, Robert T. Matsui, Democratic Representative from California and member of the House Ways and Means Committee, was watching the ultra-conservatives set themselves up for a counterattack, and he was busy doing the required math. He knew that low wage workers have trouble paying their own bills, let alone the nation's bills. That left one large group of people, middle-income working Americans, who were bound to take the hit. "The president is making the case that people

who earn between $50,000 and $75,000 a year should be paying a third more in taxes," said Matsui, "I'd love to debate him on that."[17]

A War Boost for Tax Cut II

The Democrats had a chance to get stirred up and confront the Republicans with a strong and unrelenting message about economic inequality. Initial public reaction to Bush's tax plans in early 2003 had been negative; the Pew Foundation found that most Americans did not approve of Bush's tax policy and there were signs of retreat by the administration. By the end of February 2003, Glenn Hubbard, the flat tax and dividend exemption man, suddenly resigned his job as the president's advisor and said he might return to academic life. The costs of an impending war in Iraq had moderately conservative Republicans in the Senate— Snowe and Collins of Maine, McCain of Arizona, and Voinovich of Ohio—wondering how the government was going to combat growing deficits if it drastically reduced taxes again.

Symbolic of the administration's difficulties was President Bush's visit to a trucking company in St. Louis where he plugged away for "jobs and growth." His highly professional staging crew, which included former producers and cameramen from Fox TV and ABC, had carefully arranged a theatre set for Bush. He was surrounded by piles of boxes that the company was going to ship all over the country. The boxes were prominently labeled "Made in USA," a symbol of the new jobs Bush claimed he would create. Unfortunately for the stage crew, curious reporters peeled off the labels and found the name of the real manufactuing source underneath—the boxes were stamped "Made in China." This was a severe embarrassment, especially because it reinforced the argument that American unions had been making since Tax Cut I was put in place in 2001: tax cuts for the rich were not producing more employment, especially in the manufacturing sector, which had lost over 2 million jobs since 1998.

At a time like this it was handy to have a nasty guy named Saddam in the wings. A change of focus and a quick U.S. victory in Iraq gave the administration a big boost. The Bush Gang was able to bluster their way into waging an aggressive war, pummel a hapless opponent into submission, and celebrate an inevitable imperial conquest as the triumph of democracy. They easily swayed public opinion with a grab-bag full of innuendos and misleading information concerning "weapons of mass destruction." As these reasons were proved untrue, the Gang simply changed their justification for war and said Saddam Hussein was a brutal dictator. This was something everyone knew in the first place, but it was definitely not the reason for invasion that had been sanctioned by the United Nations.

No problem for the Bush Gang—we won, didn't we? "Mission accomplished," said George W, and the message was echoed by the banners that were fluttering behind him on the aircraft carrier. He strutted around in his "Top Gun" flight suit in a magnificent piece of stagecraft orchestrated by his handlers and readied himself for his next act.

If blustering our way to war abroad was so successful, then why not try the same thing at home with a "war on taxes?"

The President, his confidence renewed, hit the tax cut campaign trail again with a series of fresh photo ops. In Albuquerque on May 12, 2003, he claimed that his program would be a boon to small businesses: "Oh, you'll hear the

talk about how this plan only helps rich people. That's just typical Washington DC rhetoric, is what that is. That's just empty rhetoric." Many Democrats, who had difficulty opposing the war effort, now found themselves on the defensive about taxes, too. "Democrats are just scared of class warfare," a Senate Democratic aide conceded to reporter Jonathan Weisman of *The Washington Post*.[18]

Friends, Romans, Countrymen, Lend Me Your Ties

When Bush spoke to a pre-arranged crowd in Indianapolis the following day, May 13, he alternated between bragging about the victory over the sinister threat in Iraq and appealing to Americans to band together for another battle—defeating economic malaise through his "stimulus" package. The orchestration of the event was meticulous: "White House aides went so far as to ask people in the crowd behind Mr. Bush to take off their ties, according to WISH-TV in Indianapolis, so they would look more like the ordinary folk the president said would benefit from his tax cut."[19]

While it was audacious to keep repeating this propaganda—that a massive tax reduction for the rich was really a "jobs and growth" program for working Americans—there was little evidence that cash in the hands of millionaires and billionaires would create new jobs. In fact, if the behavior of the rich over the previous several years was any indication, they would be much more likely to pour their newfound funds into the most wasteful kinds of gambling, such as hedge funds, or keep rewarding CEOs for cutting jobs and moving their headquarters to tax-free destinations such as Bermuda and the Cayman Islands. The lack of upper class interest in investing in employment had already been well-established during the first 28 months of Bush II and Tax Cut I.

George W. Bush was on course to become the first president since World War II to oversee a period of job destruction instead of job creation. Even his father, who had a terrible economic record, had seen some small employment gains during his tenure. Katrina vanden Heuval, editor of *The Nation*, looked at evidence compiled by the International Association of Machinists, then pinned a new label on Bush the Second—"Top Gun at Job Destruction."[20]

As shown in the following table, the evidence against him was convincing.

JOBS: THE PRESIDENTIAL RECORD[20]

Average Monthly Gain in Jobs by Presidency Since World War II

Truman	+87,000 per month
Eisenhower	+38,000 per month
Kennedy	+122,000 per month
Johnson	+206,000 per month
Nixon (Ford)	+117,000 per month
Carter	+218,000 per month
Reagan	+166,000 per month
George Bush I	+52,000 per month
Clinton	+239,000 per month
George Bush II	**–69,000 per month**

Since the record of 69,000 jobs lost each month was compiled over the first 28 months of Bush II's stay at the White House, there remained the possibility that results would improve over the remainder of his term (20 more months) and nudge him into positive territory. This was not going to be easy, however. Unemployment increased again in the 29th and 30th month of the Bush II presidency and busi-

ness leaders continued to report very low utilization of American productive capacity. In a June 4 talk to German Bankers, Federal Reserve Chairman Greenspan reported that there was no "major evidence" of a speedy economic recovery—"the monthly data, indeed the weekly data, have got to start to move in a positive direction fairly quickly." he said. "We haven't seen that yet." This was one reason that the handful of moderate Republicans that remained in Congress were wary of the big gift to the wealthy represented by Tax Cut II in 2003. Their constituents would not be happy if the new Bush tax plan was as ineffective at creating jobs as the Tax Cut of 2001.

As for the hard-right Republicans and the Bush Gang, they were not going to let reality get in the way of what they wanted. Since the original price tag on Tax Cut II was looking too expensive at $726 billion, why not make it look cheaper by slapping a different label on it—how about $550 billion? This was the approach taken by Bill Thomas, chairman of the House Ways and Means Committee, when he offered a fresh version of the bill in May 2003. It gave corporate stockholders a smaller break on their dividends, cutting their tax to 15% instead of eliminating it altogether. The White House was ready to bless this "reduction" as an appropriate compromise for Tax Cut II because it was not really a reduction at all. On closer examination Thomas' bill proved to be even more favorable to the rich than the original Bush version.

Analysis by the Tax Policy Center at the Brookings Institution and at the Center on Budget and Policy Priorities indicated that the $550 billion figure was a smokescreen. The total impact of the legislation was obscured behind a number of time limits or "sunset" provisions inserted in the text, measures that Congress was very likely to overturn in the future. These critics calculated that the real price tag of the Thomas measure was going to be twice the advertised amount, or $1.1 trillion. [21]

Similar shenanigans were conducted by the Republicans in the Senate, who barely passed their own version of Tax Cut II. While purporting to chop the President's proposal in half, to around $350 billion, this alternative was also laced with time limits and "sunset" provisions that were unlikely to be enforced. The Center on Budget and Policy Priorities demonstrated that the real cost was likely to be $660 billion. Senator Max Baucus of Montana, senior Democrat on the Finance Committee, described the sunset language as "a huge yo-yo tax provision, now you see it, now you don't."[23]

Some options in the revised tax cut plans were even more favorable to the rich than the original, particularly in the House bill. It not only cut the dividend tax rate to 15%, but it also chopped the rate on capital gains income down to the same percentage. This idea had been central to the overall strategy of the Bush Gang for a long time; a 15% tax on capital gains was exactly the figure that George Bush I had dreamed about from 1989 to 1992. He could not get the reduction passed by Congress at the time because of the enormous federal deficits that he

had helped to amass. The fact that the capital gains tax was targeted again in 2003 was indicative of the consistency of the Bush program and the overwhelming upper class desire to abolish taxes on capital altogether.

The House bill and the final compromise offered a pay-off for each millionaire in the first year that was even higher than George W's original plan—a $93,500 tax cut as opposed to $89,500. The overwhelming favoritism of the plan was best demonstrated by the fact that the combined benefit for 184,000 millionaire households over a ten-year period was going to be equal to the amount returned to the great majority of Americans, the 116 million households who earn less than $95,000 per year.

President George W. Bush pressed the House and the Senate to come up with a conference bill as quickly as possible, so the Congress dutifully emerged with the worst possible compromise: the finished piece of legislation closely approximated the House proposal in terms of its total gifts to the rich, but it was still labeled with the misleading price tag conjured up by the Senate. Analysis by Robert Greenstein, Richard Kogan, and Joel Friedman of the Center on Budget and Policy Priorities (CBPP) summed up the result: "The tax-cut package tentatively agreed to by the White

BALANCED BY BUSH: THE SCALES OF ECONOMIC JUSTICE 2003-2013

$139 billion in tax cuts for those with incomes over $1 million	$139 billion in tax cuts for those with incomes under $95,000
184,000 households (about one-sixth of 1% of the population)	116 million households (89% of the American people)

(Source: Center on Budget and Policy Priorities analysis of House tax cut plan, 2003-2013)[22]

House and House and Senate Republican leaders carries an 'official' cost of $350 billion
through 2013, but does so only through massive
use of budget gimmicks....the cost through 2013
will be $807 billion to $1.06 trillion, depending
on how one measures the cost of extending the
bill's business depreciation tax cut."[24]

Most Republican leaders did not seem to
be embarrassed about the fact that the "temporary" benefits for the rich were a charade and
were likely to be made permanent; Speaker of
the House of Representatives, Dennis Hastert,
more or less agreed with CBPP assessment of the
real cost of Bush II's Tax Cut II: "The $350 [bil-
lion] number takes us through the next two
years, basically. But also it could end up being a
trillion-dollar bill, because this stuff is extend-
able." Republican Senators Olympia Snowe and
John McCain refused to vote for the bill because
they thought it was irresponsible and because
the sponsors were lying about the total costs.

Citizens for Tax Justice plugged the numbers into their sophisticated computer programs
for tax analysis and came up with the result for
different households. Even with the tax credits
for families with children, which presumably
would benefit a wide range of Americans, the
bottom 60% of the population was going to
receive only 8.6% of the tax cut, or less than
$400 per household over a period of four years.
The top 1% of the population, on the other
hand, was slated to receive 38% of the total
benefit, or $107,095 over the same period. And
after the year 2006, with the provisions for very
low taxes on dividends and capital gains scheduled to be kept in place, the take of the richest
1% was due to increase to 52%.[25]

On the day before the legislation passed,
Nobel Prize winners in Economics Robert
Solow and Franco Modigliani tried to send

Congress a warning with a critique published by
The Boston Globe. The real purpose of Tax Cut
II had very little to due with economic stimulus,
they wrote, and everything to do with supporting the privileged: "Bush has claimed that his
proposal would have a favorable effect on
investment through higher after-tax profitability. In reality the impact would likely discourage
investment. The current tax on dividends
amounts to a subsidy for investment financed by
retained earnings, reducing the cost of capital.
The elimination of the dividend tax would ter-
minate this incentive, discouraging corporate
saving and investment." They summed up their
argument in very plain terms: "The real intent is
a continuation of the old struggle to enrich the
wealthy at the expense of ordinary people,
including future generations."[26]

While the great sums of money redistributed to the rich were unfair and unproductive in
themselves, there was an additional overall
effect that was very detrimental to the economy.
Tax Cut II was sure to induce new kinds of eva-
sive behavior among wealthy taxpayers and the
legions of accountants and lawyers who serve
them. The great disparity between the highest
income tax rate on regular income—it was lowered to 35%—and the ridiculously low rate on
dividends and capital gains—15%—was destined to lead to a new wave of tax shelters and
tax loopholes that would continue to befuddle
the underfunded Internal Revenue Service.
Wall Street Journal analyst David Wessel warned
of the results as the final bill was being passed,
"The capacity of companies and rich investors
to exploit, and sometimes create, tax loopholes
appears almost unbounded. Taxing one kind of
income a lot more than another creates incentives for tax games. Eliminating or sharply
reducing the tax on dividends, without making

sure that companies pay taxes, can offer all sorts of opportunities to the tax-averse." It was possible that George W's Tax Cut II might artificially pump up the Dow Jones average, but it was not necessarily going to creat more job opportunities in America—with one exception. The maze of misleading regulations and time provisions in the tax bill favored those endowed with a particular kind of economic ingenuity; Wessel predicted a bright future for those who devise "clever ways to use the new law to help wealthy clients avoid taxes."[27]

A Big Victory and Dangerous Repercussions

> President Bush seems to have decided that the biggest problem facing America today is that the rich don't have enough money.
>
> —Robert S. McIntyre,
> Citizens for Tax Justice

Bush solved the problems of the rich when he signed Tax Cut II on May 28, 2003. He hailed the victory that his forces had achieved, "We have taken aggressive action to strengthen the framework of our economy."

Grover Norquist of the ultra-conservative Americans for Tax Reform worked very closely with White House aides on pushing the tax cuts along and was delighted by the future prospects. He predicted, "You'll have a tax cut every year."[28]

Others were not so enthusiastic. Veteran tax and budget expert Peter R. Orszag predicted that Tax Cut II would only exacerbate the problems caused by Tax Cut I and called attention to the negative appraisals of Bush's program: "Various analysts and institutions that have studied the 2001 tax cut, including the Congressional Budget Office, economists at the Federal Reserve, and economists at The Brookings Institution, have generally found that the long-term negative effects of the tax cuts due to larger budget deficits (and reduced national saving) will offset and potentially outweigh any positive effects on future output from the impact of reduced marginal tax rates."[29]

In fact, the potential effects of Tax Cuts I and II were staggering. The Congressional Budget Office had calculated that the effect of the 2001 cuts had already caused a $126 billion loss to the federal treasury in 2003, thus helping to push the deficit up toward $300 billion for the year. The estimated deficit rose to more than $450 billion when the 2003 tax cuts were enacted. One analysis of the loss of revenue caused by Tax Cuts I and II predicted losses in federal revenue that would be more destructive than the Reagan/Bush deficits of the 1980s and early 1990s:

> In total, the costs from 2001 through 2013 of the tax cuts enacted to date and the additional tax-cut agenda reflected in the new budget amount to $4.6 trillion, including interest payments. In 2013, the combined revenue losses would constitute a larger share of the economy than did the Reagan tax cuts of the early 1980s.[30]

Still clinging to the same course they had pursued two decades earlier, the Bush Gang was so devoted to promoting the concentration of wealth and power among America's upper class that they were disregarding the threat of crippling federal deficits. The political posturing that equated the fortunes of the rich with the preservation of good jobs for average Americans was dishonest. The same could be said for George W. Bush's claim that his 2003 tax cut would provide the "average American" with savings of "$1,000 per year." When the bill finally passed he broke into his cheerleading mode and announced to the American people, "You've got more of your money to spend!" This was only true in a very warped sense.

There were some wealthy Americans who thought that the way Bush pandered to their interests was definitely not in the best interests of the country. Warren Buffett, the savvy investor with the nation's second largest fortune (estimated at $30 billion in 2003), was one of them. He tried to warn the president about the wrong-headedness of the tax plan that was

YOU'VE GOT MORE OF YOUR MONEY TO SPEND!

(Bush Delivers on His Promise, May 2003)

Tax Cut Beneficiaries	Dollars Per Household Per Year
American Millionaires	$93,500
Middle 20% of US households	$217
Bottom 20% of US households	$1

(Source: Center on Budget and Public Policy)[31]

pushed through Congress and pointed out that real economic stimulus was possible only if ordinary people were able to spend the money: "Enact a Social Security tax 'holiday' or give a flat-sum rebate to people with low incomes, he suggested. Putting $1,000 in the pockets of 310,000 families with urgent needs is going to provide far more stimulus to the economy than putting the same $310 million in my pockets."

Since he suspected the Bush Gang would not listen to his warning, Buffett also predicted the likely long-term result of Tax Cut II—more fiscal burdens for working Americans:

When you listen to tax-cut rhetoric, remember that giving one class of taxpayer a "break" requires—now or down the line—that an equivalent burden be imposed on other parties. In other words, if I get a break, someone else pays. Government can't deliver a free lunch to the country as a whole. It can, however, determine who pays for lunch. And last week the Senate handed the bill to the wrong party.[32]

In the next decade, if left to their own devices by a weak Democratic Party, the Bush Gang will tack on Tax Cuts III, IV, and V until there is no longer any taxation of capital. They will continue to shift more and more of the costs of operating our society onto the backs of working people by instituting a flat income tax or a national sales tax, and multiplying the government interest payments necessary to pay the mounting deficits.

The culminating blow will come in 2010, when the federal estate tax, or inheritance tax, is due to be extinguished. The current law provides for the automatic restoration of the estate tax in the following year, but it is unlikely to be invoked if the Bush Gang is still in power in 2011. George W. Bush is looking forward to the day when he and his multimillionaire and billionaire friends will be able to inherit their parents' estates and not pay a penny in taxes. Plutocratic control of the American government will be assured. Then the Bush Gang can lock up the Temple of Democracy and throw away the key.

Twenty-One

Rounding Up the Bush Gang

We can have just our usual flag, with the white stripes painted black and the stars replaced by the skull and cross-bones.

—Mark Twain, 1901, suggesting a new flag
appropriate for the US conquest of the Philippines. [1]

Somehow the madness must cease ... a nation that continues year after year to spend more money on military defense than on programs of social uplift is approaching spiritual death.

—Martin Luther King, Jr., April 4, 1967,
the day he led the largest anti-war march in U.S. history

Over a period of more than two decades, there has been a profound rightward shift in the United States that has affected our economy, our political system, and our society. The economic power of our wealthy upper class and the corporations and financial institutions which they control has been immeasurably enhanced. There has been, not surprisingly, a parallel rise in the political power of ultra-conservative Republicans who support unfettered capitalism and the rule of the rich. This fusion of economic and political power, whether it is called a plutocracy or a corporate oligarchy, can be personified by one family and their henchmen, the Bush Gang. For generations the Bush family has been intimately connected to the American aristocracy of wealth and the highest levels of the Republican Party. Since George Bush I and George Bush II are apt symbols of corporate and upper-class greed, this warrants some fun at their expense. The reader should not forget, however, that these characters represent a very serious threat to ordinary Americans. The ruthless nature of our present political economy requires pirates at the top, and this reality has driven the Bush Gang to institute policies that are nothing short of criminal.

On a good many issues, we cannot necessarily prove the criminal *intent* of the Bush Gang. For all we know, the two Georges and their backers have genuine beliefs about government that go back to Alexander Hamilton and some of the Federalists, beliefs that suggest that it is wise to put severe limits on democracy and keep an elite class in charge of the country's economic assets and institutions. But in other important matters—for example, when the members of the Bush crew actually encourage wealthy citizens to practice various forms of tax evasion, shield corporate figures from criminal investigations, or lie to Congress about clearly illegal practices in the realm of foreign affairs—the consequences *and the intentions* of the Bush Gang are criminal.

Does this mean they should they be impeached for high crimes and treason? While their misdeeds warrant more attention than did the sexual peccadillos of Bill Clinton, impeachment is not the answer.

Over and above the various acts of thievery, fraud, and deception generated by the Bush Gang and their corporate allies, there is the *mega-crime* that is not a prosecutable offense. There has been a massive and intentional redistribution of income and wealth from working-class and middle-class Americans to our richest citizens. If the American people want to end this extended campaign, the misappropriation of 10% to 15% of all personal income in the United States, then we must discipline the richest 1% of the population and remove their most prominent agents, the Bush Gang, from power.

Blame the rich? Exactly. When Bush II let the words "class warfare" and "class war" slip off his tongue in January 2003, he was betraying his growing anxiety about a populist uprising. The only proper response to "Class Piracy," the undeclared war perpetrated by a tiny minority under the flag of Skull and Bones, is to call those who have looted the economy to account.[2]

The vast majority of Americans, who are very slow to anger about such things, did not quite comprehend the scale of the attack that was waged against them during the 1980s and 1990s. In the year 2000, when some of the public were realizing that CEO earnings had gone up 1,000 times faster than the average worker's wages over the previous two decades, popular

grumbling increased. By 2003, most people knew about the magnitude of the crimes perpetrated by many of these chief executives, who had pumped up the stock market and looted it before it collapsed. The economy was in sad shape and consumer confidence was falling. The question now was: who would speak for the people?

While the corporate upper class and the Bush Gang were staging their raids on American society for over twenty years, the ultra-conservative turn of U.S. politics eviscerated the Democratic Party. The Republicans continued to control the political agenda even when Clinton was president. And sometimes the Democrats, bereft of ideas and a sense of moral direction, joined the Republicans as willing accomplices of the richest citizens and corporations as they looted the economy.[2] Political commentator and television host Bill Moyers summed up the situation as of March of 2003:

> In no small part because they coveted the same corporate money, Democrats practically walked away from the politics of struggle, leaving millions of working people with no one to fight for them. We see the consequences all around us in what a friend of mine calls "a suffocating consensus." Even as poverty spreads, inequality grows, and our quality of life diminishes, Democrats have become the doves of class warfare.[3]

While the Democrats walked away from the notion of struggling on behalf of ordinary Americans, the Republicans honed their weapons for class piracy and pushed ahead with a vengeance. The story of this book, essentially, is a review of their sustained raids on the American public under the leadership of the Bush Gang. Everything they did—lowering income tax rates, deregulating business, punishing middle-income and poor people—was explicitly designed to favor the elite class that controls investment capital at the expense of those who live from their labor. What is more, even those who buy into the elite logic—that the rich must rule so that capitalism can prosper—must admit that the upper class and the Bush Gang failed miserably in this regard. As the pirates piled up their treasure, a large amount was flaunted on luxuries, and a great deal more was simply wasted through a combination of fraud and stupidity.

The rich, without a doubt, have been increasing their monopoly on the financial assets that are key to capital accumulation in the political economy of the United States. Yet, in recent decades they often neglected the task of building and sustaining productive industrial enterprises, preferring short-term, speculative gambles instead. Wealthy investors experimented with the near-weightlessness of paper entrepreneurship and financial derivatives, then flew off into the vaporous realm of the "dot.com" internet companies in the 1990s. Their attraction to the insubstantial was compounded by a process of criminal and negligent behavior—plundering the banking system, privatizing public savings, hedging against other market investments—that led to the destruction, not the multiplication, of our national assets. The conservative sponsors of unrestricted capitalism failed to deliver even when they were allowed to operate on their own terms.

The Economic Crisis and U.S. Leadership of a Capitalist World

Around 1992, after the U.S. economy suffered a severe economic downturn under the Bush I administration, it seemed that the United States was struggling and failing to grow as quickly as other highly industrialized countries. The ascent of the economies of Japan, Germany, and most of Western Europe from 1950 to 1990 had been remarkable. These nations seemed poised to leave us behind, precisely because they were taking much better care of their people at the same time that their societies were becoming more productive.

Now, more than a decade later, it is becoming clear that something more frightening has happened. In the 1990s, the United States grabbed hold of the gears of corporate globalization and seemed to recover from its economic doldrums. Because of the Clinton administration's failure to reverse the rightward shift initiated during the Reagan/Bush years, private financial institutions and giant corporations were allowed to maintain or extend their advantages over working people all over the world. Agreements and economic standards adopted by NAFTA and the International Monetary Fund did not result in the development of good jobs and social security in either rich nations or poor nations, but contributed instead to regimes of austerity everywhere. The forces unleashed by international finance capital pushed living standards downward in many parts of the world.

"Free Market Capitalism," the idealized construct of economists like Milton Friedman and other American conservatives, was supposed to mean "the freedom to choose." In the U.S. and many other places, the freedom of political choice barely exists any more. Thus the freedom to choose is reduced to two concepts. One, for the consumers in advanced capitalist countries, is the freedom to choose between the varieties of corporate products that sit on the supermarket shelf. The other, for international investors, is the freedom of capital to choose to intrude wherever it pleases. Capital has the power to move quickly from continent to continent, searching for cheap labor disciplined by authoritarian regimes, or more commonly now, by the austerity measures set in motion by the IMF and the World Bank. The world's business leaders are becoming more internationalized, too. Most do not show loyalty to the working and middle classes in their own countries. Instead they are succumbing to the creeping ideology of the right that dismisses the aspirations of working people and assumes that most of the world's citizens will have to get by with less in the future.

The dominant economic trends promoted by the United States—as typified by Wal-Mart, Tyson Foods and the meat-packing industry, the private health corporations, and the host of down-sizing, overpaid chief executives—are the favorites of capitalist investors and represent the potential downfall of more egalitarian societies. Although the weakened remnants of social democracy in Europe may survive for a while, they are unlikely to do very well if companies supported by international investors (Americans, Europeans, and Japanese alike) keep filling the world's markets with cheaper products produced by the Chinese, Indonesians, Thais, Vietnamese, Filipinos, and others in the vast new workhouse of Asia. In this chaotic world system, the regimes specializing in authoritarianism and austerity have become the models for modern development.

China, the ultimate labor resource, has replicated some features of the "Asian Tiger" economies—South Korea, Taiwan, Hong Kong, and Singapore—that over the past two or three decades were the world's best examples of super-

charged economic development based on production for export. As Chinese exports have multiplied, the U.S. economy has been gratuitously shutting down much of its own productive capacity—jobs in manufacturing dropped sharply by 2.5 million from 1998 to 2002. Much of this drop-off is due to our policy of favoring low wage production everywhere else in the world, which in turn has led to an extraordinary negative trade balance—$432 billion in 2002, with about one quarter of that going to China. While Chinese goods keep filling up our Wal-Marts, this steady movement of capital to locations outside of the United States also reduces our capacity to invest in good jobs for Americans, whether in manufacturing or some other sector of the economy.

Until recently, few economic commentators in the mainstream media in the United States have paid attention to the ways that "free-trade" ideology can undermine real freedom. Most have failed to appreciate the dark portents described by Jeff Faux, former president of the Economic Policy Institute, who in February of 2003 described the American "corporate-government strategy" that compels "workers of *all* countries to compete with each other in a downward spiral of lower wages and worsening working conditions."[4] The result for the United States is an increasingly low-wage service economy fueled by massive amounts of consumer and corporate debt.

Elsewhere authoritarian models of enforcing work discipline have gained prominence because they support industrial production at the lowest possible wages. Their adoption in China over the past two decades has accelerated that nation's rapid transformation into a more advanced economy. This kind of development, however, is not foreign to the United

States. In addition to having our own history of harsh industrial development in the 19th and early 20th centuries, the United States supported a modern version of undemocratic industrialization when it backed the so-called "Asian Tigers." In South Korea and Taiwan, American military and economic power were used to promote long-term projects of a "lite-fascist" variety—we backed brutal right-wing, anti-democratic regimes in those countries from the 1950s to the 1980s. Their draconian management style was exportable, as were their long hours and harsh working conditions. By the 1990s, while Taiwan and South Korea were becoming more democratic, industrial managers from these countries could be found running some of the most exploitative factories in the world, whether they were in other parts of Asia or faraway Central America.[5]

A New Round of Imperialism Instead of Progress at Home

Five years ago, I wrote about the failure of the Clinton administration to reverse the trends that the Bush Gang and conservative business corporations had set in motion. I was concerned about the steady erosion of democracy and equality in the United States and the possibility that we were moving toward a grim future:

> If Arkansas, which looks suspiciously like a center of third world development within the United States, is the economic and political model stuck inside our President's head, then we are already in trouble. And if Singapore is the model state for globalizing high-tech development in the eyes of the world's investing class, then we are drifting toward something worse: an illusion of democracy called 'authoritarian democracy'.[6]

At the time there was a discernable trend toward authoritarianism in countries that claimed to be democracies—Singapore was an example of a place where economic modernization was being hailed but democratic freedom was steadily suppressed. Arkansas, the poorest U.S. state, was the breeding ground for the kinds of low-wage, anti-worker corporations that were beginning to dominate the U.S.—Wal-Mart, Tyson Foods, and Beverly Nursing Homes originated there. These developments were taking us back to a more primitive level of economic development and undermining liberty and prosperity in the United States.

In 2003, the situation is much more alarming. A much more rapid attack on American values has been generated ever since September 11, 2001. We are being attacked by our own government.

The threat to American society from the Bush Gang, or more broadly, from the economic and political interests that they represent, grows with each passing day that they hold power. They are determined to keep militarizing the United States, bullying the rest of the world, and implementing a variety of authoritarian controls over daily American life. The decision to put our own Christian fundamentalists in charge of law enforcement at home, while giving a sub-gang of neo-conservatives the opportunity to engineer the conquest of Muslim nations and oil wells abroad, is a scary proposition. If we give the Bush pirates license to plunder the world at will, especially after they have rejected any need to comply with international laws and agreements, then the repercussions from the edges of the new American Empire will be constant. Angry militants of various persuasions will strike out at American interests and citizens, so that we in the United States will feel a constant urge to keep arming our garrisons around the world and shielding our own citizens at home. In the aftermath of September 11, American freedoms are already being restricted. If we attempt to extend our influence according to the unbounded aggressiveness suggested by the Bush Doctrine and the plans of the Project for the New American Century, the American people will always feel unsafe and subject to attack from "alien people."

In a previous chapter, I mentioned that Alexis de Tocqueville feared that the most formidable threat to democracy in America would be the "manufacturing aristocracy" that he saw developing in the early days of U.S. industrialization. The factory system of the 1830s degraded working people's lives. This system was later expanded to many sectors of our economy, first by the Robber Barons in the late 19th century, then again by the reactionary behavior of American corporations in the late 20th century. While de Tocqueville anticipated the emergence of a "manufacturing aristocracy" that elevated the likes of the Bush family into the corporate upper class, he also noted another threat to democracy. He suspected that the American people might relinquish their freedoms voluntarily, that they would long for law and order and the strong hand of government if they feared that their security was threatened.

> A nation that demands from its government nothing but the maintenance of order is already a slave in the bottom of its heart; it is a slave of its well-being, and the man who is to chain it can arrive on the scene.[7]

This combination of anti-democratic tendencies—the desire of the owning class to dominate the people and the secret longing of some of the people to accept authoritarian domina-

tion—is what makes the ascendance of the Bush Gang so frightening. The Bush elite are perfectly willing to stand by and watch most Americans suffer a declining standard of living. Or rather, they are more than willing to help that process along with a host of regressive tax measures and the continuing deregulation of corporate behavior. Moreover, they do not care if democratic participation and freedom of expression are usurped by the corporate state. For them, it is of little consequence if the long-term result of such a course is to hollow out the American industrial base, deprive workers of retirement funds, health benefits, and various public amenities, and otherwise demoralize the American people.

Why? Because the Bush pirates are pushing off from the shores of the United States and readying themselves for a different kind of plundering. They are waving the Stars and Stripes as if it were the Skull and Bones, the flag that declares the unchallenged privilege of a few to disregard international law and seize the resources of the world. Just before George W's election, in "Rebuilding America's Defenses: Strategy, Forces and Resources For a New Century," the Bush Gang expressed its rationale for guarding the world's resources with U.S. armed forces. It called them "the cavalry on the new American frontier."[8]

Bush loyalists have been plotting this course of open imperialism for some time. Richard Haass, who served in the National Security Council under George Bush I, joined the Bush II administration in 2001 as director of policy planning at the State Department. Just before he took over the new job he presented a paper called "Imperial America" that argued that the American people ought to "re-conceive their role from a traditional nation state to an imperial power." He suggested that "the U.S. role would resemble 19th century Britain… Coercion and the use of force would normally be a last resort."[9] The underlying political philosophy was clear—the United States would be permitted to roam the globe, imposing its own system of order, and taking whatever it wanted.

Both of the George Bushes and many of their retinue are, first and foremost, people who have gained wealth by extracting things from the earth. They are heir to a certain Christian tradition, once proudly called Manifest Destiny within the continental United States, but similarly justified over the past 500 years by the Spanish, Portuguese, Dutch, and British in their various Catholic and Protestant crusades to monopolize the gold, silver, spices, tea, diamonds, and oil of the world. This particular Western religious/economic tradition—one can hardly call it "civilization"—entitled armies and merchants of European ancestry to invade, bribe, settle by force, commit fraud, or engage in any other coercive behavior that gained control of resources and territories around the world. God, according to the perpetrators of this doctrine, gave them permission to subdue recalcitrant natives—be they "Indians" in all regions of the Americas, Indians in Asia, blacks in Africa, or the whites of Ireland (the first people to be labeled "natives" by the English)—by various brutal means, annihilating them if necessary.

This is, historically speaking, why empires have existed—they use their unrestrained power to seize territory and wealth from others. Our current leaders are people who want to ignore the environmental despoilment of the earth's ecosystems, develop many kinds of new and deadly weapons, exempt themselves from the rule of the International Criminal Court, and step around the United Nations' efforts to solve crises peacefully. Their determination is so great that suddenly, just since the Bush clique re-took power in 2001, a vocal contingent of American apologists for empire has appeared. Some of them simply believe that might makes right. Others expect that the United States will come up with an updated form of "Benevolent Assimilation," creating an empire that somehow wields its muskets in a peaceful way.

This imperial hubris borders on the ludicrous, as demonstrated by the way that both conservatives and liberals have endorsed the new imperialism by referring approvingly to Rudyard Kipling's poem, "The White Man's Burden" (the infamous doggerel that was written specifically in praise of the U.S. conquest of the Philippines). Max Boot, formerly in charge of editorial features at *The Wall Street Journal* and now with the Council on Foreign Relations, has used one of the Kipling lines, "*Savage Wars of Peace*," as the title of an article and a book that celebrate the American Empire.[10] Liberal professor Michael Ignatieff, head of the Human Rights Center at Harvard, entitled his January 5, 2003 cover article in *The New York Times*, "American Empire: The Burden." Ignatieff praised a new kind of American exceptionalism, somehow assuming that we have the moral superiority that will allow us to become the first empire in world history that can rule through kindness instead of brutality.

While these supporters cheered on the Bush administration as it readied itself for "preemptive" war in Iraq, the growing voices of protest around the world forced the Gang to hesitate. An unprecedented wave of pre-war protest also mounted within the U.S., but it could not deter the Bush Gang. They already had weapons and troops lined up and ready to go. The president and his crew ignored the clamor, expecting that most Americans would rally round the flag once troops were sent into battle. They were right.

Open Piracy: a Rational Choice or Capital Gone Mad?

The irony is that capitalism, which was supposedly reaching its maturity as a rational system of economic interchange, seems to be rapidly devolving to its most primitive stages. At home in the United States and in many newly industrializing countries, the coarser forms of exploitation of wage labor are coming into favor again. Even more regressive is the urge to engage in outright plunder of the globe and fill up the imperial treasure chests with riches stolen from others. The Bush Gang has determined that the United States ought to embark on the most ambitious military adventure of all time, extending a Pax Americana over all the earth. Americans are beginning to wake up to the fact that this is not entirely sane, no matter what their political perspectives.[11] If Mark Twain were present today, he would surely be talking about "The Blessings-of-Civilization Trust," his name for the giant enterprise in plundering that the United States embarked upon a century ago.

Mark Twain penned his most famous anti-imperialist essay, "To a Person Sitting in Darkness," in response to the war the United States was waging against the Filipinos, who had just won their struggle for independence from Spain. He was also answering the hypocritical presidential platform of the Republicans, who wanted a colony in the Pacific and promised "to confer the blessings of liberty and civilization upon all the rescued peo-

ples." Twain served as vice president of the Anti-Imperialist League, which included such people as philosopher William James, industrialist Andrew Carnegie, and Samuel Gompers of the AFL. The League tried to stop our murderous foreign adventure in the Philippines, where more than 200,000 people were slaughtered in the name of Christianity and American democracy. Twain wrote:

> The Person Sitting in Darkness is almost sure to say: "There is something curious about this—curious and unaccountable. There must be two Americas: one that sets the captive free, and one that takes a once-captive's new freedom away from him, and picks a quarrel with him with nothing to found it on; then kills him to get his land."
>
> "Of course, we must not venture to ignore our General MacArthur's[12] reports—oh, why do they keep on printing those embarrassing things?—we must drop them trippingly from the tongue and take the chances:
>
> During the last ten months our losses have been 268 killed and 750 wounded; Filipino loss, three thousand two hundred and twenty-seven killed, and 694 wounded.
>
> We must stand ready to grab the Person Sitting in Darkness, for he will swoon away at this confession, saying: "Good God, those 'niggers' spare their wounded, and the Americans massacre theirs!" We must bring him to, and coax him and coddle him, and assure him that the ways of Providence are best, and that it would not become us to find fault with them; and then, to show him that we are only imitators, not originators, we must read the following passage from the letter of an American soldier-lad in the Philippines to his mother, published in Public Opinion, of Decorah, Iowa,

describing the finish of a victorious battle: 'WE NEVER LEFT ONE ALIVE. IF ONE WAS WOUNDED, WE WOULD RUN OUR BAYONETS THROUGH HIM.'

And as for a flag for the Philippine Province, it is easily managed. We can have a special one—our States do it: we can have just our usual flag, with the white stripes painted black and the stars replaced by the skull and cross-bones."[13]

A century later, as we invade the Middle East, Mark Twain's redesign of the American flag seems perfect for the occasion. The Gang, having robbed us blind for years, is now intent on robbing "them"—the rest of the world. Somehow Twain must have anticipated that the Bush pirates would require a banner that includes black stripes representing oil, topped off by the Skull and Bones logo from their Yale club. By investing in history's most advanced and deadly weaponry the Bush Gang wants to establish a world empire, focused first of all on the trillions of dollars of oil that lie beneath the Middle East. At a time when American industry can no longer satisfy the kinds of profit margins that American capitalists desire, the owners of capital are looking favorably on a new project. The pirates have proposed "The Project for the New American Century," a plan ideally suited to chasing down the world's valuable resources and rounding them up within a vastly expanded network of military bases and technological outposts.

The 21st century is beginning, just as the 20th century did, with a renewed cycle of "Resource Wars" (to quote the title of Michael Klare's enlightening book).[14] Except this time, we are not helping our Robber Barons break out of our Hemisphere and chase after the other imperialist countries—England, France, Germany, and Russia—which a century ago

were already busy plundering the world. This time we will be cruising the globe as the only imperialist country, making up ad hoc rules for controlling natural resources, granting economic access or military assistance to the lesser countries of the world, and threatening the nations that displease us. Oil looms large, but so do a host of other diminishing mineral and forest resources, not to mention the simplest, but potentially the most valuable resource of all—water (currently many multinational corporations are increasingly active in buying up and controlling water rights and water systems). From a certain point of view—that of the artificial person known as the corporation, which only "lives" as long as it maximizes the return on invested capital—it does not look so crazy to employ an enormous military machine in the service of a new empire. The human point of view is something else entirely. Why should other nations of the earth tolerate this? And, even if many of them asquiesce to the Bush Gang's imperial desires, why would the people of the United States want to sustain such a project?

The major media corporations, being part of the multinational corporate web, effectively limit real debate about our choices in foreign and domestic policy. And in anticipation of the war in Iraq, they beat the drums for war almost as effectively as William Randolph Hearst did one hundred years ago. So naturally many people have swallowed the scary nonsense peddled by the Bush Gang in the name of patriotism. Our government wants to keep frightening American parents with constant images of impending terror, while simultaneously training our children to be gendarmes guarding our growing outposts and new colonies. They are told that they can be heroes who will protect American interests and freedom. One option for young citizens, as there are fewer prospects of good employment at home, is to become legionnaires or centurions who venture out into the empire. In so doing they will face the same moral problem that faced American soldiers in the Philippines in 1900 and later in Vietnam. The new centurions may be asked to do many things "for the homeland" that are reprehensible.

If there is a long series of "oil wars" (followed by metal wars, water wars, electricity wars, ad infinitum), this could enable the Bush Gang to keep eliminating necessary jobs in our public sector, while encouraging private investors to abandon domestic production in favor of more profitable extraction of resources abroad. This in turn will continue to drive down the incomes of ordinary Americans, thus making employment in the imperial forces ever more attractive. The harsh discipline of corporations, the bombast of war, the over-aggressiveness of management, and the greed of investors are the perfect combination for putting the squeeze on both blue collar workers and middle-class salary earners.

The great-grandchildren of the Robber Barons are dancing to Mark Twain's satirical theme: "Get money. Get it quickly. Get it in abundance. Get it in prodigious abundance. Get it dishonestly if you can, honestly if you must." As the frenzied drumbeats of amoral, impatient capital mingle with the rumbles of aggressive, "pre-emptive" war, the sound has a distinctly patriotic rhythm for the Bush Gang. Some of them, including the President, live within a closed cocoon of opinion provided by their advisors. For all we know, George W. Bush may feel he is pursuing his goals as an earnest Christian who wants to protect America. But such sentiments matter little if his economic programs and initiatives (like those of his father and the rest of the gang) are used to systematically steal from

working Americans at every turn.

Whether Bush knows it or not, he is a pirate. With regard to foreign policy, the question of sincerity is entirely irrelevant. When President William McKinley told the Methodist ladies missionary society, "I went down on my knees and prayed Almighty God," and learned that his God wanted him to seize the Philippines, did it really matter if he believed what he was saying? Truth or lie, the justification served an imperial purpose. One hundred years later, President Bush has also succumbed to the delusion that he is on the mission of a messianic warrior. "I'm in the Lord's hands," he said to *Washington Post* reporter Bob Woodward, and he also predicted that "This will be a monumental struggle between good and evil."[15]

Stopping the Big Heist

In some parts of the world, the frightening prospects of international class piracy, pre-emptive wars, and increasing environmental degradation are mobilizing many people against the policies of the Bush Gang. At home, however, if progressives hope to gain the attention of their fellow American citizens, then their pleas for global social justice must be accompanied and superseded by direct appeals to people's feelings about economic fairness within the United States. Without a broad-based populist rebellion that includes voters of all social classes, the Bush Gang will continue to push forward with their agenda, keeping a firm grip on the wealth that has been looted from the bottom 90% of the population and pursuing a militant posture as they seek to loot the whole globe.

Just before Labor Day 2003, the Congressional Budget Office issued a detailed report that again confirmed the scale of the domestic robbery. The share of income collected by the richest 1% of Americans more than doubled from 1979 to 2000. Their after-tax incomes increased 201% over twenty-one years. On the other hand, the after-tax incomes of middle-income families grew only 15%, even though they worked many more hours per year in 2000 than they had two decades earlier. This astounding shift in economic resources, the mega-crime of our era, was reflected in the way the economic pie was divided. In 1979 the bottom 60% of the American population received 35.6% of all after-tax income, nearly double the 18.1% share taken by the top 5%. By 2000, this advantage had disappeared. The richest 5% devoured such a large slice of the pie, 27.5%, that they almost surpassed the bottom 60%, whose diminished portion only amounted to 29.2%.[16] For the Bush Gang, which had set this process in motion in the 1980s, this was not a problem. They decided to keep encouraging the ravenous appetites of the very rich by doling out huge tax cuts in 2001 and 2003.

The response to this thievery, whether it comes from the Democrats, the Greens, or other independent political groups, must be strong and to the point. We must say 1) we don't like being robbed, 2) we can do a much better job of sharing the fruits of our labor, and 3) we do not want to rob the rest of the world.

If we do not speak out, "The Money Power" will get to decide where it can profit most easily, and the interests of our nation will become synonymous with the interests of an expanded empire. Does George W. Bush understand this? Perhaps. Perhaps not. But certainly his close associates have decided that the American posture must be so aggressive that it frightens the rest of the world. And they have convinced Bush that it is necessary to say, "We will export death and vio-

lence to the four corners of the Earth in defense of our great nation."[17]

This frightening image, conjured up by men cloistered in their war rooms, is absolutely the wrong goal for Americans. We citizens of the United States can find much better pursuits, including peaceful ways to rebuild our own country. If we must fight, let's mount a peaceful struggle to curtail the over-concentration of corporate power that has corrupted business values and wiped out many productive assets that once resided in the hands of ordinary citizens. Let's reinvent a variety of human enterprises that are not tied to the highest return on capital investment, thus allowing real persons and small businesses to operate without being crushed by the "artificial persons," the corporations that overwhelm us with their sprawling monopolies and oligopolies. Real democracy requires that we develop ways to share wealth and power, and create institutions that give human values more room to thrive. Outside of our borders, the United States can promote democracy if we join other nations in guaranteeing fair economic development instead of unleashing free-market chaos and war throughout the rest of the world. Let's heed the words of one of our greatest 20th century heroes, the man who spoke as eloquently for economic equality as he did for racial equality. He insisted that the struggle for justice had to include a commitment to bettering the lives of all working Americans and ending U.S. imperialist adventures in other parts of the world.

> There is nothing, except a tragic death wish, to prevent us from reordering our priorities, so that the pursuit of peace will take precedence over the pursuit of war.
>
> —Martin Luther King, Jr.,
> April 4, 1967

Notes

CHAPTER ONE

1   Clay F. Richards, "George Bush: 'co-president' in the Reagan administration," United Press International, March 10, 1981.
2   *Washington Post*, March 22, 1981.
3   Internal Revenue Service, individual tax statistics 2000 (the last year for which the Internal Revenue Service has released complete statistics); see chapter 4 for more information on income changes.
4   Kevin Phillips, *Wealth and Democracy: A Political History of the American Rich*, New York: Broadway Books, 2002, p. 309.
5   Steve Brouwer, *Sharing the Pie*, three editions, each quite different, but each focused on the magnitude and causes of economic inequality in the United States. *Sharing the Pie: A Disturbing Picture of the U.S. Economy*, Carlisle PA, Big Picture Books, 1988 and 1992; *Sharing the Pie: a citizen's guide to wealth and power in America*, New York: Henry Holt, 1998. To name only a few of many important books concerning the shift of resources and power from the people to the rich: William Greider, *Who Will Tell the People*, New York: Simon and Schuster, 1992; Kevin Phillips, *The Politics of Rich and Poor*, New York: Random House, 1990; The Center for Popular Economics; Nancy Folbre, *A Field Guide to the American Economy*, New York: The New Press, 1995; and David M. Gordon, *Fat and Lean: The Corporate Squeeze on Working Americans and the Myth of Managerial Down-sizing*, New York: The Free Press, 1996.
6   Deficits are a bad idea when they are incurred in order to serve the wealthy or pay for an oversupply of military hardware, especially when the degree of public indebtedness eliminates other spending options. After the Reagan/Bush administrations ran up a very large deficit in just this manner from 1981-1992, there was some undue deficit hysteria that lasted through the 1990s and obscured the fact that deficits can be a positive tool of government. Two of the best books for putting government borrowing and spending in perspective were written by the late Robert Eisner, professor of economics at Northwestern University: *The Misunderstood Economy*, Harvard Business Press, 1994, and *How Real is the Federal Deficit?*, The Free Press, 1986. Positive deficit spending occurs when the government borrows to invest in our country and its people—for instance, spending on education programs and public infrastructure. This is a wise use of borrowing power, analogous to taking out a mortgage to build a house. The Bush Gang is totally disinterested in this kind of deficit.

CHAPTER TWO

1   Robert Brenner, "Towards the Precipice," *London Review of Books*, February 6, 2003.
2   James K. Glassman and Kevin A. Hassett, *Dow 36,000*, New York: Times Business, 1999. This book was influential enough to get many investors and some other business writers believing that the magic number 36,000 was more than a pipe dream; they seemed to think the market could keep leaping higher without ever crashing again. In the race for greedy readers, others book titles of 1999 kept upping the ante, to *Dow 40,000* and even *Dow 100,000*.
3   "CEOs Skewer the Books, Cook the Rest of Us," United for a Fair Economy, August 2002, posted on their website, www.faireconomy.org

4   Mark Gimein, "The Greedy Bunch: You Bought, They Sold," *Fortune*, September 2, 2002.
5   United for a Fair Economy, "CEOs at Defense Contractors," April 28, 2003, <www.faireconomy.org>.
6   Center For Responsive Politics, <www.opensecrets.org>.
7   Robert Trigaux, "Bush Success Built on Harken Sale," *St. Petersburg Times*, July 21, 2002. There are now many good web collections of information on Bush and Harken and they keep expanding; see for instance, "George W. Bush and Harken Energy" at <www.cooperativeresearch.org>; Harvard Watch has helped bring attention to Harvard Management Fund, which invests the University's giant endowment, it became a major investor in Harken (so was billioniare George Soros) during the time of Bush's sale of stock and may have been the never-revealed, secret buyer of his shares. Michael Kranish of the *Boston Globe* has also pursued this angle.
8   Robert Trigaux, op. cit. And see Paul Krugman, *The New York Times*, for a series of columns in 2002 on Bush's tricks.
9   Peter Behr, "Bush Sold Stock After Lawyers' Warning," *The Washington Post*, November 1, 2002.
10 Quoted in Molly Ivins, Lou Dubose, *Shrub: the Short but Happy Political Life of George W. Bush*, New York: Random House, 2000. This was my favorite of the pre-2000 election biographical treatments of George W. Bush; for other Bush books that can supply many more tidbits about the pre-presidential life of George W. Bush, see titles listed in Steve Brouwer, *Baby Bush and the Baby Boomers*, a book review/political essay in *Frigate* <www.frigatezine.com>, the online literary magazine, issue one, August 2000.
11 Martin A. Lee, "The Campaign Issue That Wasn't: Cheney's Oil Company in Shady Business Deals with Iraq," *San Francisco Bay Guardian*, Nov. 13, 2000.
12 Mary Williams Walsh, "Shriveling of Pensions after Halliburton Deal," *TheNew York Times*, September 10, 2002.
13 Greg Palast, *The Best Democracy Money Can Buy*, Plume, 2003; "Memo Shows Enron Division Headed by Army Secretary Thomas White Manipulated California Electricity Market," *Public Citizen*, May 8, 2002. The range of estimates of the total cost to California citizens due to the energy price gouging led by Enron was summed up by Representative Bob Filner of California in the *Congressional Record* of February 26, 2002: "the theft of between $20 and $40 billion from California ratepayers."
14 Robert Scheer, "A Walk in the Valley of Greed," *Los Angeles Times*, January 29, 2002.
15 Russell Mokhiber and Robert Weissman, "Bowling for Baghdad," posted on <www.Common_Dreams.com> October 19, 2002.
16 Sidney Schama, "The Dead and the Guilty," *The Manchester Guardian*, September 11, 2002.

CHAPTER THREE

1   "Income Inequality in the U.S., 1913-1998," paper by Thomas Piketty, CEPREMAP, Paris, and Emmanuel Saez, Harvard University, 2002.
2   While the years 1973 to 1979 were bumpy compared to the preceding two and a half decades, they have a reputation for economic failure that is not really deserved; the average rate of growth for those six years, 1.9%, was still higher than the average rate of growth over the next twenty years, 1980-2000.

3   Leonard Ross and Peter Passell, "Mr. Nixon's Economic
        Melodrama," *The New York Review of Books*, September 23,
        1971.

4   M. P. Crozier, S. J. Huntington, and J. Watanuki, *The Crisis of
        Democracy: Report on the Governability of Democracies to the
        Trilateral Commission*, New York University, 1975.

5   Kevin Phillips, *Wealth and Democracy*, p. 91.

6   This was a relative change in incomes compared to the
        extreme inequality of the 1870s -1920s (see next chapter). In
        the 1950s and 1960s the U.S. still remained the most unequal
        society among all highly industrialized nations; Western
        Europe, Japan, and Canada, by following a social democratic
        path after World War II, had achieved much more equal dis-
        tribution of income and wealth within a very short time.

7   Donald L. Bartlett and James B. Steel, *America: Who Really
        Pays the Taxes?*, New York: Simon & Schuster, 1994, pp. 17-
        18, p. 295.

8   See Citizens for Tax Justice, <www.ctj.org>, Spring, 2002. In
        1992, the last year of Bush I before Clinton took office, the
        deficit was slightly lower as a percent of GDP, 6.0%. Since this
        does not change the picture, I am using the 1991 figures as cal-
        culated by Robert McIntyre.

9   Steve Brouwer, "Writing About Progressive Economics for a
        Broad Audience," Eastern Economic Association, February 23,
        2001; Tamara Sober Giecek, *Teaching Economics as if People
        Mattered*, Boston: United for a Fair Economy, 2000.

10   Thomas B. Edsall, "Bush Has a Cabinet Full of Wealth," *The
        Washington Post*, September 19, 2002.

11   Citizens for Tax Justice, "Year by Year Analysis of the Bush Tax
        Cuts," <www.ctj.org>June 12, 2002.

CHAPTER FOUR

1   "Income Inequality in the U.S., 1913-1998," paper by Thomas
        Piketty, CEPREMAP, Paris, and Emmanuel Saez, Harvard
        University, 2002. Their work is based on painstaking historical
        research of IRS records. I am taking liberties with the years
        between 1900 and 1913, because there were no IRS statistics;
        however, all historical evidence indicates that the income
        shares were at least as favorable to the very rich during the first
        decade and a half of the 20th century as they were from 1913
        to 1940. The IRS income statistics for 1999 and 2000 demon-
        strate that those two years fit in on the high end of the pattern
        described by Saez and Piketty.

2   There is a rough correlation of unionization and income equal-
        ity in Europe even today. Countries in Scandinavia tend to
        have very high rates of labor organization and much lower dis-
        parities of income (as well as very low poverty rates, etc.), but
        all European countries have stronger labor movements and less
        income inequality than the U.S. The Luxembourg Studies are
        one of the best sources for comparing European societies with
        the United States. While all of them have shifted somewhat to
        the right in recent decades, they still tend to have a much
        wider variety of political expression than the United States
        and much more egalitarian economies and social programs.
        Although only a few countries, such as Switzerland, are richer
        on a per capita basis, all of them have a much smaller propor-
        tion of truly poor people. This is in spite of the fact that few of
        these countries were democracies until sometime in the 20th
        century and most were much poorer than the United States
        until recently. Higher commitments to social spending have

        not slowed them down, since they continually gained on the
        United States over the past half century in terms of labor pro-
        ductivity and quality of life.

3   U.S. Census Bureau, "Selected Measures of Household Income
        Dispersion: 1967-2001," Table A-3, 2002. Please note that the
        shares shown for each of these groups are not as great as the
        overall shift in incomes I am describing. This is because
        Census methods of collecting income data cannot adequately
        account for the high incomes of the very rich, but are quite
        accurate for the rest of the population. Other more accurate
        methods of tracking high incomes show much larger shifts in
        favor of the rich—Saez and Piketty have relied heavily on the
        high income tabulations of the IRS, which reviews high
        income tax returns very closely; they and other experts in the
        field of income and wealth, such as Professor Edward N. Wolff
        at NYU and experts at the Federal Reserve Board, also rely on
        data gathered from the Fed's Surveys of Consumer Finances
        (completed every three years), and other records that pertain
        mostly to wealthy Americans, such as estate taxes and differ-
        ent kinds of large-scale capital gains and property transactions.

4   Mishel, Bernstein, and Boushey, *The State of Working America,
        2002-2003*, p. 90.

5   Saez and Piketty, Table II. Their calculations are confined to
        the top 10% of the population, so they offer no direct compar-
        ison with the lower quintiles of income measurement.

6   CBO, "Capital Gains Taxes and Federal Revenues," October
        9, 2002. Note that capital gains taxes generated as a propor-
        tion of all taxes, 12%, and capital gains as a proportion of all
        income, 10% (following paragraph), are measuring two differ-
        ent things.

7   The Federal Reserve Board Survey of Consumer Finances
        showed those with incomes at the 95th percentiles averaged
        $50,000 in stocks and $87,000 in mutual funds. Wealth hold-
        ers at the 95th percentile (which would include more citizens
        who had retired) averaged $122,000 in stocks and $140,000 in
        mutual funds in 2001. Both groups then lost approximately
        15% of these amounts by October 2002 due to the stock mar-
        ket crash.

8   Unpublished study by Edward N. Wolff cited in *The State of
        Working America, 2002-2003*, pp. 288-290, in Tables 4.10 and
        4.11. James Poterba calculated that in 1998 the huge majority
        of Americans, the 90% at the bottom of the wealth pyramid,
        only owned 8.9% of all directly held shares of stock; their own-
        ership only increased slightly, to 13.9%, when all kinds of
        direct and indirect stock ownership were considered—his 2000
        study cited in Table 4., *The State of Working America, 2002-
        2003*, p. 286.

9   Analysis of the 2001 Survey of Consumer Finances was pub-
        lished by the Federal Reserve in January 2003, but as of this
        writing no economist (such as Wolff or Poterba) has analyzed
        the holdings of the those who make up the top 10% (the
        Federal Reserve does not divide the top 10% into rich and
        upper middle class segments) in order to determine accurately
        the amount of stock owned by the top 1% in 2001-2002. There
        is no indication that the proportion of the holdings of the rich-
        est 10% declined in spite of the stock bubble bursting in 2000-
        2002; but there is evidence that the small average holdings of
        middle income Americans did decline slightly. See "Recent
        Changes in U.S. Family Finances," by Ana M. Aizcorbe,
        Arthur B. Kennickell, Kevin B. Moore, *Federal Reserve
        Bulletin*, January 2003, and their estimates of the effects of
        equity (stock) losses in the financial markets in 2000-2002.

10   From IRS tables giving in-depth review of high income returns for 2000, the most recent year available as of this writing.

11   Congressional Budget Office, "Effective Federal Tax Rates, 1979-1997," October 2001, Table 1.2c, p. 134; the numbers for 2001 come from preliminary figures issued by the U.S. Census Bureau and the IRS figures and are adjusted for inflation in line with the CBO figures.

12   Quote comes from Holly Sklar, ed., *Trilateralism*, Boston: South End Press, 1982, in her concluding chapter, p. 560. Also see economist William Tabb's chapter, "The Trilateral Imprint on Domestic Economics," for discussion on policy of major banks in insisting on interest rate hikes that would increase their profits while driving up unemployment rates. A short and informative discussion of the major conservative shift beginning in the Carter years can be found in later editions of Howard Zinn's, *A People's History of the United States*, for example the 1999 edition from HarperCollins, chapters 20 and 21.

13   For more details, see Steve Brouwer, *Sharing the Pie*, 1998 edition form Henry Holt, particularly Chapter 8, "The War Against Workers,"and Chapter 9, "Labor Discipline: Taking it Out of Their Hides." For readable, in-depth offerings on capital's assault on labor, see first-class academic writers with differing viewpoints from the left: Bennett Harrison, *Lean and Mean*, New York: Basic Books, 1994; and the late David M. Gordon, *Fat and Mean*, New York: The Free Press, 1996.

14   There have been many good analyses of the current long crisis of capitalism, which is usually dated from 1973 to the present day, 2003. One recent book that explains the continuing economic crisis and the most recent economic downturn is Robert Brenner's *The Boom and the Bubble: the U.S. in the World Economy*, London: Verso, 2002. Brenner is Professor of History and Director of the Center for Social Theory and Comparative History at UCLA and writes from an innovative Marxist perspective. Other good radical explanations of the crises of capitalism could be found over the past two decades, for instance Samuel Bowles, David M. Gordon, and Thomas E. Weisskopf's *After the Wasteland: A Democratic Economic for the Year, 2000* (Armonk, New York: M.E. Sharpe, 1990).

15   For instance, see Martin Jay Levitt, *Confessions of a Union Buster*, Crown, 1993.

16   Jack Beatty, review of Robert Brenner's book, mentioned above, in *The Atlantic*, July 2, 2002.

17   Mishel, Bernstein, and Heather Boushey, *The State of Working America, 2002-2003*, p. 189-191.

18   Mishel, Bernstein, and John Schmitt, *The State of Working America, 1996-1997*, p. 148, Table 3.9. *The State of Working America* is published every two years (first authored by Larry Mishel and Jared Bernstein in 1992 (the *1992-93* edition), published by M.E. Sharpe through the mid-1990s and by Cornell University Press ever since.

19   Including, of course, the highest paid in corporate law firms and other auxiliary services of corporate America. In the popular imagination, of course, the public entertainers and ballplayers are the ones who stand out. Naturally they are overpaid, since taxes are so low and profits are so high for owners that they will keep bidding up the price of the stars they employ. If we reinstate very high marginal tax rates on income—see chapter 19 on political solutions—the highest salaries will drop quickly. It is my view that sports stars would happily play for $500,000 or $200,000 per year, but no athlete (or singer or actress) wants to take that kind of money if a close competitor is getting paid twenty times as much by the likes of George Steinbrenner. In a limited sense, executive compensation if also competitive, for each top CEO compares his salary and perks with what his rivals are getting. The big difference is that the individual sports heroes often have very short careers and can prove that they are very skilled at their work. This is not necessarily true at the highest levels of CEO pay, where business analysts have usually been at a loss to find connections between high levels of corporate performance and the highest levels of executive pay. Unlike the sports world, the heavy hitters think they are stars even if they have terrible statistics. A great many CEOs batted .200 or less over many seasons, ruined the companies they managed, and still demanded, and received, the highest salaries (see chapter 8).

20   EPI estimate from *The State of Working America, 2002-2003*, p. 9.

21   Mark Weisbrot, "Globalization Fails to Deliver," column written for the Knight-Ridder Tribune Information Service, Aug. 26, 2002.

22   *The State of Working America, 2002-2003*, p. 170.

23   *Ibid.*, p. 79.

24   Obviously not all rich Americans agree with the conservative politics of the Bush Gang or the ruthlessness that has predominated among the corporate elite. Warren Buffett, though not a liberal, has generally supported higher taxes on rich Americans, particularly on capital gains. Bill Gates' father has worked with a liberal/left group, United for a Fair Economy, in an attempt to keep an estate tax on the highest fortunes (see book by Chuck Collins and Bill Gates, Sr., *Wealth and Our Commonwealth: Why America Should Tax Accumulated Fortunes*, Boston: Beacon Press, 2003). Then there are a few among the well-to-do who openly identify with the struggles of ordinary Americans; among the most visible are actors such as Paul Newman, Danny Glover, Susan Sarandon, Martin Sheen, and Harry Belafonte, who have poured much of their energy and money into openly progressive causes for many years.

25   Sarah Anderson and John Cavanagh, "Top 200: The Rise of Corporate Global Power," *Institute for Policy Studies*, December 4, 2000.

26   For variations in slavery and economic calculations about the lives of slaves, see Sidney Mintz, "Slavery and Emergent Capitalisms," in *Slavery in the New World*, ed. Eugene Genovese, Prentice Hall, 1969; Richard Sutch, "the Breeding and Reproduction of Slaves," in *Race and Slavery in the Western Hemisphere*, ed. Eugene Genovese, Princeton University Press, 1975; and B.W. Higman, *Slave Populations of the Caribbean, 1807-1834*, Baltimore: Johns Hopkins University Press, 1984. On slaves and mortality in Jamaica, see Eric Williams, *History of the Caribbean*, New York, Harper and Row, 1971. Also see two very short chapters on slavery in Steve Brouwer, *Conquest and Capitalism, 1492-1992*, Carlisle, PA: Big Picture Books, 1992.

CHAPTER FIVE

1   Based on Edward N. Wolff, unpublished analysis of Survey of Consumer Finance, cited in table 4.5. p. 281 of *The State of Working America, 2002-2003*; I have updated from 1998 to 2002 according to "family net worth" tabulated in Survey of Consumer Finance 2001, with downward adjustment for stock market losses as recommended on page 7 of "Recent Changes

in U.S. Family Finances," by Ana M. Aizcorbe, Arthur B. Kennickell, Kevin B. Moore, *Federal Reserve Bulletin*, January 2003.

2   Kevin Phillips, *Wealth and Democracy*, p. 118.

3   Edward N. Wolff, *Working Paper 300, Levy Institute, 2000*.

4   James M. Peturba, "Stock Market Wealth and Consumption," *Journal of Economic Perspectives*, 2000.

5   Joseph Nocera, *Piece of the Action: How the Middle Class Joined the Money Class*, New York: Simon & Schuster, 1994; heralded the "money revolution" that allowed middle class Americans to get access to credit cards, mutual funds, and retirement accounts. Nocera, who wrote a personal finance column for GQ, never defined the middle class.

    This is why this book tries to keep middle-income Americans (those near the median or average incomes (20th to 80th percentiles) distinct from middle class or upper-middle class Americans (either the 19% or the 9% below the truly rich). I prefer the 9% figure because their advantages of income and wealth are much greater than those in the 80th to 90th percentiles, who are most often families with two full-time workers who pull down decent, but not high wages.

6   I arrive at this figure by taking Edward N. Wolff's calculations of wealth for 1998 (in Table 4.5, p. 281 of *The State of Working America, 2002-2003*, which are based on the SCF), then looking at the preliminary findings from Federal Reserve Board's Survey of Consumer Finances for 2001, see endnote above. I have used their figure of wealth growth for the top 10%, and their suggested loss due to the stock market, as a reasonable guide to what happened to the top 1%. It seems quite possible, given the huge capital gains reaped by the very rich in 2000-2001 (see previous chapter), that the top 1% may have gained at a greater rate than the rest of the top 10%.

7   Edward N. Wolff, unpublished analysis of Survey of Consumer Finance, cited in Table 4.5. p. 281 of *The State of Working America, 2002-2003*.

8   See downward adjustment for stock market losses as recommended on page 7 of "Recent Changes in U.S. Family Finances," by Ana M. Aizcorbe, Arthur B. Kennickell, Kevin B. Moore, *Federal Reserve Bulletin*, January 2003.

9   Dean Baker, "The Run-up in Home Prices: Is it Real or Another Bubble?" CEPR, August 5, 2002.

10 Raymond J. Michalowksi, *Order, Law, and Crime*, New York: Random House, 1980.

11 Fred Tasker, "There's Nothing New About Greed," *Miami Herald*, August 1, 2002.

12 See Steve Brouwer, *Sharing the Pie*, chapter 15, Carlisle, PA: Big Picture Books, 1992.

13 Stephen Pizzo, "Whitewashing the Bush boys," *Mother Jones*, March 1994.

14 *Business Week*, September 16, 1985.

15 Joseph B. Treaster, "Prudential to Pay Policyholders $410 million for its Sales Tactics," October 12, 1996.

16 "SEC is said to plan fraud case against Merrill Lynch," *The New York Times*, September 20, 1996.

CHAPTER SIX

1   Most of the sharp reduction in corporate taxes in one year, 2000-2001, however, probably had more to do with the stock market crash than the Bush favors.

2   Tom Petska, Mike Strudler, IRS, "Income, Taxes, and Tax

    Progressivity," Internal Revenue Service paper, April 4, 2000; 2001 figure from Citizens for Tax Justice.

3   To be fair to Greenspan, the increase in Social Security taxes was necessary to meet future shortfalls in the program. The unfair part was that a huge shortfall in other revenue was permitted—the big deficit of the 1980s—in order to reduce the taxes of much more prosperous taxpayers.

4   "Who Pays State and Local Taxes," The Institute on Taxation and Economic Policy, 2002 edition, January 7, 2003.

5   David Cay Johnston, "Key Company Assets Moving Offshore," *The New York Times*, November 22, 2002, p. C3.

6   Richard Stevenson, "Bush to Get Options on Revamping Tax System," *The New York Times*, Oct. 15, 2000.

7   Robert McIntyre, "The Taxonomist," *The American Prospect*, October 21, 2002.

8   David Cay Johnston, "Focus on Farms Masks Estate Tax confusion," *The New York Times*, April 8, 2001.

9   Ibid.

10 Joel Friedman and Andrew Lee, "Permanent Repeal of the Estate Tax Would be Costly...," Center on Budget and Public Policy, 2002.

11 Gates and Collins, *Wealth and Commonwealth: Why America Should Tax Accumulated Fortunes*, Boston: Beacon Press, 2003.

12 Barry W. Johnson, Martha Britton Eller, "Federal Taxation of Inheritance and Wealth Transfers," Internal Revenue Service publication, March 7, 2001.

13 Edward N. Wolff, *Top Heavy*, New York: The New Press, 1996, p. 90.

14 David Cay Johnston, *The New York Times*, August 8, 2002.

15 Robert S. McIntyre, "Free Money: Take Some," *The American Prospect*, April 8, 2002. He wrote: "But if we want the IRS to crack down on tax-evading corporations and rich people, we should worry about all the resources the IRS diverts to (poorly) monitoring the EITC." Sometimes these claims result from fairly innocent situations, such as when two low income parents are separated or divorced and each takes the EITC credit without consulting the other. But Robert McIntyre of Citizens for Tax Justice reports that flat-out cheating by low-income workers does occur—as when they simply invent fictional children in order to qualify for the EITC—and says the practice must be discouraged if this program is to maintain its integrity. The EITC was one of the few measures strengthened during the Clinton years that actually helped make up for the extreme downward pressure on working people's wages.

16 Max B. Sawicky, Economic Policy Institute, "Where the Money Isn't," October 15, 2002.

17 David Cay Johnston, "A Tax Break for the Rich Who Can Keep a Secret," *The New York Times*, September 10, 2002.

18 *The American Prospect*, Nov. 4, 2002.

19 Andrew Ross Sorkin, "Tyco Shareholders Vote to Keep Headquarters in Bermuda," *The New York Times*, March 6, 2003.

20 David Cay Johnston, "Key Company Assets Moving Offshore," *The New York Times*, November 22, 2002, p. C3.

21 Daniel Gross, *MSNBC* on line opinion page, "Corporate Tax Dodgers," February 17, 2002.

CHAPTER SEVEN

1   Dean Baker and Mark Weisbrot, *Social Security: The Phony Crisis*, Chicago: University of Chicago Press, 2000.

2   *LA Times* poll, December 18, 2002.
3   Economic Policy Institute, "Social Security is Not Broken: Why Does Wall Street Want to Fix It?" 1998.
4   Dean Baker and Mark Weisbrot, *Social Security: The Phony Crisis*, Chicago: University of Chicago Press, 2000.
5   Young Americans and Social Security," Peter D. Hart Research Associates, July 1999; the young people polled were in favor of government-sponsored retirement investments in the stock market, but only if they were an additional benefit and Social Security benefits were kept at their current level.
6   Polls conducted by the Zogby International Institute.
7   For an interesting exchange of ideas among left/liberals on Social Security, who do not always agree on solutions to such issues, see letters between Mark Weisbrot of Center for Economic and Policy and Robert Greenstein of Center on Budget and Policy Priorities; their disagreement is more about politically feasible solutions than about the health of Social Security. Go to <www.cepr.org>.
8   Cited in *The State of Working America*, 2002-2003 p. 247.
9   Edward N.Wolff, *Top Heavy*, New York: The New Press, 1995, p. 64.
10   See Federal Reserve flow of funds.
11   Dean Baker, "Dangerous minds," Center for Economic and Policy Research, December 2, 2002.
12   Ibid.
13   Dean Baker, "The Cost of the Stock Market Bubble," Center for Economic and Policy Research, November 27, 2000.
14   Steve Brouwer, *Sharing the Pie: A Citizen's Guide to Wealth and Power in America*, New York: Henry Holt/Owl Books, 1998.

CHAPTER EIGHT

1   Edward Chen, "Bush Aims to Privatize Many Federal Jobs," *Los Angeles Times*, Nov. 15.
2   David Kotz, "Neoliberalism and the U.S. Economic Expansion of the '90s," *Monthly Review*, April 2003. This is an excellent summary of the right wing response to declining economic performance in the U.S. in the last quarter of the 20th century.
3   "How High Can CEO Pay Go?" *Business Week*, April 22, 1996.
4   John A. Byrne, senior writer at *Business Week*, in *Chainsaw: the Notorious Career of Al Dunlap in the Era of Profit-at-Any-Price*, New York: Harper Business, 1999.
5   Bill Gallagher, "'Chainsaw Al Undisputed King of Greed, Corruption, and Creepiness," *Niagara Falls Reporter*, Sept. 17, 2002.
6   Lisa Takeuchi Cullen, "Where Did Everyone Go?" *Time*, November 18, 2002.
7   Ibid.
8   Ibid.

CHAPTER NINE

1   "The New Jungle," *US News and World Report*, September 23, 1996.
2   Note: manufacturing wages as a whole did not go up over the past twenty-five years, so there was no question of meat-cutting industries being left behind by other more prosperous sectors. Exploitation, pure and simple, drove wages down.
3   Eric Schlosser, "The Chain Never Stops," *Mother Jones*, July/August 2001

4   Elizabeth Becker, "Feedlot Perils Outpace Regulation, Sierra Club Says," *The New York Times*, August 13, 2002.
5   The Center for Science in the Public Interest (CSPI), February 2002.
6   Eric Schlosser, "Bad Meat: The Scandal of Our Food Safety System," *The Nation*, September 16, 2002.
7   David Migoya, "ConAgra beef eyed in illness," *Denver Post*, July 11, 2002.
8   Eric Schlosser, "Bad Meat: The Scandal of Our Food Safety System," *The Nation*, September 16, 2002.
9   Ibid.
10   Donald L. Bartlett and James B. Steele, "The Empire of the Pigs," *Time*, November 11, 1998.
11   *The AgBiz Tiller Online*, March 1997.
12   Elizabeth Becker, "Feedlot Perils Outpace Regulation, Sierra Club Says," *The New York Times*, August 13, 2002.
13   Ibid.
14   Cat Lazaroff, "Hog Hell in North Carolina," February 9, 2000 (Environmental News Service).
15   From "Migration Dialogue," a very good source of information about the status of food workers, agriculture, and corporate crimes against immigrants and workers alike; it is found on an online service of the University of California at Davis; they cited the following articles: Nancy Cleeland, "Union Decries Conditions at Pilgrim's Pride Chicken Plant," *Los Angeles Times*, February 27, 2002; Dane Schiller, "Tyson claims unfair targeting," *San Antonio Express-News*, February 14, 2002; John Taylor, "New election is possible at beef plant," *Omaha World-Herald*, January 3, 2002; Carey Gillam, "Tyson charges 'tip of the iceberg,' *Houston Chronicle*, December 31, 2001; Jim Schoettler, "Immigrants admit labor scheme," Jacksonville (Fla.) *Times-Union*, January 16, 2002; and Kevin Sack, "Under the counter, grocer provided immigrant workers," *The New York Times*, January 14, 2002.
16   Eric Schlosser, *Fast Food Nation*, New York:Houghton Mifflin Co., 2001, p. 159.

CHAPTER TEN

1   Lisa Featherstone, "Wal-Mart Values: Selling Women Short," *The Nation*, December 16, 2002.
2   Steven Greenhouse, "Suit says Wal-Mart forces workers to toil off the clock," say company forces unpaid overtime," *The New York Times*, June 25, 2002.
3   Lisa Featherstone, "Wal-Mart Values: Selling Women Short," *The Nation*, December 16, 2002.
4   Mark Gimein, "Sam Walton Made Us a Promise," *Fortune*, March 18, 2002.
5   Ibid.
6   Ibid.
7   Lisa Featherstone, "Wal-Mart Values: Selling Women Short," *The Nation*, December 16, 2002.
8   *The State of Working America*, 2002-2003, p. 407.
9   From "uni" on the internet (www.union-network.org); other sources include UFCW site. Most impressive is the amount of the grassroots rebellion on the web—there are now literally hundreds of anti-Wal-Mart sites on the internet, most set up by former workers and community activists who have kept Wal-Mart out of their towns. Simply go to Google and ask for Wal-Mart.
10   Jim Hightower, in his newsletter, "Hightower Lowdown,"

April 26, 2002.

CHAPTER ELEVEN

1   Martin Gottlieb and Kurt Eichenwald, "A Hospital Chain's Brass Knuckles, and the Backlash," *The New York Times*, May 11, 1997.
2   Claire M. Fagin in a letter to *The New York Times*, August 20, 1996.
3   Testimony of the American Nurses Association on "The Nursing Shortage and Its Impact on America's Health Care Delivery System," before the Subcommittee on Aging Committee on Health, Education, Labor, and Pensions, February 13, 2001.
4   Steven L. Dawson, President of the Paraprofessional Healthcare Institute of the South Bronx, "Safety in Numbers: national deficiency in nursing home staff," at <www.movingideas.org> May 9, 2002.
5   Quoted by Congressman Pete Stark, a staunch opponent of managed care, May 5, 1999.
6   Kurt Eichenwald, *The New York Times*, December 17, 2002.
7   "Costs of Health Care Are Seen Rising by 15%" reported Dow Jones/AP dispatch on October 15, 2002.
8   James Adams, "Rex Morgan's prescription: socialized medicine in U.S.," *Toronto Globe and Mail*, August 29, 2002.
9   *Orange County Register*, December 1, 2002.
10 Steffie Woolhandler and David Himmelstein, *Bleeding the Patient*, Monroe, Maine: Common Courage Press, 2001, p. 221.
11 "Dividing up health care by income class," *Boston Globe*, August 19, 2002.
12 The report was available on the consulting company's website.
13 Steffie Woolhandler and David Himmelstein, *Bleeding the Patient*, Monroe, Maine: Common Courage Press, 2001, pp. 193-97.
14 Ibid., p. 197.
15 Ibid., p. 143.
16 Ibid., pp. 59-61.
17 Robert Pear, "Critics Say Proposal for Medicare Could Increase Costs," *The New York Times*, May 6, 2003.
18 J. Robert Warner, Americans for Insurance Reform, began reporting on the national trend in late 2001, and then produced very precise analysis of the situation on a state-wide basis, for instance, *Stable Losses, Unstable Rates in West Virginia*, January 6, 2003. Go to the Public Citizen website to read analyses of the situation and factual responses to the "medical malpractice crisis" in Pennsylvania, New York and other states (for example, "Medical Misdiagnosis in Pennsylvania," January 2003); as of this writing the state medical associations have not supplied any accurate information to refute these arguments.
19 *The Wall Street Journal*, June 24, 2002, p. 1.

CHAPTER TWELVE

1   Kurt Eichenwald, *The New York Times*, June 30, 2002.
2   Quoted in Harry Magdoff, "The American Empire and the U.S. Economy," *Monthly Review*, November 1966.
3   Ibrahim Werde, "LTCM, a hedge fund above suspicion," *Le Monde Diplomatique*, November 1998.
4   See Roger Lowenstein, *When Genius Failed*, New York: Random House, 2000.
5   Joseph Kahn and Peter Truell, "Hedge Fund's Bets Top $1.2 Trillion," *The New York Times*, September 26, 1998.
6   Ibrahim Warde, "LTCM, a hedge fund above suspicion," *Le Monde Diplomatique*, November 1998.
7   Russell Mokhiber and Robert Weissman, *Corporate Predators: The Hunt For Mega-Profits and the Attack on Democracy*, Monroe, Maine: Common Courage Press, 1999.
8   "Will Hedge Funds be Overrun by all the Traffic?" *Business Week*, March 11, 2002.
9   Adam Shell, "Hedge funds attract crowd," *USA Today*, February 11, 2002.

CHAPTER THIRTEEN

1   Thom Hartmann, *Unequal Protection: The Rise of Corporate Dominance and the Theft of Human Rights*, Rodale, 2002, p. 52.
2   George Monbiot, *The Captive State: the Corporate Takeover of Britain*, London: Macmillan, 2000.
3   See the history of the British East India Company, for instance <www.theeastindiacompany.com>, and Thom Hartmann, *Unequal Protection*, for more on the subject of profits from trade and piracy, and the origins of the limited liability corporation.
4   Thom Hartmann, *Unequal Protection: The Rise of Corporate Dominance and the Theft of Human Rights*, Rodale, 2002.
5   Quoted in Alfons, J. Beitzinger, Edward G. Ryan, *Lion of the Law*, Madison: Wisconsin State Historical Society, 1960.
6   Emanuel Hertz, *Abraham Lincoln: A New Portrait*, Horace Liverwright, 1931, Vol. 2, p. 954.
7   Hartmann, *Unequal Protection*, p. 49.
8   David Cole Martin, "The Corporation and Anti-Trust Law Policy," in Warren J. Samuels and Arthur S. Miller, eds., *Corporations and Society: Power and Responsibility*, Westport, CT: Greenwood Press, 1987, p. 212.
9   Howard Zinn, *A People's History of the United States*, New York: HarperCollins, p. 255.
10 Martin J. Sklar, *The Corporate Reconstruction of American Capitalism, 1890-1916*, Cambridge: Cambridge University Press, 1988.
11 Trevor Coleman, "Walsh's Verdict: Federalist Society can Divide Judiciary," *Detroit Free Press*, July 8, 1999. Lawrence Walsh also mentioned the dangerous character of the Federalist Society in his book *Firewall: The Iran/Contra Conspiracy and Cover-up*, New York: W. W. Norton, 1998.
12 Karl Rove, at White House news conference, January 22, 2003. Bush was asked about his three favorites while campaigning in 2000—Christopher Caldwell, "Tagging After Teddy," *The Atlantic Monthly*, March 22, 2000.

CHAPTER FOURTEEN

1   David Starr Jordan wrote an influential book on eugenics, *The Heredity of Richard Roe: A Discussion of the Principles of Eugenics*, Boston: American Unitarian Association, 1911. The American Breeders' Association would later be renamed the American Eugenics Society under the leadership of Irving Fisher and Madison Grant. Like many others in the field, Jordan was not averse to exterminating "unfit" human beings and quoted approvingly from one of his contemporaries: "the true function of charity is to ... allow those unfit from heredi-

ty to become extinct with as little pain as possible"(p. 141).

2 Stefan Kuhl, *The Nazi Connection: Eugenics, American Racism, and German National Socialism*, New York: Oxford University Press, 1994.

3 Beth Mintz, "The President's Cabinet, 1897-1972," *Insurgent Sociologist*, Spring 1975.

4 *Arizona Republic*, ``Skull for Scandal: Did Bush's Father Rob Geronimo's Grave?" 1988.

5 Webster G. Tarpley and Anton Chaitkin, *George Bush: the Unauthorized Biography*, Washington DC: Executive Intelligence Review, 1992

6 See Christopher Simpson, *The Splendid Blond Beast*, Monroe, ME: Common Courage, 1995; Charles Higham, *Trading With the Enemy: The Nazi - American Money Plot, 1933-1949*, Delacorte 1983.

7 Evan Thomas and Walter Isaacson, *The Wise Men*, New York: Simon Schuster, 1986.

8 For instance, when Prime Minister Mossadegh, the democratically elected leader of Iran, nationalized the oil companies and incurred the wrath of Britain and the United States in 1951, it was Harriman who was dispatched to chat with him. Harriman told Mossadegh he had better resign his office.

9 Alexandra Robbins, "Knight of Eulogia," *Atlantic Monthly*, May 2000.

10 John T. Bethell, "Roosevelt at Harvard," *Harvard Magazine*, 1936.

11 Not all aspiring pirates had to go to Yale, for plenty of opium money had also been invested at Harvard by other wealthy New England privateers, such as the Perkins family.

12 The reader will find that the internet is now a source for Skull and Bones information, as well as entertaining and wild speculation (and not-so-wild speculation) about all kinds of secret activities that the Bonesmen might have undertaken—the Tarpley/Chaitkin book noted above can be found on the web and has a vast compendium of useful information, but I would take the implied conspiratorial leads with a grain of salt. In general I would advise the reader to be skeptical of most conspiratorial theories about Bush and Co., even intriguing ones like the CIA-Yale connection, because they generally indulge in such broad musings about suspected links that they do not necessarily hold up under detailed analysis. I would suggest that the studies of the "power elite" by Domhoff and C. Wright Mills are more fruitful for understanding how wealthy families make connections that protect their capital, promote their political agendas, and recruit intelligent allies from the middle classes.

13 E. Digby Bartzell, *An American Business Aristocracy*, New York: Collier, 1962.

14 G. William Domhoff, *The Power Elite and the State*, New York: Aldine de Gruyter, 1990.

15 Molly Ivins, "The Weasels Sneak into the Henhouse," *Chicago Tribune*, November 14, 2000.

16 Peter Daniels, "Chief Justice's Daughter," World Wide Socialist Web, Nov. 30, 2002.

17 Madison Grant, *The Passing of the Great Race: The Racial Basis of European History*, New York: Charles Scribner's Sons, 1916.

18 Jonathan Marks, "Eugenics: Breeding a Better Citizenry through Science," Department of Sociology and Anthropology, University of North Carolina Charlotte.

19 G. William Domhoff, *Who Rules America: Power and Politics*, New York: McGraw Hill, 2002.

CHAPTER FIFTEEN

1 Albert Einstein, "Why Socialism," *Monthly Review*, 1949.

2 Eric Boehlert, "Fox guarding the henhouse," *Salon*, November 15, 2000.

3 Russ Baker, "Murdoch's Mean Machine," *Columbia Journalism Review*, May/June 1998.

4 Neil quoted by Jim Naureckas in "From the Top," *Extra!*, July/August 1998.

5 Alex Patterson, *The Economist*, March 20, 1999.

6 *The Washington Post*, January 21, 2001.

7 "How a Prominent Lawyer's Attack Memo Changed America," Jerry M. Lindsay, <www.mediatransparency-.org> August, 20, 2002.

8 Ibid.

9 Christopher Georges, "Conservative Heritage Foundation Finds Recipe for Influence," *Wall Street Journal*, August 10, 1995.

10 Robert Kuttner, *Everything for Sale*, New York: Knopf, 1996, p. 341.

11 Jon Wiener, "Dollars for Neo-Con Scholars," *The Nation*, January 1, 1996.

12 M. P. Crozier, S. J. Huntington, and J. Watanuki, *The Crisis of Democracy: Report on the Governability of Democracies to the Trilateral Commission*, New York University, 1975.

13 John B. Judis, in his book, *The Paradox of American Democracy*, New York: Pantheon, 2000.

14 Ibid.

15 Venezuela-Unida, news website, profile on Cisneros, <www.nodo50.org/venezuela-unida>

CHAPTER SIXTEEN

1 Quoted by Bob Woodward in *Bush at War*, New York: Simon and Schuster, 2002.

2 Bush Sr. had to produce pages of his diary in 1992 for Special Prosecutor Lawrence Welch's investigation of Iran-Contra.

3 Robert Parry, "Guatemala, Reagan & Guatemala's Death Files," *iF magazine*, May/June 1999.

4 Thomas Bodenheimer and Robert Gould, *Rollback*, Boston: South End Press, 1989. This book is excellent for understanding the genesis of "war on terror" themes under Bush Gang I.

5 Robert Scheer, "Many a U.S. President Pays the Pardon Piper," March 6, 2001, *Los Angeles Times*.

6 Jim Lobe, "Neo-conservatives consolidate control over U.S. Mideast Policy," *Foreign Policy in Focus*, December 6, 2002.

7 Saul Landau, "Bush Vision and the Culture of Power," *CounterPunch*, December 11, 2002.

8 Mark Danner, "The Truth About El Mazote" *The New Yorker*, December 6, 2001.

9 Jim Lobe, "Neo-conservatives consolidate control over U.S. Mideast Policy," also see David Corn, "Iran/Contra Rehab," *The Nation*, March 11, 2002, and Tom Barry, *CounterPunch*, December 6, 2002.

10 Conn Hallinan, "Caesar's Wife: Negroponte and the War on Terrorism," *San Francisco Examiner*, October 20, 2001.

11 Duncan Campbell, "Friends of Terrorism," *The Guardian*, February 8, 2002, and "The Bush Dynasty and the Cuban Criminals," *The Guardian*, December 2, 2002.

12 Conn Hallinan, "Caesar's Wife: Negroponte and the War on Terrorism," *San Francisco Examiner*, October 20, 2001.

13 Tom Barry, "American Beacon of Freedom," *Project Against the*

14   *Present Danger*, November 2002.

14   Jim Lobe, "Bush Channels Conservative Vision," *Alternet*, February 27, 2003. Lobe, associated with Foreign Policy in Focus, wrote "A Rightwing Blueprint for the Middle East," *Alternet*, April 4, 2002.

15   James Zogby, "Understanding America's Right Wing," *Washington Watch*, Part I and Part II, May 13 and June 3, 2002.

16   Samuel Huntington, *International Security*, Summer 1981.

17   Maureen Dowd column in *The New York Times*, April 20, 2003.

18   Bush made this remark to reporters on the White House lawn on Sunday, September 16. Because of immediate angry responses from Europe and Muslims around the world, White House Press secretary Ari Fleischer denied two days later that the president had meant any religious offense. Similarly the Pentagon's initial name for the War on Terrorism, "Operation Infinite Justice," had to be changed and removed from the Pentagon web-site after September 20 when Muslim critics pointed out that only Allah was capable of infinite justice. The Bush administration then realized they had better soften their rhetoric. However, the use of these words with their offensive (in both senses) religious overtones, reveals the depth of their own right-wing theological/political zeal. To put this response in context of earlier American "wars against terror" under the Reagan/Bush administrations see Robert Parry, "Bush's 'Crusade,'" *Consortium News* September 25, 2001.

19   Steve Brouwer, Susan D. Rose, and Paul Gifford, *Exporting the American Gospel: Global Christian Fundamentalism*, London, New York: Routledge: 1996.

CHAPTER SEVENTEEN

1   Emily Eakin, "'It takes an empire,' say several U.S. thinkers," *The New York Times*, April 2, 2002.

2   Daniel Yergin, *The Prize*, New York: Simon and Schuster, 1991.

3   Jonathan Glancey, "Gas, chemicals, bombs: Britain has used them all before in Iraq," *The Guardian*, April 16, 2003.

4   Ibid.

5   Ibid.

6   David Hackworth, "Please, No More Made-in-the-USA Monsters," syndicated column, *The Sentinel*, Carlisle, PA, April 15, 2003.

7   Peter S. Goodman, "U.S. Adviser Says Iraq May Break With OPEC," *The Washington Post*, May 17, 2003.

8   *Wall Street Journal*, July 11, 1996

9   See PNAC archives for articles such as: "Congress Versus Iraq," "The UN Rewards Saddam."

10   John Donnelly and Anthony Shadid, "Iraq War Hawks Have Plans to Reshape Entire Mideast," *Boston Globe*, September 10, 2002.

11   Jim Lobe, "Woolsey's Role Crucial to Impact of Occupation," *Foreign Policy In Focus*, April 8, 2003.

12   Bush administration's "National Security of the Untied States," 2002, p.15.

13   Jim Lobe, op. cit.

14   Martin Merzer, "Poll: Majority oppose unilateral action against Iraq," Knight Ridder, January 12, 2003.

15   Nicholas Arons, *Foreign Policy in Focus*, April 2001.

16   Joe Conason, "Our Man In Iraq," *New York Observer*, April 9, 2003.

17   Joseph Schumpeter, *Imperialism and Social Classes*, New York: Augustus Kelley, 1951, p. 66.

18   Maggie Burns, "The enemy of my enemy is my customer: Iraq and the Bush administrations," *Online Journal*,September 5, 2002.

19   Jeremy Scahill, "The Saddam in Rumsfeld's Closet," <www.Common-Dreams.org> August 2, 2002.

20   Bob Herbert, "Spoils of War," *The New York Times*, April 10, 2003.

21   Ibid.

22   William Blum, "A brief history of U.S. interventions," *Z Magazine*, June, 1999; *Killing Hope: U.S. Interventions in the Third World*, Monroe, ME: Common Courage Press, 1995 and *Rogue State: A Guide to the World's Only Superpower*, Monroe, ME: Common Courage Press, 2000. In the wake of the Iraq War, ex-CIA professionals have formed a group called VIPS—Veteran Intelligence Professionals for Sanity—in order to call attention to abuses within the spy agencies which are only getting worse. They are very critical of the false intelligence that was manufactured in order to justify the Iraq War.

23   William M. Arkin, *Los Angeles Times*. October 27, 2002, also see Dan Dupont, Inside the Pentagon report, "Secrecy News," Federation of American Scientists, October 28, 2002.

24   Ahmed Rashid, *Taliban:Militant Islam, Oil and Fundamentalism in Central Asia*, Yale University Press, 2001; *The Rise of Militant Islam in Central Asia*, St. Martins, 2003; also, for a related set of antagonisms set loose by U.S. policy in the Middle East, see Stephen Zunes, *Tinderbox: U.S. Middle East Policy and the Roots of Terrorism*, Monroe, ME: Common Courage Press, 2003.

25   Chalmers Johnson, *Blowback*, Henry Holt, 2000. Another word for more or less the same phenomenon, "boomerang", has been used by Mark Zepezauer, *Boomerang! How Our Covert Wars Have Created Enemies Across the Middle East and Brought Terror to America*, Monroe, ME: Common Courage Press, 2003.

26   David Martin, <www.CBS News.com>, September 4, 2002.

27   Bruce B. Auster, Mark Mazzetti and Edward T. Pound, "Truth and Consequences: New Questions about U.S. Intelligence Regarding Iraq's Weapons of Mass Terror," *US News and World Report*, June 9, 2003.

28   Seymour Hersh, "Selective Intelligence," *The New Yorker*, May 12, 2003.

29   Ibid.

30   Ibid.

CHAPTER EIGHTEEN

1   Greg Palast, "The Great Florida Ex-Con Game: How the 'felon' voter-purge was itself felonious," *Harper's, March*, 2002.

2   *"Bad Boy: The Life and Politics of Lee Atwater."* Copyright 1997 by John Brady. To be published by Addison Wesley Longman.

3   William Greider, "The Power of Negative Thinking," *Rolling Stone*, January 12, 1989.

4   *FDR's Fireside Chats*, R. D. Buhite and D. W. Levy, Eds., Penguin Books, 1992.

5   Ibid.

6   For details, see Steve Brouwer, *Sharing the Pie*, New York: Henry Holt/Owl Books, 1998.

7   Ruy Teixeira and Robert Borosage, "The Politics of Money," *The Nation*, October 21, 1996,. based on data from poll con-

ducted by Lake Research in July 1996.

8   Joel Rogers and Ruy Teixeira, *The Forgotten Majority: Why the White Working Class Still Matters,* New York: Basic Books, 2000.

9   Voter News Service data, *The New York Times,* December 12, 2000.

10   Greg Palast, *Salon,* November 1, 2002.

11   *St. Petersburg Times* editorial, "Zones Hinder Free Speech," November 9, 2002.

12   David Cole, "Secret Court Takes the Fourth," *Counterpunch,* November 22, 2002.

13   Stuart Taylor, Jr., "Let's Not Allow a Fiat to Undermine the Bill of Rights," *National Journal,* "Legal Affairs," *Atlantic Online,* July 23, 2002.

14   Bob Herbert, *The New York Times,* September 11, 2002.

15   *USA Today,* October 16, 2002.

16   Adam Clymer, "Government Openness at Issue as Bush Holds On to Records," *The New York Times,* January 3, 2003.

17   Dean Schabner, "Conservative Backlash," ABC News, March 12, 2003.

CHAPTER NINETEEN

1   Robert Reich, *The Observer,* December 15, 2002.

2   Jennifer King, "Demron?" *The American Partisan,* February 1, 2002.

3   Daniel Gross, "How Global Crossing Spun Political Gold," *Tech Investor,* <www.Business2.com>, March 25, 2002.

4   Neil Boortz, "Terry McAuliffe is a Socialist...No, Wait, He's a Capitalist?" January 31, 2002, <newsMax.com.>

5   Bill Moyers, *NOW with Bill Moyers,* March 7, 2003.

6   The high income tax rates of the 1950s and 1960s were effective in discouraging super-high executive salaries; the capital gains rates for the very rich were often at much lower rates. The best solution is to keep the rates high on salary income, investment income, and corporate income because this will help limit the endless proliferation of tax dodges and loopholes as the wealthy try to shift their income from one category to another.

7   See Brouwer, *Sharing the Pie,* Chapter 18, "Social Democracy Works," and chapter on international comparisons in *The State of Working America.*

8   I feel it is fair to blame the "rich" as a group because they own most of the investments, but of course there are many obvious individual exceptions. Warren Buffett, the second wealthiest man in the U.S., is one. See his articles in *Fortune* warning about the insane level of interest in high-tech stocks (1999) and the neglect of employee pension funds by corporations (2001).

CHAPTER TWENTY

1   Warren Buffett, "Dividend Voodoo," *The Washington Post,* May 20, 2003.

2   Franco Modigliani and Robert Solow, "Dangers of the Dividend Tax Cut, *The Boston Globe,* May 22, 2003.

3   Robert S. McIntyre, Citizens for Tax Justice, January 8, 2003, preliminary analysis of Bush's tax plan.

4   Center on Budget and Policy Priorities, "Who Belongs to the Investor Class?" January 6, 2003; "Contemplating a Dividend

Tax Cut," *The New York Times,* January 7, 2003; analysis from The Tax Policy Center, a non-profit research center run jointly by The Brookings Institution and the Urban Institute.

5   *The New York Times,* February 10, 2003.

6   "Notes from the editors," *Monthly Review,* March 2003.

7   Robert S. McIntyre, Citizens for Tax Justice, January 8, 2003, preliminary analysis of Bush's Tax Plan.

8   Elisabeth Bumiller, "Nurturing the Tax Cut Idea Since the Era of Reagan," *The New York Times,* January 7, 2003.

9   Lawrence Mishel, Jared Bernstein, Heather Boushey, *The State of Working America: 2002-2003,* Ithaca: Cornell University Press, 2003, Table 7.9, p. 410; also see Brouwer, *Sharing the Pie,* and the Luxemburg Income Studies.

10   Jonathan Weisman, "New Tax Plan May Bring Shift In Burden, Poor Could Pay A Bigger Share," *The Washington Post,* December 15, 2002.

11   Robert S. McIntyre, Citizens for Tax Justice, December 16, 2002 at <www.ctj.org>.

12   Based on the most recent data available. IRS figures for high income taxpayers are 20.3% in 1999 and the 20.8% in 2000; for 2001 McIntyre of Citizens for Tax Justice cited a preliminary figure of 18.1%, down slightly because of a reduction of capital gains (probably due to stock market losses), but he then estimated that the real figure would be significantly higher, over 20%, when final income adjustments were accounted for.

13   The author's chart based on the income figures in Robert S. McIntyre's analysis, Citizens for Tax Justice, December 16, 2002. Effective tax rate for 1979 comes from the IRS study by Tom Petska and Mike Strudler, "Income, Taxes, and Tax Progressivity," Internal Revenue Service paper, April 4, 2000.

14   Jonathan Weisman, "New Tax Plan May Bring Shift In Burden, Poor Could Pay A Bigger Share," *The Washington Post,* December 15, 2002.

15   Ibid.

16   Ibid.

17   Ibid.

18   Jonathan Weisman, "Bush Blunts 'Fairness Question' on Taxes: President's 'Class Warfare' Rhetoric Brings Support for Cuts Skewed to the Wealthy," *The Washington Post,* May 13, 2003.

19   Elisabeth Bumiller, "Keepers of Bush Image Lift Stagecraft to New Heights," *The New York Times,* May 16, 2003.

20   Katrina vanden Heuvel, "Top Gun at Job Destruction," *The Nation,* May 5, 2003.

21   Robert Kogan, Richard Greenstein, and Andrew Lee, "Tax Policy Center and CBPP Analyses show that Thomas Plan Would Be More Tilted Toward the Very Wealthy—and More Expensive-than the Bush Plan," CBPP, May 7, 2003.

22   Isaac Shapiro, "Millionaires and the Ways and Means Tax Plan," CBPP, May 5, 2003.

23   David E. Rosenbloom, "Plan to Suspend Tax on Dividends Passes the Senate," *The New York Times,* May 16, 2003.

24   Robert Greenstein, Richard Kogan, and Joel Friedman, "Conference Agreement on Tax Cuts Makes Heavier Use of Gimmicks than House or Senate Bills: Nearly Every Provision in Bill Has Artificial Expiration Date, With True Cost Likely to be $800 Billion to $1 Trillion Through 2013," Center on Budget and Policy Priorities, May 23, 2003.

25   Citizens for Tax Justice, "Final Tax Plan Tilts Even More Toward Richest," May 22, 2003.

26   Franco Modigliani and Robert Solow, "Dangers of the Dividend Tax Cut, *The Boston Globe,* May 22, 2003.

27   David Wessel, "Dividend-Tax Cut Runs Risk of Opening Doors to New Shelters," *The Wall Street Journal*, May 22, 2003.

28   Dana Milbank and Dan Balz, "GOP Eyes Tax Cuts as Annual Events," *The Washington Post*, May 11, 2003.

29   Peter R. Orszag, "New Joint Committee on Taxation Study," Center on Budget and Policy Priorities, May 14, 2003.

30   Joel Friedman, Richard Kogan and Denis Kadochnikov, "Administration's Tax Cutting Agenda Would Cost $2.7 trillion through 2013," Center on Budget and Policy Priorities," March 7, 2003.

31   Robert Greenstein, Richard Kogan and Joel Friedman, "The New Tax Use Gimmicks to Mask Costs," Center on Budget and Policy Priorities, June 1, 2003.

32   Warren Buffett, "Dividend Voodoo," *The Washington Post*, May 20, 2003.

CHAPTER TWENTY-ONE

1   "To a Person Sitting in Darkness," January 1901, *The Sun* (New York); see a collection of Twain's anti-imperialist writings compiled by Jim Zwick at <www.boondocksnet.com>

2   Though the Democrats deserve to be held to account for instances in which they betrayed average Americans, their overall efforts seldom reached the level of the Republican thievery. Although they often rewarded their wealthy political contributors in unseemly ways, they sometimes succeeded in some efforts to raise taxes, raise the minimum wage, and protect workers' rights. And when Clinton did cave in to the right—helping to end many welfare programs, lowering the capital gains tax, and pushing NAFTA—many Democrats in Congress did not go along with him.

3   Bill Moyers, *NOW*, PBS, March 7, 2003.

4   Jeff Faux, "Manufacturing: Key to America's Future," presentation to the Industrial Union Legislative Conference, February 4, 2003.

5   Steve Brouwer, *Conquest and Capitalism, 1492-1992*, Carlisle PA: Big Picture Books, 1992, and Brouwer, Gifford and *Rose, Exporting the American Gospel: Global Christian Fundamentalism*,London: Routledge, 1996. See the chapters on Guatemala and South Korea in particular.

6   Steve Brouwer, *Sharing the Pie: A Citizen's Guide to Wealth and Power in America*, New York: Henry Holt, 1998.

7   Alexis de Tocqueville, *Democracy in America*, Book II, Chapter XIV.

8   A Report of the Project for the New American Century, September 2000.

9   Richard Haass, "Imperial America," paper delivered at the Atlanta conference, November 11, 2000 <www.brook.edu>.

10   Max Boot, *Savage Wars of Peace: Small Wars and the Rise of American Power*, New York: Basic Books, 2002; and article of that title in *Hoover Digest*, 2002, no. 3.

11   The volume of criticism from old-line conservatives and the libertarian right was very heavy before the invasion of Iraq began. A wide compilation of views can be found at the website of <www.antiwar.com>.

12   The father of the other General Mac Arthur who was in the Philippines during World War II.

13   "To a Person Sitting in Darkness," January 1901, *The Sun* (New York), the title of what is probably Twain's most famous anti-imperialist essay. The word "niggers" in Twain's text reminds us how the racial prejudices of the day helped justify the conquest of the Philippines; racism was still with us in the Gulf War of 1991, when American soldiers called Arabs "sand-niggers" and "rag heads."

14   Michael T. Klare, *Resource Wars: The New Landscape of Global Conflict*, New York: Henry Holt, 2001.

15   Bob Woodward, *Bush at War*, New York: Simon and Schuster, 2002.

16   Congressional Budget Office, *Effective Federal Tax Rates: 1997-2000*, August 2003. See Tables B1-A, B1-B, and B1-C, and analysis by Robert Greenstein and Isaac Shapiro, "The New, Definitive CBO Data on Income and Tax Trends," Center on Budget and Policy Priorities, September 23, 2003. These studies show that the after-tax income share of the top 1% more than doubled, from 7.5% in 1979 to 15.5% in 2000. This increase almost exactly parallels the increase in income as measured by IRS tax return data, which showed that the top 1% share of adjusted gross income also more than doubled, from 10.08% in 1979 to 21.73% in 2000 (Thomas Piketty and Emmanuel Saez, "Income Inequality in the United States, 1913-1998," National Bureau of Economic Research, Working Paper 8467, September 2001, with updates from Professor Emmanuel Saez's website <http://emlab.berkeley.edu/users/saez>). Please note that these two measures of drastic income change (from the IRS and the CBO) confirm each other. The IRS percentages (such as those that are used earlier in this book) are higher than the CBO percentages because the IRS does not measure all the sources of non-taxable income that the rigorous CBO study takes into account—for example, Social Security income, welfare and other transfer payments that go to poor and middle income Americans. For 2001, preliminary IRS figures showed that the income share of the richest 1% dropped somewhat, to about 18% of all income, on account of the stock market collapse and falling capital gains income. Most likely, this is a temporary setback and will not change the overwhelming advantages that the very rich have accrued over the past 25 years.

     The CB0 study cited above gives further proof to the arguments made on pages 44-45 of this book which were based on a similar CBO study completed in 2001. The tremendous income gains of the last two decades went almost exclusively to the top 1% of the population. The gains of the next 4% (the 96th-99th) were significant (53%), but only slightly above what everyone would have received if the average income gain (40%) had been shared among all income groups (as was the case between 1947 and 1979.)

17   Ibid.

Index

About the Author

Steve Brouwer has been writing about economics, politics, and American culture since the 1980s. His books, *Sharing the Pie: A Disturbing Picture of the U.S. Economy* (1988 and 1992 editions) and *Sharing the Pie: A Citizen's Guide to Wealth and Power in America* (1998), explained the connection between the startling increase in economic inequality in the United States and the extreme rightward shift in the political scene. In *Conquest and Capitalism: 1492—1992*, he explored the predatory history of European/North American capitalism in the Western Hemisphere. With his wife, sociologist Susan Rose, he co-authored *Exporting the American Gospel: Global Christian Fundamentalism*, a book that examines American-style Christian fundamentalism and its aggressive propagation in many parts of the world.

For many years, the author was a carpenter, builder, and designer of houses. In the process he engaged in successful enterprises that practiced democratic, egalitarian approaches to business and economics. He has organized housing cooperatives, founded a worker-owned construction company, and developed a community-owned rental housing program.

Brouwer is the father of four and grandfather of one and lives with his family alongside the Conodoguinet Creek in Pennsylvania.

For updates, statistics, sources and links see:
www.stevebrouwer.com